ANIMAL LESSONS

Animal Lessons

How They Teach Us to Be Human

KELLY OLIVER

Columbia University Press   *New York*

Columbia University Press
Publishers Since 1893
New York   Chichester, West Sussex
Copyright © 2009 Columbia University Press
All rights reserved
Library of Congress Cataloging-in-Publication Data
Oliver, Kelly, 1958–
Animal lessons : how they teach us to be human / Kelly Oliver.
p.   cm.
Includes bibliographical references and index.
ISBN 978-0-231-14726-2 (cloth : alk. paper)
—ISBN 978-0-231-14727-9 (pbk : alk. paper)
—ISBN 978-0-231-52049-2 (ebook)
1. Animals (Philosophy)   2. Human-animal relationships.   3. Human beings—Animal
nature.   4. Philosophical anthropology.   I. Title.
B105.A55045 2009
113'.8—dc22
2009019725
⊗
Columbia University Press books are printed on permanent and durable acid-free paper.
This book is printed on paper with recycled content.
Printed in the United States of America
c 10 9 8 7 6 5 4 3 2
p 10 9 8 7 6 5 4 3 2
References to Internet Web sites (URLs) were accurate at the time of writing. Neither the author nor
Columbia University Press is responsible for URLs that may have expired or changed since the manu-
script was prepared.

This book is inspired by, and dedicated to,
the memory of my beloved companion Kaos (1988–2006),
whom I affectionately called "the porpoise of life."

KAOS, THE PORPOISE OF LIFE

I called him Kaos poody, silly willy, and bandini.
I called him funny bunny, budrella and hoodini.
I called him principiccio, Buddah-udah, and the snortus,
But if I dare tell the truth, he gives life sweetest porpoise.

He wasn't like McCavity, and neither was he Wizard,
Defying laws of gravity, and deftly catching lizards.
The Kaos pood-pood-nicky, fastidious with his locks,
Wasn't bad-boy Yuki, who stinks outside the box.

Yukiyu will taunt yah, and so did Kaos too.
Both can sit like Buddah, though Yuki jumps at boo,
Unlike that poopasorus, who runs throughout the house
Kaos poodie oodie, could never catch a mouse.

He was Mr. Cheivious, playing poody games,
Some of them were devious, always without aim.
Even supercilious, that teaser entertained.
Kaos Trouble Poody, it was his middle name.

He nibbled on the rubber plants, they always made him sick.
Too lazy to go chasing ants, wet saucy food he licked.
Don't let him near the plastic, and ribbon's even worse,
He swallowed it fantastic, too messy for this verse!

I called him Kaos poody, poodini and poop-snort.
I loved him more than anything, his life was much too short.
I prodded and I poked him, jelly belly stayed amorphous,
Though Nietzsche taught me many things, he gives life sweetest porpoise.

Toilet paper he unwound, to watch it piling up.
Trinkets ever lost he found, tried drinking from your cup.
He jumped in the Jacuzzi, to see if he could swim.
He spoiled pancakes for Suzi, and wrecked the plate for Tim.

Walking on the table, sleeping on the desk,
His fur was soft as sable, and smelled sweet gingeresque.
Wearing furry slippers, sliding 'cross the floor,
Giving gifts of gentle purrs, I loved to hear him snore.

Blue eyes like sapphire planets, magic stuff of dreams,
Attracting folks like magnets, this cat's not what he seems.
Some confounded people, fearing an attack
Had the gall to ask me, isn't that a yak?!

Escaping like Hoodini, nonchalantly sauntered out.
Hiding like a meanie, 'til I heard his snorting snout.
Riding magic carpets, then choreographed a dance.
I'm forever in his debt, for furry-covered pants.

The Limpet was not graceful, he ruined Wizard's hunt
By rushing at a chipmunk, impulsive silly stunt.
Then Wizard had to slap him, and right across the face,
A lover not a fighter, he laughed without disgrace.

I called him Kaos poody, silly willy, and bandini.
I called him the snooda, tuna-luna, and zucchini.
I called him seal-point princess, burry furry, and the orkus,
To all of my philosophies, he gives life sweetest porpoise.

Unlike a dog he wouldn't come, whatever name I used.
Just seeing him uplifted me, my spirits he amused.
I miss that snortus porpoise, I cry for him at night,
His regal presence haunts me, but I must not lose sight.
All roly-polyed into one: wisdom, calm, and strife,
Most beautiful companion, the porpoise of my life.

CONTENTS

ACKNOWLEDGMENTS

Although I would have to write poetry, if only I could, to even begin to express my gratitude, I extend my heartfelt thanks to my family, especially Beni, Yuki, Hurrican, and Mayo; and to Rosario, who not only appreciates the importance of Kaos but also has shown how poetry can approach the depths of love.

I would like to thank Kalpana Seshadri-Crooks, who on an outing with her beautiful collies and me, suggested that I write a book on animals. Her feedback on a version of the first two chapters is also appreciated, especially because it led to the notion of *animal pedagogy*. I would also like to thank Fred Evans, Leonard Lawlor and Eduardo Mendieta for their extremely thoughtful and helpful comments on an early draft of the manuscript. I am grateful for Wendy Lochner's encouragement throughout this project. Many others have helped me along the way, including Ellen Armour, Walter Brogan, Ed Casey, Tina Chanter, Beth Conklin, Colin Dayan, Lara Giordano, Lisa Guenther, Adrian Johnston, Elissa Marder, Elaine Miller, Mary Rawlinson, Alison Suen, Lisa Walsh, Cynthia Willett, David Wood, and Emily Zakin.

I would also like to acknowledge that parts of chapters 8 and 9 appeared as "Strange Kinship: Heidegger and Merleau-Ponty on Animals" in *Epoché: a journal of the history of philosophy* (fall 2009); parts of chapter 10 appeared as "Stopping the Anthropological Machine: Agamben with Heidegger and Merleau-Ponty" in *Phaenex* (an electronic journal (spring 2008); parts of chapter 4 appeared as "Tropho-Ethics: Derrida's Homeopathic Purity," *Harvard Review* (fall 2007); and parts of chapters 2 and 3 appeared as "Animal Pedagogy: The Origin of 'Man' in Rousseau and Herder," *Culture, Theory and Critique* 47, no. 2 (2006):107–31. Thanks to those journals for allowing me to use this same material here.

ANIMAL LESSONS

Biting the Hand That Feeds You

The Role of Animals *in Philosophies of* Man

On October 3, 2003, after years of performing in the Las Vegas show *Siegfried & Roy*, Montecore, a white tiger, attacked Roy Horn and nearly killed him. The attack sparked a debate about why the tiger bit Roy and dragged him off stage by the neck. Some people claimed that the tiger was trying to protect Roy, who had tripped and fallen; others speculated that the tiger sensed Roy's impending stroke; some blamed a "big-haired" woman in the front row; others suggested a thyroid disorder; and some insisted that a tiger is an unpredictable wild predator who will attack without reason or warning. Late-night television was full of jokes about the big cat. Later, Roy insisted that the tiger was trying to protect him, possibly sensing his stroke. He maintained that the tiger was acting on a benevolent instinct, perhaps a sixth sense unavailable to humans, and intended no harm. Roy still calls Montecore his "lifesaver." Was the attack inevitable or a freak accident?

These speculations about Roy's "accident" suggest that questions of the animal mind, and of the animal more generally, are still unanswered. Indeed, we could say that Roy performs our conflicted relationship with animals: his seemingly paradoxical attempt to master them through love, his sense of himself so closely connected to his animals, and the fact that he made his living by exhibiting them and training them. Roy's accident reveals the illusionist's most profound illusion: that he can master animals. That is, the accident was a *symptom* of the animal accidents at the heart of everything we take to be distinctively human that assures us of our mastery over all other creatures and the earth. (*Symptom* also means "fall," "chance," or "accident"; from *symptoma,* meaning "accident.") Montecore and Roy, trained tiger and circus trainer, set the stage for a discussion of the way that animals have performed in the texts of philosophers, particularly when they bite back.

The Way to Man's Origin Is Through His Stomach

In the history of philosophy, the necessity of human existence has been justified with appeals to an eternal realm of forms or reason, divine providence or design, nature or natural laws, and perhaps the most influential alternative to the hand of God: the hand of Nature through the law of natural selection. What these religious and secular accounts of the origin of man share is their insistence on necessity over chance, providence over accident. Man's existence is preordained by God or Nature; it is *not* an accident. In part 2, I turn to a moment in the history of philosophy in which the obsession with nature's providence may be the most dramatic, and explore animal accidents at the heart of human necessity in the pre-Darwinian Romantic myths of the origin of man in texts by Jean-Jacques Rousseau and Johann Gottfried Herder, with an eye to how the animals in these texts "bite back." In those passages in which they delineate what distinguishes man from animals, both Rousseau and Herder turn to animals to illuminate their arguments. Their animals do not merely serve as examples against which they define man. Rather, these animals belie the very distinction between man and animal that their invocation seeks to establish. As we will see, the examples and metaphors of animals that inhabit these texts ape or mock assertions of any uniquely human characteristics.

Animals appear in these texts as either ideal or abject ancestors and, as such, are corralled into a past belonging to man. I diagnose slips in the philosopher's attempt to "train" his animals, which reveal both the ways in which the notion of human necessity is dependent on animal accidents and the ways in which that dependence is absorbed into myths of human origin as animal sacrifice. Ultimately, on the conceptual level *the animal* is sacrificed for *man,* and on the literal level, animals are sacrificed for the sake of men. Animals metaphorically and literally fortify and sustain man. Despite their differences, for both Rousseau and Herder, men become civilized, that is, become man, in relation to *eating* animals. Rousseau identifies the evolution of men in terms of what they eat; he says that grain eaters are the most civilized and that the cake was the first form of communion. Man's superiority to other animals is based on the fact that he is an omnivore and can eat everything. In contrast, Herder distinguishes man from animal insofar as man eats fine foods and animals eat coarse foods, which makes man fine and animals coarse. Unlike Rousseau, Herder prefers domesticated animals, particularly sheep, which teach man to speak. For both Rousseau and Herder, man becomes human by eating and assimilating animals. If man becomes human by eating animals, he becomes a speaking being by assimilating animal voices through imitation. In a close reading of particular texts, language and other characteristics unique to man, including spirit, reason, understanding, recollection, recognition, free will, and even fire, are *responses* to animals whom men ape or imitate. Like the circus trainer, however, the philosopher cannot fully domesticate his metaphorical animals.

In the interview "Eating Well," Derrida argues that we cannot avoid assimilating the other, that we need to eat and that eating is good. For him, the question becomes *how* to eat, not *what* to eat (which is why he can claim to be a vegetarian in his soul, even though he eats meat). In chapter 4, I examine the distinction between what and how, since *how* we eat is determined by *what* we take something to be. As Cora Diamond might say, it is not because people are capable of reason or language or because they can suffer that they do not eat them (1978). Rather, we do not eat people because we do not consider people food. If we did not consider animals *good* to eat, we wouldn't consider them food, and vice versa. We eat animals because we consider them food. Returning to Rousseau's notion of what is good to eat, which for him is inherently related to what is morally good, I explore the limits of Derrida's own discourse of purity in terms of eating well and good taste (in both the sensory and moral senses). I investigate his notions of pure forgiveness, hospitality, and gift in relation to what I call the *homeopathic purity* of his hyperbolic ethics, or ethics of limits. Derrida says in *The Animal* that he is concerned with what "feeds" the limits of the man/animal binary. Taking off from his discussion of one of these limits, *trophe*, I nibble at a precarious distinction between two senses of the term, nourishment and trophy, which offer different ways to assimilate and/or eat the other. We can eat only what we need to eat in order to nourish ourselves while nurturing relationships with others so that assimilation is as nourishing as possible. Or we can kill animals for the sake of conquest and mount our trophies on the wall, dissect them and write about it in journals, or train them to jump through hoops of fire on a Las Vegas stage. The primary warning of Derrida's hyperbolic ethics is that we cannot be certain which is which. We cannot always distinguish between nourishment and trophy, which is why hyperbolic ethics requires constant vigilance over not only *how* and *what* but also *why* we eat and/or assimilate the other. From Rousseau and Herder to Freud and Kristeva, philosophers suggest that the human and humanity are determined by what we eat. Whether they think that we are what we eat (like Rousseau and Herder) or that we are not what we eat (like Freud and Kristeva), man becomes human by eating animals. Indeed, Kristeva's *Powers of Horror* is devoted to rituals and prohibitions that govern what counts as food and how we become who we are in relation to what we eat. How "we" define "ourselves" is determined by what and how we eat and/or assimilate.

I begin this project by looking back at eighteenth-century notions of humanity and animality that define man according to what he eats or assimilates, in order to set the stage for investigating the ways in which philosophies of otherness from Freud through Kristeva repeat romantic gestures that exclude and abject animals. By examining texts as varied of those of Jean-Jacques Rousseau, Johann Herder, Sigmund Freud, Martin Heidegger, Jacques Lacan, Maurice Merleau-Ponty, Simone de Beauvoir, Jacques Derrida, Giorgio Agamben, and Julia Kristeva, we see that concepts of subjectivity, humanity, politics, and ethics continue to be defined by the double movement of assimilating and then disavowing the animal, animality, and animals. Even nineteenth- and twentieth-century thinkers who explicitly reject romantic notions of humanism rely on an opposition between human and animal born out of this double movement to describe a divided subjectivity constituted in relation to alterity. Even in their attempt to undermine or decenter the Cartesian self-sovereign subject by revealing its dependence on the other, they use and efface the animal other and other animals. Animals are so radically other, it seems, they cannot even stand in the place of the other in relation to the subject of philosophy. Yet in significant ways, animals remain the invisible support for whatever we take to be human subjectivity, as fractured and obscure as it may become. Just as philosophers from Aristotle through Kant have used animals to support a notion of the unified or autonomous subject, in philosophies of alterity the abstract concept *animal* continues to work along with animal metaphors, examples, illustrations, and animal studies to support alternative notions of a split or decentered subject. Even as these thinkers challenge the Cartesian subject and the concomitant notions of rationality, sovereignty, and individuality, they continue to rely on the divide between human and animal. Even Deleuze and Guattari, whose notion of "becoming-animal" is intended to unseat the Cartesian subject, show little concern for actual animals. And although they draw attention to the fluidity and relationality of the human, they also use the concept of becoming-animal to reconceive the human subject. In this way, the animal is again put into the service of man. Perhaps this is unavoidable in any attempt to imagine new modalities of human–animal relations. They do insist that the becoming other of the subject transforms its others. So, man's becoming-animal also necessarily changes his animal others. Still, for Deleuze and Guattari, animals become a human mode of being-as-becoming that corresponds to "zones of liberated intensities" (1986, 13). Their animals signal the fluidity and intensity of a "human all too human" experience.

Moreover, even though philosophers of difference attempt in various ways to rethink ethics based on otherness, alterity, and difference, rather than on identity and sameness, they do not recognize the differences among animals or the possibility of ethical relations with them. On the contrary, the very notions of humanity and ethics continue to be formed through a disavowal of their dependence on the animal and animals. In various ways and to different degrees, these philosophers of alterity continue to erect fences to keep animals out. Animal difference is too different, too other, too foreign, even for these thinkers of alterity. As a result, their philosophies remain conservative and traditional in this regard. Like their predecessors, with few exceptions they accept something like the Cartesian notion of the animal even while they reject the Cartesian notion of the human subject. But we cannot decenter the human subject without also calling into question the animal other. To try, as these thinkers do, is to disavow our dependence on the animal, animality, and animals. It is to disavow what I call *animal pedagogy*— the ways in which animals through these philosophical discourses teach us to be human. It disavows the ways in which human kinship and community depend on the absolute foreclosure of animal kinship and community. In other words, it repeats the very power structure of subject and object, of us versus them, of human versus animal, that the ethics of difference is purportedly working against, or working through (in the psychoanalytic sense).

By uncovering the latent humanism in antihumanist texts, we continue to witness the ambivalence toward animality and animals that has defined Western philosophy and culture. This ambivalence is all the more striking in these philosophies of ambivalence. The very psychoanalytic notion of ambivalence itself is linked to the history of using and disavowing animals. Engaging with animal figures in these texts, however, reveals the dependence of man, human, humanity, and subjectivity on animal, animals, and animality. Looking to the animals in these texts can help us acknowledge our dependence on animals on all levels of our existence, physical, imaginary, and symbolic. As animals make their way into these texts, they cross through fences erected to keep them out. They bite the metaphysical hand that feeds them. It is telling that the violence toward animals in these philosophies of otherness—like the romantic philosophies of man before them—correlates with how vehemently they reject the proximity between the animal and the human. Nonetheless, some of these philosophers of ambiguity challenge the traditional opposition between man and animal in favor of a more complicated set of boundaries. Merleau-Ponty and Derrida, in particular, insist on more fluidity between humans and animals in the case of the former, and on "thicker" distinctions in the case of the later, than the man/animal binary allows. Deleuze and Guattari imagine human–animal hybrids and becomings. In her attempt to vindicate woman, de Beauvoir tries to redeem all female animals. Kristeva addresses some of the ways in which man defines what is properly human (and what is properly food) through rituals involving killing and eating animals.

We could say that like Roy Horn, some philosophers of ambiguity and otherness replace with love the chair and whips of previous animal trainers. From loving your symptom and embracing the other within, to learning to love the otherness of others and developing an ethics based on difference rather than sameness, these thinkers try to come to terms with ambiguity rather than bury their heads in the sand denying it. Like Roy, they have come to see that the other, and in some cases even the animal other, is not and cannot be trained. In Roy's own words, "This is like any other relationship. It doesn't always go as planned" (Friess 2003, 16). Of these philosophers, Derrida in particular continually tries to show how mastery of either the other or oneself is an illusion; it is—to quote the title of Roy's memoir—to try "mastering the impossible." In his first posthumously published book, *The Animal That Therefore I Am* (2008), Derrida reminds us of the menagerie of creatures that he calls on to witness the beastliness of the categorical, oppositional, and exclusionary thinking of Western philosophy. Not so much a Doctor Doolittle as a shape shifter who signs in the name of various animals, Derrida himself is a master of the impossible, or more precisely, he is the master of demonstrating the impossibility of mastery. With masterful consistency, he points to the impossibility of the sovereign subject of Western philosophy's "I can," whether it is the "I can" of "I can train the others/animals" or of the "I can love the others/animals," which amount to the same thing if love is a matter of knowing, understanding, sovereignty, individuality, autonomy, possession, mastery, law—those values at the center of the Cartesian subject, not to mention Western ideals of citizenship, rights, morality, and politics. Derrida insists on the uncertainty, impossibility, and ambiguity inherent in Western attempts to maintain categorical oppositions between man and animal. This opposition gives rise to many other dichotomies in whose name we torture and murder one another, whether it is man/woman, white/black, citizen/foreigner, pure/impure, righteous/infidel. Even the binaries love/hate, justice/injustice, and giving/taking come under scrutiny when Derrida insists that we cannot always distinguish one from the other, that our ways of loving can also be ways of killing.[1] He is not proposing that we stop loving or giving or seeking justice but that we cannot stop. We cannot rest in our quest to love or give, but this vigilence requires questioning our history, our motivations, our sense of ourselves as sovereign agents in pursuit of these goals. In *The Animal That Therefore I Am (That I Follow)*, this pursuit is the pursuit of the animal.[2] Here Derrida examines the various ways in which we follow the animal, both coming after the animal and being after the animal, as in tracking it. It is this ambivalence toward the animal, animality, and animals that I pursue in this book.

Sciences of Man and Animals: "Mastering the Impossible"

Derrida's following or coming after the animal resonates with Roy Horn's description of his relationship with animals. The media describe Roy as a modern-day Doctor Doolittle who is able to communicate with animals. This is an image fostered by Roy himself, who, in his memoir *Mastering the Impossible,* says, "My certainty of unconditional trust, unconditional emotion and unconditional strength—comes from my animals. . . . My animals are the friends who will accept me always for what I am—rich or poor, fat or thin, dumb or intelligent" (see Achenbach 2003, D1). Roy implies that his certainty of himself—"what I am"—comes from his animals. His account of his dependence on his animals for his very sense of himself suggests that his "therefore I am" follows from his relationships with animals. The title of his memoir, however, implies a mastery over the animals that he achieves through this special relationship. The sense of himself that comes from his relationships with animals thus includes a sense of mastery over them, and his trust and love are built on this mastery. His relationship with animals gives him confidence in himself. As one article put it, he was "a boy who found love among the animals" (Achenbach 2003, D1). Roy has mastered the impossible, the "unconditional" nature of Nature, the animality of the animal. He claims that his mastery does not come from violent domination of the big cats with whips or chairs but from love, what he calls "affection conditioning." In the words of fellow Vegas entertainer Penn Jillette (of Penn and Teller), "Every other animal trainer has this macho feeling of control over the beasts. It's chairs and whips and yelling. It's like 'I'm going to bitch-slap them into submission.' Roy's style was, 'I love these animals so much, they do whatever I want them to do'" (Achenbach 2003, D1). Given the traditional associations between women and animals, it is noteworthy that Jillette refers to violent training techniques as "bitch-slapping," since "bitch" is both a derogatory name for women and the designation of female dogs. Roy's love, his way with animals, allowed him to domesticate wild tigers without "bitch-slapping" them and to create the illusion of his mastery over them; at least it did until that fateful October evening when Montecore sank his teeth into Roy's neck and bit back.

My project here is to indicate various ways in which, despite philosophers' attempts to domesticate the animal, animality, and animals like Montecore, animals break free of their textual confines and bite back. For the most part, the animals in these texts have been tamed, even maimed, in the name of philosophy or science and for the sake of determining what is proper to *man* or, in the case of Simone de Beauvoir, *woman*. For example, the entire first section of de Beauvoir's seminal *The Second Sex* is devoted to biology, especially zoology, which she (inconsistently) uses both to vindicate females of all species and to uncouple the traditional associations between woman and animal. Both Merleau-Ponty and Lacan (who were close friends) are especially fond of citing animal studies to develop theories about perception, imagination, and consciousness in man. Animal studies, particularly one involving the dissection of a bee, figure prominently in Heidegger's comparative analysis of animals and Dasein. The development of the emerging science of ecology influenced the later work of Heidegger, Merleau-Ponty, and Lacan. In chapters 8 and 9, I show that Heidegger and Merleau-Ponty use zoology, biology, and ecology in their attempts to navigate between mechanism and vitalism toward a theory of humanity that takes us beyond Cartesian dualisms of mind and body or subject and object. But their interpretations and use of the life sciences takes them on divergent paths and leads them to radically different conclusions regarding the relationship between man and animal. For example, whereas Heidegger sees in contemporary biology an emphatic insistence on the uniqueness of man, Merleau-Ponty sees proof of the continuity between man and animal; although biology confirms Heidegger's insistence on the rupture and irruption of Dasein, it only further substantiates Merleau-Ponty's insistence on a type of continuity that cannot be reduced to biological continuism. Whereas Heidegger sees an abyss between man and animal, Merleau-Ponty sees kinship. And although both object to Darwinian theories of evolution, they do so for very different reasons. Ultimately, however, both of them engage in what I call "animal pedagogy" by using animals, the animal, and animality to teach us about men, the human, and humanity. Moreover, both treat their animal examples in ways that betray their attempts to avoid conceiving of humans as dominating subjects standing against objects or other beings as their lord and master, concerned with them only insofar as they have a use or value for their own projects.

In *This Is Not Sufficient*, Leonard Lawlor lays out the dangers of both biological continuism and metaphysical separationism, which he sees as the extreme positions in debates about the relationship between man and animal (2007, esp. 25–26, 52). *Biological continuism* is the position that humans and animals are fundamentally the same, that their differences are no more than degrees of the same kinds of things, whether it is consciousness, emotions, pain, or linguistic systems. (This is the position of many philosophers of animal rights and animal welfare.) *Metaphysical separationism* is the position that humans and animals are fundamentally different types of beings whose similarities are superficial at best or anthropomorphisms at worst. (This is the position of much of the history of philosophy that justifies man's dominion over animals.) On the surface, Merleau-Ponty could be regarded as a biological continuist, and Heidegger could be regarded as a metaphysical separationist. In both cases, however, their analysis of the relationship between humans and animals is more nuanced than either of these positions suggests. As Derrida's critical engagement indicates, Heidegger's "abyssal kinship" with animals is fraught with conceptual dependencies that belie his attempts to keep humans and animals ontologically separate. As we will see in chapters 9 and 10, Merleau-Ponty's notion of "strange kinship" should not be read as straightforward biological continuism. The strangeness of our relation with animals, along with what he calls the thickness of flesh, both connects us and distinguishes us as and from animals.

De Beauvoir and Lacan also use animal studies and animal examples in ways that oscillate between continuism and separationism and thereby demonstrate a certain ambiguity toward the animal, animality, and animals. For de Beauvoir, we are *not* born as but become man or woman; however, along with other animals, we *are* born female or male. She begins her discussion of biology claiming that female animals have gotten a bad rap, suggesting that setting the record straight by using the black widow spider and the praying mantis, we can also reform our views of female human beings. In the end, however, she merely replaces the man in the man/animal opposition with woman. Ironically, it is woman's weakness and pain in service to the species through childbirth that makes her distinct from other animals. As Derrida might say, it is her fault that makes her superior to other animals. De Beauvoir does not revalue the feminine as it has been linked to denigrated animality; rather, she calls on women to transcend their animality to become equal to men. Given her ambivalence toward the animal, animality, and animals, it becomes clear that de Beauvoir turns to animals not to vindicate them in their own right but only to use them to help redeem woman, and then only as far as they become more like man.

Lacan, as well, identifies a weakness in man's constitution that separates him from other animals. As I show in part 4, if fragility for de Beauvoir makes the woman, duplicity for Lacan makes the man. According to Lacan, in addition to man's "premature birth," he differs from other animals in his ability to prevaricate. Like de Beauvoir, Lacan frequently turns to animals to make his case. Although generally—we might say in the flippant tone Lacan himself often employs—he doesn't give a rat's ass about empirical science, particularly behavioral psychology;

he loves animal studies. Consequently, he uses animal studies and animal illustrations to point to a continuation between man and animals, on the one hand, or to insist on the radical separation between man and animals, on the other. In some texts, it seems that what separates man from animals is man's imagination; in others, animals share imagination but lack access to the symbolic; and in still others, although they have some access to the symbolic, they are unable to lie. Whereas man can erase his tracks and make what is true appear false (and vice versa), animals can make false tracks, but they can neither erase their tracks nor make true ones appear false. Derrida analyzes the irony in making man's duplicity his hallmark and questions the distinction between merely lying and lying about lying or erasing one's tracks and making the true appear false. Following Derrida, I challenge the distinction between reaction and response, which for Lacan becomes the ultimate stinger in the man/animal opposition.

Heidegger, Merleau-Ponty, Lacan, de Beauvoir, Freud, and Kristeva all use empirical science to support and substantiate their speculative theories. Even as they challenge the distinction between fact and value, they use animal studies to make their work appear more scientific, more factual. In other words, they use animal studies as facts that anchor their theories about the evaluative and interpretative nature of man. For example, as we will see in chapter 8, despite his criticisms of instrumental reason, Heidegger uncritically uses animal studies to prove his speculative hypotheses about Dasein. De Beauvoir challenges the distinction between nature and culture in regard to woman using the nature of animals as evidence. In chapter 6, I analyze the ways in which de Beauvoir's analysis undermines the traditional distinction between fact and value, even though she continues to use it in regard to animals. Facts of biology may always be framed by interpretations, but animals still occupy a natural world cut off from the world of human culture. As I point out in chapter 11, Freud and, in a more complicated way, Lacan struggle with the status of psychoanalysis as a science. As a result, their science envy leads them to use, and not occasionally abuse, data from zoology and, in Freud's case, anthropology. In *Powers of Horror*, Kristeva refers to contemporary anthropology to revise Freud's theory of the uncanny, which becomes her notion of the abject. Chapter 12 shows that although Kristeva is more self-reflective about her use of the "sciences of man," she too accepts its findings as "fact" in a human world otherwise filled with interpretation. These theorists use animals, animal studies, anthropology, and biology to make their work appear scientific so that they can more persuasively outline the dynamics of the uniquely human psyche. In other words, they use animals to add rhetorical force to their descriptions of the distinctive qualities of the human. We see logic familiar from the history of philosophy, in which animals are used to shore up the borders of man. In other words, animals are called as witnesses to man's superiority. According to this logic, animals are more than what is excluded from the category *human*. They also teach man how to be human: man is human by virtue of animal pedagogy.

The use of animals in science is well known. Animals serve as "guinea pigs" for all sorts of experiments that teach us about ourselves. Usually, however, these animals do not fare well, because scientists' techniques are invasive and violent. Because our biology and medical science depend on animals (and now our design and engineering depend on animals), our relationship to animals continues to be ambivalent. Most of the sciences at best consider animals awesome spectacles that teach us about ourselves and the world, and at worst they are mere objects to be used and abused for human purposes. We rely on animals not only for food but also, among other things, for complex computer programs and intelligence, which traditionally have been seen as the unique domain of humans. Designers have turned to animals to see what they can learn about everything from computer modeling and complex delivery routes to car design and search-and-rescue robots. Bees and ants teach us how to communicate important information quickly and efficiently. Lizards teach us how to get water to dry regions. Humpback whales teach us how to increase wind power from windmills. Sharks teach us how to design aerodynamic swimwear (see Mueller 2008). The study of "swarm intelligence" indicates that "almost any group that follows the bee's rules will make itself smarter" (Miller 2007, 138). Of course, the human means of "learning" is violent and often involves killing and dissecting its teachers. These animals are regarded as cool specimens rather than fellow creatures that we imitate, learn from, and follow. Certainly, there must be other models of pedagogy we might adopt, models that do not involve eating and dissecting the teacher, or at least doing so in more metaphorical and less literal ways, in more thoughtful and less violent ways. Echoing Derrida's sentiment, if we want to assimilate what animals can teach us, perhaps we should attend to how we learn from, and how we should thank, our teachers.[3] We need to examine the role that animals play in the sciences of man. We need to interrogate the ways in which our lifestyles too often depend on extinguishing theirs.

Although Giorgio Agamben is not so much concerned with animals themselves, he scrutinizes the role of science, particularly the sciences of man and the science of ecology, in his analysis of what he calls "the anthropological machine." In *The Open,* Agamben examines various ways that philosophies and science have created *man* against *the animal,* which he claims operates as the constitutive inside of the concepts *man* and *human.* That is, the categories *human* and *man* contain a subhuman other that can be figured as *animal* and thereby excluded from the polis, even killed. In chapter 10, I turn to Agamben's critical engagement with the man/animal dichotomy and "the anthropological machine" to illuminate the political stakes of animal pedagogy and animal kinship. Agamben is primarily concerned with the ethical and political consequences of producing the concept *human* in relation to the concept *animal*. He suggests that a by-product of the anthropological machine is the subhuman, or the human being deemed animal to justify its enslavement and genocide. Although Agamben does not extend his analysis to the "enslavement or genocide" of animals, his conclusion that in order to stop the anthropological machine, we need a "Shabbat" of both man and animal clearly has implications for the animal side as well as the human side of the dichotomy. In the end, I examine Agamben's call for "Shabbat" by returning to a discussion of the role of science, now in relation to religion, in philosophies of animality. But rather than turn away from science and back toward religion, as Agamben suggests, I return to Merleau-Ponty's philosophy of nature to find resources for reconceiving the mysteries of science so that its objects are not merely specimens under the microscope of human mastery but instead are fellow creatures, our teachers, our companions, our kin, even if it is a "strange kinship."

Trotting Out the Animals, or Tigers on Cue

Certainly, philosophies and sciences of man have treated animals as specimens for study, more often than not for the sake of discovering something about humans and not for the benefit of animals themselves. Rousseau, Herder, Freud, Heidegger, de Beauvoir, Lacan, and Kristeva, as just a few examples, are concerned with animals only insofar as they can teach us something about humans. Although some of them—especially Rousseau, Freud, and Lacan—mention animals in nearly everything they wrote, those animals are put in the service of their theories about human language, human society, and human desires. In various ways, these philosophers dissect, probe, exploit, and domesticate animals to shore up their notions of human and humanity. Moreover, they disavow the animal pedagogy at the heart of their philosophies of man. Rather than acknowledge the role of animals in the philosophies and sciences of man, they erase their tracks as soon as they make them. Like the circus trainer, they trot out the animals to perform on cue for the sake of man. But the functions that these trained and domesticated animals perform in their texts exceed their stated ends. They are never mere examples, illustrations, or animal studies. Rather, they are the literal and metaphorical creatures by virtue of which we become human subjects. Like Roy's white tiger Montecore, we cannot know for certain whether or not these animals-on-cue are following the script, have missed their mark, or are carrying us off stage for their own ends. By looking closely at where they show up and how they are used, my analysis reveals the unpredictability of the animal effects in these texts. Even as they create the illusion of something proper to man, on closer examination they reveal the secrets to the philosopher's success in apparently mastering the impossible, turning wild animal metaphors into domesticated beasts of burden to prove their theories about man. Examining the animals in these texts reveals the smoke and mirrors behind the philosophers' tricks, particularly when they rely on pulling a metaphysical rabbit out of a metaphorical hat.

One Vegas producer hit the mark when speaking of Siegfried and Roy's success with the white tiger extravaganza: "The show's success was based largely on the illusion that the duo could turn exotic, wild beasts into obedient, docile pets" (Friess 2003, 16). The duo's symbol was

the white tiger, but look closer—it's a white tiger hitting its mark. It's the tiger on cue. For years, Montecore walked within feet of the audience, unleashed, never declawed, and he always hit his mark. According to [Steve] Wynn, he did so even on that terrible night when he left the stage with Roy in his mouth—"exactly on his mark, where the blocking is, at the exact speed he walks off every night." (Achenbach 2003, D1)

It is the tiger-on-cue that turned Siegfried and Roy's show into the longest-running live show in history. The duo's show was at the heart of the first casino—Steve Wynn's Mirage—that moved from gambling and glitz to spectacle and family entertainment and thereby revitalized Las Vegas. In a sense, the new Las Vegas strip was built on the white tigers. The white tigers breathed new life into Vegas.

Paradoxically, as Roy's memoir, *Mastering the Impossible,* demonstrates, part of the tigers' appeal is that even while they are mastered, conditioned, and commoditized, the tigers represent natural purity uncontaminated by human exchange, uncontaminated by Vegas. Even as they helped "remake" Las Vegas from sin city into spectacular family entertainment, these animals are imagined as being outside the market as representatives of the sheer power of life, the *unconditional* whose *impossibility* makes them all the more marketable. Roy's accident reveals that the duo's success, along with the revival of Las Vegas itself, was dependent on this illusion of mastering the impossible. Montecore's actions forcing the cancellation of the most profitable show in Vegas history reveals how Roy—and all of us—profits from his/our relationship with these animals. The question becomes, In what ways do we profit? Do we profit from their exploitation? Or do we profit from acknowledging our dependence on them and the importance of what they teach us? Do we profit from the illusion that we can understand and control them, if not through violence or scientific observation, then, like Roy, through love (many media reports of Montecore's attack maintained that the one man who could say why the tiger attacked was lying in the hospital fighting for his life)? Why would the tiger literally bite the hand that fed and loved him (Montecore bit Roy's arm before he took him off stage by the neck)? These questions point to a more fundamental way in which we profit from our relationships with animals who sustain us: the constitution of our humanity is dependent on animal pedagogy, a dependence that is projected onto the animal, who seemingly becomes dependent on man as his benefactor or lord, the shepherd of beings. In this way, our indebtedness to animals is disavowed. And it is this dependence, this indebtedness, that is disavowed by the notion that we can master animals or animality itself. The tension between Roy's mastery of, and his love for, his animals points to the ambivalent position occupied by the animal, animality, and animals in Western thought. What surfaces in Roy's intimate relationship with the tigers, and the accident that belies it, is the illusion that animals exist for us, for our entertainment, that we can own them, "my animals" as Roy says.

Like Roy, Freud is especially fond of trotting out animals to perform the Oedipal drama. Freud stages the Oedipal complex, along with castration, anxiety, neurosis, and the primary processes, using animals, which appear on cue whenever his theory is in doubt. Of the veritable zoological compendium running through Freud's work, he puts the spotlight on a few animals that, like Roy's white tigers, made him famous, namely, the rat, the wolf, and the horse. Among Freud's most famous cases are The Rat-Man and The Wolf-Man, both named for the animals of their phobias. Along with Little Hans, who is afraid of horses, these animal phobics take center stage in Freud's development of his most important concepts, especially the Oedipal and castration complexes. Indeed, it seems that whenever Freud needs to prove the reality of the castration threat, he trots out the animal phobias, full of scary animals that threaten to bite off the penises of bad little boys. I argue in chapter 11 that Freud's use of these animals both supports and undercuts his theory of the Oedipal family romance. Freud attempts to domesticate these animals in order to cure his patients. But as I will show, in significant ways they escape their natural enclosures to bite back. The threats represented by these animals have as much to do with womb envy and sisterly identifications as they do with paternal castration threats. Not coincidently, these feminine figures remain linked to the natural world of the animal even as they are used to play up the prominent role of the masculine members of Freud's cast. In chapter 11, I attempt to unleash both the animal and feminine figures that work as beasts of burden in Freud's development of psychoanalysis. I show how they bite back even while hitting their mark.

Kristeva develops and extends the connection between the feminine and the animal associated with Freud's uncanny. In *Powers of Horror,* she develops the notion of abjection in food prohibitions, which regulate how we eat animals, in relation to the role of the maternal body and its representatives. The questions of how and what we eat become, in her analysis, rituals for regulating the power of maternal authority in a battle between the sexes. As I argue in chapter 12, even as she uncovers this repressed maternal authority and complicates the maternal function as it operates in psychoanalysis, she perpetuates the association between woman and animal. In addition, although she diagnoses how repressed animality returns to the "speaking animal" through the maternal figure, she does not acknowledge the role of animals themselves even when they are eaten in rituals of purification. Her notion of the abject devouring mother is a reflection of a figure that remains in the shadows of her analysis, the abject devouring animal. Her theory of abjection both enacts, and reveals a slippage between maternity and animality in psychoanalysis. In this regard, we could say that psychoanalysis is an animal by-product.

The Science of Kinship

In my engagement with Freud's *Totem and Taboo,* and Kristeva's notion of the abject, I consider the slippage from the literal flesh and blood of animals to the metaphorical flesh and blood of human kinship. As I argue in chapter 11, Freud's use of the anthropology of kinship in *Totem and Taboo* undermines his notion of what he calls the "real family" with its Oedipal drama. The logic of totemism on which his analysis of the origins of civilization rests is based on the possibility of kinship with animals. Indeed, Freud defines kinship in terms of the totem animal and goes to great lengths to substitute the metaphorical flesh and blood of the nuclear family for the flesh and blood of animals worshipped through totemic religions. In Kristeva's analysis (which, in an important sense, is an update of Freud's *Totem and Taboo*), because the human body is no longer considered literal flesh and blood for consumption, it becomes the metaphorical flesh and blood of kinship. What she does not consider is that animal flesh becomes the nourishing substitute on which human kinship ripens. As I argue in chapter 12, for Kristeva animals are never more than the representatives of human relations; they become symbols through which human relationships are created. Disembodied and drained of their blood, these symbolic animals are assimilated so that we can live. The literal consumption of their bodies that feed ours is accompanied by the symbolic assimilation that allows us to become speaking animals, animals who sublimate. As it does with Freud, the animal lies behind Kristeva's primary processes, but in Kristeva's reinterpretation of Little Hans's phobia, the role of the

Freudian father is now played by the mother. Although its human referent has changed, the role of the animal remains the same. It stands in for what we cannot think and what we cannot accept about ourselves. In this Freudian scenario, we eat what we are not, and vice versa. We do not eat our kin, and if we do, it isn't kin. Human kinship is the result of animal sacrifice.

In *The Animal,* Derrida wonders whether we can call an animal "brother." Discussing the biblical story of Cain and Abel, he asks,

What happens to the fraternity when an animal enters the scene. . . . Or, conversely, what happens to the animal when one brother comes after the other, when Abel is after Cain, who is after Abel. Or when a son is after his father. What happens to animals, surrogate or not, to the ass and ram on Mount Moriah? (2002, 381)

It seems that when brothers are after each other, animals get the worst of it. Think of Freud's account of the transition from primal horde to a band of brothers enacted through animal sacrifice (see chapter 11). Kinship with animals is sacrificed for the sake of human kinship. In other words, our notion that we are kin or that fraternity is possible between human beings is dependent on the absolute foreclosure of the possibility of kinship between human beings and animal beings or of proper kinship between animals.

The foreclosure of animal kinship is especially apparent in Heidegger's comparative analysis of humans and animals, in which animals live with us but cannot exist with us as true companions. Merleau-Ponty's notion of our "strange kinship" with animals, in contrast, says that fraternity between humans and animals is possible, which thereby transforms our traditional notion of kinship. This "strange kinship" attempts to balance relationships and communion between human and animal beings with respect for the differences between them: differences that extend to individual human or animal beings in ways that ultimately explode the dichotomy between man and animal. If Heidegger insists that the animal is captivated by the world in the sense of being captured by it, Merleau-Ponty allows for the possibility of animal captivation as a type of appreciative fascination for fellow creatures. By looking critically at the work of Rousseau, Herder, Beauvoir, Lacan, Heidegger, Merleau-Ponty, Freud, and Kristeva, we learn that human kinship is also a "strange kinship" forged through animal bodies. If the so-called brotherhood of man and human fraternity depend on animal sacrifices and the sacrifice of the animal, within the discourse of these texts it is the animals themselves that lead the way. We become the "family of man" by excluding the possibility of any animal family. As it turns out, however, because of its dependence on the denial of kinship with animals, human kinship itself is precarious. I argue that either kinship with animals is possible or kinship between humans is impossible (and perhaps both). Either way, we must rethink the very notion of kinship, making it strange rather than familiar.[4]

Kinship and Sexual Difference

Phrases like the "brotherhood of man" and "fraternity" do not grate on the ears just because they exclude animals but also because they exclude sisterhood, woman, and sorority.[5] As we know, within the patriarchal imaginary, woman and maternity are closely related to animal and animality; women's bodies have been imagined as subject to, and determined by, natural processes that make them closer to animals than to men. Chapter 11 demonstrates how Freud's theories conflate animals, sisters, and mothers and then disavow their importance in favor of sons and fathers. Like the animals, however, these sisters "bite back." It seems more surprising that feminist and postfeminist thinkers like de Beauvoir and Kristeva continue to employ notions of "brotherhood" and "fraternity" when pointing to the future of humankind. Although de Beauvoir loosens the man/animal binary by considering female animals and their relations to woman, and Kristeva stages the return of the repressed maternal body, Derrida perhaps most evocatively suggests a sexual difference "worthy of its name." In chapter 5, I again follow Derrida in thinking through the relation of sexual difference and animal difference. Rather than attempt to vindicate women, as de Beauvoir does, by placing them on the side of men in the man/animal divide, I approach the issue from the other side, the side of the animal. Recognizing the nearly infinite diversity of animal species that have been corralled into the concept *animal* may also help open the other side of the binary, *man*. In other words, if there are infinitely more differences on *the animal* side of the divide, there may be infinitely more differences on the *man* side of the divide. By opening up the *animal* to difference, including sexual difference, perhaps we can open up *man* to difference, including varieties of sex, sexuality, and genders.

In a striking scene in *The Animal*, Derrida talks about his embarrassment in front of his female pussycat, who, he says, is looking at his naked sex: "I often ask myself, just to see, who I am—and who I am (following) at the moment when, caught naked, in silence, by the gaze of an animal, for example, the eyes of a cat, I have trouble, yes, a bad time overcoming my embarrassment" (Derrida 2008, 3–4). His shame and embarrassment in front of his cat fly in the face of the history of philosophy in which while we look at them, animals do not look at us. In more contemporary philosophy, while the gaze of the other may recall us to ourselves and our freedom, that gaze does not emanate from the eyes of an animal, since supposedly animals are incapable of any encounter as such, and furthermore, they may not even have faces, properly speaking. Certainly, in the history of philosophy—unless it can be used to prove the superiority of man over woman—the sex of animals has been irrelevant. (Many of the jokes on late-night TV after Roy's accident with Montecore were jokes about sex and the big pussycat.)

Compare Derrida's embarrassment in front of his female cat with Merleau-Ponty's indifference to the gaze of a dog:

In fact the other's gaze transforms me into an object, and mine him, if we both make ourselves into an inhuman gaze, if each of us feels his actions to be not taken up and understood, but observed as if they were an insect's. This is what happens, for instance, when I fall under the gaze of a stranger. But even then, the objectification of each by the other's gaze is felt as unbearable only because it takes the place of possible communication. A dog's gaze directed towards me causes me no embarrassment. (2004a, 160)

Strangely, for Merleau-Ponty it is the human gaze become inhuman, and human movements become like an insect's—or perhaps a dog's or a cat's—that objectify us. When the gaze animalizes, then it makes us uncomfortable and recalls to us the possibility of a properly human exchange. For Merleau-Ponty, there is no embarrassment in front of a dog because communication is not possible there; because there is no possibility of an encounter, there is no shame. Here Merleau-Ponty forecloses the possibility of an encounter with an animal even as he imagines an inhuman gaze that turns humans into insects. This foreclosure, built as it is on animal metaphors (the insect), animal examples (the dog), and an opposition between human and inhuman, is yet another symptom of our ambivalence toward the animal, animality, and animals. Merleau-Ponty denies being embarrassed by this ambivalence. But it is precisely what gives Derrida a bad time when he sees himself through the eyes of his cat, as he says, naked as a jaybird. No wonder this bird feels threatened by the gaze of a cat, a gaze that has been disavowed. It is no surprise, therefore, that we are bewildered when the cat looks—or bites—back. For what if the human is by virtue of the look of the cat? What if the human subject comes to itself through the eyes of a cat? What if the human being speaks in response to the meow of a cat (à la Rousseau) or the baah of a sheep (à la Herder)? Derrida asks, What if the animal responded? Here I ask, What if the human responded? Can animals be our kin, our brothers, sisters, fathers, mothers, sons, and daughters? Diagnosing his animal phobics, Freud seems to think so. So does a New Yorker who kept a

Siberian tiger in his apartment until authorities took it away, who lamented, "I miss him a lot. He's like my brother, my best friend, my only friend, really." A bipolar Missouri man registered his parrot Sadie as a "service" animal because she says "Jim, I love you" when he starts having anxiety attacks. And what are we to make of a recent survey in which one-third of the women agreed with the statement "If my dog was a man, he'd be my boyfriend!"[6] Is this puppy love or the real thing? In the words of Cole Porter, "Is this real turtle soup, or only the mock?"

Women's Rights, Animal Rights

The connection between women and dogs runs deep. Donna Haraway wrote several essays on her connection with dogs and dog training, along with the various ways in which dogs and humans have developed through a relationship of mutual influence. Real estate mogul Leona Helmsley left $12 million to her Maltese, named Trouble (which led to death threats against the dog!), and $5 billion to $8 billion to the dogs of New York. One article reporting her doggie love was entitled "Rhymes with Rich," indicating yet another deep-seated connection between women and dogs.[7] Curiously, another arena in which animals have been compared with women is discussions of animal rights and animal welfare in mainstream analytic philosophy. Philosophers like Peter Singer and Tom Regan compare animal liberation with women's liberation. If animal rights and equality are analogous to women's rights and equality, then animal rights advocates could learn something from feminist criticisms of rights discourse. As I argue in part I, focusing on rights or equality and extending them to animals does not address more essential issues of conceptions of *the animal, man,* or *human.* It does not challenge the presumptions of humanism that makes man the measure of all things, including other animals and the earth. Insofar as it leaves intact traditional concepts of man and animal and the traditional values associated with them, it cannot transform our ways of thinking about either. The consequences of Western conceptions of man, human, and animal are deadly for both animals and various groups of people who have been figured as being like them. Without interrogating the man/animal opposition on the symbolic and imaginary levels, we can only scratch the surface in understanding exploitation and genocide of people and animals. As Agamben declares,

The very question of man—and of "humanism"—[that] must be posed in a new way . . . it is more urgent . . . to ask in what way—within man—has man been separated from non-man, and the animal from the human, than it is to take positions on the great issues, on so-called human rights and values. (2004, 16)[8]

Although Agamben is more concerned with separating the animal from the human in order to prevent treating people like animals than he is with the treatment of animals, he is right that we cannot begin to address the ways in which we denigrate some groups of people that we consider subhuman or nonhuman—that we consider or compare with animals—until we explore our ambivalence toward the animal, animality, and animals themselves.

Before we can fully appreciate what we mean by either animal rights or human rights, we must investigate what we mean by *animal* and *human,* particularly as the man/animal binary has been elemental in the development of the very notion of *rights.* In the following chapters, I examine the ways in which the animal, animality, and animals have been used in the history of philosophy, especially by philosophers expressly concerned with otherness and difference, in order to demonstrate how notions of man, human, pedagogy, and kinship are intimately linked to animals. As we will see, it is the animals that break free of the philosophical confines of these texts that teach us to be human and allow us to be kin. Although this book is not explicitly about animal rights, the first chapter demonstrates how the issues at stake here come to bear on mainstream discussions of animals rights and animal welfare. Here I explain how extending rights and equality to animals makes more obvious the paradoxes of rights discourse.

Considering animals opens a menagerie of problems that affect almost every aspect of our lives. On a philosophical level, the very conceptions of animal and human, rights and intelligence, are at stake. On a social level, giant global capitalist enterprises such as factory farming and much of the pharmaceutical industry, are relevant. On a personal level, what (or who) we eat, what (or who) we wear, and whom (or what) we call friends and family hang in the balance. In fact, our use of pronouns may need an overhaul depending on whether we conclude that animals are things (what) or persons (who). The stakes of bringing animals into our philosophical thinking about ethics and politics are mammoth. Indeed, much of the history of philosophy, particularly in ethics and politics, has depended on an explicit or implicit commitment to the man/animal dichotomy that defines man against animals.

In sum, in the rhetorical gestures of certain philosophical texts, man learns to be human from those very animals against which he defines himself. It is not just that the concepts of *human* and *animal* are intimately and essentially related in these texts but also that animals themselves show man how *not* to be one of them. It is not just that the *animal* and *animality* remain the constitutive outside of the concepts *human* and *humanity* or that the animal and animality are the abjected other against which what is properly human and humanity are defined and maintained. Certainly this is the case. What is as striking in these texts is the various ways in which they rely on examples, illustrations, metaphors, and studies of animals that belie their central theses about the human subject and humanity. It seems that the more adamantly these authors insist on an absolute distinction between man and animal, the more their arguments depend on *animal pedagogy*. Despite the explicit message of these texts—that humans are radically distinct from animals—animals function to teach man how to be human. Not surprisingly, then, this animal pedagogy is not acknowledged. To acknowledge the dependence of *man* and *humanity* on *animal* and *animality* is to undermine man's sense of himself as autonomous and self-sovereign. For, if anything, in the history of Western thought, man trains animals and not the other way around.

My point in examining some of the ways in which philosophers disavow the dependence of the human on the animal and humans on animals is not to argue that in the end, animals are like us. Rather than look to qualities or capacities that make them the same as or different from humans, like Deleuze and Guattari, I am interested in the *relationship* between the human and the animal, humans and animals.[9] To insist, as animal rights and welfare advocates do, that our ethical obligations to animals are based on sameness reinforces the type of humanism that leads to treating animals—and other people—as subordinates. Our consideration of animals makes it more pressing than ever not to repeat exclusive gestures that justify our treatment of animals based on what we take to be salient about their nature or behavior. Can we learn to appreciate animals for their differences from us and not just their similarities to us? It seems that an ethics of difference or alterity is what we need at this point. My analysis here suggests, however, that even an ethics of difference may not be adequate to considering animals. If the recent history of philosophies of alterity are any indication, we can acknowledge difference without also avowing our dependence on animals or including animals in ethical considerations. We can talk about both identity and difference without examining the relationship between them. Perhaps, then, we need to move from an ethics of sameness, through an ethics of difference, toward an ethics of *relationality* and *responsivity*. Animal ethics requires rethinking identity and difference, by focusing on relationships and response-ability.

By exploring the conceptual relations between *animal* and *human* and between animals and humans, we may come to see both animals and humans in a different light. Certainly we will have to reconsider how we relate to the animal, animality, and animals on a conceptual level as well as a practical level. Acknowledging the ways in which we are human by virtue of our relationships with animals suggests a fundamental indebtedness that takes us beyond the utilitarian calculations of the relative worth of this or that life (so common in philosophies of animal rights or welfare) or economic exchange values to questions of *sharing* the planet. This notion of sharing does not require having much in common besides living together on the same globe. But it does bring with it responsibility. The question, then, is not what characteristics or capacities animals share with us but how to share our resources and life together on this collective planet.

My aim in this book is not only to propose an animal ethics but also to show how ethics itself is transformed by considering animals. In this regard, I am not arguing for animal rights but suggesting that our entire conception of rights, based as it is on assumptions about autonomous human individuals, is altered by animal pedagogy and animal kinship. We must reconsider our notions of autonomy and freedom in relation to animals and ourselves. Obviously, the very conception of "ourselves" or "we" comes under scrutiny when we consider animals, not just because we may decide to include animals in those designations, but also because we acknowledge that animals always have been formative parts of our self-conception, an avowal that necessarily transforms it.[10] My project challenges assumptions about the individuals, autonomy, and identity around which most of the work on animals in philosophy revolves today. It looks to an animal ethics that disarticulates the ways in which the concepts of animal, human, and rights all are part of a philosophical tradition that trades on foreclosing the animal, animality, and animals. But as we have learned from psychoanalysis and poststructuralism, these barred animals always leave traces; they cannot be erased. The repressed always returns. Indeed, even within the confines of various philosophical texts, animals cannot be contained. They break free of the roles defined for them by philosophers and, like the white tiger Montecore, bite back. Whether a love bite, a rescue attempt, an enraged reproach, or just the distraction of a big-haired woman in the front row, we cannot be certain; we will never know. Perhaps animals bite back because it is man who first bites the hand—or paw, claw, talon, hoof—that feeds him. What philosophy can learn from Roy's accident is that mastering the animal, animality, and animals is an illusion. As this book shows, the animals who escape from the confines of these philosophies force us to rethink notions of humanity, animality, pedagogy, and kinship in ways that will have significant consequences for reconceiving our relationships to the earth, the environment, animals, and "ourselves."

PART ONE

What's Wrong with Animal Rights?

CHAPTER ONE

The Right to Remain Silent

Philosophical debates over the status of animals have exploded, making a survey of the literature overwhelming. With the exception of a few continental philosophers, most philosophers discussing animals today still do so in terms of animal suffering or animal intelligence, which in turn lead to discussions of animal rights or animal welfare.[1] Most of these discussions revolve around the ways in which animals are—or are not—like us and therefore should—or should not—be treated like us. Most of them measure animals against humans in an attempt to delineate similarities and differences that may help us decide something about our ethical or political obligations to animals. Throughout this literature, animal rights are likened to (or distinguished from) civil rights for women and people of color. Animal liberation—also the title of Peter Singer's seminal book—is compared with women's liberation and the liberation of other oppressed groups; speciesism is on par with racism or sexism; and factory farms and slaughterhouses are analogous to concentration camps and gas chambers. What these philosophers do not consider when making *analogies* between women and animals is that the exploitation and denigration of people traditionally involves viewing them *as* animals, treating them *like* animals, and justifying their "inferior" status on the basis of their supposed animality or proximity to animals. This was (and is) the case with women, who traditionally have been considered closer to nature and to animals, especially in their reproductive and child-rearing functions. This was the case with slaves, who were treated like cattle or oxen to be bought, sold, and used on plantations. This was (and is) the case with people of color who have been stereotyped as hypersexual, immoral, or irrational like animals. The proximity between oppressed peoples and animals is not just a contingency of history but a central part of Western conceptions of *man, human,* and *animal.*[2] As a result, overcoming the denigration of oppressed peoples and revaluing them on their own terms may require attention to the man/animal opposition as it has operated in the history of Western thought.

It is not news that historically, with few exceptions, Western philosophy was developed and practiced by privileged white men who regarded themselves and their own situations and values as universals. The human subject—until relatively recently referred to as "man"—was conceived of as free, autonomous, self-sovereign, and rational. It also is not news that this conception of *man* or *human* was/is built and fortified by excluding others who were viewed as man's opposite, particularly animals and those associated with animals, who were/are conceived of as determined by natural law to be dependent and irrational. It is not by accident that Descartes uncovered this disembodied thinking subject by shutting out the world around him, for this subject is assumed to be detached from its surroundings, history, and social context. Feminists and others have argued that there is no subject apart from its social and historical context and that therefore the Cartesian subject is a myth. The illusory nature of this subject has been challenged from quarters as distinct as feminist care ethics, functionalist philosophy of mind, and poststructuralism.

Why, then, do most philosophical discussions of animals, and the relationship between man or human and animal, assume the Cartesian subject that has been part and parcel of the history of the denigration of animals and that, in turn, is used to justify the denigration of people figured "like them"? For the most part, in philosophical discussions, the ethical, moral, or political consideration of animals revolves around issues of animal rights and animal equality that assume some notion of interests or capacities linked to the Cartesian subject. The twin questions, then, for animal rights and equality discourse—and rights and equality discourse more generally—are, Can we assume the Cartesian subject (autonomous, sovereign, individual) without also assuming the Cartesian object (automata, determined, inferior)? Can what was once considered the Cartesian object become the Cartesian subject? In other terms, can those considered other or man's opposites, including women and animals, be included in the category *man?*

As we know, for Descartes, animals are automata like machines that merely react to stimuli but do not have any true responses; because they don't have language, they don't have souls. They are the opposite of humans who are free, rational, and have souls. In the Cartesian scenario, the automatic actions of animals assure us of the freedom of our own—we are not animals; therefore, we are not automata. Animals not only operate to assure us, but they also make us *certain* about what is clearly and distinctly different between man and animal. In the history of philosophy, the opposition between man and animal has consistently been used to delineate the nature of humans and humanity against the nature of animals and animality. Indeed, the very notion of *nature* is linked to animals, whereas humans transcend nature. The distinction between nature and culture itself is a product of the oppositional thinking that sets man against animal. Although the notion of natural rights—what Jeremy Bentham called "nonsense on stilts"—is out of vogue in legal theory, it is implied by many of the proponents of animal rights. The natural identity of animals is what is at stake in determining their rights: if they have interests and the capacity to suffer, to feel, or to reason, then they deserve rights. Rights follow from their natures. The same has been said about human rights. But as contemporary legal theorists have argued, whatever their justifications in "nature," rights are political entities conferred by law. The very word *right* denotes law, and the history of philosophy bears this out. For example, according to Aristotle, the fact that man makes civil laws for himself, that he is self-governing, both distinguishes him from other animals and gives him dominion over them. The distinctions between natural law and civil law, nature and culture, fact and value, all take us back to the animal/man binary. In other words, all these distinctions so essential to the notion of rights and to philosophy are built on the backs of animals. Perhaps one step in unburdening animals is to extend rights to them, but not without reflecting on the conceptual status, along with the practical stakes, of also extending notions of sovereignty, autonomy, and freedom that have been central to man's dominion over animals.

Enlightenment ideals that make man superior to animals lay the foundation for rights discourse—whether human or animal—such as rationality, autonomy, individuality, and sovereignty, have been challenged from many quarters, including feminism, critical race theory, progressive social theory, deconstruction, and left legal theory. These ideals, as important as they are and have been to liberation movements, also fall short when addressing many of the problems of oppression and exploitation. These shortcomings are glaring when we apply Enlightenment ideals to animals, because our ability to "speak their language," find adequate translators, or avoid speaking for them is daunting, if not impossible. Indeed, the history of these ideals of rationality, autonomy, individuality, and sovereignty is built on opposing them to animality and animal nature. In this regard, it is again significant that oppressed groups of people—slaves, women, people of color— have been likened to animals to justify their exploitation. Even as Enlightenment ideals of personhood, citizen, and human subject have expanded to include women and others, they have not radically changed their parameters. Animal rights advocates may focus on animals' ability to feel rather than to reason, but they still hold onto notions of individuality and sovereignty that contribute to the continued exploitation of animals and the earth and threaten the survival of many animal species, including Homo sapiens.

Considering animal rights points to the limits of rights discourse and the need to revise our thinking about rights more generally. In the philosophical litera-ture, animal rights and animal welfare arguments are usually based on analogies with human rights and human welfare. For example, Peter Singer argues that all animals are equal and that "the ethical principle on which human equality rests requires us to extend equal considerations to animals" because animals, like hu-mans, have interests, pains and pleasures (1975, 1, 5, 7). Singer does not argue for animal rights but, rather, for animal welfare and animal liberation based on analo-gies with women's liberation and the civil rights movement. He argues that disre-gard for animals is "speciesism," just as disregard for women or African Americans is sexism or racism. Tom Regan does argue for animal rights. Like Singer, he bases his arguments on similarities between animals and humans; because they are like us, they deserve rights like us. He maintains that animals—although not all animals—are subjects of lives, which is to say that they have experiences (1983, 1987). And insofar as they have experiences, they are like us and deserve respect:

It is the similarities between those human beings who most clearly, most non-controversially have such value [inherent value and a right to be treated with respect] (the people reading this for example), not our differences, that matter most. And the really crucial, the basic similarity is simply this: we are each of us the experiencing subject of a life, a conscious creature having an individual welfare that has importance to us whatever our usefulness to others. We want and prefer things, believe and feel things, recall and expect things . . . the same is true of those animals that concern us. (1987, xx)

In this passage, Regan presumes autonomy, individuality, and sovereignty, if not rationality. First, he assumes a norm of personhood (the noncontroversial cases), which excludes the most difficult issues involving the concept of person. Moreover, he does not consider how certain *norms* of personhood have been part and parcel of oppressive logics from slavery to sexism and racism. Indeed, traditionally norms of personhood have been used to justify treating some groups "like animals" because they were considered to be more like animals than people. Next, he insists that we ignore differences—differences that might be critical to considering the specific interests of any given species or individual animal—and look at what he calls "the really crucial, the basic similarity," which is delineated in terms such as experi-encing, subject, conscious, individual, preferences, beliefs, feelings, memory, and expectations. Behind his reasoning is a commitment to the notion of individual autonomy and subjectivity such that all creatures that have value—which may not be all creatures—possess these qualities. The same could be said of Peter Singer's equality arguments. That is, creatures deserve equal protection or equal consideration, if not equal treatment, because they possess certain qualities, namely, interests. According to this logic, rights or equal consideration is deserved if one possesses certain characteristics. The connection between rights or equality and identity is a mainstay of animal rights discourse and rights discourse more generally.

Regan limits his scope to "noncontroversial" humans who have inherent value and animals who, like those "normal" humans, are a "subject of a life." Although Regan makes some suggestions, where we draw the line between normal and abnormal, subjects and nonsubjects, is ultimately unclear; it is up to empirical scientists to determine when brain science is more advanced. The kind of line drawing that plagues Regan—that is, who is normal and therefore inherently valuable and who is not, which animals have interests and which do not—is typical of animal rights and animal welfare debates.[3] The literature is full of lists of creatures that have interests or can suffer or feel pain and pleasure and those that do not. The line is drawn in different places by different thinkers. Some believe that shellfish don't feel pain. Others contend that great apes deserve more rights than other animals because their interests are similar to ours. In all these cases, the more similar these creatures are to us, the more consideration they deserve; and the more different they are from us, the less consideration they deserve. Moreover, those creatures that we consider vermin or contagious diseases may not only not have interests but also may deserve to be killed.[4]

This type of line drawing forms two sides: the haves and the have-nots, those who have what it takes to be inherently valuable and those who do not. Conceptually, this is the same kind of oppositional and exclusionary thinking inherent in the man/animal or human/animal dichotomy. And it is the same type of oppositional or exclusionary thinking that leads to oppression, war, and poverty. If the man/animal binary is part and parcel of the history of rights discourse, then how can we use that same discourse to overcome it? How can we apply the rights of persons to animals if the very distinction between animals and persons is inherent in the notion of rights? Furthermore, starting from the premise that it is our similarities and not our differences that matter, how can we even imagine any sort of ethics that encounters animals in terms of their own interests as they experience them? The conceptual and practical problems of rights discourse are compounded and magnified when we consider animals. If animal liberation is like women's liberation, as Singer, Regan, and others claim, then feminist criticisms of taking characteristics associated with men as the hallmark of human identity, or citizenship, rights, and so on, apply here too. Just as feminists ask why women have to be like men in order to be equal, we can ask why animals have to be like us to have inherent value. The notion that man is the measure of all things is precisely the kind of thinking that justifies exploiting animals, along with women and the earth, for his purposes. Considering animals takes us to the limits of assimiliationist politics and ethics based on sameness. As debates over multiculturalism have made clear, assimilationalist agendas present a myriad of problems regarding what culture sets the standards and who adjudicates them. The same could be said of adjudicating the difference between human cultures and animal cultures. Feminist political theorist Wendy Brown says that rights are what we cannot not want (2002), but are they what animals want? Indeed, we might ask, which human culture will be the standard for considering whether or not animals are like "us" and deserve rights? This is particularly problematic considering that many cultures do not even have a concept of rights.[5] The question of which humans are "us" is as vexed as the question of which animals are like us.

If we have learned anything from the civil rights and women's liberation movements, which are invoked by many animal rights or welfare activities and theorists, it is that identity politics has limits. Using the same terms of identity that were used to subordinate in order to liberate, has problems. While identifying a group of people who have been victims of oppression or exploitation opens the possibility of arguing for their liberation at the same time that it repeats their identification as victims or women or blacks. In other words, it does not change or revalue the meaning of these categories or stereotypes associated with them. For example, even as legal rights expand, we continue to use names associated with these groups as insults, especially when it comes to animals. We insult people by calling them animals: pigs, cows, asses, vipers, snakes, vermin, rats, and so on. However identity is defined in order to overcome oppression and exploitation, at the same time it excludes others who may be even more disadvantaged by patriarchal, racist, or, in the case of animals, speciesist, institutions. For feminists, this became evident when bell hooks asked, "Ain't I a woman?" in response to white feminists' complaints that they were locked in their suburban homes with their children all day, which for many women of color seemed like living the dream.[6]

Wendy Brown discusses the paradox of women's rights as either basing rights on characteristics specific to feminine or female identity and thereby reinforcing a subordinated or abjected identity, on the one hand, or basing rights on universal characteristics associated with masculine and male identity and thereby continuing to devalue femininity and female identity, on the other. She contends, "The paradox, then, is that rights that entail some specification of our suffering, injury, or inequality lock us into the identity defined by our subordination, and rights that eschew this specificity not only sustain the invisibility of our subordination but potentially even enhance it" (Brown 2002, 423). This danger is a result of the universal and abstract nature of discussions of rights—and moral principles more generally—that discount the significance of social and historical conditions and contexts. The liberal rights discourse, of which animal rights is a part, assumes that rights must be recognized as something universally true throughout history, without regard for context or social institutions.[7] This ahistorical approach risks reinscribing the subordination and denigration it hopes to eliminate by addressing the symptoms, but not the structures, of oppression, including material and economic structures, but particularly linguistic, conceptual, and cultural structures and institutions.[8] Rights may be better than nothing, but they still leave oppressive power structures and values intact. In addition, while rights of protection may be a start, they are not rights of equality or freedom. We may extend rights of protection to the great apes and other animals we deem sentient or capable of suffering, but—even if enforced—do those protections change the ways in which we value animals, consider their interests, or afford them equal treatment?

Rights defined as protections may be necessary, but they still do not address the many causes of oppression and denigration. They address neither the material nor the conceptual inequities that are part of the history of exploitative practices. As legal theorist Duncan Kennedy points out, "Rights were usually defined in terms of equality, but equality in a special sense. They did not involve the demand for equality in the distribution of income or wealth between social classes, regions, or communities, but rather 'equal protection' for individual members of previously subordinated social groups" (2002, 82). Equal protections, then, do nothing to redress the material or cultural inequities in the distribution of resources. For animals, the struggle continues between environmental and business interests over the allocation of resources for wildlife. Of course, the terms of these negotiations are always set by humans and ultimately in favor of human interests, including human interests in animals. Equal protection for oppressed people or animals does not go far enough in redistributing resources. In addition, these protective rights bring with them regulation and surveillance, if not disciplinary institutions.[9] The relationship between protective legislation and regulation, surveillance and discipline is even more obvious when it comes to animals. Defining certain animals as members of a protected class entails further regulations. For example, legislation protecting endangered species requires counting animals, capturing and tagging them, following them, tracking them, breeding them, and so on. Thus, even as such legislation goes some distance in "liberating" animals, it continues structures of power that both enable and require putting up fences and manhandling them for their own protection. Our attitudes toward animals, and the ways in which we count them, make it obvious that equal protection means increased surveillance and regulation. In addition, rights to protection do not mean rights to freedom. The recent protections of rights to life and freedom for the great apes does not prohibit their use in zoos, despite limiting their freedom by living in captivity. Even though people may not be captured, tagged, and bred in captivity, they are nonetheless measured, counted, and regulated in less conspicuous ways, particularly now with the heightened security regulations in place for our protection. The ways in which the liberty and freedom afforded by protective rights also bring increased regulations is more apparent when we consider animal rights, but they should also give us pause in terms of human rights.

So far, we have considered that although rights may be better than no rights, they also do not go far enough in addressing the structural and ideological issues that made them necessary in the first place. We have seen that reliance on identity politics means that rights discourse either uses and repeats identities that historically have been used to oppress or exploit certain groups, or it uses values associated with the dominant group as its norm. The latter is usually the case in animal rights arguments: because animals are like humans, they should have rights or equal protections. In the future, the extension of rights might begin to shift who belongs to what group, but it does not address the conceptual hierarchy of human and animal. The ahistoricism of universal rights arguments does not include the history of thought, concepts, and language that figures humans as both distinct from and superior to animals. In addition, the individualism of rights discourse is at odds with addressing the social and historical conditions that give rise to exploitation and subordination. This is particularly true when animals gain protection only if they are like humans: In their animality, they are still subordinated, but in their "humanity," they can be liberated. The power hierarchy and value systems that make animals and animality inferior to human and humanity remain in place.[10]

Considering animals makes it clear that the individualism of the rights discourse is not effective in redressing the wrongs done to subordinated and denigrated groups. Within the U.S. legal system, women's rights are treated on a case-by-case basis to protect individuals without necessarily affecting the systematic nature of sexism. Still, in Western legal systems, in principle if not in practice, women are considered individuals equivalent to men, so, for example, a woman can sign a contract in her own name.[11] Animals, however, are not currently treated as individuals. Prosecution in cases of cruelty to animals is unusual; laws are rarely enforced; and huge sectors of industry like factory farming, slaughterhouses, pharmaceutical testing, and experimentation on animals are exempted. In legal terms, animals are considered members of a class without individuals. Even if we recognize differences among species, historically and legally we do not recognize individual animals. In fact, traditionally the uniqueness of human beings, who have legal proper names, has been opposed to animals, who supposedly are all alike in their slavish adherence to natural law. Human individuality is seen as a hallmark of human freedom, which historically has defined the difference between human and animal. The lack of animal individuals in our history makes the application of individualist human rights to animals even more problematic than the application of masculine individualist rights to women. Historical reclamation projects have had limited success in recovering the records of women philosophers, writers, artists, and the achievements of great leaders of civilizations of people of color, but can we imagine historians uncovering the deeds of an individual animal? The point is not that we need to engage in such a task. Rather, the lack of historical evidence of individual animals, those with proper names, is telling in that we do not conceive of animals as individuals. Another significant fact is that when human beings are called animals or treated like animals, they are not treated like individuals.

Animals are not seen as individuals, and differences among species are either lost in animal rights discourse or become the reason for excluding some animals from equal protection. In other words, the working definition of animal is either so vague that it includes everything from amoebas to zebras without considering differences among them, or it uses the differences among them to continue to justify excluding or exploiting most of them. For example, Tom Regan defines "the word *animal*" as "mentally normal mammals of a year or more," which excludes hordes of nonmammals as well as all mammals of less than a year in age (2004, xvi). This kind of definition flies in the face of normal usages of the word *animal* and also appears arbitrary and dangerously exclusive. In this regard, an important difference between contemporary discourses about women's rights and animal rights is that while second-wave feminists have argued that women's equality should not be premised on their being just like men, animal rights arguments continue to use identity politics. Many feminists have recognized the limitations of identity politics in the crucial difference between equal treatment and fairness or justice. That is, there are differences between men and women that require differential treatment in order to be just. Given the patriarchal history of the concepts *man* and *woman,* we cannot simply extend the "rights of man" to women without encountering a dilemma. So too, given the history of the concepts *man* and *animal,* we cannot simply extend the "rights of man" to animals without encountering a dilemma. Animal rights advocates usually do not consider what an ethics or politics of difference for animals might be. How can we include them in human society without excluding their animality? How can we extend rights to them not as like us but as different from us? Is there a way to treat them as equals without treating them as *animals* or as humans in furry suits?

These questions and paradoxes point to problems with identity politics that come into focus even more clearly in the case of animals. If man becomes man by defining himself against woman, he becomes human by defining himself against the animal. If the category *woman* erases differences of social and historical situations among women, the category *animal* erases vastly diverse differences among individual animals and subgroups within species and between species themselves. Because it herds countless species into one category and then denigrates them, the category *animal* indicates the difficulty with using the identity *animal* in legal rights considerations. For example, zoologists recently discovered at least six genetically distinct species of giraffe.[12] If we disavow the vast array of animals by penning them into one concept—which is not accidentally opposed to man and human—we do conceptual violence to them as well as justify physical violence to them. Ironically, these differences between species plague philosophers of animal rights who continually try to determine which animals are most like us and which are not and which deserve rights and which do not. This raises the challenge of adjudicating rights among different species, including human beings and other animals. What happens when the interests of one group conflict with the interests of another? This is especially problematic for those theorists who base equality on interests, particularly when those interests are translated into some sort of natural right.[13] In fact, this issue has led animal rights theorists to imagine all kinds of bizarre scenarios, including burning buildings that present the choice of saving your child or the family dog, lifeboats situations that may involve throwing a million dogs overboard, casseroles made of Great-Aunt Emily, and choosing between soy milk and Kahlúa.[14]

Duncan Kennedy discusses the move from interests to rights (in terms of humans, not animals) as a rhetorical gesture that turns preferences into rules:

Once the interests of the group have been assimilated to the interests of the whole polity by recasting them as rights, the factoid character of rights allows the group to make its claims as claims of reason rather than of mere preference. Because you do or at least ought to agree that everyone has this universal right, and that reasoning from it leads ineluctably to these particular rules, it follows that you are a knave or a fool if you don't go along. To deny the validity of these particular rules make you *wrong*, rather than just selfish and powerful. (2002, 188, italics in original)[15]

Conversely, turning interests into rights disavows the power structures that privilege some interests over others and leads to the need for rights claims. Moreover, rights claims can be made by the powerful and selfish to ensure that their rights also are protected. People who enjoy eating meat and the feel of leather and fur can assert their rights to free choice and happiness against the rights of animals. The double-headed problem with these types of rights is that on the one hand, it turns preferences and interests into rules, and on the other hand, it pits interests or rights against each other without considering differential power structures. Indeed, issues of ethics or social justice can get lost in debates over conflicting rights. The rhetoric of color blindness in the United States is a good example of how civil rights designed to protect minorities and women against discrimination are being used effectively in legal arguments against so-called reverse discrimination, enabling many affirmative action policies to be overturned.

In addition, because of the exclusionary nature of identity claims, they inevitably end up justifying rights or equality for some and not others, often for an elite few. Just as rights for women and minorities in Europe and the United States were (and, in many cases, still are—think of the prison population in the United States whose rights are revoked, including the right to vote, combined with the fact that most of those prisoners are African American; remember also that most of the world's poor are women and children) extended first to a select few, usually based on class. So, too, animal rights are reserved for those most like us. This is evidenced by the Great Ape Project, which has had some success in arguing that great apes are unique among animals in that they are our closest animal relatives and possess many of our defining characteristics and therefore should have special treatment among animals and equal treatment to people at least in terms of freedom and right to life.[16] As I write, following Great Britain and New Zealand, Spain is on the verge of approving rights for great apes to comply with the Great Apes Project. A recent headline in *The Times* (London) reads, "Apes get legal rights in Spain, to surprise of bullfight activists." The article begins, "Spain is to become the first country to extend legal rights to apes, wrongfooting animal rights activists who have long campaigned against bullfighting in the country" (Vera 2008).

Asked about the exclusionary vision of the Great Ape Project, the French philosopher Jacques Derrida responded,

To want absolutely to grant, not to animals but to a certain category of animals, rights equivalent to human rights would be a disastrous contradiction. It would reproduce the philosophical and juridical machine thanks to which the exploitation of animal material for food, work, experimentation, etc., has been practiced (and tyrannically so, that is, through an abuse of power). (2004, 65)

Derrida worried that giving rights to some animals but not all would repeat the exclusionary logic of the Cartesian subject and the juridical conception of individuality and freedom resulting from it. As he pointed out, the exploitation of animals has been justified and practiced using this logic. Derrida was skeptical of extending human rights to animals, since the concept of right and rights is part of a tradition whose conceptual system trades on excluding, exploiting, and disavowing animals. He warned, "To confer or to recognize rights for 'animals' is a surreptitious or implicit way of confirming a certain interpretation of the human subject, which itself will have been the very lever of the worst violence carried out against nonhuman living beings" (2004, 65). In other words, extending human rights to animals both repeats and reinforces the notion of the human subject built on the backs of animals. Extending human rights to a few select animals and not others makes apparent the exclusionary nature of the Cartesian logic. Moreover, it suggests the way in which rights are seen as possessions or entitlements of a select group whose interests are valued more than the interests of others, particularly others defined as having no interests. The juridical notion of rights leads to calculations of whose interests are more important and whose rights trump all others. The calculus of interests and rights is particularly vexing when weighing human rights against animal rights, which is bound to happen given the oppositional nature of the concepts human and animal and the exclusionary nature of the concept of rights on which animal rights (like human rights) are based.

Although the question of animal interests versus human interests raises hordes of practical concerns about human freedoms in regard to eating, clothing, and human welfare, as well as drug testing and medical research, the fundamental problem with arbitrating rights is not the practical matter of determining the proper balance or a fair utilitarian calculus. The problem, as Derrida might say, is imagining that we *can* calculate the incalculable, that we *can* decide the undecidable, that we can be *certain* about what is just, fair, equal, or right. Delineating rights, calculating interests, and weighing the value of one life against another may be juridical necessities in civil society, but they are the antithesis of ethics. Instead of taking responsibility, they become ways of shirking it; they become principles used to justify actions rather than to think about their implications. After all, history has shown that rights discourse can be used to justify the rights of the dominant to dominate and the propertied against the propertyless. Calculating rights or interests can turn ethics into moral rules that eliminate critical thought or soul-searching from the process. They risk replacing ethical responsibility with equations and legalisms. While laws may be necessary and may go some distance in making things right, they cannot approach the ethical responsibility engendered by our relationships with others. Indeed, these calculations disavow the ambiguities and uncertainties of our experience; they disavow the ways in which we do not and cannot know for sure. They make man the measure of all things—he is the measurer and the yardstick.

In *The Animal That Therefore I Am,* Derrida argues that this type of moral principle, and application of it, disavows the animality in human morality because it becomes a preprogrammed response to an ethical problem. As such, it is not a response at all but a reaction, and it thereby belies the Cartesian distinction between reacting and responding supposedly definitive of the man/animal distinction. Ironically, in measuring according to moral rules, man is no more ethical (or free) than a calculator.[17] As we will see in subsequent chapters, in his deconstruction of the opposition between reaction and response, Derrida contends that following moral rules or universal principles becomes just as automatic as supposed animal reactions. The certainty with which we claim the right to decide on the sameness or difference of animals belies a reactionary position at odds with ethical responsibility. Moral rules and juridical legalism help us sleep peacefully at night, whereas ethical responsibility, as Levinas might say, produces insomnia. Rights can be granted, laws can be followed, but ethics and justice cannot rest there. In this sense, ethics must go beyond rights.

Given that rights discourse has assumed the Cartesian subject and that the Cartesian subject has been constructed through the sacrifice of the animal, animality, and animals, it is imperative that we consider the social and historical conditions that made the discourse of human rights possible. It is significant that the discourse of rights developed in relation to owning animals and the land on which to keep them. The domestication of animals made it necessary for farmers and ranchers to build fences or patrol property, which in turn led to land disputes and the beginning of private property. With private property came property rights.[18] The rights discourse began with private property in relation to keeping domestic animals, and other rights were granted based on the ownership of property, the rights of citizenship, for example.[19] Most of what we take to be constitutional rights began, in one sense or another, with the domestication, use, and owning of animals.[20] The exploitation of animals is deeply embedded in the history of rights. Indeed, treating other people as property, chattel, or slaves followed property laws involving animals; and those laws were justified by comparing subordinate groups with animals. Even after the abolition of slavery, wives and children were still considered the property of men. As many feminists have argued, this is only one aspect of the patriarchal association between women and animals, evidenced even today by the various names used to degrade women, including pussy, kitten, bunny, beaver, bitch, chick, fox, vixen, and cow.[21]

The connection between the degradation of women and traditional views of animals as existing for man's use complicates any easy analogy between women's liberation and animal liberation. If women's subordination is partly justified by comparing them with animals, then perhaps one reason why women's liberation has continued to meet with resistance and to bump up against the "glass ceiling" is because of our attitudes toward animals and the deep patriarchal associations between women and animals. In other words, the relation between the exploitation of animals and the exploitation of women and other oppressed groups is not just a matter of analogy. Rather, the conceptual opposition between man, on the one side—the civilized side—and animal, on the other—the natural or barbaric side—plays a central role in the oppositions between man and woman, white and black, civilized and barbaric, and so forth.[22] Until we address the denigration of animals in Western thought on the conceptual level, if not also on the material economic level, we will continue to merely scratch the surface of the denigration and exploitation of various groups of people, from Playboy bunnies to prisoners at Abu Ghraib who were treated like dogs as a matter of explicit military policy.

Feminists also have criticized rights and equality discourses as the twin problems of speaking for others and the meaning of consent, issues that are even more obvious when we consider animals. Speaking for others assumes that the speaker knows the desires and interests of the spoken for. Feminists have argued that white men speaking for women and people of color may have good intentions and still do harm. At the least, the powerful speaking for the powerless replicates, but does not change, the power structure itself. Moreover, speaking for others can be a way of silencing those others. Certainly, considering animals takes this issue to the limit. Because for the most part (except for individuals like Alex the parrot or Koko the gorilla), animals don't speak—at least not in a language we understand—the meaning of consent is a vexed issue when it comes to animals, particularly those animals we call pets, the ones we love. What does it mean to say that animals freely consent to our attentions and love? If the meaning of consent is a thorny issue when people are concerned, then it is even pricklier when we consider animals. How do we define consent in the case of animals? Feminist criticisms of liberal theories that assume the Cartesian autonomous individual challenge the notion that "free" participation necessarily means consent. Social and historical situations and expectations complicate any straightforward notion of consent in the case of women. Women have been expected to perform certain functions and to behave in self-sacrificing ways for so long that they often "freely consent" to their own subordinations. For example, Gayatri Spivak problematizes the meaning of consent in the traditional Indian ritual of *sati,* in which a widow threw herself on the burning funeral pyre of her husband (Spivak 1988). If women freely consent to social subordination by occupying traditional roles, do domestic animals? Does that question even make sense? What does it mean for our pets to consent to our care for them?

Catharine MacKinnon offers a provocative and telling example of the legal conundrums involving consent when trying to include animals in protective legislation. She discusses laws against "crush videos," a genre of pornography in which small rodents are tormented and then crushed to death by scantly clad women. Congress has outlawed the depiction of cruelty against animals if they will be harmed or killed in the making of such representations. But MacKinnon points out that there is no such legislation against harming or killing women to make a film, as long as they consent (2004, 268). In 2000 in California, a bill was rejected that would have made both crush and snuff films illegal (snuff films show women being killed while having sex). The bill would have outlawed the depiction of "the intentional and malicious maiming, mutilating, torturing, or wounding of a live animal" when the "killing of an animal actually occurred" (MacKinnon 2004, 268–69). For humans, the bill made a felony "the intentional or malicious killing of, or intentional maiming, torturing, or wounding of a human being, and intentional killing or cruelty to a human being actually occurring in the course of producing the depiction" (269). MacKinnon finds it ironic that the ACLU launched a successful campaign defending First Amendment rights to free speech against the human part of the bill only (269). In other words, because women were assumed to consent to their own maiming and torture, it was free speech; but animals were assumed not to consent, or not to be able to consent. MacKinnon concludes,

Instructively, the joint crush/snuff bill had a consent provision only for people. Welcome to humanity: While animals presumably either cannot or are presumed not to consent to their videotaped murder, human beings could have consented to their own intentional and malicious killing if done to make a movie, and the movie would be legal. Even that was not enough to satisfy the avatars of free speech. One wonders anew if human rights are always better than animal rights. Many laws prohibit cruelty to animals, but no laws prohibit cruelty to women as such. (2004, 269)

The plot thickens in the associations between animals and women.

This example makes evident the ways in which conflicting rights claims—the right to free speech versus the right to protection against torture, even killing—can lead to complications that cannot be easily resolved by appeals to either civil or natural rights, even those we take to be most basic: the rights to life, liberty, and the pursuit of happiness. We see how rights discourse and legalisms skirt issues of ethics and even justice. Free speech seems like a red herring when women are being abused and killed for entertainment, as long as they consent. But what does consent mean when it becomes a matter of freely participating in one's own suffering? Interestingly, animal welfare advocates and theorists suspicious of the liberal discourse of rights in reference to animals agree that because animals can suffer, we should not inflict suffering on them. They cite Jeremy Bentham, maintaining that the question is not whether they can speak but whether they can suffer. Because, like us, they can suffer, we have an obligation not to abuse and kill them. The question "can they suffer," however, has become an empirical question involving more experiments on animals. Even philosophers like Cora Diamond who reject Singer's and Regan's arguments for animal rights, turn to suffering as a *capacity* that we share with animals.[23] Doing so, however, risks treating suffering as yet another capacity or identity that can be possessed, used to draw exclusionary lines, and measured in terms of man.

As MacKinnon's example points out, however, even our suffering does not stop us from making others suffer, not just when conflicts of rights arise or in the context of wars, but also for entertainment. Indeed, if we include mental, emotional, and psychological suffering, we rarely go a day without either receiving or inflicting suffering on others. Of course, just because this is the case does not mean that it ought to be. We can have an ethical obligation to avoid making others suffer even if we cannot live up to that obligation every day. This may be a case of an infinite responsibility that outstrips our capacities or our identities. We are not capable of avoiding suffering, either for ourselves or for others. In the case of suffering, laws are never enough. Reducing animal ethics to questions of an ability to suffer, or capacities they share with us, leads to displacing ethical reflection onto moral rules or laws that—even though they go some distance in righting wrongs—do not bring us face-to-face with our responsibility or, more precisely, our responsibility for our irresponsibility. The ethical question that asks us to confront our own responsibility is not whether they can suffer but how we respond to the suffering of others. It is a question of response and relationship rather than a question of capacity or identity.

Shared Embodiment and the Capacity for Suffering

If this brief sketch of the thicket we enter when considering animal rights—and rights discourse more generally—alerts us to the dangers of assuming the Cartesian subject rather than interrogating it, we might look to philosophers who reject the Cartesian subject as a starting point for reconceiving what it means to be man, human, and animal. We might turn to philosophers who have "decentered" or "deconstructed" that subject and thereby challenged traditional notions of autonomy, reason, sovereignty, and freedom. We might expect to find that if man's rationality is no longer the center of the philosophical universe, then animals fare better in that world. The first posthumously published book by Jacques Derrida, *The Animal That Therefore I Am,* shows how those expectations would be disappointed (2008). We see there that giving up Enlightenment humanism does not mean giving up man's dominion over animals. Indeed, rethinking the subjectivity of man has not meant rethinking his counterpart, animal. This also is true in feminist discourses that challenge the gender specificity of the supposedly universal category of man while continuing to embrace the more inclusive category of human against the animal. Moreover, reconceiving man does not necessarily lead to reconceiving the dependence of *man,* or *human,* on *animal.* The newly conceived subject is still constructed on the back(s) of *the animal* or *animals.* And animals continue to play a similar role in these philosophies, namely, of reassuring us that we are not like them, that we are superior to them. Derrida shows how philosophers of otherness or difference, such as Heidegger, Lacan, and Levinas, continue to develop their theories of human existence against animal life. Heidegger opposes the very concept of existence—at the heart of his notion of Dasein—to life, which he identifies with animals. Lacan assumes that whereas humans respond, animals merely react. And Levinas says that animals do not have faces, the focal and inaugural point for ethics. In his ethics as first philosophy, humans become subjects by virtue of their obligations to the other, whom he often figures as the orphan or the widow, those most vulnerable, those who suffer.

While Levinasian philosophy begins with an ethical command inaugurated in our relationships with others and thereby opens philosophy to the vulnerability and suffering of others, as Derrida shows, it does not open philosophy to the animal other, animal others, or the suffering of animals. Levinas's orphans, it seems, do not include animals. The bread that we are obligated to take from our own mouths and share with others is not for the mouths of animals. In one of the only texts in which Levinas addresses the question of the animal—in the figure of the now famous dog Bobby who visited the prisoners at a concentration camp—he begins with a passage from Exodus that divides man and dog based on what they eat: "You shall be men consecrated to me; therefore you shall not eat any flesh that is torn by beasts in the field; you shall cast it to the dogs" (Exodus 22:31). Levinas suggests that men should be more concerned with what comes out of their mouths, that is, words, than what they put in them; they should be concerned not with filling their bellies but with emancipating and feeding all enslaved peoples (cf. Levinas 2004, 47–49). But much of our philosophy of man and freedom centers on what man eats, with little or no concern for animals except, as in the Exodus passage, it reassures man that he is not an animal because he doesn't eat like one. Animals are always secondary to man, even if they help man, as in Levinas's relation with Bobby, the dog who "recognizes" the humanity and dignity of the prisoners even while the Nazis treat them "like apes." The role of the good animal, the good dog, is to reassure man of his status as man. Even as he looks Bobby in the face, Levinas does not see a face or an other or an orphan who deserves the bread from his mouth. His philosophy of alterity does not consider the vulnerability of the animal as provoked by its face.

It might seem that philosophies based on embodied vulnerability and mortality would have to include animals. Surely, animals have bodies that are vulnerable, and we share mortality with animals. But for the most part, post-Levinasian philosophers of violence and vulnerability do not consider violence toward animals or their vulnerability.[24] Even as they base ethical obligations on the fact that we have bodies that can be wounded and killed, they ignore the fact that animals also have bodies that can be wounded and killed. If our ethical responsibility originates in bodily vulnerability itself, then how or why is it limited to human bodies? The terrorist attacks of September 11, 2001, led several philosophers (following popular discourse) to turn to the question of vulnerability as constitutive of humanity, ignoring the vulnerability of animals.[25]

In the Continental-inspired tradition, we are seeing new attempts to ground ethical and political obligations in embodiment and a shared capacity for suffering.[26] For example, in *Precarious Life,* philosopher Judith Butler argues that we have a primary vulnerability that comes with being human; more specifically, it comes with being born as a human infant completely beholden to others for survival. She claims that this primary vulnerability constitutes humanity (Butler 2004a, esp. xiv and 31). Although infancy lasts longer in humans than in other animals, the vulnerability of newborns is not unique to humans. The fact that we can be wounded by, or wound, others also is not unique to humans. We share this vulnerability with all living creatures. As Butler observes, if recognizing that our vulnerability is something we share with others can make us less violent toward them, then perhaps recognizing that vulnerability is something we share with all creatures can make us less violent toward nonhumans, as well as animals and other inhabitants of the earth.[27]

Butler suggests that a politics of recognition—the recognition of the humanity of others—can be founded on this primary universal vulnerability that comes with dependent embodiment.[28] In this text, her notion of the performance of recognition that brings with it the conferral of rights is based on shared embodied vulnerability.[29] She concludes her reflections on violence by insisting that

the task at hand is to establish modes of public seeing and hearing that might well respond to the *cry of the human* within the sphere of appearance, a sphere in which the trace of the cry has become hyperbolically inflated to rationalize a gluttonous nationalism, or fully obliterated, where both alternatives turn out to be the same. (2004a, 147, italics added)

She points out that we see and hear "the cry of the human" but at the same time we do not see and hear it because, as she maintains, we do not *recognize* it as *human*. What does this mean? Does it mean that we hear and see the cry as nonhuman, as animal? Butler's invocation of the human and her assumptions that bodily vulnerability is uniquely human conjures the human/animal opposition central to Enlightenment humanism and the Cartesian subject, both of which she rejects.[30] In order to make sense of this uniquely human cry, don't we have to distinguish it from the animal cry? Doing so, however, suggests that something more than bodily vulnerability makes this cry ethical, unless we allow for animal ethics.

French theorist Julia Kristeva also invokes vulnerability in *Hate and Forgiveness,* in which vulnerability does not come from having a body per se but from having a speaking body (2005). Here she associates vulnerability with otherness, whether it is an otherness prompted by encounters with other people who are different from us or encounters with our own otherness. Ultimately, the two are inseparable. Kristeva claims that along with liberty, equality, and fraternity, vulnerability is a fourth term that we inherit from Enlightenment humanism (2005, 115). Speaking of the handicapped and extending her analysis to racism, classism, and religious persecution, she states that a narcissistic wound constitutes humanity as a scar at the suture of being and meaning. It is our ambiguous position between nature and culture, animal and human, being and meaning, that makes us vulnerable and also free. What makes us human and opens up a world of meaning also makes us vulnerable. In contrast to Butler, Kristeva views our vulnerability as the result of not merely our bodily vulnerability—which we share with other animals—but also the fact that we are "speaking animals." Presumably, then, this vulnerability or scar would be apparent in any speaking being, human or not. Conversely, any speaking being would be a human being. As Kristeva describes it, this vulnerability is not primarily the result of our having been an infant whose body could be wounded by others or our having a body that could be wounded but because we occupy a place between being and meaning, between bodies and words. According to Kristeva, the gap between bodies and words, the ways in which words are never quite adequate to capture bodily experience, is figured as a wound, which is the seat of our vulnerability. We are wounding and wounded because we occupy the space between bodies and meanings. She suggests that the uncanny encounter with another puts us face to face with our own vulnerability "with and for others." It is the fear and denial of our own vulnerability that ·

cause us to hate and exploit the vulnerability of others. She raises the question of "how to inscribe in the conception of the human itself—and, consequently in philosophy and political practice—the constitutive part played by destructivity, vulnerability, disequilibrium which are integral to the identity of the human species and the singularity of the speaking subject?" (2005, 115). She asks how we can acknowledge that to be human is to be vulnerable. In other words, how can we accept our own vulnerability without violently projecting it onto others whom we oppress and torture or, alternatively, "civilize" and "protect"?

Although like Butler, Kristeva makes vulnerability one hallmark of humanity—which does not include animals—this vulnerability comes from an uneasy relationship between our own animality and whatever sets us apart from other animals. The ambiguity of the human condition as neither fish nor fowl, so to speak, makes us particularly vulnerable. In this regard, it is not just that we share bodies but that we share the awkward space between bodies and meaning, neither of which we control, neither of which is our home. We are strays, wounded animals, whose scars make us human. Even though this view embraces our animality, it does not consider other animals or the animality of animals in its ethical invocations. Even as it emphasizes Enlightenment notions of vulnerability over sovereignty and rationality, it manifests continued ambivalence toward animals, if not human animality. In addition, it distinguishes human animality from the animality of animals in that it continues Enlightenment humanism's opposition between human and animal, albeit on another level. While Kristeva's position calls on us to examine our own investments in violence towards humans and our own animality, it does not require any such investigation in regard to animals.

Once we take bodily vulnerability—which is to say the fact that we are mortal and can be wounded—as our starting point, are we delineating what constitutes humanity? Or are we setting out what constitutes all living creatures? And if we are relational, dependent beings by virtue of having bodies, then isn't this also true of animals? Moreover, if we extend the notion of dependence in the way that Butler and Kristeva do to make it a cornerstone of ethics and politics, then aren't we also obligated to consider the (material and conceptual) interdependence of humans and animal?[31] We are dependent on animals, and animals are dependent on their environments and one another. Increasingly, their habitats depend on human management and interventions, which often results in their displacement or extinction when we cannot learn to share. If we consider our shared embodiment with animals, then discussions of ethics and politics based on suffering and vulnerability would have to change to include animals. We might ask, Why talk about the suffering of animals when there is still so much human suffering in the world?

I would answer that in the history of philosophy we must consider the ways in which human suffering and animal suffering are inseparable. In this history, the human is consistently and continually defined against the animal. Even now, philosophers of consciousness, like Daniel Dennett, define human cognition and intelligence in relation to animal and machine intelligence and reserve suffering for humans; Dennett argues that animals merely feel pain and not suffering (1998).[32] Moreover, ethical and political theories have often used the distinction between man and animal to define the realm of ethics and the domain of the political as uniquely human. As we have seen, discussions of human rights are, in an important sense, based on explicit or implicit invocations of an opposition between humans and animals. But it is not just in philosophical discourse or theory that justice and rights turn on the man/animal binary. As we know, in popular parlance, colonization, oppression, discrimination, and genocide are usually, if not always, justified by an appeal to the animality of the victims. These supposedly subhuman groups do not deserve human rights or human justice because they are figured as inhuman monsters, beasts, or dogs. Recall the Abu Ghraib photographs of Private First Class Lynndie England with a leash around the neck of an Iraqi prisoner. Reportedly, the guards were ordered to treat the prisoner like "dogs," even making them bark like dogs. It seems that we cannot talk about recognizing the humanity of others or about conferring human rights on them without relying on, or at some level presupposing, an opposition between humans and animals. The histories of the suffering of humans at the hands of other humans and the suffering of animals at the hands of humans are intimately connected. In order to postulate an ethics whose obligations originate in a recognition of suffering, whether human or animal, we must ask, What kind of capacity is the ability to suffer? And what does it mean to recognize it as either uniquely human (as Butler and Kristeva do) or as what we share with animals (as Bentham-inspired advocates of animal welfare do).

The Limits of the Human

In *The Animal,* Jacques Derrida takes up Bentham's question: Do animals suffer? Along with Bentham-inspired animal rights advocates like Singer and Regan, Derrida suggests that the capacity to suffer is something we share with animals.[33] Because we are embodied, we are vulnerable; and because we are vulnerable, we are open to suffering. That is, we are open to others, including parasites, bacteria, and viruses, along with enemy combatants and suicide bombers, or, in the case of animals, hunters and slaughterhouses. Yet Derrida asks what kind of *capacity* is this *ability* to suffer? What kind of *power* is the power to suffer? What is the power to be vulnerable to others, even others within one's own body? What kind of capacity is it that makes the body other-to-itself, whether it is the physical body or the social body (which Derrida discusses in terms of autoimmunity)? In a sense, the capacity to suffer is an impotent power, a powerless power, the power of interdependence, which Derrida suggests may be definitive of humanity and all of life.[34] It is an incapacitated capacity, a disabled ability. It is not the hallmark of an autonomous self-sovereign rational subject but the limits of that subject— that subject as it is opened to others, whether it likes it or not. It is not the kind of ability that animal welfare advocates cite in order to prove that animals are like us and therefore deserve rights like ours. It is not an ability or capacity that we possess or control. Rather, we are possessed by it.

Embodied vulnerability, then, is what we share with animals and also what limits our own sovereignty and autonomy. It is the limit of the human in the face of the animal. In this sense, it takes us beyond either Butler's or Kristeva's notions of a uniquely human vulnerability in that it is also what strips us of our humanity. Cary Wolfe identified the paradox of embodied vulnerability in two types of passivity and vulnerability in Derrida's interpretation of Bentham's question of whether animals could suffer:

The first type (physical vulnerability, embodiment, and eventually mortality) is paradoxically made unavailable, *inappropriable* to us by the very thing that makes it available— namely, a second type of "passivity" or "not being able," which is the finitude we experience in our subjection to a radically ahuman technicity or mechanicity of language, a technicity which has profound consequences, of course, for what we too hastily think of as "our" concepts, which are therefore in an important sense not "ours" at all. (2008, 25–26, italics in original)

The emphasis on the uniqueness of human language—that we are speaking beings or speaking animals, as Kristeva might say—paradoxically indicates the limits of our autonomy and self-sovereignty. Moreover, because we are subject to language and not masters of it, the distinction between response and reaction so central to the distinction between man and animal becomes suspect. As we will see, psychoanalysis with its unconscious processes further challenges the sovereign subject who supposedly masters language and, with it, himself and all the other creatures of the earth. Our embodied vulnerability and our uneasy place between meaning and being become limitations on the Cartesian autonomous self-sovereign individual. We cannot, like Descartes, escape the world and others by meditating in our dressing gowns. We are affected by others and our surroundings, and we are subjects of experience or subjects of a life, as Regan might say, only through our responses to them. Of course, in the history of philosophy, the ability to respond has been reserved for humans and withheld from animals or machines.

It is noteworthy that in contemporary biological and medical sciences and current popular parlance, human behavior and physiology are defined in terms of machines and computers. From "that really turns me on" and "she knows how to push my buttons" to "gene machines" and "hardwired into the brain," humans have become machines. In a fully automated world, we are constantly interfacing with the mechanisms of everyday life. Recent philosophy also figures humans as machines. From Gilles Deleuze and Félix Guattari's assemblages and apparatus and Michel Foucault's disciplinary techniques to Daniel Dennett's computer brain, philosophers have rejected Descartes' thinking subject in favor of complex networks of actions and reactions described by machine metaphors. The machine throws a wrench into the man/animal dichotomy, depending on who is the machine. In other words, if we are like machines, then can we be so certain that we are autonomous rather than automatons?

In *The Animal*, Derrida probes the "auto" in relation to the human/animal binary from both sides. Unlike proponents of animal rights, he does not argue that animals deserve consideration because they share some characteristic with humans. Rather, he is interrogating the borders and limits between the two sides of the binary. He argues that we cannot draw an absolute borderline between human and animal because there are multiple, shifting, unstable borders between different sorts of animals, including human animals. We use the term *animal* to refer to vast numbers of different species from ants to zebras, which effaces the multiplicity of nonhuman animals, some of which may have more in common with humans than they do with one another. In addition, as Deleuze and Guattari point out, "A race-horse is more different from a workhorse than a workhorse is from an ox" (1987, 257).[35] In contrast, humans may not have the capacities or abilities that historically have assured us of our uniqueness and superiority. Derrida challenges the man/animal opposition by suggesting that animals have interests or that they can suffer and also by pointing to the limitations of the human:

There is not one opposition between man and non-man; there are, between different organizational structures of the living being, many fractures, heterogeneities, differential structures . . . none of the traits by which the most authorized philosophy or culture has thought it possible to recognize this "proper of man"—none of them is, in all rigor, the exclusive reserve of what we humans call human. Either because some animals also possess such traits or because man does not possess them as surely as is claimed. (2004, 66)

Given that we are waging endless war, that species are disappearing from the earth at an astounding rate, and global warming threatens the health of the planet, perhaps it is time to think about our own limitations and the limits of the human and humanity. It is time to check our hubris and see what we can learn from the animal and animals, not to dissect them and examine their brains to learn something about our own. Not to unlock and master the secrets of life. Not to make them trophies to hang on the wall or to document in scientific journals. But rather to humble ourselves before fellow creatures that accompany us in life and through which we become human.[36] Perhaps what we need is a sustainable ethics, one based on responsibility to our founding possibility, the earth, animals, and other people, without which we could not live. We need a meta-ethics that goes beyond rights or recognition to the conditions of embodied life on a shared planet and the obligations those conditions entail. And in thinking about an ethics of relationality and responsivity that obligates us to share, we must interrogate the ways in which the man/animal binary sets up an oppositional and exclusionary way of thinking about our relationships to animals and to the earth that ultimately justifies violence toward animals and violence toward people figured as animals.

Whatever the problems with Immanuel Kant's moral justifications for republican federalism, it is instructive that he founded the connection between morality and politics on the limited surface of the earth. In his essay "Perpetual Peace," in the section on universal hospitality, he stated,

The stranger cannot claim the right of a guest to be entertained, for this would require a special friendly agreement whereby he might become a member of the native household for a certain time. He may only claim right of resort, for all men are entitled to present themselves in the society of others by virtue of their right to communal possession of the earth's surface. Since the earth is a globe, they cannot disperse over an infinite area, but must necessarily tolerate one another's company. (1970, 106)

Over the last two hundred years, if we have learned anything—and one wonders—it is that the "communal possessions" of which Kant speaks are the *fruits* of the earth that belong to everyone.[37] What if we go a step further and question what it means to belong—whether human or animal—not as property but as inhabitants of a shared planet?

PART TWO

Animal Pedagogy

I have studied many philosophers and many cats.
The wisdom of cats is infinitely superior.

—HIPPOLYTE TAINE

CHAPTER TWO

You Are What You Eat

Rousseau's Cat

> An animal's eyes have the power to speak a great language. . . . Sometimes
> I look into a cat's eyes. . . . The beginning of this cat's glance, lighting up
> under the touch of my glance, indisputably questioned me: "Is it possible
> that you think of me? . . . Do I really exist?"
>
> —MARTIN BUBER, *I AND THOU*

In both *A Discourse on Inequality* (1755) and "On the Origin of Languages," Jean-
Jacques Rousseau describes "civilized man" as the result of the evolution from
savage hunter, through barbaric herdsman, to civilized farmer.[1] Las Vegas per-
former Roy Horn—who defines himself in terms of his animals and who makes
his living using them—could be just the latest stage in the development of man
described by Rousseau: savage hunter, barbaric herdsman, civilized farmer, Vegas
entertainer. The different social organizations described by Rousseau correspond
to "man's" livelihood and, more specifically, to his relation to animals: "The savage man is a hunter (*chasseur*), the barbarian is a herdsman (shepherd/*berger*),
and civil man is a tiller of the soil (ploughman/*laboureur*)" (1966, 38; 1993, 89).
Rousseau (a vegetarian) describes the savage men as "terrible meat eaters" (*ter-
ribles dévoreurs de viande*) who hunt and kill animals (1966, 35; 1993, 86); barbaric
herdsmen are a step forward because they cultivate and domesticate animals for
food; and civilized men have learned to use animals both directly and indirectly
for food through harvesting crops using animals to till the soil. The movement
from spontaneity to convention, from savage to civilized, is a movement away
from chance and toward necessity. It is a movement away from the accidental
nature of man to nature's determination of man as the dominant animal. Rousseau imagines animals in the state of nature as man's own animal ancestors before
his Fall into civilization.

Even Rousseau's most romantic description of the birth of love, and thereby
of nations, is related to animal needs: the girls come to the watering hole to fetch

water and the boys to water their herds. "Feet skipped with joy, earnest gestures no longer sufficed, being accompanied by an impassioned voice; pleasure and desire mingled and were felt together. There at last was the true cradle of nations [or people, *des peuples*]: from the pure crystal of the fountains flow the first fires of love" (1966, 45; 1993, 96). Language is not only from, but also for, passion; "stirring the heart and inflaming the passions takes words" (1966, 8). Language becomes part of a mating ritual that gives birth to love. But as we will see, the fire of love is not far from the fire necessary to cook the cattle that the boys are herding; and the stirring of hearts comes from the stirring of pots into which the girls have poured their bounty. Where there is love, there are animals, especially those boiling in stews.

In Rousseau's account, human society is organized according to providence in accordance with its provisions. In other words, we are what we eat. Savages eat wild animals, so they are wild. Herdsmen eat domestic animals, so even if they are still barbaric and their manners are crude, they have been domesticated. Civilized men eat cultivated grain, and through their cultivation of the soil, they become cultivated: "Concerning agriculture, which is slower to come into being: it is connected to all the arts; it leads to property, government, and laws, and gradually to the misery and crime that are inseparable for our species from the knowledge of good and evil" (Rousseau 1966, 37). For Rousseau, civilization is both the highest development of man and the fall of man into misery, crime, and evil. Civilization, then, is a symptom, an accident waiting to happen.

Not only are the human and humanity constituted in relation to the animal and animality, but also and more specifically for Rousseau, men constitute themselves as humans by using animals directly and indirectly for food, by eating them. At one point Rousseau suggests that humans are separated from animals through their ability to make and use fire, but actually fire is motivated by the need to cook meat. Again, the ability to cook other animals and eat them becomes a sign of our distinctiveness and intelligence. In a footnote, Rousseau remarks,

No one would say that any beast, wild or domestic, has acquired the skill to make a fire in the same way that we do. Thus these rational beings who are said to have formed a short-lived society before man, still did not reach a level of intelligence at which they were able to strike a few sparks from a flint to make a fire, or even to preserve whatever random fires they might come across. (1966, 41)

Here, the ability to make fire is seen as a sign of intelligence and of man's capacity for reason. But in the paragraph to which this footnote is appended, Rousseau claims that the stomach and intestines of man are not made to digest raw meat and that "with the possible single exception of the Eskimos . . . even savages cook their meat" (1966, 41). So, given the constitution of man's gut, fire is not a sign of intelligence as much as a natural necessity. Rousseau goes on to say that people gather around fire because the flames are useful and pleasing, "and on this simple hearth burns the sacred fire that provokes in the depths of the heart the first feeling of humanity" (1966, 41). Humanity, then, is born from man's need to cook and eat animals (even though for Rousseau, civilization was born from man's overcoming the need to eat animals). In this passage, man's intellectual superiority over animals appears as a consequence of man's need to cook his meat. Again, the providence of nature gives man a necessary advantage over animals when it comes to fire, and the proof of this advantage is that men can kill, cook, and eat animals.

Man also has the advantage that unlike animals, he is not a picky eater. Because men will eat anything, they are more adept at survival than other animals. Again, Rousseau links man's distinctiveness to his digestive track and eating habits, which, it turns out, he appropriates from other animals:

Man dispersed among the beasts, would observe and imitate their activities and so assimilate their instincts, with this added advantage that while every other species has only its own instinct, man, having perhaps none which is peculiar to himself, appropriates every instinct, and by nourishing himself equally well on most of the various foods the other animals divide among themselves, he finds his sustenance more easily than do any of the others. (Rousseau 1983, 92–93; 1984, 81–82)

Men learn what and how to eat from animals. Through this *animal pedagogy*, they are able to imitate animals and assimilate animal instincts. And unlike animals (who eat only what is natural to them), men (owing to their imitation of all of them) eat everything. In fact, Rousseau's argument for man's freedom from animal instinct hinges on his observation that men will eat everything, whereas animals have more restrictive diets. It is noteworthy that it is not animal in general or animality that teaches men what is edible; rather, the assortment of animals in their midst teach them about different food-stuffs that may be eaten. It is only by learning lessons from various animals that men develop the multifarious diet that gives them the edge through which they become human. Men eat and/or assimilate animals both literally as food and figuratively when they ape animals' eating habits. In Rousseau's discourse on inequality, this argument takes many forms involving diet and food, including the fact that unlike other animals, man does not serve as food for another (1984, 83) and that he is distinctive in that he eats but is not eaten by other animals (the tiger mauls but does not eat Roy). Rousseau also cites differences in human and animal infancies and maternal feeding practices as reasons for human sociality: he claims that human mothers are able to carry their young to feed them at all times while other animals cannot (1984, 84). Ultimately, though, man is distinguished from animals by his "free will," which is based on the freedom to eat anything, whereas "a pigeon would die of hunger beside a dish filled with choice meats and a cat beside a pile of fruits or grain, even though either could very well nourish itself with the foods it disdains, if only it were informed by nature to try them" (1984, 87). Man's resistance to "the call of nature" is the result of his ability to appropriate instincts from a variety of other animals that allows him to eat their foodstuffs indiscriminately. It is man's assimilation of animal instinct, therefore, that enables him to transcend instinct, which amounts to the freedom to eat as he will, which he learns from animals (1984, 87).

Given Rousseau's stance on eating meat, the sign of more civilized men should not be that they can eat anything but that they can choose what they eat. In *Émile,* Rousseau repeatedly condemns meat eating, especially in children and nursing mothers. He claims that children fed a vegetarian diet are less likely to get worms and colic because farinaceous foods produce more blood than meat and they are less likely to rot (2003, 28). He extols the virtues of milk, which (along with cheese, judging by his recollections in *Confessions*) is one of his favorite foods; he proposes that "milk, although manufactured in the body of an animal, is a vegetable substance; this is shown by analysis; it readily turns acid, and far from showing traces of any volatile alkali like animal matter, it gives a neutral salt like plants" (2003 29). As further proof of the benefits of a vegetarian diet, he says that the milk of herbivores is sweeter than that of carnivores. He argues that a diet of vegetables is healthier than a diet of meat and also is more natural. As proof that eating meat is not natural, Rousseau claims that children don't like to eat meat (2003, 140). As he does so often, he points to the behavior of other animals to demonstrate what is natural to human animals: "Women eat bread, vegetables, and dairy produce; female dogs and cats do the same; the she-wolves eat grass. This supplies vegetable juices to their milk. There are still those species which are unable to eat anything but flesh, if such there are, which I very much doubt" (2003, 29). That all animals eat vegetables is proof that it is natural to do so. As we have seen, although meat eating is natural to savage man, the more civilized man becomes, the greater the distance from his "prey" also becomes. Conversely, the more that man distances himself from the animals that he eats, the more civilized he becomes. Recall that the third stage of man's development, as Rousseau describes it, is the plowman, who cultivates grain instead of cattle. At this point, there are two possible directions for man: he can continue to eat meat but now distance himself from killing his animal food in order to disavow his killing, or he can choose not to eat meat. Grain becomes either a means to feed animals for man's consumption or a means by which man makes the transition from carnivore to herbivore. Rousseau begins by arguing that the vegetarian diet is healthier, then he claims that it is more natural, and finally he makes a connection between taste and morality: vegetarianism is a moral choice that is evidence of man's freedom not to eat meat. Unlike other carnivores, man can choose to become an herbivore. Unlike animals, eating enables humans to rise to moral inclinations. For Rousseau this is another reason why the child's diet is important. Given his statements on taste, animals should have a better moral sensibility than humans, in a paradoxical sort of way. I will return to the connection between taste and morality in chapter 4.

Rousseau maintains that "the first cake to be eaten was the communion of the human race" (1966, 35). It is cake that brings men together; cake is the basis of human society. No other animal can make a cake, which for Rousseau is the result of the cultivation of fields, the beginning of all art and artistry (never mind that Rousseau doesn't talk about the making, but the eating, of cake, ignoring that other animals can eat cake and that even cavemen painted pictures). Sowing for harvest requires ownership of land, tools, foresight, and community, all of which hunters and shepherds lack (1966, 33–34). Although animals are used for farming and many of the early tools for tilling the soil required oxen and horses, Rousseau imagines the civilized man as a grain eater who begins to separate himself from the animals that he consumes, which are raised and slaughtered elsewhere and for which he trades his harvest. In this regard, the distance between man and his animal eating is a sign of civilization. He no longer hunts wild animals or slaughters his domestic animals; now he uses animals to produce crops that he can exchange for animals once they have become meat and other commodities. This is the beginning of property, which Rousseau identifies with the beginning of dependence, bondage, servitude, and the inequality of men (e.g., 1984, 105–6). We could say that for Rousseau, as man disavows his dependence on animals and his diet of animals by shielding himself from their production for food, by turning them into commodities—meat instead of animals—he becomes more civilized (and more corrupt). Human society, then, is based on the double sacrifice of animals: first the killing of animals for food and then the concealing of that killing so that man can continue to eat animals without guilt. Rousseau's text seems to suggest that vegetarianism might be a sign of higher development.

The *Natural Man* seems to be this higher stage in the development of man, going beyond the agricultural cultivation of the earth toward the cultivation of his own nature. In *Émile,* Rousseau describes the education of the Natural Man, whom we might call *postcivilized* in that he does not so much return to nature as learn from it. Rousseau suggests that the Natural Man resolves the contradiction between nature and culture because he lives with others in society yet emulates the vigor and vitality of nature (2003, 9). He lives among other men but learns from plants and animals. Just as plants require cultivation in relation to society, so does man in the form of education (2003, 6). The natural man overcomes the arbitrariness of fate, the accidental situation of man in society, by learning from nature. This renewed relation to nature is a type of "second nature" that Rousseau describes as *habit* (2003, 7). He explains that just as plants habitually grow toward the sun, whatever their training, the natural man should develop habits that keep him in harmony with nature. The education that Rousseau describes in *Émile* is designed to cultivate these habits so that "in vain will fate change his station, he will always be in his right place" (2003, 10). If civilization is an accident that transgresses natural law, then the cultivation/education of the natural man is an attempt to bring him "back" to the laws of nature, only now within his social milieu. Natural man learns about the laws of nature from plants and animals, who teach him the ways of the world of necessity by accident and bring him back to himself, so to speak. Rousseau sees this education as teaching life in general and manhood in particular: "In the natural order men are all equal and their common calling is that of manhood. . . . Life is the trade I would teach him. . . . When he leaves me . . . he will be a man" (2003, 10).

Again, animals play an essential role in the education of man. Unlike the savage, the herdsman, and the plowman, the natural man looks to animals for food and for lessons in life. Rousseau begins *Émile* by stating that man is like a saddle horse or a tree that needs to be trained and shaped (2003, 5). Throughout this immense book, he describes how he will teach Émile the ways of the animal. For example, Rousseau says: "I shall be told that animals, who live according to nature, are less liable to disease than ourselves. Well, that way of living is just what I mean to teach my pupil; he should profit by it in the same way"—the way of the animals (2003, 26); and

the other animals possess only such powers as are required for self-preservation; man alone has more. Is it not very strange that this superfluity should make him miserable? . . . If a man were content to live, he would live happily; and he would therefore be good, for what would he have to gain by vice? (2003, 53)

While the savage, the herdsman, and the plowman increasingly disavow their dependence on and relation to animals, the natural man cultivates respect for animals and refuses to eat them. The natural man learns from the animals and imitates them until his animal actions become second nature or habit.

For Rousseau, however, imitation and habit are not enough to make the natural man a good man; as Derrida points out, imitation must be supplemented with understanding and love (1967, 205). Throughout *Émile,* Rousseau insists that natural man must be educated by example, imitation, and experience rather than with words or lectures; but he also maintains that even monkeys imitate, and animals, too, learn by experience (2003, 81, 193, 33). He argues that actions are good only if they are felt and understood and not just imitated. Although the child (or monkey) can imitate without understanding, the child also must be able to love the good for his actions to be truly good. The child must have good intentions to supplement the good action that he or she imitates. The monkey example, however, is an odd moment in *Émile,* since throughout the text Rousseau is adamant that (children's) knowledge is on the level of sensation and not understanding and that teaching words is not teaching (2003, esp. 84–86). Rousseau states that children learn through imitation, as monkeys do, and that only when they enter the age of reason that comes with adulthood can they begin to understand. The education that he describes begins with imitation and is followed by habit and finally understanding and love, which come only later. Monkeys imitate, but in man imitation can become parody and ridicule, which Rousseau condemns. Even plants have habits, but in man habits can become bad habits. What is good in nature can become bad in man.

According to Rousseau, corrupt forms of imitation display their mimetic talents as ends in themselves or for the sake of debasement, whereas natural imitation is a form of respect and eventually of response. The monkey imitates man because he fears him and "thinks what is done by his betters must be good," whereas the lower classes imitate the higher as a form of debasement and ridicule evidenced, according to Rousseau, in their choice of models (2003, 81). That is, the people that these men take to be their betters are poor models for emulation. Rousseau's work suggests that we would be better off imitating monkeys than rich, propertied fat cats. As usual with Rousseau, there seems to be a form of imitation that he criticizes—the one through which we attempt to "escape from ourselves" and our environment—and a form of imitation that he endorses—the one through which we learn to be responsive to our environment (cf. 2003, 81). The bad form of imitation comes from envy and the product of man's ability to compare himself with others that begins with property ownership. The good form of imitation is the result of the natural urge to respond to one's fellows and environment. Émile's education is based on teaching responsiveness: Rousseau presents him with new experiences, tries to surprise him and not to spare him pain, in order to teach him to be responsive. This is why he denounces learning by rote, since it cannot teach Émile how to respond to different situations, that is, how to live. "The only habit the child should be allowed to contract," says Rousseau, "is that of having no habits" (2003, 34). "The natural man is interested in all new things," and therefore children must be exposed to different sorts of experiences (2003, 34). Rousseau maintains that they should not be protected from terrible things and that they should not be allowed to get used to anything. Nothing should take place at fixed hours, to avoid making the child rigid in his expectations; rather, variation nourishes responsiveness to new situations. Imitation and example are valuable insofar as they teach response-ability, and conversely, response-ability begins with trained reactions.

Rousseau describes Émile's education as a series of training exercises designed to accustom him to different situations and, more than that, to make him responsive to his environment and those around him. What starts as habit and reaction gives way to morality and response-ability. Émile is trained as an animal would be trained, by a kindly trainer, through love, repetition, and food. Like Roy, Rousseau prefers to reward his pupil with carrots rather than sticks. In fact, often when Rousseau extols the benefits of example and imitation, he describes a stimulus/response type of behavior modification that uses food as a reward. For example, the lessons of astronomy become useful only when they help Émile find his way back to lunch (2003, 173). Ice cream is used to teach cold (2003, 199), and cakes are indispensable to teaching the value of exercise and ambition, judging distance, and generosity (2003, 134). Rousseau describes at length the cake pedagogy with which he teaches a lazy boy to love running and eventually to love sharing the rewards of competition. As we have seen, cake also plays a crucial role in the development of savages into humans.

Rousseau's writings suggest that choosing to eat cake instead of eating animals is a sign of the natural man's higher evolution. Rousseau also identifies the inequality of men in society with differences between foods that didn't exist with natural or primitive man:

Now if we compare the prodigious diversity of upbringings and of ways of life which prevail among the different classes in the civil state with the simplicity and uniformity of animal and savage life, *where everyone eats the same foods,* lives in the same style and does exactly the same things, it will be understood how much less the difference between man and man must be in the state of nature than it is in society. (1984, 105, italics added)

Eating the same foods is the first characteristic of the equality among animals, including savage men. Like the differences between animals and man, differences among men are evidenced in the differences in what they eat. Again, Rousseau describes freedom as the freedom to eat what one will, to eat freely from a variety of foods, while servitude (whether it is to instincts, in the case of animals, or to other men, in the case of humans) is evidenced in not having a choice about what one eats.

Ironically, in *Émile,* it is man's freedom that both distinguishes him from the animals and makes him misérable and capable of evil. In the beginning, the child's freedom is no more than the animal's, which is to say, freedom of movement. In fact, the animal has greater freedom than the child, who, as Rousseau complains, is too often wrapped in tight blankets and clothing that impair its natural freedom. Unlike in animals, however, in humans freedom of movement eventually gives rise to freedom of will. In "A Discourse on the Inequality," it would seem that men enslaved by other men have been denied a fundamental human freedom, the freedom to eat everything and thereby to live more like animals. Rousseau's discourse on inequality suggests as much when it repeatedly invokes metaphors of animals to conjure images of the inequality among men. The enslavement of men is compared with the domestication of animals, who are more robust in nature:

One might say that all our efforts to care for and feed these animals have only succeeded in making them degenerate. The same is true even of man himself; in becoming sociable and a slave, he grows feeble, timid, servile; and his soft and effeminate way of life completes the enervation both of his strength and his courage. (1984, 86)

Suggesting that our "animal ancestors" are more powerful in nature before they have been domesticated, Rousseau continually uses animals to make his claims about men. For example, to show that slavery is not natural but a result of socialization, Rousseau gives the example of a horse who "rears impetuously at the very approach of the bit, while a trained horse suffers patiently even the whip and spur," so too "savage man will not bend his neck to the yoke which civilized man wears without a murmur" (1983, 157; 1984, 125). Both men and horses can be domesticated, trained to endure the whip. Rousseau compares the accumulation of slaves as property with the collection of cattle. And he insists that the rich are like "ravenous wolves, which, having once tasted human flesh, refuse all other nourishment and desire thenceforth only to devour men" (1984, 120).

It should not be surprising, then, that for Rousseau, man's relation with animals sets the stage for his relation with humans—we mistreat one another because we mistreat animals. For example, collecting and owning cattle prepares man to collect and own human slaves (1984, 131), and from hunting and killing animals man learns war and conquest; "war and its conquests is just a kind of manhunt" (1966, 36). Herding cattle teaches men to herd men; hunting wild animals teaches men to hunt men. Man's cruelty to other men echoes his cruelty to animals. The rich can be "like wolves" and "devour" men only because men first prey on wolves. We could say that inequality among men is a symptom of man's relation to animals. Conversely, we can learn about human relations from our relations with animals. Again Rousseau claims that man's character is formed in relation to what and how he eats: flesh eaters are cruel, while flower eaters are gentle (2003, 140–41). He asserts that "all savages are cruel, and it is not their customs that tend in this direction; their cruelty is the result of their food. They go to war as to the chase, and treat men as they would treat bears. . . . Great criminals prepare themselves for murder by drinking blood" (2003, 140–41). As part of his argument in favor of a vegetarian diet in *Émile*, Rousseau maintains that it is not only for health's sake that children should avoid eating meat but also for their characters (2003, 140). He proposes that eating flesh begins and ends in cruelty. Quoting Plutarch, he gives a forceful account of the barbarity of killing and eating animals:

How could his hand plunge the knife into the heart of a sentient creature, how could his eyes look on murder, how could he behold a poor helpless animal bled to death, scorched, and dismembered? . . . Thus must he have felt the first time he did despite to nature and made this horrible meal; the first time he hungered for the living creature, and desired to feed upon the beast which was still grazing. When he bade them slay, dismember, and cut up the sheep which licked his hands. It is those who began these cruel feasts, not those who abandon them, who should cause surprise, and there were excuses for those primitive men, excuses which we have not, and the absence of such excuses multiples our barbarity a hundredfold. (2003, 141)

Barbarity toward animals begets barbarity toward fellow humans; hunting and killing animals is a training ground for hunting and killing men; war is a natural outgrowth or at least a side effect of slaying animals: Flesh eaters make war. Rousseau's position is worth considering, since as we have seen recently, dietary restrictions against eating flesh or certain animals are broken as a means of torture in war; think of American prison guards forcing Iraqi prisoners to eat pork. In the United States, hunting has been almost mandatory for presidential candidates, shown on television with guns walking through marshes to reassure us that they are tough enough for the job.

Even as he describes man's distinguishing characteristics—capacity for free will, spirituality of soul, faculty of self-improvement—Rousseau's repeated use of animal metaphors belies the distinction between man and animal. Men are compared with horses, cattle, wolves, monkeys, and crows, and these animals are put in the service of his argument that civilized men are different from them.

Although Rousseau gives us a continuum of animals in relation to a continuum of humans in progress or degeneration and he idealizes animal nature as man's potential for coexistence, his animals still serve as romantic and ideal ancestors for man, man's better half, rather than coexisting companions. When animals do coexist with men, they are killed, cooked, and eaten.

Rousseau uses animals in his attempts to distinguish natural man from civilized man in order to demonstrate that inequalities among men are not natural. He bases his argument that inequalities among men are not natural on what appears to be a natural division between man and animal. Man, once an animal himself, becomes man by dominating other animals. This inequality between man and animals becomes the basis for Rousseau's arguments from nature that ground his claim that inequalities come from cultural, not natural, differences. We can see those differences among men as cultural only because we see the differences between man and animals as natural. We can see that inequalities among men are accidental because inequalities among animals are preordained. But Rousseau's animals refuse to be domesticated. His metaphors and illustrations of animals bite back and cause his texts to chase their own tails when they are used to characterize human nature. They are the animal accidents at the heart of human providence, the accidental origin of humanity, the animal pedagogy to which humanity is beholden.

The origin of language and thereby humanity or civilization is the main focus of Rousseau's essay "On the Origin of Languages," in which he claims that "conventional language is characteristic of man alone. That is why man makes progress, whether for good or ill, and animals do not" (1966, 10). While animals may have some form of communication or natural language ("the speech of beavers and ants"), they do not (and cannot) have conventional language (1966, 10). Here again, however, there are signs in Rousseau's text that conventional language is a *response* to animals. Beginning, as Rousseau does, with the assumption that human language was acquired, then presumably man's original encounter with other savages or primitive men must have been animal encounters. As Rousseau describes it, man's language, like the "speech of beavers and ants" or the language of "crows or monkeys," was originally gestural and only later became proper speech, beginning with figurative utterances motivated by passion (1966, 6–7, 111–12). If the first language was figurative, then according to his analysis, those primitive figures must have been animals (along with the plants and trees in the midst of humans).

In his essay on looking at animals, citing Rousseau, John Berger claims that

the first subject matter for painting was animal. Probably the first paint was animal blood. Prior to that, it is not unreasonable to suppose that the first metaphor was animal. . . . If the first metaphor was animal, it was because the essential relation between man and animal was metaphoric. Within that relation what the two terms—man and animal—shared in common revealed what differentiated them. And vice versa. . . . What distinguished man from animals was the human capacity for symbolic thought, the capacity which was inseparable from the development of language in which words were not mere signals, but signifiers of something other than themselves. Yet the first symbols were animals. What distinguished men from animals was born of their relationship with them. (1980, 5–6)

The acquisition of language, which supposedly sets man apart from animals, is the result of man's relation with animals, in the sense of both the significance of animal proximity to the lives of primitive men and the provision of species against which man could identify himself as man. Claude Lévi-Strauss comments that

it is because man originally felt himself identical to all those like him (among which, as Rousseau explicitly says, we must include animals) that he came to acquire the capacity to distinguish *himself* as he distinguishes *them* i.e., to use the diversity of species as conceptual support for social differentiation. (1962, 101, italics in original)

Lévi-Strauss believed that man could distinguish himself from animals only because he first learned to distinguish animals from one another. It is precisely this *difference among* animals that the philosopher buries in the concept of "the animal" or "animality."

As we have seen, much of Rousseau's discussion of the difference between man and animal revolves around food; men literally assimilate animals by eating them and thereby establish their dominance over them. Moreover, men secure their ability to eat all things by imitating and assimilating animal instincts; men watch animals and eat what they eat (1984, 81–82). It is as if the assimilation of animal flesh becomes the assimilation of animal sounds. Man's assimilation of the animal/animals takes place on a figurative as well as a physical level; man assimilates and imitates animal sounds and cries, animal "speech," and eventually develops conventional language, which is born from the "voice of nature" (cf. 1966, 58; 1984, 70, 93). Man's ability to figure, to figure animals, comes through his imitation of animals; man substitutes words for animal speech (both his own gestural language and the sounds he assimilates from other animals). The logic of substitutability, the logic of metaphor itself, begins in this substitution of sounds for animals. Metaphoricity, then, also is a response to the animals. The logic of metaphor that makes men human is a response to the animals in their midst. These animals show or demonstrate the process of assimilation that men ape by substituting human symbols for animal signs, homologos for zoölogos. This logic is taken to its extreme when, like a cat digging in sand, man covers up the animal sign that fertilizes his imagination and teaches him the capacity for metaphor, that is, what he imagines distinguishes him from the animal. In this sense, man's disavowal of animal pedagogy and of those animals that gave him words and thereby a world, albeit accidentally, is engendered by animals. In Rousseau's account of the origin of languages, however, it is not simply the case that what men and animals shared revealed their differences and thereby allowed man to name himself (and the animals). It is also not simply that the relation between man and animal is metaphorical, so that his first metaphors were of animals. In addition, the very possibility of metaphor, that is, the very possibility of language, depends on the substitution of man for animal: language itself operates through the assimilation and/or imitation of animals and the subsequent disavowal of that animal pedagogy. This mimetic logic is itself metaphorical in the sense that it substitutes one thing for another and thereby confounds identity and difference. In order to become human, men act like animals, eat what animals eat, and say what animals say, only now with words.

Rousseau argues that for uncivilized men, sensation does not have moral meaning, whereas for civilized men, intellect and moral reasoning give sensations their meaning. He criticizes the view that sensations have meaning in themselves and insists that their meaning comes from emotions and feelings familiar from culture. More than the influence of culture, it seems that the most refined and cultured sensations—fine music—pull at the heart of the most cultured men in ways that they do not in the uncultured. Rousseau says that "the ear does not so much convey pleasure to the heart as the heart conveys it to the ear" (1966, 61). His argument leading up to this conclusion is that familiar sounds and sensations will have meaning but unfamiliar ones will not. He gives the example of the healing sounds used to cure tarantula bites, which he maintains cannot be particular sounds but must be sounds familiar to the inflicted: "Italian tunes are needed for Italians; for Turks, Turkish tunes. Each is affected only by *accents* (des accents) familiar to him" (1966, 60; 1993, 112, italics added).

Rousseau begins his argument about the importance of feeling or moral sentiment by describing his own attempt to imitate his cat's voice. At first, his attempt appears successful when his cat perks up its ears to listen, but soon the cat recognizes Rousseau's accent and goes back to sleep:

When my cat hears me imitate a mewing, I see it become immediately attentive, alert, agitated. When it discovers that I am just counterfeiting (*contrefais*) the voice of its species, it relaxes and resumes its rest. Since there is nothing at all different in the stimulation of the sense organ, and the cat had initially been deceived (*trompé*), what accounts for the difference? Unless the influence of sensations upon us is due mainly to moral causes, why are we so sensitive to impressions that mean nothing to the uncivilized (*des barbares*)? (1966, 59; 1993, 111)

This passage is remarkable in several respects. First, Rousseau imitates his cat: he meows! Next, the cat realizes after initially being deceived that the meowing is not another cat. Then Rousseau takes up the question of what accounts for the difference for the cat between deception and recognition. Finally he concludes that recognition gives meaning to sensations that mean nothing to the uncivilized. All this suggests, however, that either Rousseau's cat occupies the place of the civilized man because it can distinguish a fake from a real meow or Rousseau's meowing is itself the language of the civilized man that his cat cannot appreciate because it is not familiar with the sound of a "civilized" meow. So either the cat is civilized, or civilized language is one that imitates the sounds of animals, which, as we have seen, resonates with what we might call Rousseau's animal pedagogy. In either case, much of Rousseau's discussion of the importance of familiarity to meaning rests on his cat and its ability to distinguish a familiar meow from Rousseau's uncanny imitation. The cat is put into the service of Rousseau's argument that human meaning cannot be reduced to animal sensation.

At this point, it may be helpful to compare Rousseau's cat with Derrida's cat. In "The Animal That Therefore I Am (More to Follow)" (2008), Derrida introduces his own cat. He insists that he is talking about "a real cat, truly, believe me, *a little cat.* It isn't the *figure* of a cat" (2008, 6, italics in original). Later he teases his reader by saying that perhaps he is only quoting from Lewis Carroll's *Through the Looking Glass* while pointing out that one French translation gives us "pussy" (*chatte*) for cat. Earlier, he quoted Montaigne "playing" with his pussycat (*chatte*) in the context of describing a feeling of shame in front of his female cat looking at his "sex . . . without touching yet, and without biting, although that threat remains on its lips or on the tip of the tongue" (1999, 254; 2008, 4). Here he stops himself, saying that he "wanted to bite his tongue" (*j'avais voula me mordre la langue*) because it seems as if he was about to admit what the symptom cannot admit, namely, that it is an accident (symptom).

Even while continuing the wordplay with *à suivre* (more to follow, to be continued), Derrida is explicit that we "follow" or "come after" the animal: "being-after-it in the sense of the hunt, training, or taming, or being-after-it in the sense of a succession or inheritance? In all cases, if I am (following) *after* it, the animal therefore comes before me, earlier than me. . . . The animal is there before me" (Derrida 2008, 10–11). Derrida suggests that the "I" in the cogito follows the animal, that self-reflection is conjured in the look of the animal, especially in his case, the look of his female cat before whom he is recalled to himself in the shame of his nakedness. He describes chasing himself out of the room and biting himself in the presence of his cat. He becomes an animal captured by the look of another animal. By recalling him to his animality, the look of the cat also recalls his humanity, which follows, comes after, the animal, here his cat. Derrida concludes by asking whether his cat can be his "primary mirror" (*mon premier miroir*) (2008, 51). This discussion is in the larger context of criticizing Levinas's insistence that the human face-to-face encounter founds ethics (not a Sartrian look and particularly not the gaze of an animal) and of indicating suspicions of how Lacan traps animals at the mirror stage.

In what almost seems like a stray paragraph in a text that revolves around the "to follow" or "comes after," Derrida interrogates the "to follow" and multiplies it (in opposition to Heidegger) in "being alongside," "being near," "being with," "being huddled-together" (2008, 10). Despite this gesture toward being-with, Derrida's invocation of the mirror at the end of the essay—not to mention his sexual fantasies of his cat—indicates that we are back to his analysis of Rousseau in *Of Grammatology,* in which all contact with the other, including conversation, comes back to autoaffection (e.g., 1974, 165–66). Derrida's perverse pussy, a voyeur threatening castration, seems a far cry from Rousseau's clever cat, who isn't fooled by her "master's" attempts at "cat language." Whereas Rousseau sees the cat as a potential interlocutor, Derrida sees himself captured by the menacing look of the cat after his sex. I will return to Derrida's cat in subsequent chapters.

Rousseau introduces his cat toward the end of "On the Origin of Languages" to contend that our most lively sensations are produced by moral impressions, which distinguish civilized man from uncivilized man, if not man from animals. If not as threatening as Derrida's cat, Rousseau's cat is another spot where the text begins to chase its own tail on the question of the distinction between man and animal, and not just because, as Derrida points out, Rousseau allows for moral sentiment in "the animal" but, stranger still, because he is attempting to talk to his cat in its own language, by meowing. Rousseau's deceived yet discerning cat may be a different breed from Derrida's nasty-looking cat in that she shows up to illustrate the significance of accent rather than of language itself. In chapter 4, I return to the relation between accent and articulation as Derrida describes it in his analysis of Rousseau in *On Grammatology,* in relation to what I call his "taste for purity."

With Rousseau's cat, it is not just a question of speaking cat language (or any language) but of speaking with a credible accent. For Derrida, it seems that response is tied up with an (in)credible translation of the name: he asks what would it mean for an animal to respond in its own name. In turn, this could suggest that this animal gives itself a name in its own tongue or responds in the name that humans have given it, that is, in our tongue, or to be truly its own, it would have to be its proper name. This focus on the name of the animal is revealing because the proper name of each singular animal would remain the same in every language, except in terms of its accent. In *The Animal,* Derrida points out a translatory supplement, the insertion of the word *response* (*répondre*), into French translations of Lewis Carroll's Alice complaining about kittens: "Whatever you say to them, they *always* purr" and "But how *can* you talk with a person if they *always* say the same thing?" (2008, 8). If translation is the substitution or supplementation of one language for another (which may also work to domesticate wild or stray phrases), then accent is not a matter of substitution but of inflection, so that always "saying the same thing" can in fact say different things and to different people, including cats. This tone of voice or accent seems to be implied in Alice's debate with the Cheshire cat over purring versus growling.

Rousseau's cat, along with menagerie of other animals that appear in his texts, serve to create the illusion of arguments grounded in experience, in natural facts. These animal examples and metaphors are not as domesticated or well trained, however, as his arguments make them out. Like Roy Horn's domesticated wild cat, Montecore, Rousseau's cat is unpredictable. It doesn't always perform as its human would like; and sometimes its effects demonstrate that human mastery is the illusion at the heart of man's relation with animals. As we have seen, in his account of how man becomes civilized by moving beyond animal needs or instincts, Rousseau continually slips "back" into animal needs to make his case, specifically the need to eat, and what we eat is definitive of what we are: wild, domesticated, or cultivated. Man's gut becomes the guiding principle behind the providence of human destiny. Even language, with all its attendant capacities that make man uniquely human, turns out to be the assimilation of animal language, or man acting like an animal (like an ass, as in asininity). Just as men assimilate animals by eating everything animals eat and then by eating them and thereby forming human societies, they assimilate animal sounds and thereby form human language. Society and language are responses to animals with whom men share the world and from whom men learn to be human. The wild and domesticated animals in Rousseau's texts leave signs of the accident playing possum at the origins of human necessity.

And Say the Human Responded?

In Rousseau's discussions of civilized man, the tension between natural law and conventional law is apparent in his writings and in the commentaries on them, particularly those by Jacques Derrida and Paul de Man. One of the ways that this tension plays out in Rousseau's accounts of the origin of society and of language is in what we might call the *paradox of freedom:* either human society and language are the necessary results of the progress of nature and subject to—that is, determined by—natural law, or they are accidental to nature and man is free to break natural law—that is, he is not determined by natural law, but free. If what we take to be human freedom is the result of natural law and determined by it, then in what sense is it free? How are humans any different from animals? Conversely, if human society breaks with natural law in order to become free of it, then in what sense are human beings natural? Are we aberrations of nature? How can we be both free and natural at the same time? Given Rousseau's idealization of Nature, this is a question that vexes most of his work and the commentaries on it. Is man necessary or an accident? Rousseau seems to struggle somewhere in between the either/or dichotomy of this question and a both/and that might ease the tension between the two poles of necessity and accident. This is not news to Rousseau scholars. But what may come as a surprise is that when Rousseau is most diligent in arguing for man's freedom from natural law, he invokes animal metaphors and illustrations that recall the natural need or law on which that freedom depends. These moments suggest that man's freedom is the result not only of natural law but also, and more specifically, of animal pedagogy. For Rousseau, as we have seen, man learns to become man from the animals.

The Gamekeepers

It is noteworthy that the "founding fathers" of what is known as *deconstruction,* Jacques Derrida and Paul de Man, disagree about the role of nature in Rousseau. One privileges his insistence on natural law, and the other privileges his insistence on conventional law. As Rousseau describes it, human language both evolves from nature and replies to it. It is the tension between the notions that language/civilization evolves from nature and that it erupts from nature that marks both Derrida's and de Man's readings of Rousseau. Whereas Derrida argues that Rousseau's philosophy continues the metaphysics of presence of his predecessors, de Man argues that it is not presence but absence at the heart of Rousseau's writing. Derrida maintains that Rousseau tries to protect the plenitude and purity of Nature by figuring absence and corruption as accidental to it, but de Man claims that Rousseau prefers evolution to eruption. Interestingly, while trying to deconstruct metaphysical binaries, these two critics chose sides in relation to Rousseau.

As fascinating as this debate may be, there is a larger reward for rehearsing this decades-old disagreement. More productive than choosing sides in this debate over to which pole we tether Rousseau, attending to the ambiguities in Rousseau's writings as a hallmark of listening and responsiveness offers alternative ways to conceive of both man and animal. As we know, Rousseau repeatedly claims that conventional language is a response to the "voice of nature" (*voix de la nature*) (cf. 1966, 58; 1983, 80; 1984, 70, 93). If man learns to speak from nature, more specifically from the animals, doesn't he first have to listen? And if nature or animals speak first, then isn't listening as essential to man and definitive of him as speaking? I believe that these questions are perhaps best answered by another of Rousseau's commentators, Jean Starobinski, whose readings of Rousseau were mentioned and dismissed by both Derrida and de Man. Starobinski helps us understand the role of listening and responsivity in Rousseau's account of language. The role of listening and responsivity implies that we are morally obligated to other life-forms on whom we depend for our survival as animal bodies and for our conception of ourselves as distinct from other animal bodies. Conceiving of humanity as a capacity for listening and responding brings with it ethical obligations to all living beings with whom we share the earth, and perhaps to the earth itself.

In "The Rhetoric of Blindness," Paul de Man concludes that Derrida's "story" of Rousseau surreptitiously smuggling the "truth" into the "precinct he was assigned to protect" is a good one because it turns out that it is "the game-keeper himself who is here doing the poaching" (de Man 1983, 119). But that is not the only plot twist: it turns out that the truth that Rousseau is smuggling is the absence at the heart of the presence of truth, that the truth is not what it appears, or more accurately, it is only appearance. The familiar story of the poacher become gamekeeper is a popular scenario in Hollywood Westerns, in which the outlaw becomes a virile organ of justice more powerful than the law itself, is reversed. Here, according to de Man, it is the law that turns out to be the criminal, which also is a familiar plot twist in Hollywood films. This ambiguity between law and transgression is precisely what is at stake in both Derrida's and de Man's readings of Rousseau. Reaching opposing conclusions, they both attempt to explain the ambiguities of Rousseau's texts on the question of the status of Nature.

At length, Derrida argues that Rousseau "declares" the presence of Nature in the origins of man and society but that he "describes" absence in that same place. As de Man's essay points out, Derrida's text is inconclusive regarding whether or not Rousseau intentionally "conjures" absence "in contraband" even while declaring presence, or whether the supplementary structure of language beyond Rousseau's control "governs" his discourse (de Man 1983, 117; cf. Derrida 1967, 345). Although de Man means that Derrida falls prey to the same smuggling and ambiguities as Rousseau does (e.g., on whether the ambiguity in Rousseau's texts on origin originates in Rousseau's intentions or in the structure of language), he warns that "we would be falling into a trap if we wanted to show Derrida deluded in the same manner that he claims Rousseau to be deluded" (de Man 1983, 122). De Man himself, however, cannot help falling into that trap, especially when he argues that "Rousseau's text has no blind spots" and goes on to explain "Derrida's blindness." Note that he does not say the blindness of the text, but Derrida's blindness (1983, 139). One of de Man's moves in deconstructing Derrida's text (or Derrida himself) is to adamantly proclaim that "there is no need to deconstruct Rousseau" (1983, 139). "Rousseau's text has no blind spots" and "there is no need to deconstruct Rousseau" seem to appear in de Man's essay as incantations designed to erase the "disturbing parts of the work" with which he began the essay. Like Obi wan Kenobi's incantations in *Star Wars*, it is as if the hypnotic effect of the phrases themselves could make it so ("these are not the ones we are looking for; let them go").

Both de Man and Derrida try to show that it is no accident that absence is the origin of presence, that there is no origin, and that because of this, all interpretation has its blind spots, that all seeing is blind to its own limitations. In relation to Rousseau, de Man claims that Rousseau saw the accident as necessary and that an insightful reading of Rousseau demonstrates that he does not contradict himself on the question of origins. Rather, a more truthful reading of Rousseau shows that he discovered the duplicity at the heart of language, which begins in error compounded by lie. Derrida, in contrast, contends that Rousseau did not see the accident at the heart of origin, which he nevertheless describes. According to Derrida, Rousseau tries to separate the accident from Nature in order to protect its innocence: Nature is good and true, while all evil and falsehood are the result of man, whose origin is accidental. Is the accident an accident, or is it necessary? And if it is necessary, as both de Man and Derrida insist in their own ways, then hasn't it been assimilated into the very history of metaphysics of presence that both theorists criticize? When the accident becomes part of the necessary structure of language and origin, then hasn't it been recuperated for the sake of presence, now at the structural or syncratic rather than historical or diacratic level? Since the tumultuous times of the publications of these texts, there have been volumes of commentary, especially on Derrida's early work. Although these texts and the differences between de Man and Derrida are interesting in themselves, my point in coming back to this seminal moment in philosophical criticism is to revisit Rousseau's writings in order to track the multitude of different animals present in his texts that are missing in both de Man's and Derrida's readings of Rousseau's Nature. Putting a different spin on de Man's figures of speech, we might ask, "Is the gamekeeper here doing the poaching?" and "What about this *trap* that the critic/reader falls into?"

Commentators on Rousseau's writings have to contend with vast inconsistencies and stray remarks. As de Man argues, most either reduce the ambiguities in the texts to contradictions or read them away in the name of consistency. If de Man does the latter—there are no contradictions or blind spots in Rousseau—Derrida does both at the same time. He does, as de Man points out, set up binary oppositions in order to knock them down (he constructs them in order to deconstruct them), and by so doing, he effectively assimilates ambiguity and tensions in Rousseau's texts into the narrative of the primacy of absence over presence. Derrida deconstructs the binary by reversing the hierarchical valuation of its terms. It is as if even as they highlight the ambiguity in the texts and in language itself, they cannot help but recuperate it into a coherent structure—even a structure that undoes itself is better than none—to echo a Nietzchean sentiment. But perhaps this is the point.

By revisiting the shadows of Rousseau's animals in Derrida's and de Man's readings, I would like to suggest an alternative to reading binaries into Rousseau, which may shift the possibilities for thinking ethics. Although I don't want to pretend that my writing is not also falling into traps right and left or that I am not also unknowingly "poaching in the name of gamekeeping," I hope to bring into relief certain figures and patterns in these texts that may be instructive in thinking about relationships between subjects, whatever or whoever they are. By setting our sights on the issue of the role of animals and the concept of the animal or animality in these texts, the questions of subjects and concepts of the subject or subjectivity themselves become prey. The hunt for the animal is necessarily also a hunt for the subject, and any attempt to delineate the animal or animality from the human or humanity must dissect the meaning of "subjectivity." The precarious and ambiguous space between human and animal is the ecosystem of contemporary discussions of so-called animal rights, of environmental ethics, and of ethics more generally.

Poaching on Rousseau's Nature

From the perspective of humanity (so to speak), particularly philosophies of the human, ambiguity eventually takes us (back) to the animal, who serves to protect against the very ambiguity that it conjures. The concept *animal* signifies all living creatures that are not human and thereby secures the identity of man against brute, and at the same time, it covers over differences among vast numbers of species and their proximity to or distance from man. Binary oppositions such as body/mind, passion/reason, biology/culture, determinism/freedom, and reaction/response recall the more primary and threatening opposition between animal and human. Man's status as the "rational animal" puts him at the same time in an ambiguous space as animal but not animal. In the history of philosophy, bodies and passions threaten *regression* to animality, which is associated with man's abject animal ancestors (think of the phrases "animal lust" or "animal magnetism"). Animality in man is seen as base and evil (think of the metaphors of bestiality associated with war). We may attribute our bad behavior to animal instinct, but animality is usually no excuse in the face of law. As we have seen, in Rousseau's writings, the tension between law and instinct, between civil or symbolic laws and the laws of nature, is the philosophical meat of arguments over the relation between man and animals. Unlike many other figures from the history of philosophy, Rousseau's texts make explicit this ambivalence about animals in the philosophy of man. The animals—the monkeys, crows, cattle, horses, pigeons, dogs, and cats—that populate Rousseau's texts can be seen as symptoms/accidents that haunt the necessity of man and his dominion over all others. But because Rousseau also credits the animals and the voice of nature for the response they elicit from man, his writings at least implicitly acknowledge the active role of animals in conventional language. The tension between natural and conventional law or language points up an ambiguity at the heart of Rousseau's thinking, that rather than pinning him to one pole or the other, as in Derrida's or de Man's readings, may open a space for thinking about responsivity and the role of listening in both Rousseau's theories of language and more generally in what we consider definitive of humanity, if not in metaphysical terms (which Derrida and de Man teach us to suspect), then in ethical terms.

Which Comes First, Listening or Speaking?

Given de Man's passion in taking on Derrida, it is ironic that the most prominent "traditional" interpretation of Rousseau, on which both Derrida and de Man comment, that of Jean Starobinski, may suggest the most productive way to navigate between the two poles—accident or necessity, conventional or natural, absence or presence, supplement or original—without either choosing sides or reducing one side to the other. Jean Starobinski's prose is almost as romantic as Rousseau's. He reads all of Rousseau's writings as confessions and alternately chides Rousseau for his arrogance and praises him for his brilliance. He claims that "out of respect for the real Jean-Jacques," "we must be careful not to fill gaps in his arguments," although arguably his strong interpretation of (and seeming identification with) Rousseau in many places does just that (1988, 274). Starobinski's remarks about "the voice of nature," however, offer a dynamic alternative to either the evolution model or the eruption model of the origin and role of language. Starobinski describes Rousseau's voice of nature not as an instinct or binding natural law but as "an injunction that involves the moral being, that is, man's free will, his ability to disobey nature's law" (1988, 306). In the same passage, Starobinski moves away from the language of command and proposes that nature's voice is an "intimation" which "becomes an internal language, a language to which man pays heed because it is *spoken* within him" (1988, 306, italics in original). He goes on to say, however, that because "the voice of nature whispers so close to man's ear," it is confused with man's inner voice, which whispers that man's inner voice may be a *response* to the voice of nature, it is not identical with it (1988, 306). Starobinski maintains that "nature speaks *inside* him because he himself is *in* nature" (1988, 306, italics in original). In the sense that man is part of nature, part of his environment, and not separate from it, the voice of nature is also his inner voice.

This is only the beginning of the oscillations in Starobinski's reading of Rousseau on the voice of nature. He also claims that "the fact of perceiving that language [the voice of nature become man's internal language] is the first sign of morality, which distinguished man from the animals even though their behavior remains identical. Man is defined in the first instance not by his ability to speak but by his ability to listen" (1988, 306). Starobinski emphasizes that it is not information that man hears when he listens to the voice of nature; it is not a message or a statement. Rather, as he insists throughout his reading, it is a moral injunction or intimation.

When civilized man creates his own conventional language in response to the voice of nature, he also distances himself from that voice, which he now perceives as outside himself (and presumably not applicable to him as *man*, free and rising above natural instincts). This is when it becomes necessary for man to "recover the voice of nature by means of a kind of interpretative archaeology" (1988, 307). Starobinski concludes that the interpreter of this voice is the philosopher. The ability to listen gives way to the ability to interpret, which both distances and recovers the voice of nature. So it seems that it is not the ability to listen that is unique to man and not the animals but the ability to interpret. Both require the ability to respond. Man responds to nature and his environment because he is part of them. He responds to the animals because he, too, is an animal. He responds to other living creatures, because he, too, is a living creature. According to Starobinski, this ability to respond begets a moral obligation or responsibility. The voice of nature issues a moral injunction to which man is obligated to respond. Responsibility itself is his moral obligation. More specifically, he has a responsibility to respond to his environment with respect (just as Starobinski claims to have an obligation to respond to Rousseau with respect). Starobinski proposes that ethical obligation begins in the "conversation" between man and nature. It is relational and a matter of responsivity; that is, it is not merely on the side of man. It also complicates the relation between need and desire; desire is no longer only on the side of man, opposed to need on the side of nature. Responsivity—the ability to respond—begets responsibility. Perhaps for Rousseau, responding respectfully to the voice of nature obligates us to listen, to interpret, and to acknowledge our indebtedness to other living creatures in our midst.

Émile substantiates the idea that listening is essential to man. Rousseau claims to teach Émile to be a man, more precisely a natural man, a man who listens and responds to the voice of nature. Throughout *Émile,* Rousseau insists that education should proceed by experience and not with words and that teachers should teach by example. But what is really at stake for Rousseau in experience and example is what both can and cannot be learned: responsivity. He claims that children should be exposed to all sorts of experiences and should not be sheltered from pain or suffering (cf. 2003, 16–17). Recall that ultimately the only habit that children should learn or acquire is the habit of not having any habits (2003, 34). In other words, learning to respond to different experiences, different places, and different people is crucial to becoming a natural man and defines the natural man. Living in nature and culture require attentive responsivity to one's environment and other creatures. Here Rousseau suggests that man can learn attentiveness to his environment by watching animals.

Rousseau also emphasizes action; the child must learn to act in a way appropriate to his or her environment. To act is to respond. The natural man is at home in the world only when he learns response-ability, the ability to respond to his environment, to live anywhere with anyone. Rousseau wants to teach Émile flexibility and adaptability, to avoid fixity and routines. Freedom, which Rousseau maintains is also definitive of man, is freedom of movement that allows a variety of responses. For Rousseau, variety truly is the spice of life (ironically, perhaps, except when it comes to food—there he prefers a steady simple diet). The natural man, then, is defined not in terms of his properties but his relationships. This relational model of man circumvents the binary opposition between substance and accident that forces us to choose between the necessary or accidental nature of man and his relation to Nature.

If the relationship between man and nature is one of response rather than (or in addition to) evolution or eruption, then the terrain between necessity and accident begins to open. The binary oppositions between evolution/eruption and necessity/accident lose their mutual exclusivity (becoming both/and rather than either/or for Derrida), and moreover, an alternative topography appears in which these two monuments lose their significance. At stake in Rousseau's account of the origin of languages—and Derrida's and de Man's reading of it—is the role of imitation. Both these critics focus on the ambiguity of whether the literal or figurative comes first in Rousseau's writing. Derrida maintains that Rousseau declares that the literal comes first but describes the opposite; that is, Rousseau declares an original (presence) but describes a chain of substitutes (absence of origin). De Man claims that Rousseau declares that the figurative comes first because he is not searching for a literary narrative, not literal origins, which in turn demonstrates that all language is narrative or figurative. But if we shift the terrain slightly and rethink Rousseau's account of the origin of languages in terms of responsivity, specifically man's response to the animals, these binary oppositions begin to lose their force. Perhaps, as Derrida's later discussion of the animal in the history of philosophy postulates, the binary merely shifts to that between response and reaction: Does man respond and animals merely react? How can we distinguish response from reaction? Isn't reaction a prerequisite for response? We will return to these questions later when I take up Derrida's "deconstruction" of Lacan's distinction between reaction and response.

Derrida argues that for Rousseau, language and humanity are the products of instantaneous substitution, on the one hand, and gradual development, on the other (presumably evidenced in the animal sounds that turn into words when aped by man). Derrida works this tension in Rousseau's texts to conclude that the origin is "always already" a supplement, that the correction comes before the defect. He says that "substitution has always already begun" (1967, 215). Although Derrida seemingly turns Rousseau's text upside down and shakes every last dust mite from even the tiniest pockets, ultimately what catches his attention from the resulting pile of plants, animals, and humans is concepts. He opens the interval between nature and culture, animal and man, by demonstrating that as concepts, one is implied in the other: "Everything in language is substitute, and this *concept* of substitute precedes the opposition of nature and culture: the supplement can equally well be natural (gesture) as artificial (speech)" (1967, 235, italics added). There is a sense in which the concept—not just the concept of substitute, but the concept itself—becomes "originary" for Derrida. Perhaps this is why in *Of Grammatology* he can thoroughly dissect Rousseau's "zoonotology" without seeing the trees for the forest (or, in this case, the animals for the animal). He tracks "the animal" in Rousseau's writing without stopping to distinguish the cats from the beavers and without even acknowledging their presence. In his search for the absence at the heart of Rousseau's notion of presence, he ignores the veritable menagerie of animals that appear in Rousseau's texts. For Derrida, *the animal* stands for everything he wants to describe:

Animal language—and animality in general—represents here the still living myth of fixity, of symbolic incapacity, of nonsupplementarity. If we consider the concept of animality not in its content of understanding or misunderstanding but in its specific function, we shall see that must locate a moment of life which knows nothing of symbol, substitution, lack and supplementary addition, etc.—everything, in fact whose appearance and play I wish to describe here . . . a life without différance and without articulation. (1967, 242)

Even while criticizing the function of the concept of animality in the history of philosophy in general and in Rousseau's writing in particular, in which animality functions as the imaginary other out of and against which humanity is constituted, in this early work, Derrida does not attend to the difference between animals and their various functions in Rousseau's texts. Even as he attempts to discount the quest for origins by doggedly insisting on the "always already" of supplementarity, his text puts origin and supplement into a "which came first, the chicken or the egg" relationship. In *Blindness and Insight* (1971), Paul de Man suggests as much when he claims that Derrida's use of the vocabulary of origin leaves him, like Rousseau, looking forever for "deeper" origins, evidenced by phrases like "need before need" (1971, 122). While changing the conjunction from *or* to *and,* as Derrida does—before *and* after, more *and* less—does throw a wrench into Rousseau's sometimes teleological account of the progress (or degeneration) from animal to man, as well as into the logics of noncontradiction (which, as we will see, motivates Herder's notion of the opposition of man to animal), it also does away with animals. For their own good, animals are again sacrificed to the concept of animality to show how they have been used, even abused, in our own account of our origins as human. If the human is always already in the animal and the animal is therefore always already in the human as its other, then where are animals in themselves or even in our midst? The relationship between humans and animals is nothing more than a conceptual one that remains haunted by the romantic notion of the animal ancestor. Only now, that ancestor from our past is actually from our present/presence, but it is no more a cohabitant or companion than it was before.

Consider Derrida's reading of just two passages central to my analysis. To make the point that for Rousseau's text (here working against what it explicitly says), the "faculty of supplementarity" "is the true 'origin'—or nonorigin—of languages," Derrida quotes a long passage from the "Essai sur l'origine des langues" (Essay on the Origins of Languages) in which Rousseau says, and Derrida emphasizes with italics, "That those animals which *live and work in common, such as beavers, ants, bees, have some natural language for communicating among themselves, I would not question*" (Derrida 1974, 241). Although he highlights the individual animals or species mentioned by Rousseau, Derrida concludes from this passage that "animal language—and *animality in general*—represents" plentitude; he thereby substitutes the concept of animal—*animality in general*—for Rousseau's beavers, ants, and bees (Derrida 1974, 242, italics added).

To make the point that there is a tension in Rousseau's text between an eruption of language and a gradual acquisition of language, Derrida uses a passage in which Rousseau mentions a barking dog and describes the encounter with his cat as an example showing that moral sentiments are already present in animals (Derrida 1974, 207). Again, Derrida never mentions the dog or the cat—or even animals, for that matter—but replaces them with "the animal": "one must admit that 'moral impressions' through signs and a system of differences can always be already discerned, although confusedly, in *the animal*. [Derrida quoting Rousseau:] 'Something of this moral effect is perceivable even in *animals*'" (1974, 207, italics added). Derrida replaces Rousseau's "animals" with "the animal." It is striking that Derrida not only does not see the animals in Rousseau's text but also effaces them by substituting the animal, disregarding the ways in which Rousseau delineates differences among species in relation to language and humanity. Man learns different things from different animals, and for Rousseau, men become human man only through a multitude of animal guides.

Decades later, in *The Animal*, Derrida attempts to re-dress animals with his essays on animal autobiography, in which he questions "the philosophers'" use of the animal:

It follows from that that one will never have the right to take animals to be the species of a kind that would be named the Animal, or animal in general. Whenever "one" says, "the Animal," each time a philosopher, or anyone else, says "the Animal" in the singular without further ado, claiming thus to designate every living thing that is held not to be human. . . . [E]ach time the subject of that statement, this "one," this "I," does that he utters an *asinanity* [*bêtise*]. He avows without avowing it, he declares, just as a disease is declared by means of a symptom, he offers up for diagnosis the statement "I am uttering an *asinanity*." And this "I am uttering an *asinanity*" should confirm not only the animality that he is disavowing but his complicit, continued and organized involvement in a veritable war of the species. (2008, 31)

This "I am uttering an *asinanity*" in Derrida's lectures on animal autobiography reads almost like a confession to the blindness of his earlier work. He argues that we use the word *animal* to "corral a large number of living beings within a single concept," justifying this conceptual lasso by characterizing *animals in general* as those without the word, without language (2008, 32). The philosophers ride their high horse in relation to animals because, according to Derrida, they assume that animals are "deprived of language. Or, more precisely, of response, of a response that could be precisely and rigorously distinguished from a reaction" (2008, 32). Much of *The Animal* is concerned with what it would mean for the animal or an animal to respond (in its own name). In his analysis of Lacan's "animal," entitled "And Say the Animal Responded?" Derrida asks how we can be so certain that we can tell the difference between responding and reacting so that we, as human beings, can respond rather than merely react (2003, esp. 137–38). Following Derrida, yet straying too, I would propose "And Say the Human Responded?" I will return to Derrida's autobiographical analysis of animals in *The Animal* in subsequent chapters.

Elsewhere, I have argued that subjectivity is responsivity and that the ability to respond brings with it ethical responsibilities (Oliver 2001). In that subjectivity is the ability to respond, then in its conception, what we take to be human subjectivity is linked to ethical responsibility. Responsibility has the double sense of opening up the ability to response—response-ability—and ethically obligating subjects to respond by virtue of their very subjectivity itself. Response-ability is the founding possibility of subjectivity and its most fundamental obligation, which reformulates Eva Kittay's analysis of relations of dependency, a subject who "refuses to support this bond absolves itself from its most fundamental obligation—its obligation to its founding possibility" (1998, 131). Certainly, both human beings and animal beings respond. Even plants respond to their environment and perhaps even to human voices or touch. Living beings are responsive beings; and living beings are dependent on their environment for their very survival and for the quality, perhaps even the meaning, of life.

In light of my project on animal pedagogy, we must consider what it means in terms of both subjectivity and ethical responsibility that we respond to animals. We must consider what it means that in the history of philosophy, our dependence on, and indebtedness to, animals as our founding possibility has been denied. The question is not just Derrida's "and what if the animal responded?" but "what if the human responded?" This question, as we will see in subsequent chapters, becomes problematic whenever we attempt to distinguish human response from animal reaction. What happens to what I call elsewhere the "ethics of witnessing" when we acknowledge that we are addressed by, and can address ourselves to, animals? (see Oliver 2001). What happens when we consider that we respond to and can, in turn, elicit a response from animals? Indeed, for animal pedagogy and animal kinship, these questions have everything to do with what we take to be both blindness and insight.

Reformulating de Man's questions to Rousseau and Derrida, we could ask, Are we blind to animal pedagogy and animal kinship by nature or by convention, by necessity or by accidents of history? Indeed, in a sense, don't the very categories of blindness and insight, like those of nature and convention, or necessity and accident, trade on the presumed and fundamental distinction posited throughout the history of philosophy between animal and man? Throughout the rest of this book, engaging with various philosophers, I describe some of the consequences of our blindness to animal pedagogy and animal kinship and how they come to bear on what we consider human insight. Once animals enter the scene of philosophy, its terms necessarily begin to shift. The shifting terrain of metaphysics and epistemology has huge implications for ethics, particularly animal ethics and notions of obligations to the earth and all its inhabitants.

CHAPTER THREE

Say the Human Responded

Herder's Sheep

If Rousseau treks through the animal kingdom trying to identify man's distinguishing features because he denies any definitive border between man and animal, his German contemporary, Johann Gottfried Herder, avoids particular animals in favor of the animal in general because he is certain of the abyss between man and animals, a border that is both definitive and dangerous. Crossing the boundary between man and animal puts man on uncertain footing; for here, man all too easily slips "back" into the animal. Once that happens, the necessity of the human, civilization, and man's dominion over nature fall into the abyss. Rousseau's analysis of the origins of man prefigures Darwin's theory of evolution and gives a glorious idealized animal ancestor, whereas Herder's ultimately denies evolution even while imagining with horror the ape as man's abject alter ego.[1] If Rousseau flirts with the danger in engaging with various wild and domestic animals, Herder prefers the animal in general and resorts to particular animals only when cornered, and even then he prefers only the most domestic, servile, and harmless of animals, the lamb or sheep. But the few appearances of Herder's sheep are telling. Indeed, Herder's sheep threatens to unravel his entire argument that man is by nature human and therefore independent of "the animal" and of animals in general.

Here again, the question of the origin of man turns on the question of the relation between man and animals. In "Abhandlung über den Ursprung der Sprache" (Essay on the Origin of Language, 1772), Herder maintains that both Condillac and Rousseau give erroneous accounts of the origin of language because they have confused the relation between man and animals: "Condillac and Rousseau had to err in regard to the origin of language because they erred, in so well known a way and yet so differently, in regard to this difference (between animals and men): in that the former turned animals into men and the latter men into animals" (1966, 103). In response to these theories that Herder thinks confuse the question of the distinction between man and animal, he argues that "every animal has its sphere to which it belongs from birth, into which it is born, in which it stays throughout its life, and in which it dies" (1966, 104). Unlike other animals, man (individual men as well as the whole species) is born a rational and linguistic being and remains in the sphere of human language all his life. Unlike other animals, though, man is not born with the instinctive use of language, whereas other animals speak by nature, by instinct—"the bee hums as it sucks; the bird sings as it nests"— man "does little or nothing entirely by instinct, entirely as an animal" (1966, 107). Rather, the entire human species "stands above the animals not by stages of more or less but in kind" (1966, 108). Even if animals have some form of "language," theirs is different in kind, not in degree, from man's. Man's reason and language are not higher forms of animal reason or animal speech, but altogether different forms of reason and language.

Herder bases his argument on the fact that animal activities and lives have a narrow scope, whereas man's are broad and far-reaching; and man's activities and lives can be improved forever, whereas animal's cannot (1966, 109). So even if man cannot build honey cells as well as bees can or cobwebs as well as spiders can, he has powers of conception that he uses and on which he relies precisely because, unlike the bee or the spider, he doesn't build or spin by instinct but through reflection (1966, 109). If an animal does have the capacity for reflection, then it is a man. Conversely, if a man can build or spin like a bee or a spider, even if for only an instant, "he is *ipso facto* no longer a man in any thing, no longer capable of any human act" (1966, 111). It seems that you won't catch Herder's civilized man meowing like a cat or devouring other men like a wolf. And if Herder had a cat, it wouldn't be clever enough to discern accents based on rudimentary moral sentiments (or to serve as a mirror for his humanity by staring at his sex). Indeed, for Herder there are no essential distinctions between savage and civilized men. Whether considered as individuals or as a species, men are men from birth to death:

For if reason is not a separate and singly acting power but an orientation of all powers and as such a thing peculiar to his species, then man must have it in the first state in which he is man. In the first thought of the child this reflection must be apparent, just as it is apparent in the insect that it is an insect. (1966, 112)

Ultimately there is no essential continuity between man and animal: "The difference is not one of degree nor of a supplementary endowment with powers; it lies in a totally distinct orientation and evolution of all powers" (1966, 110). What for Rousseau is a matter of degree, for Herder is a difference in kind.

But *man* and *animal* are not just essentially different, they are opposites, mutually exclusive beings. To be a man is not to be an animal, and vice versa. What for Rousseau was a matter of the logic of mimesis or metaphor, for Herder is a matter of the logic of noncontradiction. For Herder, reason and instinct cannot exist together in the same being because one cancels out the other. This opposition is the basis of Herder's argument for the distinctiveness of man. Herder begins with the premise that man is man and animal is animal, which in his logic of noncontradiction leads him to the conclusion that man is not animal and animal is not man. Thus he can conclude that "if man was not to be an instinctual animal, he had to be—by virtue of the more freely working positive power of his soul—a creature of reflection" (1966, 112). This conclusion is based on his claim that

if man had the drives of the animals, he could not have what we now call reason in him . . . if man had the senses of animals, he would have no reason; for the keen alertness of his senses and the mass of perceptions flooding him through them would smother all cool reflection. (1966, 111)

Man must compensate with reason for what he lacks in drives and sensations. Herder's presumption that animal drives and sensation are all-consuming and therefore opposed to reason is possible only because he deals with an abstract generalized animal and an abstract generalized man (another can of worms, which I barely touch in this book). If he considered individual animals or individual humans and compared them, he would have had to allow for more variations and continuity *between* them. Herder chastises philosophers for dividing the soul and man's capacities into categories or chapters, "metaphysical abstractions" convenient to "feeble minds" unable to conceive of the whole undivided activity of the soul, yet he employs abstract metaphysical notions of man and animal in order to stake his claim that man does nothing in the way that an animal does (1966, 110–11). Animals in general and the abstract animal function in Herder's texts to dismiss individual animals and the difference among animal species so prominent in Rousseau's texts.

Beautiful Man, Ugly Ape

As Rousseau does, Herder wavers on the significance and possibility of animal language and animal influence on human evolution. While they share roman- tic notions of Nature, Herder's struggle to distinguish man from animal seems motivated by an abhorrence of "the animal" precisely because of its closeness to man. For Herder, any ambiguity between man and animal, any mixture of the two, is a disgusting abomination of nature. Herder maintains that we must "ar- raign Providence" "for suffering man to border so nearly on the brute" (1800, 124). Whereas Rousseau idealizes the "primitive," including both savage men and animals, Herder prefers the beauty of trees and plants and frequently uses floral metaphors when describing man's difference from animals. For Herder, the pri- mary difference between man and animals is that men are beautiful and animals are grotesque; and the closer they are to men, the grosser they are; these gross ap- proximations of man only highlight the refinement or "fineness" of man. The ape in particular, with its powers of imitation and similarity to man, has an uncanny effect on Herder, which prompts him to sketch man with a fine point while paint- ing apes with slobbering rhetoric to draw a bold line between them:

Why has the father of human speech done this? Why would he not permit the all-imitative ape to imitate precisely this criterion of human kind, inexorably closing the way to it by peculiar obstacles? Visit an hospital of lunatics, and attend to their discourse, listen to the jabbering of monsters and idiots; and you need not be told the cause. How painful to us is the utterance of these! How do we lament to hear that gift of language so profaned by those! And how much more would it be profaned in the mouth of the gross, lascivious, brutal ape, could he imitate human words with the half-human understanding, which I have no doubt he possesses! Disgusting tissue of sounds resembling those of man com- bined with the thoughts of an ape—no: the divine faculty of speech was not to be thus debased, and therefore the ape is dumb; more dumb than his fellow-brutes, each of which, down to the frog and the lizard, has his own peculiar voice. (1800, 88)

Those gross, lascivious, brutal, disgusting apes mock man with their powers of imitation; they reflect back to man his animality in ways that threaten the neat border between them. The extreme rhetoric of abjection in Herder's text suggests that his description of the apes is overdetermined by the threat that these creatures so similar to man pose to his theory. The ape recalls man's own animality and therefore must be abjected and expelled from the human world in no uncertain terms. The ape, man's alter ego, is the disgusting side of man's own nature, the side Herder turns his back on in his romantic picture of beautiful man versus ugly ape.

Describing the physical differences between man and ape in great detail, Herder locates the "base, disgraceful aspect" of the ape in the fact that it cannot stand erect as a man can. In man, the baseness of the ape becomes "the beautiful free formation of the head for the upright posture of man":

Let this point be otherwise disposed, beautiful and noble will be the whole form. The forehead will advance forward big with thought, and the skull swell into an arch with calm exalted dignity. The broad brutal nose will contract, and assume a higher and more delicate figure: the retreating mouth will be more beautifully covered, and thus will be formed the lips of man, which are wanting to the most cunning of apes. The chin will sink to round the fine perpendicular oval: the cheeks softly swell: and the eye look out from beneath the projecting forehead, as from the sacred temple of mind. (1800, 74)

Herder's description of the head of man is as lofty as his description of the head of apes is base. Everything disgusting in apes becomes dignified in man.

In "Essay on the Origin of Language," criticizing Rousseau, Herder contends that "the ape may forever be aping, but never did he emulate" because mimicry in man is the result of reflection and therefore becomes emulation, while in apes it is merely organic (1966, 125; cf. 1800, 232). Martin Heidegger interprets Herder's distinction between aping and imitating as one between mere instinctual reaction without grasping the other being and its voice as such, on the one hand, and the self-determined recognition of the other being and its voice as such, on the other (1999, 126). In *Outlines of a Philosophy of the History of Man* (1784), Herder maintains that man's power of imitation is the result of the "exquisite" organization of the human body which allows, even necessitates, that imitation-cum-emulation become speech (1800, 232). He concludes that "man did not attain the artificial characteristic of his species, reason, by all this mimicry: he arrived at it by speech alone. . . . Speech alone has rendered man human" (1800, 232–33). The ape does not have the bodily organization or organs for speech. And while some animals, parrots for example, can imitate human speech, Herder insists that these animals are further from the possibility of human thought than apes are, which is why Nature has given them voice and song. Herder maintains that these lower animals, so far from human understanding, are no threat to man's dominion over all other species:

The tongue of some is so formed, as even to be capable of pronouncing human words, the signification of which they do not understand. . . . But here the door is shut, and the manlike ape is visibly and forcibly deprived of speech by the pouches Nature has placed at the sides of the windpipe. (1800, 88)

The more similar to man a species is, the greater will be the necessity that it be mute. Because Herder regards speech as definitive of humanity, it is imperative—a necessity of divine Providence—that animals capable of thought are not capable of speech, and vice versa. Herder is repulsed by the idea of a speaking ape; nature would not insult man by allowing such a coarse and grotesque creature to speak. But if apes could speak, then they would be men, and that mixing of the human and animal would be unacceptable, even abject. It would threaten Herder's entire philosophy of the divine uniqueness of man and man's legitimate dominion over the earth. Claiming that each species has its own voice intended for itself alone, Herder is haunted by the liminal ambiguous mixtures of humans and animals that his texts explicitly argue against:

As little, then, as the nightingale sings—as some imagine—to entertain man, so little can man ever be minded to invent for himself a language by trilling the trills of the nightingale. And what a monstrosity: A human nightingale in a cave or out in the forest with the hunt! (1966, 136) [*Und was ist doch für ein Ungeheuer, eine menschliche Nachtigall in einer Höhle oder im Walde der Jagd?*] (1772, 52; note that the translator replaced Herder's question mark with an exclamation point, making the passage seem even more passionate)

Herder's dogged insistence on a categorical segregation between man and animals is repeatedly belied in his texts by the fantasies with which he patrols the borders, human nightingales, speaking ape-men, budding souls, and other "abominations." In these places, Herder's own "monstrous" illustrations ape or mock his attempt to protect man from the threat of animals.

For Herder, the distinction between man and animals is a distinction between pure and abject that repeatedly appears in his texts as the distinction between the fine and the coarse. Herder says that "man is organized for finer Instincts, and in consequence to Freedom of Action" (1800, 89). Reason, language, and freedom are the result of man's fineness, and the lack of these is the result of the ape's coarseness. The coarse animal, however, is not abject in itself so much as it is abject in relation to man, abject as the specter of man's own animality, abject insofar as it conjures the "monstrosity" of the in-between, ambiguity, or mixture of human and animal. It is not the coarse in itself, but mixing the fine and the coarse that is abhorrent to Herder. Apparently both fascinated and repelled, he cannot resist conjuring images of monstrous fine/coarse human/animals.

In accordance with this phobic logic motivated by the threat of ambiguity, it should be no surprise that Herder prefers plants, especially flowers, to animals. Plants are far enough from the human not to threaten the borders between human and nonhuman (or, in this case, vegetable). Mixing floral and human, however, is precisely what he does repeatedly in order to shore up the distinction between man and animal. In a sense, the monstrosity of a speaking ape or a human nightingale is forestalled by human plants, metaphors of the soul and human reason, and understanding as beautiful, divine flowers budding and blossoming under the glorious sun. Herder describes the movement from "inferior" forms of life, "the brute," to the superior human form:

The bud of humanity, benumbed by cold, and parched by heat, will expand in its true form, in its proper and full beauty. . . . Nature had similar purposes in all earthly wants: each was to be matrix of some germe of humanity. Happy is it when the germe buds: it will blossom beneath the beams of a more glorious sun. Truth, beauty, and love are the objects. (1800, 124)

The hybrid human flower defends against the greater threat of the monstrous human animal. Opposed to the realm of coarse and grotesque animals, humanity blossoms like a flower, fine and beautiful.

We Eat What We Are

Remarkably, the distinction between fine and coarse comes back to food: to eat coarse food is to be coarse, and to eat fine food is to be fine, and vice versa. To both Rousseau and Herder, we are what we eat (and we eat what we are). As Rousseau does, Herder talks about the assimilation of both animal sounds and animal flesh in conjunction with the origin of language. But unlike Rousseau, he figures this assimilation as the conversion of matter into higher forms and ultimately into the highest form, the soul. Rousseau sees assimilation as based on imitation, a form of animal pedagogy, whereas Herder sees it as the digestion and transformation, even purification, of lower life-forms. Herder uses the caterpillar's metamorphosis into butterfly to show that the death of the coarse body frees the beautiful soul for a different form of life:

Behold, there crawls the despicable caterpillar, obeying the gross appetite of eating. . . . His whole structure is altered: instead of the coarse leaves, on which he was at first formed to feed, he drinks the nectarous juice of flowers from their golden cups. Even his destination is changed: instead of obeying the gross appetite of hunger, he is moved by the more refined passion of love. (1800, 126)

This passage is noteworthy in several respects. First, the distinction between forms is characterized as a distinction between coarse and fine, which is defined in terms of eating; coarse leaves give way to refined passions through flower nectar. Sipping is in itself more refined than chewing. Next, the butterfly's beauty—"adorned with all the splendid hues, that can be produced beneath the sun: the waft the creature as it were on the breath of zephyr"—corresponds to the beauty of its sup—"nectarous juice of flowers from their golden cups" (1800, 126). This beauty in itself produces love beyond appetite. This distinction between coarse and fine is aesthetic, and Herder prefers the aesthetics of "beautiful" butterflies and flowers to "ugly" apes and parrots. Again, we see that his rhetoric is full of romantic images of fine beauty opposed to abject images of disgustingly coarse appetites.

For Herder, like Rousseau, one of man's advantages over other animals is that he can eat almost anything. But for Herder, by so doing man transforms what he eats/assimilates into a higher form (lest he be contaminated by ingesting abject animal forms). In an interesting turn of phrase, Herder suggests that by eating plants, animals "animalize" them:

The animal stands above the plant, and subsists on its juices. The single elephant is the grave of millions of plants; but he is a living, operative grave; he animalizes them into parts of himself: the inferior powers ascend to the more subtle from of vitality. It is the same with all carnivorous beasts: Nature has made the transition short, as if she feared a lingering death above all things. She has accordingly abridged it, and accelerated the mode of transformation into superior vital forms. The greatest murderer among all animals is man, the creature that possesses the finest organs. He can assimilate to his nature almost every thing, unless it sink too far beneath him in living organization. (1800, 115)

Nature operates according to the principle of "active improvement" through which animals "animalize" plants and presumably humans "humanize" animals by eating them. This assimilation of lower forms into "superior" forms guarantees that although man is the "greatest murderer" among all animals, he remains uncontaminated by ingesting all other animals. The fact that Herder mentions animals that might be too far beneath man to eat raises the specter of contamination by inferior species. Rousseau's man can eat everything and still be a man (although he may be a more uncivilized man, depending on what he eats); whereas the humanity and not just the civility of Herder's man is threatened if he eats something too coarse, base, or abject. For example, while the juices of plants can be transformed into higher powers in animals who make use of "vegetable powers" to "enliven parts of a vegetable nature" now serving animal purposes, the juices of animals—blood—"enliven rapaciousness, beastliness, and barbarousness" in both animals and man, which is why Herder says that "the establishment of nations has made it one of the first laws of human feeling, not to desire for food a living animal with its blood" (1800, 116). Sheepishly, Herder concludes from this analysis that spiritual powers do not come from the corporeal sources of animal juices even if animal powers come from vegetable juices as "the scale of improvement ascends through the inferior ranks of nature" (1800, 116). The prohibition against ingesting blood or living animals is a sign/symptom of a spiritual power among carnivores, unique to man. Although for Herder, man is not a vegetarian by nature, he can abstain from eating (previously) living flesh and blood. As Rousseau points out, man prefers, nay needs, to cook his meat.

In Herder's logic of natural accession from inferior to superior powers and forms through assimilation, cannibals pose an interesting problem. The cannibal eats other people and therefore can be seen engaging in the highest form of assimilation, the assimilation of humanity into greater spirituality—the cannibal humanizes the human just as the animal animalizes the vegetable. Indeed, in trying to account for how we get from the carnal to the spiritual in this dog-eat-grass chain of being, almost in spite of himself Herder cannot help but lead us to the cannibal. He says that "the cannibal, thirsting for revenge, strives, though in a horrible mode, for a *spiritual* enjoyment" (1800, 120, italics in original). In this same chapter of *Outlines of a Philosophy of the History of Man*, even while he insists that ideas in the mind are "altogether spiritual, and not corporeal," Herder compares food for the body to ideas for the mind and concludes that the "same laws of assimilation, growth, and production," only now in a spiritual rather than corporeal manner, obtain in the soul as in the body (1800, 119). But he struggles to describe how man crosses the canyon between the corporeal and spiritual, sides that stand opposed to each other. His solution is to propose that although they are opposed and one does not generate the other, they still operate according to the same logic of assimilation, through eating and digesting nutriments. They share the same logic and the same processes of growth and production, but on different levels. Like the body, so too the mind can "overgorge itself with food, which it is incapable of appropriating and converting into nutriment" (1800, 119). According to Herder, however, if the transition from corporeal to spiritual is not organic, then it must be mimetic: The mind must imitate the body in its operations of assimilation to produce food for thought; and "devouring" ideas with the passion and appetite equal to that of the rapacious beasts, we become human, eventually able to pick the bones of the most delicate argument morsel by morsel along with Herder. Despite his "bitter" judgment, mimicry becomes emulation; appetites of the body become appetites of the mind; and animals become human.

In Herder's account, the transformation from corporeal to spiritual in man is coexistent with the transition from assimilation to appropriation. Through his assimilation of animal food, behavior, and, most important, animal sounds, man becomes "lord of every thing in nature" (1800, 240). To Herder, the invention or acquisition of language that separates man from beast depends on both the assimilation and appropriation of animals. Language, of course, is man's crowning glory, and by naming the animals he lords over them:

For in every one of his appropriations he does nothing in reality but mark the characters of a tamable, useful being, to be employed for his own convenience, and designate it by language or pattern. In the gentle sheep, for instance, he remarked the milk sucked by the lamb, and the wool that warmed his hand, and endeavored to appropriate each to his own use. (1800, 240)

By naming the animals insofar as they are useful to him, man not only secures his dominion over them but also justifies it. The sheep is named in conjunction with men's appropriation of it for their own purposes: It is reduced to milk and wool. For Herder, naming is the assimilation of animal sounds in the service of the appropriation of the animals themselves.

The animals introduce themselves to man through their own tongues, figured as the tongues of vassals and servants deferring to the divine superiority of man:

Each one has its name on its tongue [*jedes trägt seinen Namen auf der Zunge*] and introduces itself to this concealed yet visible god as a vassal and servant. It delivers to him its distinguishing word to be entered, like a tribute, into the book of his dominion [*seiner Herrschaft*] so that he may, by virtue of its name, remember it, call it in future, and enjoy it. (1772, 46; 1966, 130)

Unlike Rousseau's noble animals, from whom man learns to be human, Herder's present themselves as servants before the god-man. The distinguishing mark through which man comes to know the animals is the voice of the animals themselves, whose "language" is translated into "the natural scale of the human voice" (1966, 137). Just as the assimilation of "inferior" forms of life into the body through eating transforms them into higher forms, inferior forms of language are transformed into the highest form, the human form, through the mouth of man. Man "humanizes" animal language simply by speaking it with his beautiful, finely formed mouth, which is beautiful as a result of his beautiful finely formed soul. This transformation or translation is automatic. For Herder, human language is not a different inflection of the voice of nature as it was for Rousseau; rather, it is an appropriation, even an exploitation, that transforms it into something else, an altogether different kettle of fish.

The Sheep Bleats and Man Responds

At the heart of Herder's theory that language is natural and necessary to the human soul is a bleating sheep in response to whom man learns to invent language. Indeed, as Herder describes it, man himself begins to "bleat" (*blöken*) out with his lips what his soul had bleated within when he heard and responded to the sheep's bleating: "The sound of bleating perceived by a human soul as the distinguishing mark of the sheep became, by virtue of this reflection, the name of the sheep," and he began to

bleat out with his lips [*mit den Lippen vorblöken*] this distinguishing mark of reflection for another, his soul—as it were—bleated within [*seine Seele hat gleichsam in ihrem Inwendigen geblökt*] when it selected this sound as a sign of recollection, and it bleated again as it recognized the sound by its sign. Language has been invented! Invented as naturally and to man as necessarily as man was man [*die Sprache ist erfunden! ebenso natürlich und dem Menschen notwendig erfunden, als der Mensch ein Mensch war*]. (1772, 33–34; 1966, 118)

The sheep's bleating becomes the founding metaphor for Herder's theory of the uniqueness of man and his distinctiveness from the animal kingdom through the invention of language. Like the sheep from his *Outlines of a Philosophy of the History of Man,* this sheep assures Herder of the necessity of human naming as the beginning of man's dominion over animals. There the "gentle sheep" demonstrates that man appropriates the sheep for his own convenience and use by designating it (1800, 240). In his *Outline,* Herder defines the sheep in terms of its gentleness and passivity, but in "Essay on the Origin of Language," the sheep actively speaks so that man can respond in kind. In his "Essay," quite against Herder's bullish insistence on the origin of language in man's soul itself, the sheep *teaches* man to speak. The sheep at the heart of Herder's text acts up and belies man's relation to his own animality and to his own dependence on animals. Man learns to speak, and thereby becomes human, in response to animals. The sheep bleats and man responds with his own bleating. And say the human responded? Looking carefully at Herder's description of man's relation with this sheep, it becomes clear that man's unique capacity for understanding, knowing, reason, transcending instinct, emulation, speech, differentiation, observation, recognition, recollection, and ownership—everything that defines man as man and as human—comes through an encounter with the sheep (1966, 116–118; cf. 129, 132, 138). Man is man by virtue of the lamb—think, too, of Christian metaphors of Christ as the lamb of God.

Clearing Before Hearing

It is noteworthy that in his lecture course on Herder's essay, Martin Heidegger completely disavows the role of the sheep in man's acquisition of language. Heidegger also criticizes Herder for not making the difference between man and animal absolute and essential. According to Heidegger, despite Herder's conclusions about the uniqueness of man (and his abjection of animals), the gap Herder draws between man and animal is not wide enough. In a section of his course entitled "The Sheep Bleats," Heidegger focuses on the ear as the teacher, and the sheep becomes "merely" an exemplar of being (e.g., 1999, 17, 120, 174). Heidegger claims that the bleating of the sheep is the object of "pure disinterested contemplation" (1999, 17). What is essential to the example of the sheep for Heidegger is the *being* of the sheep *as such*. Man says to the sheep, "You are the one that bleats," and the verb *to be, are,* or *is,* is the focus of Heidegger's analysis. It is not that man responds to the sheep's bleating but that man sees in the bleating a being that bleats, the being as such. Heidegger argues that man's own bleating, even if he also says "baah," is already a representation and not a response to the sheep's voice: "The 'baah' is never a mere tone in the sense of hearing . . . but it is always being and representation. . . . We hear beings by representing" (1999, 138).[2] Man no longer responds to the sheep by repeating its "baah" after listening to its bleating. For Heidegger, man grasps, takes, and penetrates its being as such by representing it. The difference between a responsive relation in which man learns from the sheep and the controlling, seemingly violent relation in which man disinterestedly takes from the sheep is striking.

Herder describes how man listens to the sheep and to nature and thereby learns to speak—man is the listening animal.[3] Taking his cue from Herder yet leaving behind the animal voices, Heidegger insists that this hearing is originally a hearkening. Emphasizing Herder's claim that man is a hearkening, attentive creature, Heidegger is not content with Herder's search for the origin of human language in its beginnings. Instead, he reinterprets the search for origin as a search for essence. He concludes, echoing Herder, that language is originally or essentially making manifest, announcing. But according to Heidegger, this making manifest, or announcing, is not merely the sound of bleating or "baah" but also of the bleating or "baah" as such. It is the "as such" that marks what is distinctive about human language. Heidegger argues that this is why Herder returns to the sheep example a second time: "'Why does the sheep appear for a second time?'. . . At first the sheep was only an example of an encountered being; but now it unveils its own example character: It is a being that is encountered, which resounds" (1999, 158). Heidegger concludes that the sheep reappears in Herder's essay in order to signal the double nature of man's grasping with words: the sheep is a being as such, and it is a being that sounds for the sake of man's resounding as such. For Heidegger, Herder's sheep is not the soft, white, wooly creature that man touches, sees, and relies on for milk and wool. Rather, the sheep becomes nothing more than a bleating being as such, an object of disinterested contemplation. Furthermore, when repeated by man, its bleating becomes a representation, a sign. Man's "baah" is not like the sheep's "baah." Not because as Rousseau's cat example might suggest, man does not have the proper accent to "speak sheep"; but because for Heidegger, man's "baah" is language and the sheep's "baah" is mere noise.

Heidegger also discounts Herder's claim that hearing is the medium through which man acquires language. First, Heidegger suggests that by hearing, Herder really is referring to all the senses, that since listening is a matter of attending to, man listens through all his senses (1999, 104). Second, Heidegger criticizes Herder for pointing in the direction but not seeing where he is going. That is, Herder recognizes man as a hearkening, attentive creature and still reduces this hearkening to the sense of hearing: "He [Herder] does not even see the essence of hearing as hearkening and still less the inner *connection* of hearing *as hearkening with being attentive* (reflective awareness, perceiving); he does not realize that he sees the 'sense of hearing' already as *essentially* different" (1999, 108, italics in original). Although Herder does insist that the sheep's bleating affects man's soul and not just his ears, Heidegger does not think this goes far enough away from the bleating animal or man's own animality. Heidegger argues that what Herder does not see is the clearing necessary for hearing in the sense that distinguishes human hearing and hearkening (and speaking) from animal hearing (and noise making). Unlike man, animals' ears cannot hear the ontological difference between themselves and humans. Man, however, can "hear" this ontological difference because he is a hearkening, attentive creature who can contemplate the unsaid in the said, the silence of being as such, the clearing of being: "Hearken—to be still, to enter into silence of the there—. Hearken—not only: 'be all ears,' but be one who perceives-by-taking, who you already are, without fathoming and even only knowing and ground your 'being'" (1999, 120). "To be all ears" is not merely to hear but also to attend to the differences that ground the very possibility of listening. For Heidegger, Herder's sheep signals that in the clearing that is open to man alone . . . there is bleating (1999, 119).

Heidegger criticizes Herder for drawing an analogy between humans and animals. He rejects any type of comparative analysis between humans and animals, insisting that there is an essential difference, an ontological difference, that cannot be described as a sort of ontic continuity (1999, 8, 23, 145). As we will see in chapter 8, in his engagement with Herder, Heidegger reaffirms his conclusion from his own comparative analysis of humans and animals in his 1929/1930 lecture course, namely, that there is no comparison. Heidegger contends that although Herder claims that the difference between man and animals is one of kind and not degree, "Herder appears to remain in what is animalistic because he thinks from the beginning within the animal economy" (1999, 145). Because Herder begins his analysis of the origins of human language by talking about animals and continues to base his conclusions about man on a comparison with animals, Heidegger believes that he misses the essential difference, which is precisely that human beings have language and that "the word has the human being" (1999, 135). Heidegger insists that this is more than a mere reversal; it is also a transformation. He says that it strives for a more original understanding of the essence of language in relation to the essence of human being. He suggests that human beings recognize themselves as such only through language. Indeed, he says that human beings recognize themselves as animals only through the word *animal*. To Heidegger this proves that "the human language is therefore distinguished in terms of quality from that of the animal; it can therefore also have only a non-animalistic ground of origin" (1999, 136). We can recognize ourselves as Herder's "reflective animals" only because the essence of human being and human language is not animal.

When comparing Herder's analysis of the narrow circle binding the animal to its natural instinctual life with man's wide open circle and its resulting self-determination and freedom, Heidegger argues that because humans are different in kind but not in degree, they cannot differ from animals merely in the size of their circles. As we will see later, this discussion of circles in which animals are "wrapped" is also reminiscent of Heidegger's analysis of the captivation of animals in their *Umwelten* (environments).[4] As Heidegger says, "We will still see that this is not the spatial circle of the animal, to which the drives are somehow 'tailored' subsequently, but the drives themselves co-determine first what 'circle' means here" (1999, 137). In other words, the circle is not an ontic feature of animal life but is essentially definitive of it, is ontological. But Heidegger doesn't just insist that humans and animals are different kinds of beings with different ways of being in the world. He also says in regard to Herder that while animals are encircled by their instincts, human beings are not encircled: "If essential distinction means: to be different in kind, which cannot be determined through that of the animal, one could say, then Herder should not start with 'small circle—big circle,' but should pose the distinction: circle—no-circle" (1999, 146). What in Herder is an ontological difference (despite what Heidegger sees as its inconsistencies), in Heidegger becomes an opposition: circle—no-circle. Animals are limited by their narrow circles, but humans have no such limitations. This difference become opposition seems to fly in the face of much of Heidegger's thinking about differences that cannot be reduced to a simple law of noncontradiction. Where Herder sees a difference in kind established through analogy, Heidegger sees an ontological difference as an abyss that no analogy can possibly bridge.

Heidegger turns Herder's listening responsivity to the sheep, such as it is, into "taking," "grasping," "penetrating," "standing against," "standing free," standing "erect." Heidegger's metaphors belie a sense of human dominion over other beings, more ruthless than the innocent Shepherd of Being he imagines elsewhere. Perhaps the Shepherd of Being steps into the clearing and guards the Being of beings only by forsaking them. Heidegger seems to herd Herder's sheep into the controlling dominion of human grasping with understanding, which here displaces the hands of slaughter, but is just as violent in their own realm as those literal grasping hands are in theirs. I will return to Heidegger's hands and his insistence on the abyss in chapter 8. Heidegger and Herder share the emphasis on standing erect. For Heidegger, human standing, particularly its being-there (or there-being, Dasein) is what makes humans unique and separates them from animals by an abyss. For Herder, man's literal upright posture is definitive in the human ability to perfect himself and move beyond animals. Heidegger repeatedly talks of humans "erecting into free-standingness" (e.g., 1999, 105, 119, 163). According to him, man's relation to the sheep is one of "erecting up" and "standing against" (1999, 119). Discussing the development of man's senses against the animal, Heidegger states, "We interpret development as the course of the erection into the free-standingness of the human being" (1999, 163). Herder also is fascinated with erection, claiming that "the posture of man is upright; in this he is unique on earth. Admittedly, the bear has a broad foot and fights in an erect position, and apes and pygmies sometimes run or walk upright. Yet only man is naturally and continuously in the erect position" (1969, 255). Because man is the only creature that has the purview afforded by his erect posture, he can take the distance from his environment necessary to reflect on it. Herder maintains, "The upright posture of man is natural to him alone; indeed it is the organizing determinant of man's activities and the characteristic which distinguished him from all other species. No nation on earth has been found walking on all fours" (1969, 257). This passage suggests that man is a political animal, as Aristotle says, because of his upright posture, because he is a two-legged creature. Herder concludes:

With grateful eyes let us contemplate the blessing of the hallowed act by which our species became a human species. We cannot but note with a sense of wonder the peculiar organization of powers, deriving from the erect posture of man by which, and by which alone, he became what he is: man. (1969, 257)

Heidegger, of course, is concerned with that "is," insisting that man became human by standing against or erecting himself against beings, including his own being, *as such*.

Leaving Heidegger for the time being (so to speak), as different as their conclusions about the origin of language may be, both Rousseau and Herder rely on animals to make their cases for the uniqueness of man as either degenerate or godly, respectively. In sum, while Rousseau proposes that only from a multitude of different animals can man learn to become human, Herder prefers the sheep because it is easily domesticated to feed and clothe man and because its innocent bleating initiates in man—despite himself—man's own bleating. If Rousseau idealizes animals in the state of nature, Herder abhors them. Yet in a crucial sense for both Rousseau and Herder, man becomes human as a response to animal pedagogy. Even while Herder's discourse assimilates and appropriates animals as examples, illustrations, facts, and metaphors to demonstrate and justify the necessity of man's dominion over animals, the animal, and animality, his discourse and justifications are betrayed by that one innocent sheep in response to whom man bleats. In Rousseau's less dogmatic account of the origin of languages, even with its attention to the plurality of languages and accents, his menagerie interrupts his attempts to present a coherent account of the origin and development of human civilization. The necessity of man is premised on his various animals: apes, nightingales, butterflies, sheep, horses, cattle, beavers, ants, pigeons, bees, dogs, and cats. These animals are made to serve the argument that man is essentially distinct from the animal. Like Siegfried and Roy's trained tigers, these animals step in on cue to domesticate wild arguments and round up stray thoughts. We catch a glimpse of these animals when the philosopher, like the circus trainer, slips and falls back on man's animal instincts to make his case that man is human by transcending these animals. Man's soul, reason, language, and self-reflection appear in these texts as responses to the animals. In this regard, the animals do not so much bite back as teach man to be himself. Like the illusionist, the philosopher summons the animals on cue and names them, as if to demonstrate his mastery over them, only to conjure, by accident, the symptom of his own illegitimate birth. Everything he takes for his own is not preordained by nature but is contingent on animal pedagogy, as if in the animal kingdom, man is not king but merely an accident waiting to happen.

PART THREE

Difference "Worthy of Its Name"

When you notice a cat in profound meditation,
The reason, I tell you, is always the same:
His mind is engaged in a rapt contemplation
Of the thought, of the thought, of the thought of his name:
His ineffable effable
Effanineffable
Deep and inscrutable singular Name.

—T. S. ELIOT, "THE NAMING OF CATS"

CHAPTER FOUR

"Hair of the Dog"

Derrida's and Rousseau's Good Taste

In his early work, Derrida probes the limit set up between man and his others, including the animal and the divine, in order to challenge the "mythic purity" of concepts (Good or Evil) on either side of the divide: "Man *calls himself* man only by drawing limits excluding his other from the play of supplementary; the *purity* of nature, of animality, primitivism, childhood, madness, divinity. The approach to these limits is at once feared as a threat of death, and desired as access to a life without différance" (1967, 244, second italics added; cf. 1967, 235, 290). At its core, Derrida's deconstructive project challenges the investment in the purity of concepts that drives the history of philosophy. In his late work on animals, he describes his project as a "limitrophy" concerned with what "feeds" (at the) limits.

In light of the ways that until his death, Derrida prodded conceptual limits and the limits of concepts, his insistence on the "purity" of certain concepts like hospitality, forgiveness, and the gift seems puzzling. In this chapter, I explore the limits of Derrida's own discourse of purity as it works against more traditional discourses of purity in terms of what I call its *homeopathic* properties essential to his hyperbolic ethics. Returning to *Of Grammatology* and Derrida's analysis of Rousseau's notion of purity, I consider both Derrida's and Rousseau's "taste for purity." The double meaning of "taste" becomes obvious and significant in that they link eating and morality. Even while challenging Rousseau's commitment to the purity of Nature, Derrida echoes his sentiments about eating well, sharing one's food, and the importance of nutrition over trophies. In *Of Grammatology,* although Derrida "deconstructs" Rousseau's romantic vision of the purity of nature, purity becomes central to the hyperbolic ethics of his later work. Derrida, too, associates this purity with eating, more precisely with eating or assimilating the other. More self-conscious than Rousseau about the politics of his own commitment to purity, Derrida is suspicious of his "taste" for purity but continues to use the discourse of purity for the sake of "good taste," which for him becomes associated with an ethics of the extreme: extreme obligations in the face of extreme uncertainty.

In this chapter, I argue that Derrida uses the concept of purity *homeopathically* in his later writings on hospitality and forgiveness. There Derrida embraces a notion of *pure* forgiveness and *pure* hospitality, which seems to be in tension with his criticisms of discourses of purity in his early work. The concept of *purity*—or, we could say, the purity of concepts—that he employs in his later work, however, is intended to counteract the history of philosophy's adherence to a notion of pure Nature as distinct from impure or corrupt culture: "a bit of the hair of the dog that bit you," we might say. To illuminate what appears as a shift in Derrida's attitude toward purity, I delineate various ethical stakes of Derrida's use of *purity*. I begin by examining the ways in which eating and food operate as pedagogical tools for Rousseau, for whom the ultimate lesson is how to be morally good and pure. Then I turn to Derrida's discussion of eating in "Eating Well," in which eating—or the notion of eating—becomes an allegory for relations with others. Unlike Rousseau, however, the allegory of eating does not so much teach us moral lessons as it teaches us that ethics is always and necessarily in tension with morality. Finally, I analyze Derrida's own discourse of purity in relation to what he calls hyperbolic ethics both in his discussions of the pure gift, forgiveness, and hospitality, and in his complicated appeal to nudity and nakedness in *The Animal That Therefore I Am*. In conclusion, I argue that Derrida's hyperbolic ethics requires that we continue to investigate and interrogate any allegiance to an ideal of purity, even of conceptual purity or pure concepts, including impure purity.

Rousseau: You Are What You Eat

As we have seen, Rousseau describes the evolution of human society in terms of how and what men eat: wild savages hunt and kill wild animals for food; herdsmen domesticate animals and thereby domesticate themselves; and civilized or cultivated men cultivate crops. As we know, for Rousseau, there is a moral causality between food and character: "All savages are cruel, and it is not their customs that tend in this direction; their cruelty is the result of their food. They go to war as to the chase, and treat men as they would treat bears. . . . Great criminals prepare themselves for murder by drinking blood" (2003, 140–41). But recall that he also says, "The first cake to be eaten was the communion of the human race" (1966, 35). Here I am more interested in Rousseau's suggestion about the connection between diet and morality than the connection between food and civilization discussed earlier. But before moving to his remarks on pure, natural, and wholesome tastes in both food and morality, recall that Rousseau's discussion of the diet of civilized men implies that man becomes cultivated in relation to how he eats animals and also learns how and what to eat from animals.[1] As we have seen, Rousseau repeatedly describes how man imitates animals to survive and to become more human. This assimilation of animal lessons is another form of ingestion that enables human culture and morality themselves. Derrida's analysis of eating also revolves around the metonymy between eating and assimilation, and eating understood as assimilation leads him to the heart of the problematic of ethical relations with others.

For Rousseau, the process of assimilation in regard to ethics or morality is both metaphorical and literal. In *Émile* he describes in detail the proper diet to nourish both body and mind, recommending a vegetarian diet, especially for children, who, he says, are healthier when they do not eat meat (2003, 28). Recall that he extols the virtues of milk, particularly the milk of herbivores, which he says is sweeter than that of carnivores (29). Even the curds in milk are healthy because they nourish by becoming solid and therefore do not merely pass through as liquid (29). Rousseau prefers simple, easily palatable, pure foods like milk and cheese. But food is much more than nourishment for the body. In *Émile* it is also a pedagogical tool used to "lead children through the mouth" (male children are more susceptible to these techniques than female children, who are "more eager for adornment than for food," see 2003, 396, 139). Cakes, ice cream, and lunch are pedagogical tools.

Indeed, for Rousseau, what and how one eats are signs of the strength of one's mind. "Gluttony is the vice of feeble minds. The gourmand has his brains in his palate, he can do nothing but eat; he is so stupid and incapable that the table is the only place for him, and dishes are the only things he knows anything about" (2003, 139). As he describes it, we should attend to good eating habits for the sake of our bodies *and* our minds. This is because of all our senses, taste (*goût*) affects us most in that "it concerns us more nearly to judge aright of what will actually become part of ourselves, than of that which will merely form part of our environment" (2003, 138; see 1999, 172–73). Although he maintains that matters of taste (*goût*)—both physical tastes and aesthetic tastes—are physical and material, they affect the mind and character (e.g., meat eaters are cruel) and can be symptoms of a weak mind and character (e.g., gourmands are stupid).[2] We need to concern ourselves with good taste, but not necessarily with what tastes good. We can (and should) train our tastes to appreciate purity and wholesome "goods." Moreover, he observes that simple tastes are closer to nature and therefore are not just good to eat but morally good. The sensation of taste gives way to, and becomes a sign of, moral taste.

Although Rousseau says that the laws of moral taste and physical taste differ, and in one passage he claims that taste makes so little appeal to the imagination that morality must come through other senses, he repeatedly associates pure and wholesome food with pure and wholesome morals (cf. 2003, 365, 139, 368). Both moral taste and physical taste are good when they are close to nature, and both become corrupt the farther they move away from nature. In this romantic view, nature is innocent, pure, wholesome, and good and is corrupted only by man's attempts to change it. Rousseau's writing implies that if we assimilate what is pure, wholesome, and good, then we will become pure, wholesome, and good. He says that the sense of taste affects us more than the other senses because the food becomes part of ourselves. Food is one element of the environment that we cannot separate from ourselves; with food, our environment becomes part of us. Morality, too, is assimilated from the environment. Rousseau claims that the worst taste on earth is in Paris because it is corrupt, which is why he prefers the simple tastes of country folk and insists that Émile be raised in the country (2003, 367). We assimilate our environment both physically and spiritually, which is why we must become attentive to it.

A healthy and pure lifestyle satisfies itself with a healthy and pure diet: "There are no such cooks in the world as mirth, rural pursuits, and merry games; and the finest made dishes are quite ridiculous in the eyes of people who have been on foot since early dawn" (Rousseau 2003, 379). In Rousseau's romantic vision, exercise and picnics outdoors beneath a tree or alongside a river are the greatest pleasures because they are the purest, which is to say the closest to nature: "Our meals will be served without regard to order or elegance; we shall make our dining-room anywhere, in the garden, on a boat, beneath a tree" (379). The *where* and *how* of eating are intimately connected to the *what;* in natural surroundings, the pure of heart delight in simple food and a simple lifestyle. For Rousseau, taking pleasure in such simplicity is evidence of a pure heart.

When Rousseau turns his attention from physical tastes or food to aesthetic tastes, he once again insists that Émile develop simple tastes "in order to keep his taste pure and wholesome" [*pour lui conserver en goût pur et sain,* 1999, 427] (2003, 368). Even as he maintains that bodily tastes and moral tastes are two separate realms, he continues to develop the analogy or metonymy between them: aesthetic tastes are moral only if they are natural, pure, and wholesome, while food that is natural, pure, and wholesome nourishes a good body and a good mind or soul. The simplicity of taste "goes straight to the heart," literally and metaphorically (*une certaine simplicité de goût qui va au coeur*, 1999, 427; cf. 2003, 368). Rousseau concludes that good and bad tastes take shape in relations of the heart "between two sexes." This relation too must be natural, pure, and wholesome, which he says is "why good taste implies good morals," and women are experts at bodily tastes, while men are experts at moral tastes (2003, 366). In the end, one of the central lessons of *Émile* is that the natural man should develop a taste for pure, simple, wholesome nourishment for *both* body and soul.

In order to be pure, however, Émile's simple pleasures must be shared with others. Many of Rousseau's lessons are designed to teach the value of generosity: "If you have pleasure without pain let there be no monopoly; the more you leave it free to everybody, the *purer* will be your own enjoyment . . . real pleasures are those which we share with the crowd; we lose what we try to keep to ourselves alone" (2003, 381–82, italics added). Here Rousseau is discussing poachers and "ordinary sportsman, who on a good horse, with twenty guns ready for them, merely take one gun after another, and shoot and kill everything that comes their way, without skill, without glory, and almost without exercise" (381–82). His ideal estate is wild and without fences, where game is not preserved and therefore not poached or hunted without strenuous efforts. The way that one hunts animals becomes a criterion for good taste. Hunting and eating will be truly pleasurable—pure pleasures—only if they are close to nature, simple, and one has to work for them. Only then will one truly appreciate them without squandering them and without arrogance. The "good" hunter hunts for exercise and food to share and not for trophies or sport alone.

"Good taste," then, also requires that Émile give up illusions of property or ownership. His estate will have no borders to keep animals in or poachers out. He will share his wealth with others because only then will it bring him pleasure—a lesson that he has taken to heart. Émile knows that "with health and daily bread we are rich enough" and that wealth "cannot buy you pleasure." Because "his heart is purer and more healthy . . . he will feel it more strongly" (2003, 383). So for Rousseau, a pure and healthy heart is more committed to the good life, which he describes as simple and natural, without pretense or property. Conversely, the good life produces a good heart, both physically and morally. The good is related to tastes, in both food and pleasures. Moral tastes and bodily tastes, then, are intimately connected. If we eat good food, we become good men.

For Rousseau, good taste is a matter of education. Émile has a pure heart because his tastes have been properly trained. His training includes how to become accustomed to surprises or the unexpected. Rousseau claims that he would expose his pupil to all different sorts of experiences so that he can more easily adapt and adjust to variety (except perhaps in diet!). But what would it mean to learn to respond to surprises? If this lesson could be learned, would there be anything left of surprise? Or would every situation be anticipated and every reaction trained? Traditionally, man is distinguished from animal in that he can respond, whereas animals merely react, and his ability to respond makes him uniquely capable of morals or ethics. But if a pure heart is a matter of training, then we might wonder what the difference is between the reaction of animals and the habitual reactions of a properly trained Émile. If morality is a matter of training, are we any different from animals? This question brings us to the heart of Derrida's engagement with the history of philosophy on the question of *the animal*.

Derrida: How to Eat the Other

In *The Animal* (2008), Derrida tracks the figure of the animal as it founds the notions of *man* and *the subject* in the history of philosophy.[3] He argues that man and everything proper to him has been defined against the animal, both requiring and ensuring that the animal and animals are not included in the fraternity of men, and the general concept of *the animal* erases multitudes of differences between animal species and individual animals. As it operates in the history of philosophy, the man/animal dichotomy disavows the ways in which man is also an animal and the ways in which the limit between the two is not absolute or stable. Derrida's analysis suggests that covering over differences between animals in order to distinguish man from all other living creatures also works to congeal differences among "men," most obviously sexual difference, which is disavowed in the generic use of *man* to refer to all human beings. Derrida's analysis could be read to suggest that the distinction and opposition between man and animal is the beginning of the history of the disavowal of differences in the name of difference.[4] We could say that the difference between man and animal stands in for difference in general and thereby effaces differences by pitting difference in general against identity in general in a fixed binary opposition that does not allow for degrees or the fluidity of "real-life" relationships.

Derrida's hunt for the animal began at least forty years ago when in *Of Grammatology* he claimed that the concept *the animal* in the writing of Rousseau represents everything that he is aiming at in his engagement with the history of philosophy: "Animal language—and animality in general—represents here the still living myth of fixity, of symbolic incapacity, of nonsupplementarity" (1974, 242). In other words, in the history of philosophy, *the animal* represents an indivisible and innocent origin out of which (or against which) man either erupts or evolves. In Rousseau's writings, this eruption or evolution is associated with the Fall of man away from the purity of nature and toward the contamination and corruption of society.[5] Derrida's argument in *Of Grammatology* is that the concept of Nature in Rousseau (and in the history of philosophy more generally) is "always already" contaminated by evil (figured variously as divisibility, absence, alienation, mediation, culture, writing, and so forth). In sum, philosophy cannot maintain the purity of the *concept* of Nature in its attempts to define it because every articulation is "always already" mediated by language and therefore a contamination of the pure immediacy of the natural world. In his latest work, Derrida argues that in the history of philosophy, the concept *the animal* stands in for both absolute or pure innocence and absolute or pure evil, the Other against which man defines himself as rational (see, e.g., 2008, 64, 78).

L'animal que donc je suis (*The Animal That Therefore I Am/Follow*), as the title suggests, continually returns us to the hunt for the animal, the animal that I follow, that I am *after* in several senses of that word.[6] As translator David Wills points out, the French title is a

play on Descartes' definition of consciousness (of the thinking animal as human), [and] it also takes advantage of the shared first-person singular form of *être* (to be) and *suivre* (to follow) in order to suggest a displacement of that priority, also reading as "the animal that therefore I follow after." (Derrida 2008, 162)

There are, however, other senses of the word *follow* that Derrida exploits in his analysis of the man/animal dichotomy. First, and perhaps more implicitly in the text, man follows from the animal in a logical sense. This suggestion feeds Derrida's "deconstruction" of the response/reaction binary by linking man to the animal according to a logical determination that works against the freedom usually attributed to man (and not to animals). This sense of "to follow" relates to Derrida's discussion of the logical entailment of the "therefore" in Descartes' formulation of the cogito as "I think, therefore I am." In Derrida's analysis, this "therefore" has a determinative power that seems to undermine the freedom and privilege of man over the animal/machine as figured by Descartes. In addition, Derrida explicitly plays on the notion of following, as in tracking or hunting the animal. Man is *after* the animal in both chronology (specifically according to the Genesis creation story) and in chasing after it in order to eat it or to display it as a trophy. The distinction between killing to nourish and killing as spectacle or trophy is significant to both Rousseau's sense of moral or good taste (as we have seen) and Derrida's (as we will see).

In the interview "Eating Well," Derrida wonders whether a head of state (*chef d'état*) could gain office by declaring himself (or herself) a vegetarian and concludes, "The chief (*chef*) must be an eater of flesh" (1991b, 114).[7] The press made fun of Barack Obama for drinking green tea, while Sarah Palin's grit was evidenced by her ability to kill and gut a moose. In the United States, we often see our political leaders hunting, particularly bird hunting, which seems to demonstrate their manly fortitude and bloodlust that can keep us safe. Hunting itself as a trope has become a trophy of sorts in the rhetoric of political image making. And meat eating or eating flesh is a sign of strength and fortitude. It is interesting to note that unlike Rousseau, Derrida was an "eater of flesh." In this same interview, seemingly reminiscent of Rousseau, Derrida associates eating well with ethical obligations and what Rousseau might call "good actions" that separate moral and physical nourishment from trophies. Derrida maintains that the oppositional limit between animal and man, and even between living and nonliving, has been challenged to the point that the ethical question in relation to animals is not whether they are subjects, sentient or feeling, and so forth and therefore should not be killed, but how to eat them in the most respectful way:

The question is no longer one of knowing if it is "good" to eat the other or if the other is "good" to eat, nor of knowing which other. One eats him regardless and lets oneself be eaten by him. . . . The moral question is thus not, nor has it ever been: should one eat or not eat, eat this and not that, the living or the nonliving, man or animal, but since *one must* eat in any case and since it is and tastes good [*bien*] to eat, and since there's no other definition of the good [*du bien*], *how* for goodness sake should one *eat well* [*bien manger*]? (1991b, 114–15)[8]

By *eating* Derrida means not only the physical act of ingesting food but also the metonymical act of interiorizing symbols, language, and social codes. Experience and sensation also are implicated in this eating. All forms of identification and assimilation in relation to the Other (language, meaning, etc.) and others (including animals, plants, and rocks) are literal and/or metaphorical forms of eating. Derrida argues that all our relationships literally or symbolically assimilate the other. Assimilation is necessary not only for war but also for communion and love: communication depends on the assimilation of the Other (especially language and meaning) and others (friends, family, and loved ones). We learn language by assimilating words, and we understand others and communicate with them by assimilating traditions and values, and so forth. Both words and food move through the orifices of the body, particularly the mouth.

In his recent book on Derrida and animals, *This Is Not Sufficient*, Leonard Lawlor gives what he calls a "recipe" for eating well that involves the "lesser of evils" when it comes to eating others, especially animals. Lawlor argues that if we gave each animal a proper name, then we would avoid the worst violence—eating their flesh—by "eating" them symbolically instead:

Only in this way, through the name, can we welcome, make a place for the animals, internalize them, even eat them. . . . But this replacement, which does not sacrifice, would be a way of eating the animals well. Here, through the specific internalization of the name (and not the flesh of the animals), we are able . . . to advocate a kind of vegetarianism that is compatible with a minimal carnivorism, but what I am really advocating is a kind of asceticism. (2007, 105)

In this Derridian "cookbook," Lawlor proposes replacing animal bodies with animal names. Indeed, he argues that if we give animals names, we will no longer be able to stomach killing them: "And, if, after naming the animals, we ate their bodies, their flesh, their meat, in other words, if we did more than internalize them through the name, if we *really ate the animals,* how could we not suffer from bad conscience?" (2007, 107, italics added).[9] Isn't this "really ate the animals" precisely what is at stake in Derrida's analysis? Throughout his writings, Derrida maintains that the literal and the metaphorical or the real and the fantastic are inseparable. The names that we use to describe the world bring with them—in terms of their denotation if not also their evocation—prescriptions. We could say "the what" is inseparable from "the how": we treat beings differently depending on what we take them to be—what we call them—animal or man. Once we "deconstruct" the categories of man and animal, literal and figurative, real and symbolic, and show that they are inseparable, what does "really" eating animals mean?

Derrida says "as concerns the 'Good' (*Bien*) of every morality, the question will come back to determining the best, most respectful, most grateful, and also most giving way of relating to the other and of relating the other to the self" (1991b, 114). For Derrida, as for Rousseau, the *Good* of morality or ethics is explicitly linked with the *good* of eating, as in *tastes good* and *eating well.* Derrida emphasizes that one *must* eat. It is both a need and a desire, and the *must* is both a natural necessity—living organisms must eat to live—and a moral obligation. That is, in our culture, suicide, even by starvation, is considered immoral. In addition, all community or communion requires some form of assimilation—common language and customs—that Derrida metonymically links to eating. We must eat, and since we must eat by both need and desire, the question is not whether or not to eat but how to eat.

Derrida presses the question of what to eat, given that ultimately any lines we might draw between man and animal, animal and vegetable, living and nonliving, are always fluid and open to debate. The "what" of "what should we eat?" is a moving target as both our needs and desires change: we are told to change our diets for the sake of life and health, and our customs and sensibilities oblige us to change our diets for the sake of ethical obligations to other creatures and renewing the resources of the planet. Also on the metonymical level, we share languages and symbolic resources. So the question of what to eat is never answered once and for all; it has to be continually asked in the vigilant, and ultimately undecidable, way required by hyperbolic ethics.[10] Following Levinas, Derrida proposes what he calls *hyperbolic ethics* in order to insist on urgency and the necessity for constant vigilance. Its imperatives and responsibilities are hyperbolic because they demand the impossible: that we be hyperaware of the ways in which our actions and decisions fall short of our ideals. Like the infinite curve of a hyperbola, we can only continue to approach the asymptote that is our ideal. Moreover, we must be hyperaware of the ways in which our ideals themselves exclude others, even others whom we may not recognize. So although we must eat, we also have an ethical obligation to decide how to eat in a way that respects others, even those whom we ingest. Moreover, we must choose our style of eating, our lifestyle, in the face of ultimately undecidability and uncertainty about our relation to others. In other words, the question of "what" is a metaphysical question that is essentially undecidable, a question that must be answered but cannot be answered with certainty. The question "Is it good to eat?" is fraught with ambiguity in the face of which we have ethical obligations that we do not even recognize as such. If the ethical question par excellence for Derrida is not whether or what but how to eat/assimilate well, it is crucial to point out that the questions of what and how are intimately linked. We decide how to treat other beings on the basis of our presuppositions, beliefs, and conclusions about *what* they are: Are they sentient, are they human, are they capable of suffering, are they food, and so forth. *How* we treat them—or eat them—is determined in large part by *what* they are.

Discussing Derrida's ambivalence toward vegetarianism, David Wood says,

Derrida is reported to have said at the Cerisy conference in the summer of 1993, "I am a vegetarian in my soul." The proper place for vegetarianism is not in the soul but in a complex reworking of the investments of the oral sphincter and all its personal and political ramifications. Carnophallogocentrism is not a dispensation of Being toward which resistance is futile; it is a mutually reinforcing network of powers, schemata of domination, and investments that has to reproduce itself to stay in existence. Vegetarianism is not just about substituting beans for beef; it is—at least potentially—a site of proliferating resistance to that reproduction. (1999, 32–33)

Against what he suggests may be Derrida's "beautiful soul," Wood argues for vegetarianism as a "symbolic substitute for unlimited and undelimitable responsibility—the renegotiation of our Being-toward-other-animals" (1999, 32). Wood refuses to accept what seems to be suggested by Derrida's remark that "vegetarians, too, partake of animals, even of men." It is not so much that Wood denies that vegetarians also participate in systems of domination and live in various essential ways off of killing and eating animals, including other human beings.[11] Rather, on the one hand, Wood imagines a more "deconstructive" form of vegetarianism— or perhaps a more vegetarian form of deconstruction—through which we might rethink all our relationships to others; and on the other hand, he insists that there is a difference between eating beef and eating beans that cannot be so easily disregarded, even in the name of keeping vegetarians honest. In other words, although we all are implicated in killing and eating the flesh of others, it still matters ethically and politically whether or not one decides to eat beef or beans. As Wood insists (along with Lawlor in the prescriptive moments of his text), we have to be able to distinguish really eating animals from symbolically eating them. As we learn from Derrida, even if the real and the symbolic are inseparable conceptually (they have their meaning only in relation to each other), on the level of practical ethics and politics, it is imperative to keep them distinct. According to Derrida, this we can do only by acknowledging the ways that one is implicated in the other. In other words, we can separate really eating from symbolically eating only by recognizing how the two are always already mixed (cf. Lawlor 2007, 31).

In his criticisms of Wood, Matthew Calarco emphasizes this later aspect of deconstruction, namely, that we cannot stop questioning our own investments in killing others, including other animals and other people, just because we stop eating meat. Deconstruction requires ongoing self-interrogation into both how and what we eat. The ethics of deconstruction must radically question what Calarco calls "the undisclosed anthropocentric and carnophallogocentric limits of the dominant discourses in animal ethics and vegetarianism," which base human responsibilities to other animals on our similarities with them (2004a, 197). Calarco concludes that deconstruction may provide a way of thinking about our ethical obligations to animals beyond what we might call taking the easy way out by finding similarities. While deconstruction may provide a much needed antidote to rights discourse based on identity, Calarco's beef with Wood sometimes seems to degenerate into a debate over the virtues of veganism over vegetarianism. As both Calarco and Wood acknowledge, however, Derrida's point is that ultimately where we draw the line between ourselves and others is radically undecidable in any certain metaphysical terms and yet at the same time is unavoidable. Ethics cannot be founded on counting how many species are sentient or suffer, whether we eat shellfish or so-called animal products like dairy. What about bacteria, viruses, and fungus that feed on us? Aren't they living beings, too? Should we kill them? Can we be open even to the other who feeds on us? Derrida is adamant that an extreme ethics allows that we can never know from where—or from whom—we will hear an ethical call. Ethical responsibility is motivated by radical differences that multiply rather than diminish or calculate the species of ethical calls. Derrida seems to ask, "Can we eat the other in a way that nourishes her as well as nourishes us?" In other words, is there a virtuous way of eating the other? This question involves both the how and what, not to mention the why, of ethical eating.

Reminiscent of Rousseau's suggestion that physical taste and moral taste are mutually implicated, for Derrida ethics becomes the question of eating well or, in a sense, good taste. Derrida says, "The Good can also be eaten. And it must be eaten well" (1991b, 115). It is not just a matter of interiorizing or assimilating the Good—that is, learning what is good or how to imitate it as Rousseau's monkey does[12]—but learning the lesson well, taking it to heart, but not by making it second nature or habit as Rousseau's natural man does. Eating well requires vigilance and must resist becoming merely a habit. If it does become a habit, then it is no longer ethical because it does not continue to question and to "learn." If morality becomes a habit, then we are like trained animals, reacting rather than responding. Since none of us can be like Émile with his pure and healthy heart, at best we can end up like Rousseau with his self-imposed dietary restrictions. Derrida embraces Rousseau's ideal of the pure heart, but only in its impossibility; it is precisely this impossibility of the pure that separates (radical or pure) ethics from morality. Whereas for Rousseau the good heart results from properly training the senses and then waiting for those lessons to "sink into your scholar's memory till they are old enough to take it to heart," for Derrida taking to heart is an impossible ideal that can never be realized yet must be attempted anyway and always (Rousseau 2003, 80). Indeed, if it were realized in Rousseau's sense of becoming a moral or mental habit, it would no longer be ethical. Rousseau's project of training Émile to expect the unexpected—to prepare for surprise— shares the aspect of paradox (and uncertainty) with Derrida's hyperbolic ethics. In Derrida's writing, however, Rousseau's romantic faith in the purity of nature becomes a rejection of that very purity in the name of an impure purity or a taste for impossible purity, forever deferred, a purity of the future, a purity to come. For Derrida, an ethics that remains open to surprise or open to the other requires giving up moral habits along with the notion that morality is a matter of habit. Doing good as a matter of habit or convention reduces ethics to nothing more than a reaction to stimuli, and Émile becomes a well-trained horse or dog, doing clever tricks to impress his master.

Despite his departures from Rousseau, Derrida also embraces ideals of generosity that suggest the individual's inherent and intimate relations with others. Like Rousseau, Derrida says that in order to be good, food must be shared. To eat well, one must share both food and nourishment; we have an obligation to attend to the other's nourishment even as we feed ourselves:

The infinitely metonymical question on the subject of "one must eat well" must be nourishing not only for me, for a "self," which given its limits, would thus eat badly, it must be shared, as you might put it, and not only in language. "One must eat well" does not mean above all taking in and grasping in itself, but learning and giving to eat, learning-to-give-the other-to eat. One never eats entirely on one's own: this constitutes the rule underlying the statement, "One must eat well." It is a rule offering infinite hospitality. (1991b, 115)

In this regard, we could learn something about eating well at table from the metonymical "eating" of speaking, and vice versa. There is no private language, or we could say that to speak only to oneself or for oneself is to speak badly because (even when talking to oneself) language presupposes an addressee. Language entails response-ability in that it is always addressed to someone, in particular or in general, near or far, radically other (like the time capsules launched into space from earth intended for extraterrestrials) or the other-within-the-self. The "must" of "must eat" compels hospitality insofar as eating well is a social experience. Obviously, food is the heart of many social and familial gatherings and events, and it is usually the result of some sort of cooperation or exchange in that (in developed countries) very few people eat only the food that they produce themselves (indeed, it would be a mighty task for one individual alone to produce—grow, harvest, cook, and so forth—all the foodstuffs that he consumes). The ethics of eating well, then, seems to imply a politics of food through which we attend to how we acquire nourishment. Derrida's eating well may have something to say to the "slow food" and "local food" movements. In addition to food, we also share languages, cultures, customs, and love, which more obviously raise political questions about English-only policies, multiculturalism, and globalization.

Unfortunately, more often than not, the cooperation and social exchange that allow us to eat are built on exploitation in an economy of exchange that makes everything fungible. The fact that eating or speaking requires a group effort or global exchange should not be confused with hospitality. In addition, the ethical obligation that Derrida describes is not just to hospitality, to sharing food and nourishment (of all sorts) but to *infinite* hospitality. To eat well is to be infinitely vigilant in one's hospitality to the other, even the very other whom one eats. In fact, as Derrida articulates this ethical obligation, it is this "who" or "whom" that must be incessantly questioned, on the side of the "subject" and on the side of the "other": *Who* claims the rights and privileges of *whom,* of subjectivity? Who has the right to judge the subjectivity or humanity of others? Derrida ponders the ways that subjects give themselves the right to divide the world into subjects and objects/others, man and animals, those who eat and those who are eaten (both literally and figuratively).[13]

Purity and Contamination

Derrida calls this infinite hospitality "absolute" or "pure hospitality," which he envisions as the foundation of hyperbolic ethics (e.g., 2000, 25; 2005, 249). In *Of Hospitality,* he describes the rule or law of hospitality as impossible, since true hospitality cannot be dictated by law, custom, habit, or training but must come "from the heart" (as he says later):

It is as though hospitality were the impossible: as though *the* law of hospitality defined this very impossibility, as if it were only possible to transgress it, as though the law of absolute, unconditional, hyperbolical hospitality, as the categorical imperative of hospital-ity commanded that we transgress all the laws (in the plural) of hospitality, namely, the conditions, the norms, the rights and the duties that are imposed on hosts and hostesses, on the men or women who give a welcome as well as the men or women who receive it. (2000, 75, cf. 77)

Derrida plays on the fact that in French, *hôte* means both "host" and "guest," implying the fluidity of giving and receiving. That the host can become the guest, and vice versa, just as the eater can become the eaten, and vice versa, indicates both the instability of power relations and the relationality of subject positions. Derrida recounts Benveniste's semiotic chain involving hospitality, host, hostage, and hostility (1998, 14). He exploits this semiotic fluidity and ambiguity to call into question what we traditionally imagine as the sovereignty of the subject. Pure or absolute hospitality requires giving up the illusion of being at home or owning a home in which one can play host. It even can mean being a hostage in the Levinasian sense of being beholden to the other.[14] From the holy host to the parasite's host, playing host is problematized.

The impossibility of a law or habit of hospitality, of pure or absolute hospi-tality, entering into an economy of exchange is a central problematic of much of Derrida's later work, starting with his discussions of the gift and continuing through his discussions of forgiveness. In terms of the gift, what he calls the "pure gift" cannot be dictated by law or part of an economy of exchange (e.g., 2005, 143). If duty obligates you to give a gift, are you really giving? Is it really a gift? Likewise, if you give a gift in exchange for something else, is it really a gift or more like a payment?[15] As Derrida says in relation to hospitality, in order for it to be pure and absolute, hospitality cannot be given as payment for a debt or done merely out of duty to the law. It cannot become a matter of either habit or moral duty, even the duty of universal hospitality that Kant describes in "Perpetual Peace," a hospitality founded on the finite surface of the globe.[16] The purity of the gift is associated with the infinite responsibility of giving, which is beyond morality in that morality is a matter of calculation and rules. Calculation, rules, and laws turn what should be an ethical response to the singularity of the other (or the event) into a mere reaction or reflex determined by convention.

In regard to forgiveness, Derrida distinguishes unconditional or pure forgiveness from conditional or contaminated forms of forgiveness. Again, if forgiveness is given only to obtain something in return, then it is not absolute. But if forgiveness is possible only for minor offenses that are without consequence, then it is not true forgiveness, or if forgiveness is given only on certain conditions—for example, the perpetrator repents or feels remorse—then it is not true forgiveness. Once forgiveness is circumscribed within social conventions or laws, it is no longer pure: "Pure and unconditional forgiveness, in order to have its own meaning, must have no 'meaning,' no finality, even no intelligibility. It is a madness of the impossible" (2001b, 45). But this impossibility is precisely what "founds" the ethical imperative, demand, or call.[17]

If it is impossible to formulate laws or to develop habits of gift giving, hospitality, or forgiveness, would the gift, hospitality, or forgiveness have to be unrecognizable in order to be pure? Derrida answers yes: "If I say lightly, 'I forgive you' this sentence . . . is the destruction of forgiveness. . . . You have to recognize that I forgive you, and this is recognizable, which is, of course, the beginning of the destruction of what forgiveness should be" (2001c, 53). What forgiveness "should be" cannot be circumscribed by law, language, or customs, or else it becomes limited, finite, and conditioned rather than limitless, infinite, and unconditioned. It becomes a reaction rather than a response.

In their absolute and hyperbolic forms, the concepts or ideals of giving, hospitality, and forgiveness have an essentially limitless and infinite quality that Derrida constantly compares with what passes for giving, hospitality, and forgiveness in our everyday lives. He maintains that what we do recognize as gifts have meaning only in relation to this ideal of giving that is essentially unrecognizable.

So even though "pure" or absolute forms are impossible, we see "contaminated" examples of them everyday. Paradoxically, forgiveness is bound to be boundless; the ethical obligation it entails is beyond any moral rules. Or in more Derridian language, the only possible prescription for giving, hospitality, or forgiveness is that they remain imprescriptable. If they follow a script, then they are not *events* in Derrida's sense of the word as "incalculable."[18] On the contrary, if they have been contrived, they do not happen in their pure sense.

Curiously, Derrida's work on forgiveness implicitly, if not explicitly, revolves around a stake in the notion of pure forgiveness as a way to interrupt discourses of racial and ethnic purity as manifest in his prime examples, the Holocaust and apartheid. Derrida questions the possibility of forgiveness as it operates in contemporary discussion of these "crimes against humanity" while measuring them against the immeasurable concept of pure forgiveness. (In *The Animal,* Derrida asks what it would mean to imagine crimes against animality.) His analysis suggests that holding ourselves to this higher standard of pure forgiveness may serve as what I call a *homeopathic* treatment for genocidal discourses of racial and ethnic purity.[19] The homeopathic remedy entails taking a dose of the very poison we seek to neutralize. We need a dose of one kind of purity—hyperbolic purity—as an antidote to another kind of purity: one ideal of purity takes out the other. We could say that Derrida proposes a purity "worthy of its name," a purity *of* the name or *of* the concept for the sake of avoiding implementation of discourses of purity on the bodies of those deemed impure. It is crucial that for Derrida the purity that he invokes operates on the conceptual level. He imagines a purity of concepts and not a purity of bodies or blood. He uses reason against itself in this homeopathic way as an antidote to all the reasons that human beings have given to justify enslaving one another and other living creatures. In this regard, deconstruction has always been a homeopathic methodology. It has always used the text, the concepts, the history of philosophy, against itself in order to make it ethical, that is, in order to imagine an ethics that might be as Derrida says "worthy of its name."

A Taste for Purity

The impossibility of gift giving, forgiveness, or hospitality is not a reason to give up hope but is what gives hyperbolic ethics its pull. These pure concepts seem to work like Kantian regulative ideals in that they are the ideals for which everyday forms of forgiveness aim and which give the everyday forms their meaning. But they are "beyond" Kantian ideals in that they are beyond all duty, law, sovereignty, or will. Derrida says that he is more Kantian than Kant (2001c, 66). These more-than-Kantian ideals are necessarily, but simultaneously cannot be, deferred. There is an urgency in Derrida's appeal to hyperbolic ethics that requires that we act now, even though we cannot be certain, we cannot know; indeed, we cannot; our response to the ethical call is not an "I can" of a sovereign autonomous subject but the blood that flows through such possibilities. In *Rogues,* Derrida describes the impossible ethical demand requiring that we attend to what might be possible and therefore is demanded from us:

This im-possible . . . is not what I can indefinitely defer . . . it precedes me, swoops down upon and seizes me *here and now* in a nonvirtualizable way, in actuality and not potentiality. It comes upon me on high, in the form of an injunction that does not simply wait on the horizon. . . . Such an urgency cannot be *idealized* any more than the other as other can. This im-possible is thus not a (regulative) *idea* or (regulating) *ideal.* It is what there is most undeniably *real.* And sensible. Like the other. Like the irreducible and nonappropriable différance of the other. (2005, 84)

The ethical injunction "swoops" down on me like a bird of prey, and my response is just as urgent. In the words of Leonard Lawlor, "This urgency is why Derrida rejects both the phenomenological concept of horizon and Kantian regulative ideals" (2007, 90). Lawlor points out that this provides another sense of Derrida's the animal that I follow, the animal that I am. We follow the animal in the sense that we are waiting to respond to the call from the animals through no agency of our own. He says, "The animal I am following, that I am, has already, is actually turning on me, menacing me, accusing me," looking at me naked like Derrida's cat; or, it is the catlike aspect of Derrida himself that stalks him/us (Lawlor 2007, 91). Lawlor remarks that when he is writing aporias, "he most resembles a cat pacing back and forth before a door, waiting to be let out or to be let in" (2007, 78). We all are waiting to be let out or to be let in, as are all the animals. Derrida's invocations of a different soft tone, a lexicon or grammar to come, naked speech from the heart, are attempts to let the animal in, and out.

With a new twist, Derrida's notion of purity takes us back to Rousseau's pure heart, which also beats in the background of Kant's goodwill. For Derrida, as for Rousseau, the pure heart is an ideal that cannot be trained or simply taught by conventions, but at the same time it cannot exist outside conventions. In this sense, the pure heart is simultaneously impossible and imperative; it is what Derrida might call an impure purity. If Rousseau's pure heart is romantic, Derrida's is messianic. If Rousseau's is given by nature and trained by the pauper philosopher who denounces book learning and words, Derrida's is the dream of a bookworm who imagines all of life in terms of a future spelling, grammar, words, and lexicon.

Discussing the unconditionality of the incalculable, in *Rogues,* Derrida says that he resorts to this terminology because it is intelligible to the Western tradition, but he imagines that "another language will perhaps one day help us to say better what still remains to be said about these metonymic figures of the unconditional [hospitality, the gift, forgiveness]" (2005, 148). This unconditionality of hospitality, the gift, and forgiveness is "required by the purity of such concepts" and gives "meaning and practical rationality" to all that we call hospitality, gift, or forgiveness. Derrida suggests that the purity of these concepts does not come, as it does for Heidegger, from their origins, but from their future. And this future that he imagines will be better than the past still has to be found somehow in that past if it is to make any sense to us. In other words, these concepts are pure not because of some pristine origin before their contamination (à la Rousseau) but because they open the possibility of imagining that we can be better, more hospitable, more giving, more forgiving, more just. Through imagination we can see ourselves saved. Of course, we also can imagine the worst, and as Derrida is quick to point out, we cannot be certain that we can tell the difference. In this way, he makes explicit the ambiguity that remains implicit in Rousseau's writings. Echoing the language of catastrophe and metaphor of floodgates that marks his work from *Of Grammatology* onward, in *Monolingualism of the Other,* he says:

I therefore admit to a purity which is not very pure. Anything but purism. It is, at least, the only impure "purity" for which I dare confess a *taste* [*le goût*]. It is a pronounced *taste* [*gout*] for a certain pronunciation. I have never ceased learning, especially when teaching, to speak softly, a difficult task for a "pied noir," and especially from within my family, but to ensure that this soft-spokenness reveal the reserve of what is thus held in reserve, with difficulty, and with great difficulty, contained by the floodgate, a precarious floodgate [*l'écluse*] that allows one to apprehend the catastrophe [*catastrophe*]. The worst can happen at every turn [*À chaque passage le pire peut arriver*]. (1998, 47–48, italics added; cf. 1996, 80)

Even with the best intentions and the most self-control, the worst can happen: the gift is poisonous; forgiveness is a guilty debt that cannot be repaid; hospitality is a virus invading its host. Here Derrida talks of a taste for a certain pronunciation, a certain soft-spoken tone of voice, a purity of language, that still risks falling into impure ruin, of overturning itself at every turn. It is noteworthy that the word *catastrophe* comes from the Greek "to overturn" or "downturn." In Rousseau's parlance, we might say it is a turn south toward the languages of passion that don't exhibit the control and capacity for articulation of the northern languages. This is, of course, both the pleasure and danger of southern languages, as they communicate through accent and tone and the northern ones communicate through articulation and rhythmic grammar.

How can we account for Derrida's taste for purity given that the heart of deconstruction is sustained by exposing the myth of purity as a dangerous supplement, a fantastic lure? In the preceding passage, he answers that his taste for purity is not very pure; it is not a form of purism; and it is not an ethical, political, or social demand. Rather, he frames it as a matter of taste, a preference for a certain way of speaking, a way of using language, that does not offend his ear, that does not make him "suffer" from its impurity (1998, 46). He says that he desires a pure French and fancies himself as more French than the French (just as later he says he is more Kantian than Kant). Derrida even goes so far as to imagine that he is the rightful and last heir of the French language (1998, 47). His good taste in language makes him suffer when others, or when he himself, cannot live up to its demands. Unlike the discussion of unconditional incalculability demanded by the pure concepts such as gift, forgiveness, and hospitality (as he describes them in *Rogues*), this demand is for a tone of voice or accent rather than for a lexicon adequate to the task of living up to our ideals insofar as they are "worthy of their names." Derrida maintains in the earlier text that the purity he demands—or, perhaps more accurately, that language demands—"does not coincide with anything that is given (the lexicon, grammar, stylistic or poetic decorum)" (1998, 47). It is something about language as it is spoken and as it is heard; it is an embodied experience that exceeds grammar or style. What is this soft-spoken pure tone of voice that Derrida favors? Among other meanings, the word *pure* denotes a pleasingly clear and vivid sound and even refers to a vowel or consonant that is constant and unchanging in its pronunciation. In music, pure refers to a single frequency without any overtones, and in general it means unmixed. Pure can mean theory rather than practice or applications (as in pure mathematics). Several of the dictionary definitions of pure have to do with sound. Is Derrida saying that he prefers a pronunciation that is constant and free from overtones, a clear and vivid voice? If so, doesn't this reenact philosophy's prejudice against all things constant, clear, and distinct, the very prejudice that Derrida's work has signaled, if not worked to overcome?

Derrida's preference for clarity in pronunciation at the least returns us to Rousseau's accent or tone, which even resonates with his cat, who also suffers from poor imitations and impure accents, when Rousseau unsuccessfully tries to imitate a meow. "Everything," says Derrida, "is summoned from an intonation" (1998, 47). Imagining a tone before tone, the intonation that gives rise to language, Derrida speaks of rhythm, which in *Of Grammatology* was associated with articulation against accent or tone. Echoing that early text, in *Monolingualism* Derrida suggests that before the beginning of tone, there was rhythm and that he stakes everything on that rhythm (1998, 47). If there is no accent without articulation, no tone without rhythm, and yet the stakes are summoned from the intonation that always exceeds its prerequisite rhythm, then between rhythm and tone, the origin of language is incalculable. Although for Derrida, there is no tone without rhythm, or accent without articulation, tone and accent make evident both the significance and the untranslatability of the performative dimension of language.

Derrida's tone is more of a whisper than the masterly voice usually associated with philosophy, for he embraces the secret that must be told—the impossible secret, the one that is impossible to keep—but can be passed on only in hushed tones.[20] But he claims to be afraid of his own voice, especially its tone: "If I have always trembled before what I could say, it was fundamentally [*au fond*] because of the tone, and not the substance [*non du fond*]" (1998, 48). Rather than adopt the booming voice of a philosopher proclaiming eternal truths, Derrida restrains himself, demanding of himself a more modest, even self-conscious tone, that still seems to hope for the best—that language can do something—while fearing the worst—what that something might be. Does Derrida's invocation of purity throughout his later work signal the catastrophe (overturning) that he, following Rousseau's implicit lead, predicts is inherent in the voice of philosophy itself?

Derrida says that he acquired his taste for purity at school:

For, naturally, this hyperbolic taste [*ce goût hyperbolique*] for the purity of language is something that I contracted [*contracté*] at school. I am not unaware of that, and it is what needed to be demonstrated. The same goes for hyperbole in general. An incorrigible hyperbolite. A generalized hyperbolite. In short, I exaggerate. I always exaggerate. (1998, 48; cf. 1996, 81)

Like an illness, he contracted his hyperbolic taste for purity at school; it was contagious and invaded him like a virus invading its host. Yet as he claims, this illness could not have taken hold of him if it did not find in him already "fertile ground" in which to grow and flourish. He says that because he grew up between cultures, he always considered himself more and less French and more and less Jewish than any other Frenchman or any other Jew and especially any other French Jew (1998, 49). This more and less is what he calls the excess of the excess, his tendency to exaggerate for effect, to affect a tone that is both exemplary and (as such) calls into question the purity of the purity.

Like Rousseau's, Derrida's taste for purity is both learned by imitating the masters and the result of a seemingly "natural" disposition, only now always already infected by the mixing of cultures, races, and histories. Like Émile, Derrida learns to value purity (only now of language rather than of morality, although I am not sure how the two can be separated, especially given Derrida's work) through imitation and necessarily more than that. In a sense, it is not the purity of his nature that makes him insist on purity but Derrida's impure or mixed heritage, both personal and philosophical, that makes him more French than the French, more and less. Notice that he does not say more *or* less but, as he does in *Of Grammatology*, insists on the "both and" (P and ~P) of deconstruction that overturns classical logic. We could say, ironically, that this entails the catastrophe of classical logic, that the danger and the promise are that in classical logic, anything follows from a contradiction.

In his later work on the gift, hospitality and forgiveness, Derrida imports his taste for purity and hyperbole into a hyperbolic ethics that makes impossible and infinite demands on us. In those discussions, Derrida's tone is urgent and yet rigorously attentive to both what he says and how he says it. Although there is no how without the what, the intonation—the how—troubles Derrida and makes him tremble. How might his exaggerations be understood? What tone of voice is appropriate to hyperbolic ethics? If the *why* is the crux of deontological ethics and the *what* is the crux of utilitarian ethics, then the *how* is the crux of hyperbolic ethics. We are back to Derrida's question: how do we (respectfully) eat the other?

Because we must eat something, because decisions about what we eat are based on categorical distinctions among types that do not stand up to scrutiny, and because our motives for eating one thing rather than other have become suspect, the question of how we eat becomes the primary ethical question (not unrelated to the other questions). Hyperbolic ethics makes us responsible for what we eat (or say) and why and also for how. It is what we say or why and how we say it that determines its ethical import. Throughout his work, Derrida attends to this performative dimension of ethics, an arena generally ignored by traditional moral theorists. For Derrida, ethics is necessarily a matter of exaggeration. To be ethics or ethical, it must be extreme. It must be more Kantian than Kant and more Benthamian than Bentham, perhaps even more Sartrian than Sartre or more Levinasian than Levinas. The hope is that this exaggerated sense of responsibility can short-circuit violence by using extreme measures against extreme danger. But this hope is always a guarded optimism because it necessarily acknowledges that the most carefully delineated categories of what, and the most categorical imperatives of why, can still lead to the worst. Hyperbolic ethics is extreme in both its hope and its worry for the future. Indeed, there is no hope for the future if we are not vigilant in our worry—to the point of insomnia, as Levinas might say—about the dangers and violence of our own eating and saying.

Echoing Rousseau's dreamer with which he concludes *Of Grammatology*, Derrida observes that the purity he desires remains a dream "to make something happen to (this) language," the dream of "an incomprehensible guest, a new-comer," who makes language speak itself in another way (1998, 51). Language becomes an event, a happening. It does something; it makes something happen. Language becomes virtuous in the archaic sense of containing beneficial powers. Language becomes like a virtuous plant or herb that has beneficial effects on the body. Whereas Rousseau gives up on words (even while continuing to use them) and turns to botany, Derrida continues to dream of the virtues of language. In *The Animal*, this dream becomes a Doctor Doolittlesque dream of an invented grammar or an extraordinary, unheard of music that moves beyond discourses of the human, animal, or divine and takes us beyond the economies of sameness or opposition that lead to warfare, including—and especially—our war on animals: "I was dreaming of inventing an unheard-of grammar and music" [*je rêvais d'inventer une grammaire et une musique inouïes*] (2008, 64).[21] It is the dream of an accent, an intonation, which opens up an impossible language that allows us to understand without representing (see 2008, 63–64).

This new way of speaking (or singing) would bring with it a new lexicon and a new intonation through which "blood mixes with ink," and this new language would write the body (1998, 52). In "Circumfession," Derrida says that he has always dreamed "of a pen that would be a syringe" so that he could write himself into a sentence and find himself there (1993, 10).[22] In this regard, Derrida's dream is not so different from Rousseau's: the dream of immediacy, of a language that does not betray the body but speaks in its own natural language, the language of blood. In this light, it is noteworthy that various historians speculate that the first ink used was animal blood, that some of the first pens were bird quills, and that animal figures were some of the first written "language." In my project, I might ask whether in a sense we always write with the blood of animals.

Pure Heart

In *The Animal*, Derrida repeatedly says that he wants to speak "from the heart," using words that are "naked" in order to avoid the "the appearance of training [*dressage*], already, of a habit or convention that would in the long term program the very act of thanking" (2008, 1). We are conventional animals in the sense that all language—we could say all communication—is circumscribed by conventions, customs, and rules. In that sense, whatever we say is "programmed" by language and culture. Derrida's invocation of "from the heart" points to a nakedness or nudity beyond all conventions, a place from which one can respond rather than merely react according to a script preordained by conventions. Derrida imagines "naked words," words that would not be governed or determined by the laws of culture, impossible words. Derrida's naked words from the heart give a new twist to Levinas's nudity in the face-to-face relationship, the ethical relation prior to politics. The movement between the impossible, the imprescriptable, the unconditional, and the pure or naked takes on particular significance when Derrida turns to the animal. Derrida, the *philosophical animal* par excellence, works the space between pure naked thanks "from the heart" and animal instincts, between response and reaction.[23]

In one sense, the central question of Derrida's latest work is, Why does man think that among the creatures on earth, he alone responds rather than merely reacts, that he alone is not determined by instincts? Derrida is less interested in defending the animal's ability to respond—especially since he objects to the general category of *the animal* itself—than in questioning *the philosopher*'s contentions that man's response is not a reaction.[24] As Derrida puts it, the problem is not only whether an animal can respond but also whether man can respond. Abilities and characteristics traditionally considered those that distinguish humans from animals (language, rationality, morality, technology, art, clothes, love, and so forth), come back to the opposition between culture and nature or society and biology, civil law and natural law, and because they are inscribed by social conventions, including language and technology, aren't they also "trained"? We can ask with Derrida, How can true response that is not also a reaction be a matter of law or convention? When we speak, reason, create art, even make love, aren't we following conventions, traditions, or rules? If so, what is the difference between the ways that we are bound to these conventional laws and the ways that we imagine animals are bound to natural laws? How can we prevent them from becoming mere second nature or habits? How can we respond "from the heart" to each new situation, to each event, to each creature? Unlike Rousseau's Émile who should learn never to be surprised, how can we always be surprised?

Philosophers have argued that man is free to break the rules of convention but that animals are not free to break the laws of nature. Derrida approaches this dichotomy from both sides, pointing out that philosophers have been inconsistent in the ways that they use animals to set up the distinctiveness of man. He also points to places where certain texts leave open the possibility of animal response, showing how these philosophers appeal to rules and laws in order to justify the distinction between these very human rules and laws and natural animal law. In addition, once psychoanalysis enters the scene, he explains that the notion of freedom and the opposition between response and reaction becomes impossible to maintain. His goal, however, is not to reverse the poles or to collapse the distinction between man and animal, between response and reaction. Instead, he aims to challenge any one stable or unified border between man and animal in order to open up our thinking of differences between and among what we call "animal" and "man."

The philosophical rigidity and fixity of the line between man and animal becomes a symptom of "man's" own reaction to otherness. To be fixed and rigid, to be certain, to have clear and distinct ideas, is to react rather than respond to the changing situations and dynamics of life, particularly in regard to its ethical and political dimensions. In other words, the certainty of reason to which philosophers have traditionally aspired, to which they appeal to distinguish man from animals, is in tension with the ethical and political responses, also identified as uniquely human. The certainty of reason becomes a type of reaction rather than a response, and thereby more like an "animal instinct" than an ethical response, at least a response "worthy of its name." If we think that we know how others will act—or how we will act—then we are no longer relating to others but only to our own images of them. In this case, we assimilate others into our own ideas or fantasies of them in order to shore up our own sense of self-possession and certainty. We assimilate or eat the other in a triumphant celebration of our own sovereignty and certainty. As Derrida might say, we act "beastly."[25]

Derrida challenges the purity of the border between man and animal in the name of another hyperbolic purity, that of infinite hospitality. He says, "My hesitation concerns only the purity, the rigor, and the indivisibility of the frontier that separates—already with respect to 'us humans'—reaction from response and in consequence, especially, the purity, rigor, and indivisibility of the concept of responsibility that is derived from it" (2008, 125).[26] In this same text, he identifies the "pure concept (life in its pure state)" of "pure philosophy" as a symptom of the history of the opposition between man and animal, between response and reaction (2008, 22). This remark implies that the concept of purity itself is a symptom of this history and that the purity and rigidity of concepts, perhaps the whole of binary oppositional thought in Western culture, begin with the division between the categories *man* and *animal.*

This makes it all the more interesting that Derrida addresses his concern about the purity of the frontier between animal and man with a counterdiscourse of purity and contamination, that of a pure hospitality or pure gift that would unconditionally welcome the other, including the animal other or, more accurately, other animals. The purity of concepts like the gift, hospitality, or forgiveness supposedly commands attention to the singularity of each individual beyond all general categories such as *man* or *animal*. Indeed, these general categories abolish both ethical singularity and individual differences in order to strengthen the oppositional hierarchy through which some "animals," those whom we call "man," come to dominate other animals, those whom we call "animal" (or "woman" or "slave" and so forth).

Derrida's challenge to the purity of the division between man and animal leads him to question the "purity, rigor, and indivisibility of the concept of responsibility," especially in his readings of Lacan (who identifies man as the only animal capable of response) and Levinas (who sees a compelling face and its ensuing responsibility for the other only in man). Derrida suggests that this dividing line cannot be drawn in any pure or rigorous way, especially if we posit the existence of the unconscious. Even if we can distinguish unconscious motivations from animal instincts, how are they any less reactionary than instinct? Again, it is not that Derrida is arguing that there is no difference between man and animals, response and reaction, or that there is no difference between the operations of the unconscious and the operations of animal instinct. Instead, he is challenging the purity of such distinctions, especially because they lead to hierarchical binary oppositions.[27]

Derrida acknowledges that this challenge also questions the foundations of freedom and responsibility that traditionally ground ethics and morality. But, he maintains, this constant questioning of foundations is essential to hyperbolic ethics:

On the one hand, casting doubt on responsibility, on decision, on one's own being-ethical, seems to me to be—and is perhaps what should forever remain—the unrescindable essence of ethics, decision, and responsibility. All firm knowledge, certainty, and assurance on this subject would suffice, precisely, to confirm the very thing one wishes to disavow, namely the reactionality in the response. (2008, 126)

In other words, all moral certainty is reactionary in that it is not continually responding or thinking, and its reactionary character makes it the antithesis of ethics "worthy of its name."[28] The ethical question becomes, How can we respond in a way that is not reactionary? How can we respond "from the heart"? Derrida asks whether this kind of nudity is possible: Can our words ever be naked and from the heart? Paradoxically, this pure nudity is associated with animals, who supposedly cannot lie; but nudity is also distinctive of man in that only he recognizes himself as naked and covers himself in shame. Can we speak from the heart without shame? Without lies? Without the conventions that make our words appear more like the result of training or dressage?

These questions are especially poignant when we consider that Derrida insists that hyperbolic ethics is beyond sovereignty. Giving, hospitality, or forgiveness cannot be matters of sovereignty, of "I give" or "I forgive," because to Derrida, this willful subject makes giving or forgiveness into possessions that he dominates and distributes in an economy that attributes certain properties to some beings and not others. In this way, giving, hospitality, and forgiveness fall back into the contaminated forms of an economy of property and exchange. The pure forms that Derrida evokes, those that are "worthy of their names," also bring with them connotations of propriety and therefore of property. To talk of a pure giving, hospitality, or forgiveness is to talk of what is proper to the concepts themselves; it is to invoke the meaning of the name as what is proper to it, if not the essence of the name. But why does he invoke the purity of concepts in a discourse that otherwise challenges the very distinction between pure and contaminated?

Leonard Lawlor's analysis of the impossibility of the "as such" is helpful here.[29] Lawlor extends Derrida's critical engagements with Heidegger to a general argument against knowing anything "as such." We never have access to life, death, ourselves as such. Our experience is always already mediated by language and our relationships to others. Lawlor points out that for Heidegger, animals are deprived of any experience of as such; they do not know that they are animals; unlike man, they do not know they are there; unlike man, they are not Dasein. But following Derrida, Lawlor argues that man, like animals, never has an experience of himself as such, as truly there:

The fault that divides, being there in us, means that all of us are not quite there, not quite Da, not quite dwelling, or, rather, all of us are living . . . in the indeterminate place . . . about which we can say that it is neither animal nor divine—nor human—or that it is both animal and divine—and human. (2007, 69)

This Derridian "neither nor, both and" logic undermines any as such because it defies ontological categorizations that separate one type of being from another. If the animal has no access to the *as such*, neither does man. Man and animals share a fault, a similar deprivation, "a staggered analogy" (a phrase that Lawlor takes from Derrida's *Of Spirit* and makes a central and recurring theme). One of the most provocative and haunting conclusions that Lawlor draws from the impossibility of the *as such* is: "Not appearing as such, an animal exists only in dispersion. And if an animal exists only in dispersion, then when we kill one, we really don't know how many are killed. How many does it take to make a genocide? Perhaps one alone" (2007, 103). If a human never appears as such, then the same applies: a human exists only in dispersion. And if a human exists only in dispersion, then when we kill one, we really don't know how many are killed. How many humans does it take to make a genocide? Perhaps one human alone. Of course, once we admit Derrida's "deconstruction" of the separation of human and animal, then the killing of one implicates the killing of the other. In less rhetorical and less eloquent fashion, we could say that given the productions and reproductions of any given individual—that is, his or her prodigy (literally and figuratively)—when we kill one, we never know how many we have killed.

Derrida's criticisms of the *as such* shed new light on his repeated use of the phrase "worthy of its name" in relation to pure forgiveness, pure gift, pure hospitality, and so forth. In the next chapter, I return to this phrase in terms of its ethical import; but for now, I would like to consider how it inflects and affects the purity of the concepts of forgiveness, gift, and so on. If there is no forgiveness as such, no gift as such, no hospitality as such, then we cannot know the essence of these concepts. Indeed, we have to reconsider what we mean by "concept." Derrida emphasizes that these pure concepts—forgiveness, gift, hospitality— must be worthy of their names. That is, they are always already mediated by the name; in other words, there is no concept as such. Rather, there is the name and its history, its etymology. The meaning of life comes from the meaning of words. But for Derrida, unlike Heidegger, this meaning is not a matter of going back to an original meaning or even a lost meaning. Instead, it is a matter of opening ourselves to meanings to come, meanings that we cannot anticipate. This speaks to the impossibility, even paradox, of waiting for the unexpected, of anticipating what cannot be anticipated. This obligation to the future brings with it obligations to the past. We cannot forget our past but must continue to search there for alternative possible futures, including the possibility of the impossible: pure forgiveness, pure gift, pure hospitality.

By taking us back to the pure worthy of its name, Derrida interrupts one discourse of property, purity, and rigor with another. That is, he interrupts the everyday practices of forgiveness, including recent political practices like the Truth and Reconciliation Commission, by comparing them with the concept of forgiveness as it has been articulated in the history of Western thought. He sees his insistence on conceptual purity in the face of real-world contamination as a primarily ethical move. This conceptual purity, as he occasionally insists, is not very pure; it is an impure purity. Because there is no concept as such and all concepts are always already names with changing histories, they are always already contaminated. But it is this very contamination and the possibility of it that make these concepts worthy of their names ethical. Their ethical force comes from the fact that they are not eternal forms but are implicated by history, which guarantees that change is possible and even inevitable and also makes the separation of remedy and poison ultimately undecidable. On the one hand, the purity of the concepts of gift, hospitality, and forgiveness requires unconditionality—to condition is to contaminate. On the other hand, all instances of gift giving, hospitality, and forgiveness have meaning only in relation to the pure or unconditional concept. Moreover—and this is crucial to Derrida—only unconditional or infinite gift giving, hospitality, or forgiveness can make sense of the concepts of gift, hospitality, and forgiveness. The condition of being unconditional refuses the logic of the *as such* as the logic of predication. We cannot with any certainty say that S is P, that forgiveness is such and such. To do so is to give conditions. Nonetheless, we name these concepts and hold ourselves to them. Given that these concepts themselves are always already mediated by their names, they must be worthy of them. To be worthy is an impossible ethical challenge, particularly since the meaning of the name is constantly deferred into the future. The call of hyperbolic ethics is to be hospitable and giving to others, even though life necessitates eating some of them. In *Rogues,* Derrida summarizes this paradoxical consequence of his attempt to articulate what it means for a concept to be unconditional: "Only an unconditional hospitality can give meaning and practical rationality to a concept of hospitality. Unconditional hospitality exceeds juridical, political, or economic calculation. But no thing and no one happens or arrives without it" (2005, 149).[30]

As it plays in Derrida's latest work, the dynamic of purity and contamination seems to issue from this impossible relationship between the unconditional and the conditioned with regard to ethics. How can we inscribe the unconditional or infinite in the conditioned and finite? Derrida suggests that we can hope to approach our ideals, on the one hand, only by constantly acknowledging the impossibility of this task while, on the other hand, constantly recognizing that all our attempts are contaminated. The acknowledgment of impossibility or contamination should not lead to quietude or despair but to a renewed commitment to pure or hyperbolic ethics, to a recognition that our ethical obligations may be to others whom we do not yet or even cannot recognize. As I have argued elsewhere, this means that our ethical obligations are beyond recognition and that nevertheless we are still radically responsible for them.[31]

TrophoEthics: Nourishment or Trophy?

Returning to the metonymics of eating and nourishment may be illuminating at this point. Derrida suggests (2008, 3) that *thinking* begins at the limit of what we call man or animal, "when the animal looks at us" (*que l'animal nous regarde,* which also means that "the animal has been our concern"; 2008, 3). It is the encounter with an animal, not the Levinasian face-to-face encounter with another human being that presents us with the most radical ethical challenge. Throughout *The Animal,* Derrida refers to Genesis and the relationship between the animal and the Fall. It is noteworthy that Derrida interprets the role of the serpent as making man conscious of his nakedness and of good and evil rather than causing his Fall (see esp. 2008, 4, 16–20). (It is interesting in this regard that when asked whether animals have faces, Levinas gives the example of a snake.) When we see ourselves through the eyes of an animal, we see ourselves for the first time and, in a sense, from then on, take it out on the animals. Derrida puts pressure on this liminal experience in relation to the animal (the shame he says he feels when standing before his cat naked) and on the limit between man and animal. He sees himself as a thinker of limits and calls his project a *limitrophy* (2008, 29). He insists that his project is not to erase limits but to multiply them. He does not want to collapse man into animal, or vice versa, because doing so would mean disavowing the differences between them. On the contrary, he wants to multiply the differences between them. In sum, his problem with the categories of man and animal is not that they cannot be distinguished from each other but that they disavow almost infinite numbers of other distinctions among life-forms. In calling his project a limitrophy, he draws out the etymological associations of the word *trophe,* which takes us back to eating:

In the semantics of *trephō, trophē,* or *trophos,* we should be able to find everything we need to speak about what we should be speaking about . . . feeding, food, nursing, breeding, offspring, care and keeping of animals, training, upbringing, culture, living and allowing to live by giving to live, be fed, and grown, autobiographically. *Limitrophy* is therefore my subject. Not just because it will concern what sprouts or grows at the limit, around the limit, by maintaining the limit, but also what *feeds the limit,* generates it, raises it, and complicates it. Everything I'll say will consist, certainly not in effacing the limit, but in multiplying its figures, in complicating, thickening, and delinearizing, folding, and dividing the line precisely by making it increase and multiply. (2008, 29)

Derrida goes on to point out that "the first literal sense of trepho" is "to transform by thickening, for example, in curdling milk" (2008, 29). We have come full circle and then back to Rousseau's curdled milk, which is not far off the mark because for him it is the combination of fluid and curds that makes milk most nutritious. The fluidity of milk alone does not nourish as much as when it becomes semisolid, in between a liquid and a solid, thickened. Ultimately it is this borderline substance moving between fluid and solid that Rousseau finds the most satisfying, pure, wholesome, and nutritious. For him, the curds do not make the milk impure, contaminated, or unsavory; rather, they make it *trophe* in the sense of feeding and nourishing. We could say that in Derrida's limitrophy, paradoxically the purity demanded by hyperbolic ethics requires the curdling or thickening of frontiers, borders, or limits. This curdling leaves them in a liminal state between fluid and solid, which opens the border onto multiple forms beyond two defined as one side or the other of the limit.[32] Derrida seems to challenge the limits of solid borders, which appear in the history of philosophy as fixed, rigid, and pure in the name of pure fluidity, which is, of course, impossible. In the name of pure fluidity, Derrida continually points to the curds, those strange substances that cannot be properly classified as solid or liquid. Ironically perhaps, the "purest" forms turn out to be thickened or curdled, the in-between substances that are neither purely liquid nor purely solids, what Julia Kristeva might identify as the most abject of milk-like substances, the skin on top of warm fluid becoming ever so slightly solid. Derrida and Rousseau seem to share this preference for curds and curdling, Rousseau in his diet and Derrida in his concepts. In their own ways, both embrace the ambiguities of life even while maintaining notions of purity. While Rousseau finds purity in nature and the material realm of the senses, Derrida finds purity in concepts and the realm of words now become the very material of thinking.[33] Rousseau's romantic vision of the past before men were corrupted by culture provides a strangely harmonic counterpoint to Derrida's messianic dream of a future of words with new meanings—new ways of meaning—that can bring us closer to the pure gift of life curdled or thickened by its own inherent heterogeneity. Both endorse an ethics motivated by *trophe* or nourishment rather than *trophy* or conquest. For Derrida, however, the ambiguity and inseparability of the two is explicit, whereas it remains implicit for Rousseau. In a sense, Derrida spills the beans about what remains secret in Rousseau, namely, that nourishment is always at some level also conquest.

The double meaning of *trophe/trophy* may be instructive in our necessary (if ultimately impossible) attempts to distinguish eating well or good eating from devouring the other in poor taste. *Tropho, trophi,* and obsolete forms of *trophe* are associated with feeding and nutrition, whereas *trophy* is associated with the spoils of war or the hunt that have been made into monuments. Do we kill and eat the other for trophe and nourishment, or for trophy, sport, and triumph? Is our relationship with the other and with others nourishing, or is it a display of power and conquest? We can ask these questions on the literal level about hunting and killing animals or people and on the figurative level about assimilating speech and cultural conventions. Are some forms of assimilation wholesome and others merely for display? Rousseau distinguishes between hunting for sport and trophy from hunting for exercise and food. The former is unhealthy and leads to a sense of lordly power over the others that comes with property, while the latter is wholesome and healthy.[34] Derrida complicates—or, we might say, curdles—any neat distinction between the two by suggesting that there is always the danger of trophe becoming trophy, of nourishment becoming a monument to status or victory (think again of Rousseau's gourmand who eats not only because it tastes good but also to show his wealth and power). Hyperbolic ethics requires vigilance in continually asking how what feeds us becomes imbricated in relations of power and domination. Why do we have such an appetite for violence, war, and victory?[35] Why do we relish trophies as much as nourishment? Our appetite for these "manly virtues" may lead us to explore another concept at the intersection of ingestion and ethics that implies a distinction among different meanings or types of virtues. *Virtue* denotes moral or ethical uprightness and manliness or courage, as well as in its older sense, the power to affect bodies in beneficial, even medicinal ways. Mineral, plants, and animals can be beneficial in this sense. In this older sense, virtue, like trophe, implies health and nourishment, even healing. A virtuous relationship with others and the environment would be a healing one.

Derrida's hyperbolic ethics, however, would caution us not to draw this line between nourishment and triumph in a fixed or rigid way. To do so is to become reactionary rather than responsive and, moreover, to shirk an ethical responsibility to the radical openness and fluidity of all moral categories. In this sense, ethics provides a kind of corrective for morality. If morality divides the world into good and evil, then hyperbolic ethics demands that we constantly question that division and our own investment in it. Do we make such distinctions in order to foster nourishing and healthful relationships, or do we divide the world in order to conquer it and take others as trophies? In terms more familiar to recent discussions in ethics we might ask, Do we circumscribe differences to justify hierarchies and domination or to respect them and acknowledge their value?[36]

Returning to Derrida's problematic, however, forces us to ask how we can acknowledge the value of differences without assimilating them into an economy of exchange. As we have seen, he attempts to address this impossible situation with his homeopathic use of the concept of purity—pure giving, pure forgiveness, pure hospitality—as an antidote to discourses of purity that are used to justify hierarchies, domination, and the assimilation of differences into the same, as if a pure enough dose of the poison, so to speak, can make us more tolerant of foreign bodies.[37] This homeopathic purity operates according to a different logic from what Derrida calls autoimmunity. Autoimmunity, as he describes it, is an attempt to protect oneself from the poison/remedy by rejecting a part of oneself.

The suicidal tendencies of recent war and terrorism are examples of the social body turning against itself.[38] As Derrida points out, the unity and identity of the social body feed off of those very others it rejects; it both secretes its own poison and feeds off it.[39] It is purification as genocide, ethnic cleansing, and apartheid. Ingesting this poison is deadly because it is another way of excising it, only now as the constitutive outside. I am arguing that Derrida's homeopathic purity works in reverse. It is a dose of purity that works as an antidote to the autoimmunity through which we would kill the other even if it meant killing ourselves. The border between remedy and poison is a thickened, delinearized border, one that cannot be easily parsed (cf. Derrida 2008, 29). In *Rogues,* Derrida says,

If an event worthy of its name is to arrive or happen, it must, beyond all mastery, affect a passivity. It must touch an exposed vulnerability, one without absolute immunity, without indemnity; it must touch this vulnerability in its finitude and in a nonhorizonal fashion. There where it is not yet or is already no longer possible to face or face up to the unforesee-ability of the other. In this regard, autoimmunity is not an absolute ill or evil. It enables an exposure to the other, to what and to who comes—which means that it must remain incalculable. Without autoimmunity, with absolute immunity, nothing would ever happen or arrive; we would no longer wait, await, or expect, no longer expect one another, or expect any event. (2005, 152)

Autoimmunity is the body turning against itself—the catastrophe of the body— motivated by an instinct to save itself that can be deadly, even suicidal. At the same time, its own proper sense of itself feeds off the other defined as foreign body, virus, monster, or animal and thereby in a sense requires that it play host to its own "parasite." Discussing the "scapegoats" cast out of the city of Athens, Derrida remarks, "The representative of the outside is nonetheless constituted, regularly granted its place by the community, chosen, kept, fed, etc., in the very heart of the inside. These parasites were as a matter of course domesticated by the living organism that housed them at its expense" (1972, 133). In his excellent book on animality and human nature in Derrida's writings, Leonard Lawlor applies this logic to animals: "They [parasites] are part of the city's own body just as cats and dogs are. But this participation in and expulsion from the city's own body mean that the ceremony of the pharmakos is played out at the limit between inside and outside" (2007, 34). The animal plays the role of a pharmakos, both sacrificed for and constitutive of humanity; the animal is both inside and out. I argue that it is precisely this ambiguous status that makes the animal so abject and therefore threatening. Lawlor contends that in order to begin to separate the good pharmakon from its "evil twin," as he calls it, we need to sacrifice sacrifice.

In other words, we need to turn the sacrificial logic back on itself and give up our need for scapegoats and sacrificial lambs (human and animal).

Even though the border between remedy and poison is thick, we must continue to try to find a remedy, even one that requires taking a dose of poison. Derrida's purity may propose such a remedy—a homeopathic remedy—one in which purity involves admitting impurity. Once we "thicken" or "curdle" pure distinctions between self and other, man and animal, how can we continue to negotiate the precarious borders between trophe and trophy? Does a purity worthy of its name require the constant acknowledgment of its own impurity and contamination? Perhaps hyperbolic ethics is not so much distinguishing trophe or nourishment from trophies or conquests as acknowledging the impossibility of doing so in any fixed and rigid way. If this is the case, then hyperbolic ethics demands that we interrogate the ways in which Derrida's own invocation of the discourse of purity crosses the limit between trophe and trophy and lands us in another economy of the proper in which concepts conquer creatures as they are engaged in living together. Is the binary opposition man/animal replaced with the binary opposition concept/material or pure/contaminated? How can we prevent the animal, animality, and animals from falling on one side of this binary once it has been reintroduced? Derrida figures his concept of purity—or the pure concept—as purer than that of Rousseau or other philosophers who appeal to pure Nature or presence. But as Derrida repeatedly acknowledges, he cannot leave behind this tradition even as he questions it. Is there a sense in which in addition to nourishing the history of philosophy, Derrida is taking pleasure in conquering it as well (which in fact may be its preferred form of nourishment)? Does Derrida's feeding off the history of philosophy teach us to be troubled by all invocations of purity, whether conceptual or material? Does his limitrophy jostle any solid border between the conceptual and the material, in which case his appeal to purity must be homeopathically turned back on itself, so that it becomes its own catastrophe or overturning? Indeed, couldn't we say that the pure distinction between concept and matter, or pure and impure, is another symptom of the man/animal binary opposition? Perhaps this is what Derrida intends to show with his impure notion of purity and his invocations of a purity more pure than that of philosophers of purity. By showing how what philosophers have taken to be pure is actually mixed or contaminated by its opposite, Derrida curdles binary oppositions, especially that between man and animal.

Elsewhere, I argue that hyperbolic ethics requires a psychoanalytic supplement in order to be vigilant and radical enough that we continually question our unconscious motives and desires along with our conscious actions and beliefs.[40] Here, I propose that hyperbolic ethics requires that we continue to question our own investments in discourses of purity, trying to avoid any simple conquest of Derrida's thought in the triumphant moves common to philosophy. Rather, in the spirit of trophe, we thoughtfully assimilate the lessons of his work in the hope of feeding a robust ethical theory that speaks to the question of how to relate to others, including animals and other living creatures with whom we share the earth, in ways that nourish rather than conquer.

CHAPTER FIVE

Sexual Difference, Animal Difference

Derrida's Sexy Silkworm

The city of cats and the city of men exist one inside the other, but they
are not the same city.

—ITALO CALVINO

In their reading of the history of philosophy, feminists point out that "female,"
"woman," and "femininity" often fall on the side of the animal in the man/animal
divide, as the generic use of the word *man* suggests. From Plato through Hegel,
Freud, and beyond, women have been associated with Nature and instincts to
procreate, which place them in the vicinity of the animal realm. We could say
that since woman's alliance with the serpent in Genesis, Judeo-Christian traditions have remained suspicious of woman's proximity to animals. In this chapter,
following Derrida's *The Animal That Therefore I Am* (2008), I take a different tack
in tracing the origin of what is sometimes called "the war between the sexes."
Rather than separate woman from animal and align her with the other side of
the divide, whether it is man or human, I explore sexual difference from the side
of "the animal." In other words, rather than introduce sexual difference into the
history of philosophy or Western intellectual and cultural traditions by insisting
on splitting man or human into two sexes, as some feminist thinkers have done, I
propose thinking beyond the category *animal* to many different animals.

I question the age-old binary opposition between man and animal not as philosophers sometimes do by claiming that man is also an animal or that animals
are capable of suffering or intelligence but by questioning the very category of *the
animal* itself. This category groups a nearly infinite variety of living beings into
one concept measured in terms of man: animals are those creatures that are not
human, even though they may have little in common. By opening the concept
of *the animal,* we may also open the other pole of the binary, namely, man. If

animals are infinitely more diverse than the binary opposition between man and animal, then perhaps man is also more diverse than the binary. In this chapter, I am particularly concerned with the sexual difference(s) of "man." By considering the multitudes of animal sexes, sexualities, and reproductive practices, perhaps we can expand our ways of thinking about the sexes, sexualities, and reproductive practices of "man."

This project is a kind of thought experiment that may help us think beyond the sexual binary of man/woman. My argument is as follows: first, the man/animal binary erases differences among vast varieties of living creatures and among vast varieties of human cultures and individuals. Second, in Judeo-Christian myths and philosophies, the binary opposition between man and animal is intimately linked to the binary opposition between man and woman. Third, if we move beyond the overly general concept of animal to considerations of multiple species and even individuals, then we might be able to move beyond the concept of man to considerations of cultural and individual differences. Fourth, in terms of sexual difference specifically, if we consider various sexes, sexualities, and reproductive practices of animals, we might be able to reconsider the sexes, sexualities, and reproductive practices of humans beyond the tight-fitting binary of man/woman or homosexual/heterosexual. My thesis is that the binary oppositions man/animal and man/woman are so intimately linked that exploding the first has consequences for the second. Furthermore, my aim is to open the conceptual landscape to differences erased by these traditional binary oppositions. To this end, I use examples of worms or ants or monkeys, not to show that humans are like these creatures, or visa versa, but to challenge the conceptual framework that restricts us to thinking in binary terms that limit concepts to pairs, especially since these pairs so easily become oppositions, hierarchies, or enemies.

Derrida's latest work, *The Animal,* can help us imagine sexual difference beyond dualism. Throughout his work, he "deconstructs" binary oppositions in order to open philosophy and thought to incalculable multiplicity. This is why in his engagement with various philosophers, he challenges theories and rhetoric that reduce all differences to one or two dialectical relations among three terms. Finding resources in the history of philosophy itself, he questions the philosophical tendency to reduce and fix into manageable systems and categories that erase or disavow multiple differences. By putting Derrida's latest work on the animal in the context of some of his earlier work on sexual difference, an evolution of thought may emerge. By revisiting some of the most problematic aspects of his latest work, namely, his insistence on concepts (such as hospitality, forgiveness, and gifts) "worthy of their names," this chapter continues themes from my earlier analysis of homeopathic purity and attempts to provide a compelling interpretation of these notions (pure, worthy of its name) that, in Derrida's project, remain puzzling. Finally, applying Derrida's theory of the concept worthy of its name to the concept of difference may help open it to incalculable multiplicity. Like opening Pandora's box, prying open the man/animal binary may unleash as yet unimagined possibilities for pansexuality.

To set the stage for my investigation into Derrida's latest work in which he sees a connection between animal and sexual difference, I look back to some texts in which he takes up the question of sexual difference head-on or, as he might say, "frontally." The issue of sexual difference is a recurring theme throughout his work. Notably, Derrida's "deconstruction" of various philosophers, including Hegel, Nietzsche, and Heidegger, often revolve around the erasure or negation of sexual difference in their writings. For example, in *Glas,* Derrida challenges Hegel's dialectical logic, which operates through the famous triple movement from position to negation to overcoming and preserving the negative moment in the final synthesis. By demonstrating that when applied to sexual difference, the dialectical method makes woman the mere negation of man, a moment necessarily overcome by the final movement of the dialectic, which reasserts the privilege of man, Derrida calls into question Hegel's entire dialectical logic.[1] In his readings of Heidegger, Derrida challenges what he sees as a second traditional tactic with regard to sexual difference, neutralization, or erasure. Dasein is sexually neuter, and as Derrida points out, Heidegger avoids talking about sexual difference, even when confronted with it in the texts on which he comments (e.g., Nietzsche's).[2] If Hegel negates sexual difference and turns woman into man's opposite, Heidegger erases sexual difference by conceiving of a neutered or neutral Dasein. Derrida implies that the ontological/ontic distinction that grounds Heidegger's thinking can be maintained only through the erasure of sexual difference. Once Derrida resexualizes these texts, they can no longer maintain their centrifugal force.

Also in Derrida's critical reading of Heidegger's privileging of ontological difference over sexual difference, he sees another, subtler stance on the issue of the difference between the sexes. In "*Geschlecht:* Sexual Difference, Ontological Difference" (1991c) and in "*Geschlecht* II: Heidegger's Hand" (1987a), Derrida argues that on close reading, Heidegger does not erase either sexuality or even sexual difference per se but sexual difference conceived in terms of opposition. In other words, what Heidegger rejects is the tradition of turning difference into opposition, precisely the tradition that makes sexual difference into a war between the sexes.

Exploring various meanings of the German word that Heidegger uses, *Geschlecht,* Derrida traces a link among different kinds of differences, particularly the human/animal difference and the man/woman difference. In Derrida's analysis,

Geschlecht first names the historical race of man or humanity as different from the rest of living creatures. Next it names the tribes, stocks, or families within this human species, and at the same time, it names the difference between the sexes (Derrida 1987a, 186–87). In general (at least as Heidegger uses it), it names a splitting in two that sets the two sides apart and figures them as opposites or one as the negation of the other, making the duality essentially dissension, war, and violence.

The English word *difference* also carries these same denotations. *Difference* can mean "to make a distinction," "to mark a difference," "a difference perceived by the subject but not existent in the object," "a controversy," "dissimilarity," "nonagreement," "opposition," "dispute," and "quarrel," from estrangement to open hostility. The different meanings of the word *difference* led Derrida to ask: "How did difference get deposited into the two? Or again, if one insisted on consigning difference within dual opposition, how does multiplication get arrested in difference? And in sexual difference?" (1991c, 401). Derrida's project throughout his writings is to imagine *difference* differently because this too often deadly dualism breaks into a multiplication of differences or a difference "worthy of its name" that does not settle into two warring opposites.[3]

Derrida's analysis raises many more questions: Why are some types of difference unremarked? What are the ethics and politics of marking and remarking? Why is sexual difference marked and then reduced to a binary or primary difference between two? How is the distinction between two conceived as opposition or even war? Finally, how can we open the field to multiple uncountable differences and unlock the stranglehold of two warring opponents? Derrida's latest work suggests that looking to the binary man/animal may hold answers to some of these questions.

The "Gift" of Difference

Before we return to the man/animal opposition, it may be helpful to continue to explore some of Derrida's comments on sexual difference, starting with the relation between marked or remarked difference and what he calls the "gift." Derrida insists that ultimately the marking and remarking of sexual difference must remain fluid. In other words, the metaphysical question "what is it?" can be answered always only precariously and provisionally. He argues that in order to challenge the "notion of male firstness" of Western metaphysics, it is necessary to leave open all categories of sexual demarcation (cf. Derrida 1991a, 445).

Otherwise, we cannot escape the binary opposition in which either the male or the female takes priority and dominates over the other. The very marking of difference—the answer to the question "what is it?"—must be open to constant remarking, which means that on the level of metaphysics (and therefore also on the levels of ethics and politics), it remains ultimately "undecidable." We cannot know for certain the correct answer to the question "what is it?"; rather, we always can only speculate given the cultural tools available to us.

Derrida's work suggests that considering metaphysical questions as ultimately undecidable has the practical effect of forcing us to continually reevaluate what we know and how we act. So while the realms of politics and even ethics may require that we make decisions based on what we believe or imagine things to "be," we must be ready to revise not only those decisions but also what we believe and imagine. In this way, although undecidability is not synonymous with multiplicity, making it an operative principle gives rise to noncalculable diversity beyond binary oppositions.[4] In his later work, Derrida moves from insisting on undecidability to what he calls "hyperbolic ethics," which is motivated by concepts like the gift, hospitality, forgiveness, and democracy, concepts whose meaning and value are infinitely deferred to some (im)possible future that we imagine will be better (more ethical) than the past, what Derrida calls "democracy to come." This future meaning is related to past meanings in all their heterogeneity, which any careful etymology will help reveal. Derrida, following Lacan and Levinas, uses the future anterior tense, "what will have been." As Lacan might say, the past is summoned in language for the sake of the future. We can "discover" the future in the past, so to speak. We can recover an alternative meaning of difference other than opposition.

As we know, in his early work, Derrida developed the notion of *differánce* to convey operations of both differing and deferring conjured by the word *difference*. We could say that as it appears in his later work, the notion of "gift" "worthy of its name" is the evolution of *differánce* into hyperbolic ethics. The difference at the heart of the word *difference* itself is an instructive example of how future conceptions of difference might be informed by multiple meanings that have been left behind to facilitate turning difference into binary oppositions. Perhaps this is why when discussing the concept of "woman" and "femininity" in "Choreographies," Derrida says,

Such recognition [of phallogocentrism or the complicity of Western metaphysics with a notion of male firstness] should not make of either the truth value or femininity an object of knowledge (at stake are the norms of knowledge and knowledge as norm); still less should it make of them a place to inhabit, a home. It should rather permit the invention of an other inscription, one very old and very new, a displacement of bodies and places that is quite different. (1991a, 445)[5]

Like Heidegger and Nietzsche before him, Derrida looks to past meanings of words in order to find alternative futures for the concepts of giving, hospitality, forgiveness, democracy, and, most important to my purposes here, difference itself.

Although Derrida does not do so explicitly, it is instructive to apply his analysis of the gift (hospitality, forgiveness, etc.) to difference, specifically to sexual difference. As we have seen, throughout his work, Derrida maintains that the gift—a "true" or "pure" gift—cannot be given out of duty or from expectations; it cannot be given from a position of sovereignty within an economy of exchange.[6] What we usually think of as gifts are "contaminated" forms of true or pure giving, which cannot even be identified as such without falling into ruin as gifts.[7] So too, a *pure* hospitality or a *pure* forgiveness must be given without any expectations for reciprocation, outside any sort of economy of exchange—monetary, in kind, psychological, or otherwise—and without being "contaminated" by notions of sovereignty that turn giving, hospitality, or forgiveness into narcissistic power plays like "I am in a position to give this to you." Derrida invokes the quality of deferral inherent in these notions. In other words, as Levinas might say, there is always one more gift, invitation, or olive branch, to give.

In addition to the qualification "pure" (which I discussed at length in the last chapter), Derrida frequently uses the phrase "worthy of its name," as in hospitality or forgiveness "worthy of its name." This phrase adds both the dimension of value, dignity, or ethics—worthy—and the dimension of the name or word itself.[8]

Consider what it could mean to think along Derridian lines about the concept of difference itself; what would it mean to imagine difference *worthy of its name?* This question may seem odd, even out of place, in relation to Derrida's project until we consider that the erasure or negation of radical difference or alterity is precisely the operation that "contaminates" our everyday forms of gift giving, hospitality, and forgiveness. In several places Derrida explicitly discusses sexual difference in terms of the gift. For example, in "Women in the Beehive," he says,

If the gift is calculated, if you know what you are going to give to whom, if you know what you want to give, for what reason, to whom, in view of what, etc. there is no longer any gift. And in order for this chance to arise, it is necessary that there be no relation with consciousness, experience or the representation of sexual determination. When we speak here of sexual difference, we must distinguish between opposition and difference.

Opposition is two, opposition is man–woman. Difference on the other hand, can be an indefinite number of sexes and once there is sexual difference in its classical sense—an opposition of two—the arrangement is such that the gift is impossible. All that you can call "gift"—love, *jouissance*—is absolutely forbidden, is forbidden by the dual opposition. . . . This does not mean that there is the gift only beyond sexuality but that the gift is beyond sexual duality. (1990, 123)

From this passage, we learn that the gift cannot be calculated, self-conscious, represented, marked, or remarked. Love and joy, like the gift or as forms of gifts, are also beyond any economy of exchange, including symbolic exchange or language. Let's leave aside for the moment that this radical ethical "idealism" seems to set up an opposition between two realms, the realm of infinite gift or responsibility, of pure concepts, and the realm of finite exchange, or contaminated actions.[9] Instead, let's follow the Derridian question of what difference *worthy of its name* is. It would have to be a difference that cannot be calculated, self-conscious, represented, marked, or remarked. In fact, it is the marking of sexual difference as two that leads Derrida to argue that binary or oppositional sexual difference is not true difference but the erasure or negation of one in favor of the other.

Derrida is not taking an Irigarayan path that would insist on the binary, the two, only without the opposition, erasure, or negation.[10] Irigaray contends that we have never actually had two because the "second sex" has always been subsumed into the one masculine sex, and therefore the fundamental project of our age is to think of sexual difference as two. But Derrida suggests that once we split sexuality or sex into two, we are already stuck at the level of a fixed binary, pair, or couple that does not allow for multiplicity. Indeed, fixing any number of calculable differences would have a similar effect. Although binaries more easily turn into oppositions or dialectics of negation, for example, man and not-man. A marked difference becomes a calculable, self-conscious, and exchangeable difference that undermines the possibility of any true encounter with another—what Derrida also calls an event (e.g., see Derrida 2005, 148). If this is the case, then it seems that only an unremarked difference leaves open the possibility of the gift or hospitality or forgiveness or what we might call difference "worthy of its name."

Derrida argues as much when speaking of various figures of unconditionality without sovereignty. In *Rogues,* for example, he describes the pure concept worthy of its name: "A gift without calculable exchange, a gift worthy of its name, would not even appear as such to the donor or donee without the risk of reconstituting, through phenomenality and thus through its phenomenology, a circle of economic reappropriation that would just as soon annul its event" (2005, 149).

If we apply this analysis to difference, the result is that we necessarily imagine a difference that would not appear as such, an unremarked difference.[11] In terms of sexual difference, most obviously this would mean that we cannot reduce sexual difference to anatomical differences or genitalia. But more than this, it means that physical or phenomenal differences remain unidentified in terms of sex. What makes a difference in terms of sex must remain an open question. Incalculable multiple sexual differences make any binary identification difficult to maintain. Sexual marks would no longer be seen as the property of any individual or group. Rather, as Derrida describes it in "Choreographies," we would have a "mobile of nonidentified sexual marks." There, he asks,

What if we were to reach … the area of a relationship to the other where the code of sexual marks would no longer be discriminating? The relationship would not be a-sexual, far from it, but would be sexual otherwise: beyond the binary difference that governs the decorum of all codes, beyond the opposition feminine–masculine, beyond bi-sexuality as well, beyond homosexuality and heterosexuality, which come to the same thing. As I dream of saving the chance that this question offers I would like to believe in the multiplicity of sexually marked voices. I would like to believe in the masses, this indeterminable number of blended voices, this mobile of nonidentified sexual marks whose choreography can carry, divide, multiply the body of each "individual," whether he be classified as "man" or "woman" according to the criteria of usage. (1991a, 455)

On a practical level, this way of thinking about difference presents us with twin problems: (1) being able to distinguish one individual or group from another and (2) being able to identify individuals with one another. Both these operations—differentiation and identification/generalization—are necessary to language systems. On a conceptual level, it should leave us wondering how we can distinguish unremarked difference from the erasure, disavowal, or negation of difference typical of Western philosophy. By insisting on unremarked or unmarked sexual difference, don't we risk disavowing sexual difference altogether? It might be helpful to consider that in *Rogues*, Derrida describes his insistence on the unconditionality of the incalculable as a useful lexicon that serves a pedagogical purpose in relation to traditional Western thought: "My recourse to the lexicon of *unconditionality* has proven useful to me because tradition and translation facilitate its being intelligible, indeed its *pedagogy*" (2005, 148, italics added). There he also states that this lexicon could one day be replaced by another that will "help us to say better what still remains to be said about these metonymic figures of the unconditional" (148). He also insists that "only an unconditional hospitality can give meaning and practical rationality to a concept of hospitality"

(149). The notions of the "unconditional," the "pure," the "incalculable," and the concept "worthy of its name" teach us that our practical applications are always conditioned by social and political economies that disavow and marginalize even when they embrace differences. In other words, we cannot always easily distinguish giving from taking. They also teach us that hyperbolic ethics demands that we continue to measure our everyday practices in terms of these immeasurable conceptions of gift, hospitality, forgiveness, and difference. If we do not hold ourselves to this impossible and infinitely deferred "standard," we risk the dogmatism and fixity of ideology that often leads to war and violence. It is this hyperbolic aspect of unconditional ethics that makes it pedagogical; our ethical ideal is like a hyperbola that necessarily remains out of reach and, for that very reason, can continue to guide our actions.[12] The ideal is an empty set or empty concept that summons its meanings from the past for the sake of the future.

The implications of what Derrida describes as hyperbolic ethics for conceiving of an ethics of difference are immense. First, an ethics of difference cannot be fixed into a set system of discernable characteristics. Instead, what counts as different or distinct must remain an open question. Second, for that reason, this ethics cannot begin with the couple, pair, or binary. Neither can it begin with one or three, other numbers favored by philosophers. The binary, however, is especially prone to becoming opposition because it easily leads to giving priority of one pole of the binary over the other; the history of philosophy bears this out insofar as dualisms and binaries of all sorts have become hierarchies that privilege one over the other. In terms of sex, thinking of difference as an open rather than closed system means imaging the possibilities of multiple sexes, sexualities, and even multiple reproductive practices.

If we begin to ask why one characteristic determines the difference between beings, and furthermore how that characteristic becomes privileged, the floodgate may open onto all sorts of other differences that could come to play in sexual difference. Certainly advances in reproductive technologies—including cloning and so-called test-tube babies—along with research on intersex infants and the regime of male/female binaries in medical science, indicate that our multifarious realities do not easily fit into the model of the heterosexual couple defined as one man and one woman. In addition, alternative sexualities articulated through transgender and transsexuality movements suggest that real bodies are already breaking out of the claustrophobic categories of male/female or man/woman.[13] Family structures that most of the time do not mirror the ideal nuclear family, such as single-parent, woman-headed households, multigenerational, and gay or lesbian families, also indicate that our practices are much more diverse than traditional and restrictive concepts of sex and sexuality. My claim is that challenging the man/animal binary from the side of the animal can help explode the man/woman binary. Perhaps then our changing conceptual life can begin to catch up to our changing embodied life as diverse beings living among infinite variation in multitudes of creatures.

Animal Pedagogy

Derrida's latest work on *the animal* also has a hyperbolic pedagogical dimension, particularly in relation to multiplying sexual differences. One of the central arguments of *The Animal* is that the concept or name *animal* is an abomination, a "chimera," because it defines all living creatures in relation to man: animals are those creatures who are not human. In so doing, it erases vast, even infinite, differences between species and individuals. The concept *animal* operates as the negation of "man," so that the negation of that negation—we are not mere animals—quickly leads to the notion that human beings are superior to animals. Some of those creatures have more in common with human beings than they do with other animals, and taken as a whole, what we call the animal kingdom is populated with creatures that overall may have less in common rather than more. Derrida's criticisms revolve around various philosophers' use of "the animal," with the definitive article and singular noun that brands or marks all animals as one and also marks them as different from man. Within these philosophies, it is against this animal other that man sets himself apart as human (and against woman that he sets himself apart as man). Moreover, the two binaries man/animal and man/woman are intimately connected in the history of Judeo-Christian thought.

As we have seen, in remarks on sexual difference in "Choreographies" and elsewhere, Derrida challenges traditional philosophies that negate or erase the feminine and points to places in which philosophers introduce the possibility of thinking of sexual difference in other ways. In various texts, however, he shows that their limited attempts to acknowledge sexual difference continues to be based on an absolute limit between man and animal that perpetuates oppositional thinking that either negates or erases animal difference(s). When they do not set up man against woman, they set up man against the animal. In other words, if woman does not serve as man's other in these myths of origin, then the animal does. Derrida finds in those very philosophers who might be seen to open philosophy to its "others" a countermovement that continually forecloses the very possibilities for openness. In regard to sexual difference and animal difference, one is played off the other so that opening one is premised on closing the other. In this regard, we may say that philosophy is taking two steps forward and one step back. So while we may follow their lead up to a point, we must also be aware that philosophy's dance can be a dangerous one for its partners.

For example, recall Derrida's suggestion that Heidegger's neuter Dasein is presented as an antidote to thinking of sexual difference in oppositional terms. Derrida argues that on close reading, what Heidegger erases is not sexuality or even sexual difference per se but sexual difference conceived in terms of opposition (see Derrida 1987a and 1991a). In other words, Heidegger rejects the tradition of turning difference into opposition, precisely the tradition that makes sexual difference into a war between the sexes. Derrida argues, however, that even while Heidegger posits Dasein as preceding binary opposition, he places "an absolute oppositional limit" between Dasein and animals, which, like all oppositions, "effaces the differences and leads back, following the most resistant metaphysico-dialectic tradition, to the homogeneous" (1987a, 173–74). Dasein is not just different from other animals, it is ontologically different, specifically because it has hands for taking and giving. Derrida concludes: "Man's hand then will be a thing apart not as separable organ but because it is different, dissimilar from all prehensile organs (paws, claws, talons); man's hand is far from these in an infinite way through the abyss of being" (1987a, 174). The difference is an ontological difference, not a mere ontic one. The very distinction between ontic and ontological, foundational to Heidegger's thought, is presupposed and supported by the absolute limit drawn between man and animal, a limit that Derrida contends is based on supposition rather than evidence. Heidegger maintains that Dasein is distinctive in that it can grasp in a way that gives and not merely takes, but Derrida challenges the assumption that only humans give, saying, "Nothing is less assured than the distinction between giving and taking" (1987a, 176). Indeed, for Derrida ethics requires that we unceasingly question that very distinction. When is a gift really a gift? In what ways do we take by giving?

As he does with Heidegger, Derrida also sees a moment in Levinas's writings that subverts the priority of man over woman, but it, too, is still based on the opposition between man and animal. For example, Derrida points out that Levinas reads the Genesis myth of origin as presenting a neuter earth creature first and sexual difference second, after a rib is taken from the first creature to create a second (see 1991a, 450). Derrida concludes: "It is not feminine sexuality that would be second but only the relationship to sexual difference. At the origin, on this side of and therefore beyond any sexual mark, there was humanity in general" (1991a, 450). Derrida quickly points out that even this view risks privileging the masculine as first and dominant.

In *The Animal*, however, he engages Levinas on a different score, one that demonstrates how Levinas's ethical relation retains a form of "humanism" that is maintained against animal difference. Levinas describes the face-to-face encounter that commands us to be ethical as uniquely human, and when asked in an interview whether or not an animal has a face, he says that he cannot respond to this question (Levinas 1986, 169). Derrida works Levinas's nonresponse to the question in relation to a traditional division between man and animals, namely, that man can respond, whereas animals can merely react (see 2008, 122–24). Earlier in *The Animal,* Derrida showed that for Descartes, the distinction is even more specific: man can respond to questions but animals cannot. So, regarding man's distinctive ability to respond to questions, what does it mean when Levinas says that he cannot answer the question? Derrida follows this track in order to challenge Levinas's latent humanism supposing man's unique possession of the face and therefore of ethics. Derrida suggests that both these nondialectical, nonhumanist, nonoppositional thinkers, Heidegger and Levinas, in the very moments when their thinking promises to take us beyond the sexual binary, fall back into a dialectical logic of opposition, human versus animal. At the moment when their philosophies offer the possibility of a nondialectical relationship of difference that is not reduced to opposition or even to binary, they support their openness to sexual difference with close mindedness in terms of animal difference. In other words, within these philosophies, sexual difference is avowed only if animal differences are disavowed through the general and fixed category of *animal.* Releasing us from one binary trades on reinstating the other.

Naming the Animals, or the fall Before The Fall

In *The Animal,* Derrida traces the connection between sexual difference and animal difference through various aspects of Judeo-Christian thought. Like Levinas, he returns to the Genesis myth of creation, but Derrida's concern is with man's naming the animals. He argues that in the first version of the two creation stories in Genesis, Adam, who is not yet gendered and whose rib has not yet been taken to make woman, does not name the animals. It is in the second version of the creation myth that Adam both names the animals and is given woman as his companion. It is noteworthy that Adam needs a companion only because none of the other animals can offer him company or a proper mate—they are not good enough for him.[14] His sovereignty and dominion over the animals leave him lonely and with no companion worthy of his stature among the animals. Derrida associates Adam's sovereignty with his loneliness, with his "God-given" right to name the animals, over whom he presides. It also is noteworthy (something Derrida does not point out) that in this second version of the story, Adam names woman *in the same way* that he names the other animals. Indeed, he names her twice: first he calls her "woman," and after they eat from the tree of knowledge, he calls her "Eve" (see Genesis 2:23 and 3:20). His providence to name her is evidence of his dominion over her, akin to his dominion over animals.

Derrida argues that the naming of animals, particularly the word or name *animal* itself, is a type of fall before the Fall. He calls it a "contretemps," a notion that plays on a sense of embarrassment as well as a time between or before time. He suggests that naming marks and thereby produces both animal difference and sexual difference and that the marking and remarking of these differences is precisely the forbidden knowledge that leads to Adam's and Eve's expulsion from paradise. If this is the case, however, then there is a kind of fall before the Fall, in that naming marks the knowledge of man's difference, particularly his nakedness, which distinguishes him from the animals and makes him aware of his sex and his anatomical differences from woman. In other words, it sets up the possibility of the serpent's leading both man and woman to the knowledge that they are naked in a way that other animals are not, that to be naked in this way is to be ashamed, and especially that their genitalia are different, which they feel compelled to cover with fig leaves (see Genesis 3:7). Both animal and sexual difference arrive at the same time as shame, heralded first by the sovereign operation of naming and next by the serpent. Man learns that unlike other animals, he marks and remarks his territory with words or names. An animal, the snake, "teaches" man that he is distinct from other animals and from woman. This knowledge of his difference ushers in everything that we associate with humanity, from clothing and culture to time itself. Thus, in the Judeo-Christian tradition, animal difference and sexual difference are intimately associated from the beginning of time.

Derrida's Pussycat

Derrida exploits this connection throughout *The Animal,* most notably in the scene with his pussycat, who, he remarks, is a female cat and in front of whom he is ashamed of being naked. Again, this scene could be read as an implicit reference to Levinas, for whom there is a face-to-face encounter only between humans that renders them "naked" or "nude" in front of the other. The "nudity" of the face plays a significant role in Levinas's ethics of the face-to-face relationship and the obligations it entails (obligations that he denies to animals). This scene marks a complicated maneuver in Derrida's thinking about *the animal.* First, he describes a kind of face-to-face encounter with an animal, a cat, whom he says is looking at his naked sex.[15] Next, he inscribes this event with sexuality and sexual difference which, he claims, have been denied to animals. Here he is rebuking both the animal difference and the sexual difference (although in the problematic way of attributing it now to a cat rather than to a woman). He describes the shame he feels in front of his female cat, which shatters assumptions about the binaries man/animal and man/woman. He plays on this notion of shame as one distinctive mark of humanity, since only humans are ashamed of being nude. In this case, though, he is ashamed in front of a cat, to whom he attributes a gaze that makes him aware of his nudity and his sex (as the snake in Genesis did with Adam) but also makes him ashamed of the word *animal* because it separates man from all other creatures, whose differences are thereby denied. Derrida further complicates the issue of sexual difference by calling the cat a *chat/chatte* (e.g., 2006, 30), a neologism that is translated as "pussycat" (with its obvious suggestion of slang names for women's genitals) but that literally means male/female cat or boy/girl cat. Like Adam before the creation of woman, this cat's gender is ambiguous or not yet marked as one or the other gender. It is "a cat of one *or* the other sex, or of one *and* the other sex" (Derrida 2008, 11).

Derrida insists that his is a real cat and not a metaphorical or figurative cat, that it is a being whom he can encounter through shared bodily mortal existence:

If I say "it is a real cat" that sees me naked, this is in order to mark its unsubstitutable singularity. When it responds in its name [*Quand il répond à son nom* (2006, 26) also can mean "when it responds to its name"] (whatever "respond" means, and that will be our question), it doesn't do so as the exemplar of a species called "cat," even less so of an "animal" genus or kingdom. It is true that I identify it as a male or female cat. But even before that identification, it comes to me as *this* irreplaceable living being that one day enters my space, into this place where it can encounter me, see me, even see me naked. Nothing can ever rob me of the certainty that what we have here is an existence that refuses to be conceptualized. (2008, 9, italics in original)[16]

What he is trying to describe is a "naked" encounter with another creature before or beyond concepts and their names, including male or female. Implicitly challenging Levinas, Derrida also implies, however, that this nakedness may be impossible—how do we encounter one another without clothing ourselves, even cats, in words? For example, doesn't the requirement that an encounter is face-to-face or "frontal" already privilege human interaction (which relies more on sight—specifically sight resulting from eyes in the front of the head—than smell) over animal interaction? (cf. Derrida 2002, 392). Moreover, Derrida observes that perhaps nudity, like pure hospitality or forgiveness, should remain untenable . . . might we say nudity, worthy of its name? (2008, 50; 2006, 76).

Throughout his writing, Derrida complicates the connection among onto-logical difference, animal difference, and sexual difference in ways that do not allow identifying their logical or chronological primacy. Indeed, he insists on an intimate association between animal difference and sexual difference that suggests that the man/animal binary and the sex binary are mutually constitutive and that by opening animal differences to the vast varieties of animals, we might also open sexual differences to varieties of sexes, sexualities, and genders.

In *The Animal,* Derrida describes a series of metonymical associations between sexual difference and animal difference through which hierarchies are maintained that privilege man over animal and over woman. These metonymies revolve around the notion that man is distinct from animals in his upright posture or erect stance, which recalls man's erection as being what distinguishes him from woman. Although Derrida does not mention Johann Herder, recall that Herder is one of the proponents of the view that man is unique in his erection:

The posture of man is upright; in this he is unique upon earth. Admittedly, the bear has a broad foot and fights in an erect position, and apes and pygmies sometimes run or walk upright. Yet only man is naturally and continuously in the erect position. . . . No nation upon earth has been found walking on all fours. . . . We cannot but note with a sense of wonder the peculiar organization of powers, deriving from the erect posture of man by which, and by which alone, he became what he is: man. (Herder 1969, 255–57).

The metonymy between erect posture and erect phallus leads Derrida to con-clude that the modesty or shame (the French word *pudeur* can mean both "mod-esty" and "shame") that separates man from animals is concentrated on man's genitals as the distinctive trait that supposedly gives him the right to dominate animals and women. His physical uprightness in his stance and his sex give him the moral right to dominate. Derrida argues that this distinctive trait is insepa-rable from man's sovereignty as it gives him the right to rule over animals. The metonymy breaks down, however, when we consider that man's erection (like the so-called instinctive reactions of animals) cannot be feinted or dissimulated:

My hypothesis is that the criterion in force, the distinctive trait, is inseparable from the experience of holding oneself upright, of uprightness [*droiture*] as erection in general in the process of hominization. Within a general phenomenon of erection as passage to the straight verticality of the upright stance distinguishing the human from other mam-mals, one would still have to distinguish sexual erection from being-standing, and espe-cially to distinguish in turn the alternating rhythm of erection and detumescence that the male is unable to dissimulate in the face-to-face of copulation (another overwhelmingly distinctive trait of human coupling). Wherever this difference in desire can no longer rely on spontaneous pretense or natural dissimulation, modesty is properly concentrated, that is to say, by arresting or concentrating the metonymy, on the phallic zone. (2008, 61)

The question of whether or not an animal can pretend or dissimulate is at the center of Derrida's debate with Lacan in *The Animal*. Lacan argues that while animals can pretend (e.g., play dead), they cannot cover their tracks or feint a feint; unlike humans, they can't pretend to pretend or engage in second-order lying. This is because they are capable only of reactions and not responses; their pretense is a reaction to their environment. Derrida challenges the distinction between reaction and response, maintaining that we cannot so easily distinguish between the two, even in humans. What we take to be human response also contains elements of reaction. Derrida indicates that man's erection is just as much a reaction as any animal's, in that it cannot be faked. Given the attention to enabling and maintaining erections and the various "artificial" means of doing so, however, we might wonder why Derrida holds on to the phallus as the place where man cannot escape his animal nature. His invocation of the phallic zone as the concentration and end point of the metonymy between the posture that distinguishes man from animals and man's sex, along with the modesty and shame attached to the genitals and thereby metonymically to the very distinction between man and animal, not to mention the slippage between standing upright and moral rights, blurs the boundaries between nature and culture. Or according to Derrida, we should say that it multiplies the borders.

Since Freud, the essential distinction between man and animal turns on another twist of the phallic zone, castration. In orthodox psychoanalytic theory, man's psyche is formed through the circuit of desire that revolves around the Oedipal complex, in which it is the fear of castration that carries the weight of the law that separates humans from animals. Out of fear of punishment, man gives up his incestuous impulses, but animals do not. Put in another way, man is cut off from the source of satisfaction, which must be continually displaced and deferred. The unfulfillable nature of desire constitutes man as human. In this scenario (which takes us back at least to Hegel if not all the way back to the ancient Greeks), man's desire makes him distinct from animals, who have instinctual needs but not desires. Thus, man's sense of lack motivates everything that we take to be his unique ability for progress and self-improvement. Paradoxically, then, what the animal lacks that man possesses is lack itself.

Discussing various instantiations of this paradoxical position, Derrida challenges the reasoning through which it is a fault or failing in man, a lack, that gives him the right to dominate animals:

It is paradoxically on the basis of a fault or failing in man that the latter will be made a subject who is master of nature and of the animal. From within the pit of that lack, an eminent lack, a quite different lack from that he assigns to the animal, man installs or claims in a single stroke *his property* (the peculiarity [*le proper*] of a man whose property it even is not to have anything that is proper to him) and his *superiority* over what is called animal life. This latter superiority, infinite and par excellence, has as its property the fact of being at one and the same time *unconditional* and *sacrificial.* (2008, 20)

In this twisted logic, animals are sacrificed both as proof of man's superiority over them and as penance for man's fault or lack. In this thinking, man is unique among animals because only he can sin; only he can be evil; only he can lie; and paradoxically, only he can be beastly. As we have seen, one of man's greatest bestialities is the invention and use of the word *animal,* "a word that men have given themselves the right to give" (Derrida 2008, 32). Derrida concludes,

This agreement concerning philosophical sense and common sense that allows one to speak blithely of the Animal in the general singular is perhaps one of the greatest, and most symptomatic asinanities of those who call themselves humans. . . . One cannot speak— moreover, it has never been done—of the *bêtise* or bestiality of an animal. It would be an anthropomorphic projection of something that remains the preserve of man, as the single assurance finally, and the single risk, of what is "proper to man." (2008, 41)

Derrida argues that philosophers continue to use this nonsensical general singular category to corral all living creatures without regard for the most basic differences, especially including sexual differences. Or as Derrida says, the great philosophers continue to use "an animal whose sexuality is as a matter of principle left undifferentiated" (2008, 40).

The Sex of Insects and Sex to Come

In the history of philosophy, the word *animal* stands for all living creatures, whether they are cats, birds, or barnacles and whether they are male or female. It is not just that philosophers haven't been concerned whether an animal is a cat or dog or a male or female. Moreover, they haven't thought about the different sexualities of animals that might take us beyond the male/female sexual binary itself. Considering the various sexualities, sexes, and modes of sex among different animal species, not to mention the different individuals within species, might teach us to appreciate the multitude of sexualities and sexual differences beyond two (which so easily degenerates into war and domination). Insects and other animals, whose sex is not easily determined, categorized, or marked, especially fascinate Derrida.

The Animal, for example, houses several monotremic (*mono-trema:* "one-holed") animals. First there is the sexy little silkworm, whose "milk become thread" is "the extruded saliva of a very fine sperm, shiny, gleaming, the miracle of a female ejaculation . . . the secret of a marvel . . . at the infinite distance of the animal, of this little innocent member, so foreign yet so close in its incalculable distance" (Derrida 2008, 36). Quoting his own earlier text, "A Silkworm of One's Own," Derrida describes the worm as beyond the sexual binary male/female, an image that becomes the basis of a fantasy of a multiple sex of "one's own": "the spinning of its filiation, sons or daughters—beyond any sexual difference or rather any duality of the sexes, and even beyond any coupling. In the beginning, there was the worm that was and was not a sex" (2008, 36).

As an aside, Derrida's silkworm reminds me of a recent article on ocean worms that have evolved at least eighteen different ways to reproduce:

Some are pinhead-size, while certain ribbon worms stretch nearly 200 feet—the longest animals on Earth. Some filter-feed, some stalk their prey, some eat their kin, and they have evolved at least 18 different ways to reproduce, including breaking into pieces. . . . The spiny ancestors of today's marine worms were among the first sea animals more than 500 million years ago. Scientists can only guess at the number of species—estimated range from 25,000 to millions. (Jennifer Holland 2007, 122)

Although reproduction and sex are not synonymous, these thousands of worms with their thousands of lifestyles do start the imaginative juices flowing. Derrida's discussion of animal sex, or animal's sexes, seems intended to spark imagining about differences, especially sexual differences, rather than offer a comparative analysis of reproductive behaviors. Another recent *National Geographic* article suggests that in some areas, damselflies may be evolving so that they can reproduce without males:

For damselflies the world over, it's virtually the same old story: Males hang out by the watering hole, defending their territory, waiting to pounce on the first female to fly by. Then came the startling report of an all-female damselfly population in the Azores, which arrived in the wake of a study on Fijian species in which females appeared to be on the prowl for mates. "I thought I knew everything about damselflies," says Carleton University biologist Tom Sherratt. "No one had ever seen sex-role reversal before.". . . Instead of a damselfly dominatrix, they found that adult males were just extremely rare. . . . Juvenile males are being killed en masse by a fungal parasite, leaving the females to fend for themselves—perhaps the first step to not needing the males at all. (Bourne 2007, 23)

In a world where there are millions of species of worms with dozens of modes of reproducing and where damselflies can change sex or reproduce their "better half," what happens to our traditional notions of male and female, or binary sex?

Returning to Derrida's bestiary in *The Animal,* the second monotreme he mentions is associated with the Chimera, a mythical, flame-spitting monster with the head of a lion, the body of a goat, and the tail of a dragon. This animal conglomerate becomes an icon for the monstrousness of the word *animal* itself, a word that mixes so many varieties into one. Just as the chimera is an illusion, so too is the general category *animal.* With the monotreme, however, the condensation of various bodily functions into one hole becomes fascinating to Derrida, who points out that Chimera is the offspring of Echidne, the name of both a serpent and a monotremic mammal: "This mammal lays eggs, something quite rare. Here we have an oviparous mammal that is also an insectivore and a monotreme. It only has one hole (mono-trema) for all the necessary purposes, urinary tract, rectum, and genitals" (2008, 41–42).

As Derrida reminds us in *The Animal,* his writings are full of various animals with whom he identifies and in whose names he sometimes signs. There are worms, monkeys, horses, hedgehogs, squirrels, sheep, ass, wolves, birds, snakes, fish, ants, sponges, and even viruses. His writings are a regular zoo, and his interest in animals often activates his interest in sex. In "Fourmis," for example, he is once again fascinated by the sex of insects when he muses on how the sex of little black ants defies identification; there, ants embody the thousands of possibilities of reading, of interpreting, and of sexes (1994, 72). Besides animals making him wonder about sex, sexual difference apparently incites his bestiary as well. As he also reminds us,

I note in passing that almost all these animals are welcomed, in a more and more deliberate manner, on the threshold of sexual difference. More precisely, of sexual differences, that is to say, what for the most part is kept under wraps in almost all of the grand philosophical-type treatises on the animality of the animal. This opening, on the threshold of sexual differences, was the very track left by the hedgehog and the (agrammatically) masculine ant, but more than that, in the most recent text, where it is precisely a matter of nakedness, with and without a veil, the thinking of what is naked, as it is said, like a worm. (2008, 36; translator David Wills points out that in English we might say "naked as a jay bird," 165)

In one sense, the connection between sexual difference and animals in Derrida's work exploits the age-old association between woman and animal. Rather than say that women are like animals, however, Derrida intimates that sexual difference is like animal difference or, more precisely, that sexual differences are like animal differences. Derrida is not trying to blur the boundary between animals and women, or animal and humans, but to multiply the differences. In answer to a question raised by David Wood, Derrida insisted,

I am not advocating the *blurring* of differences. On the contrary, I am trying to explain how drawing an oppositional limit *itself* blurs the differences, the difference and the differences, not only between man and animal, but among animal societies—there are an infinite number of animal societies, and, within the animal societies and within human society itself, so many differences. (Derrida 1987b, 183, italics in original)

The implication of this multiplication of differences is that a menagerie of animals, with sexualities intact, appears on the threshold of sexual difference in order to show that just as there is a multitude of animals, there is a multitude of sexes and sexualities. This display of animal sex is not just intended to demonstrate that all animals cannot be divided into the binary couple male/female. In addition, it opens our imaginations to the possibility of alternative sexes and sexualities. The appearance of monkeys, hedgehogs, silkworms, and ants on the threshold of sexual difference serves the pedagogical function of allowing us to see and to imagine alternatives to the limited and claustrophobic binary that reduces sex to a war between two. Returning to the man/animal binary from the side of the animals, can "teach" us that just as there are vast varieties of animal species and animal sexes, there are vast varieties of human animals and human sexes. By opening the man/animal binary, we also open the man/woman binary. And in the exploration of nearly infinite varieties of animals and of sexes, we can begin to imagine an ethics of differences that takes us beyond binaries, dualisms, or couples that so easily degenerate into opposition, hierarchy, struggle for recognition, and war.

At the same time, however, this "thought experiment" raises the question of the implications for thinking through an ethics of differences, since by the end of this century, half of all species on earth will be extinct.[17] If we can be inspired to think of ethics beyond the face-to-face encounter, beyond two, even beyond the ideal of mutual recognition and toward an ethics of infinite differences valuable for an irreconcilability that cannot be figured as opposition or negation, then we will have to reevaluate both sexual differences and animal differences in view of an ethics of bio-diversity and evolution rather than of reduction and extinction. Perhaps difference "worthy of its name" would designate differences that multiply themselves through innumerable means so that they cannot devolve into opposition or fixity or calculation of any kind. This incalculable multiplicity would not be the simple addition of new types to the old in a series of one-plus-one-plus-one; they would be neither interchangeable nor equivalent. Rather, they would require a new lexicon that would mark and remark their differences without degenerating into calculable systems of hierarchy and domination. These would be differences that appear as gifts, differences that betoken sex(es) to come.

PART FOUR

It's Our Fault

CHAPTER SIX

The Beaver's Struggle with Species-Being

De Beauvoir and the Praying Mantis

Thou hast doves' eyes . . .
Thy hair is a flock of goats . . .
Thy teeth are like a flock of sheep that are shorn . . .
Thy two breasts are like two young roes . . .

—SONG OF SONGS, QUOTED IN DE BEAUVOIR, *THE SECOND SEX*

The most often quoted line from Simone de Beauvoir's *The Second Sex* is "One is not born, but rather becomes a woman" (1949b, 267).[1] Even though de Beauvoir insists that "no biological, psychological, or economic fate determines the figure that the human female presents in society; it is civilization as a whole that produces *this creature,* intermediate between male and eunuch, which is described as feminine," "this creature" is most certainly born female (1949b, 267, italics added).[2] She opens the first part of her seminal work by pointing out that even though man is not ashamed of his animal nature, woman is made to be ashamed of hers. It is not, she claims, woman's supposed proximity to animals that ensures her status as the second sex but because she is reduced to her reproductive function:

The term "female" is derogatory not because it emphasizes woman's animality, but because it imprisons her in her sex; and if this sex seems to man to be contemptible and inimical even in harmless dumb animals, it is evidently because of the uneasy hostility stirred up in him by woman. (1949b, 3)

As it has been used in patriarchal literature, the term *female* is an insult to women and female animals alike. De Beauvoir believes that even female animals bear an unfair and unequal burden when compared with their male counterparts. This is not only because their lives are consumed with a greater share of reproduction but also because from "the human perspective," as de Beauvoir says, females are seen as physically and/or morally inferior to males, no matter what their species. The "second sex," then, applies to all animals, including humans. In the first part of her book, de Beauvoir attempts to vindicate females of all species! As we will see, however, animals play a central, if ambivalent role, in de Beauvoir's analysis of woman's oppression.

Even while she tries to redeem all female creatures, de Beauvoir puts animals in the service of raising woman from immanence to transcendence. Even while she implicitly challenges the man/animal opposition by considering the male/female opposition in all species, her arguments for woman's equality with man rests on a necessary inequality between woman and animal. Furthermore, she links woman's oppression to her natural reproductive functions that make her a "slave" to the species, which is not truly human but animal. All the while, she expresses her ambivalence toward woman, suggesting that she has more reasons to hide her animality than man does, particularly her animal odors associated with menstruation and childbirth.[3] This ambivalence is perhaps most striking to her feminist reader, who after making it through this huge book, reads the last lines: "It is for man to establish the reign of liberty in the midst of the world of the given. To gain the supreme victory, it is necessary, for one thing, that by and through their natural differentiation men and women unequivocally affirm their *brotherhood*" [*affirment sans équivoque leur fraternité*] (1949b, 732, italics added). Referring to the passage from the Song of Songs quoted earlier, de Beauvoir says that "woman becomes plant, panther, diamond, mother-of-pearl, by blending flowers, furs, jewels, shells, feathers with her body; she perfumes herself to spread an aroma of the lily and rose. But feathers, silk, pearls and perfumes serve also to hide the animal crudity of her flesh, her odor" (1949b, 158). De Beauvoir's own ambivalence is clear: even while patriarchy makes woman into a plant or an animal and excludes her from the realm of the human and equality with man, woman's patriarchal adornments help hide what de Beauvoir suggests is her naturally crude animal odor. De Beauvoir concludes that the solution for women's equality to is make men and women "brothers," which again suggests that women must become more like men.

As other feminist commentators have argued, as important as it is to feminist philosophy and to the women's movement, de Beauvoir's *The Second Sex* does not completely escape from patriarchal images of women as domestic animals. Rather than redeem woman, femininity, or female, de Beauvoir encourages women to be like men.[4] For her, women's equality depends on their ability to transcend natural animal reproductive functions and engage in creative production, as men do. As we will see, however, the opposition between production and reproduction or creativity and repetition is unsustainable, and moreover, it is a cornerstone of the very patriarchal values that de Beauvoir is arguing against. What links woman to the reproductive function is described in terms of a fault that makes her more animal than the animals. Ultimately, de Beauvoir's insistence on an absolute and ontological distinction between human/woman and animal is belied by her repeated use of animal examples to demonstrate the contingency of woman's situation and history. Despite its limitations, however, de Beauvoir's *The Second Sex* is unique in the history of philosophy insofar as it attempts to free woman from the man/animal/woman binary by embracing the world of animal difference, even if in the end she relies on a traditional opposition between human and animal to make her case.

Animal Sisters Are Doing It for Themselves (but not *pour soi*)

De Beauvoir begins her analysis in *The Second Sex* by considering what she calls the "facts" or "givens" of biology (*les données de la biologie*); the first volume of that work is entitled *Fact and Myths* (*Les faits et les mythes*).[5] She complains that what biology gives us is overdetermined by myths, to the (further) disadvantage of females. Although females may start out disadvantaged by the biological fact of reproduction, they are further debased by the values associated with those facts. On the first page, she lists several examples of female animals that are unfairly figured according to patriarchal stereotypes, which are then used against woman:

The word *female* brings up in his [man's] mind a saraband of imagery—a vast, round ovum engulfs and castrates the agile spermatozoon; the monstrous and swollen termite queen rules over the enslaved males; the female praying mantis and the spider, satiated with love, crush and devour their partners; the bitch in heat runs through the alleys, trailing behind her a wake of depraved odors; the she-monkey presents her posterior immodestly and then steals away with hypocritical coquetry; and the most superb wild beasts— the tigress, the lioness, the panther—bed down slavishly under the imperial embrace of the male. Females sluggish, eager, artful, stupid, callous, lustful, ferocious abased—man projects them all at once upon woman. And the fact is that she is a female. But if we are willing to stop thinking in platitudes, two questions are immediately posed: what does the female denote in the animal kingdom? And what particular kind of female is manifest in woman? (1949b, 3–4)

With this beginning, it should not be so surprising that a zoologist was asked to translate the text into English.[6] Starting with female animals, de Beauvoir makes clear a split between fact and myth or value.[7] Even in the "animal kingdom," the natural activities of female animals are interpreted as suspect and sinister. It is noteworthy that the first question that de Beauvoir says will be central to her study is about the meaning of "female" in the "animal kingdom." The implication is that we can answer the second question about the meaning of "female" in humans only by first attending to the animals. De Beauvoir then turns to biology in order to sort out the facts from the myths and vindicate her animal sisters.

By calling patriarchal images of female animals a *saraband,* de Beauvoir suggests a lascivious dance between fact and myth, run amok.[8] The facts of biology are one thing, but the interpretation of those facts is quite another, which becomes for man "a kind of second nature" (1949b, 36). This second nature is problematically projected onto the first nature to make biological science something akin to myth. De Beauvoir claims that

certainly these facts cannot be denied—but in themselves they have no significance. Once we adopt the human perspective, interpreting the body on a basis of existence, biology becomes an abstract science; whenever the physiological fact (for instance, muscular inferiority) takes on meaning, this meaning is at once seen as dependent on a whole context; the "weakness" is revealed as such only in the light of the ends man proposes, the instruments he has available, and the law he establishes. (1949b, 33)

The patriarchal logic that interprets biological "facts" through the lens of assumed male superiority operates by going in circles from animal behavior to human behavior and back again. De Beauvoir points out that patriarchal values are placed on these female animals and then that valuation becomes biological data, which in turn support the patriarchal thesis that women are inferior to men. Perhaps this is why de Beauvoir's use of biology has a circular aspect as well. She uses the "facts" of biology to demonstrate that sexual reproduction is contingent and not universal. The diversity of modes of reproduction in nature points to various relations between males and females. Making her case for the relative merits of females, de Beauvoir remarks, "In many species the male appears to be fundamentally unnecessary" (1949b, 5). Indeed, she observes, "The perpetuation of the species does not necessitate sexual difference" (1949b, 7). Sexual difference, then, may be a contingency of evolution. Moreover, she maintains that "in the vast majority of species male and female individuals co-operate in reproduction," meaning that the so-called war between the sexes is a human invention. Many species, she insists, do not need males to reproduce, and many more may not need males in the future. Much of her analysis of zoological life is aimed toward establishing that when it comes to reproduction, despite the biological facts, nature does not assign hierarchical values to the different roles played by sexual partners; again, this sort of prejudice is reserved for man. De Beauvoir argues that in terms of chromosomes and gametes, neither "can be regarded as superior to the other" (1949b, 11).

De Beauvoir attempts to loosen the hold of the patriarchal imaginary on the "animal kingdom" by discussing the multiplicity of sexual relations available there. She does this, it seems, to answer the question of the role of females in the animal kingdom and to demonstrate that while woman may be governed by biological facts, she is not determined by them. The suggestion is that if female animals are the victims of both biological destiny and patriarchal stereotypes, the same holds for woman. Even as it holds out the hope of the contingency of evolution, the diversity of sexes and sexualities, and the malleability of the human perspective on them, de Beauvoir's discussion of zoology also aims to show that woman is *not* like other female animals. In other words, even as she uses animals to demonstrate that woman's condition is not universal, she insists on a universal distinction between woman and animal. She uses animals in her text to teach us something about woman and to redeem their reputations in order to redeem hers.[9] At the same time, however, de Beauvoir tries to wrest woman from the side of the animal in the man/animal divide. So even though she begins by telling her reader that woman is not debased because of her animality but because she is reduced to her reproductive function, it becomes clear that woman must transcend her animality in order to ascend to equality with man. The ambivalent conclusion is that female animals teach us something about ourselves because they are like us but that woman is human because ultimately she is not like them.

While criticizing patriarchal culture for debasing females through the interpretations it assigns to mere biological facts, de Beauvoir's analysis is full of lyrical descriptions of the plight of females of all species, who remain oppressed by their reproductive functions.[10] For example, she observes that "in the termites the enormous queen, crammed with nourishment and laying as many as 4,000 eggs per day until she becomes sterile and is pitilessly killed, is no less a slave than the comparatively tiny male who attends her" (1949b, 17). Although male ants may die after mating, she recounts the "gloomy fate" of the female who "buries herself alone in the ground and often dies while laying her first eggs. Or if she succeeds in founding a colony, she remains shut in and may live for ten or twelve years constantly producing more eggs" (18). Female mammals are especially victimized by their reproductive function in that they are "taken" by the male who penetrates and dominates them, thereby doing violence to them for the sake of the species (20–21). And if this violation is not bad enough, during gestation and birth, she becomes further alienated:

First violated, the female is then alienated—she becomes, in part, another than herself. . . . Tenanted by another, who battens upon her substance throughout the period of pregnancy, the female is at once herself and other than herself; and after the birth she feeds the newborn upon the milk of her breasts. (1949b, 22)

Only when she is free from what de Beauvoir calls "maternal servitude" can she "now and then equal the male; the mare is as fleet as the stallion, the hunting bitch has as keen a nose as the dog, she-monkeys in tests show as much intelligence as males" (23). In general, the female is the victim of the species in a way that the male is not.[11]

De Beauvoir has a particularly soft spot for the praying mantis, who has gotten a bad rap for occasionally devouring her mate after sex.[12] This image feeds the masculine imaginary with notions of femmes fatales whose sexual seductions lead to murder and castration. De Beauvoir defends the female praying mantis, who, she maintains, eats her mate only when no other food is available and when she must do so to enable the production of eggs to perpetuate the species. She argues,

It is going far afield to see in those facts a proclamation of the "battle of the sexes" which sets individuals, as such, one against another. It cannot simply be said that in ants, bees, termites, spiders or mantises the female enslaves and sometimes devours the male, for it is the species that in a different way consumes them both. (1949b, 18)

De Beauvoir believes that in the case of the praying mantis, patriarchal denigrations of females reach into the "animal kingdom," apply their prejudices there, and then use those prejudiced "findings" to justify their conclusions about woman. Again, the circular logic of patriarchy looks for evidence in the animal world to support its debased images of women by interpreting the facts of biology using those very images. It looks for evidence of woman's physical or moral inferiority and finds it everywhere it looks because it uses its skewed value system to interpret the facts. De Beauvoir's assessment of female animals seems to be an attempt to provide a different interpretation and valuation of those same facts. The lesson here is that although there are facts of biology that we cannot deny, those facts do not exist for humans without interpretation and valuation. De Beauvoir returns to the praying mantis in the conclusion of *The Second Sex* to make this point:

We have seen that in spite of legends no physiological destiny imposes an eternal hostility upon Male and Female as such; even the famous praying mantis devours her male only for want of other food and for the good of the species: it is to this, the species, that all individuals are subordinated, from the top to the bottom of the scale of animal life. Moreover, humanity is something more than a mere species: it is a historical development; it is to be defined by the manner in which it deals with its natural, fixed characteristics, its *faticité*. (1949b, 716)

For de Beauvoir, the difference between fact or facticity and interpretation or valuation defines the difference between animal and human.

Discussing de Beauvoir's praying mantis, Elizabeth Fallaize speculates about why de Beauvoir insists that the female is worse off than the male even when the male is eaten by the female. She asks why the female is never allowed her superior status, even when she clearly has a leg up (2001, 77). She argues that de Beauvoir is trying to "deconstruct" images of hostile females who are dangerous to males by virtue of their reproductive functions (77). "This is why," Fallaize concludes, the female praying mantis "has to be domesticated by Beauvoir into a friendly gentle creature who prefers not to 'dine on the male'" (2001, 77). In addition, Fallaize argues that de Beauvoir refuses to allow female dominance if this superiority is based only on reproduction. She points out that for de Beauvoir, reproduction is always at odds with individuality, which leads her to figure the female as the victim of the species and the male as "a freedom fighter against the fascism of the species" (78). Fallaize also challenges de Beauvoir's account in light of recent developments in biological science, which demonstrate that in some species, females are dominant and that in many species, females choose their mates, and not vice versa (79). She concludes, however, that de Beauvoir's analysis of the facts and myths of biology prefigures contemporary work by feminist philosophers of science, particularly Evelyn Fox Keller, in examining the metaphors of science.

After biology in *The Second Sex,* de Beauvoir moves to history. She contends that throughout history, women have been subordinated to men owing to the valuation of production over reproduction. The implication is that men's production is both material production and the production of values. Men produce (and reproduce) themselves as more valuable than women, or in de Beauvoir's parlance, man produces himself as more valuable than woman. De Beauvoir identifies women's oppression with a history that gives men the freedom to create and produce, while women are limited by their reproductive function. Overcoming women's oppression requires them to enter the productive labor force and, perhaps more important—or as a consequence—to participate in the production of values. Ultimately, however, as many of de Beauvoir's feminist critics have argued, it requires a revaluation of the production/reproduction hierarchy itself.[13] Some of de Beauvoir's feminist critics have pointed out that she often seems to accept the patriarchal devaluation of maternity and therefore encourages women to throw off their reproductive chains in order to become free.[14] In places in *The Second Sex,* however, she proposes that maternity can become a project that women choose instead of a burden that they must bear. This is possible when reproductive technologies free women from the confines of biology and transform reproduction into a proper human activity rather than a mere animal one. Even while using the opposition between production and reproduction to distinguish human from animal and transcendence from immanence, de Beauvoir's analysis hints at the contingency of that very distinction.

After scores of pages sympathetically describing the plight of various female animals and easily moving back and forth between them and their human counterparts, it is surprising when, embracing historical materialism, de Beauvoir claims that "humanity is not an animal species, it is a historical reality. Human society is an antiphysis—in a sense it is against nature" (1949b, 53). Although *The Second Sex* begins by describing the ideological injustices done to women and also all female animals, the central argument of the book is grounded on an absolute abyss between women and other female animals. Man separates himself from other animals with his ability to project himself into the future and thereby transcend his animality. In order to become man's equal, woman must do the same. De Beauvoir argues that there is no "natural hierarchy" between man and woman (1949b, 33), but as we will see, this argument is based on the assumption of a natural hierarchy between human and animal. De Beauvoir maintains that while "biological considerations are extremely important," they do not establish a "fixed and inevitable destiny" for woman (1949b, 32). She insists that "they are insufficient for setting up a hierarchy of the sexes; they fail to explain why woman is the Other; they do not condemn her to remain in this subordinate role forever" (1949b, 32–33). Biological destiny does, however, determine the animal as the generic Other for the human and the female animal as the specific Other for woman. Whereas other female animals are "victims of their species" and their behavior is fixed and static, human females (like human males) define themselves and give meaning to their physiology. Whereas other animal species can be the object of empirical studies that yield the unchanging truth of their existence, human beings are constantly changing and becoming. Indeed, de Beauvoir accepts the fundamental tenant of existentialism that there is no human nature but that the meaning of humanity is a project defined by human history, a history still in the making.[15] She claims that animals have fixed natures but humans do not. In this regard, unlike other animals, human beings can transcend evolution and become something more than their biological "destiny."

De Beauvoir concludes that the role of the species

is quite different in the case of woman, as compared with other females; for animal species are fixed and it is possible to define them in static terms—by merely collecting observations it can be decided whether the mare is as fast as the stallion, or whether male chimpanzees excel their mates in intelligence tests—whereas the human species is forever in a state of change, forever becoming. (1949b, 33)

Woman's freedom, her ability to change and become, is established against female animals' inability to change, their fixity. Following Merleau-Ponty, de Beauvoir maintains that "man is not a natural species; he is a historical idea"; "man is defined as a being who is not fixed, who makes himself what he is" (1949b, 34). Despite all her comparisons between animals and humans, de Beauvoir concludes that the human situation is unique and "cannot be reduced to any other" (1949b, 35). What is most striking in her comparative analysis of animals and humans, however, is not that she concludes that ultimately the two cannot be compared but that the gap between them is gauged in terms of human sexual difference. In other words, man and woman are different from animals in different ways. In order to be equal to man, woman has the double burden of overcoming her specific difference from other *female* animals and her generic difference from animals. In a sense, man is defined in terms of his generic difference from animals, but woman is still burdened by her specific difference from female animals.

It's Her Fault

In light of Derrida's analysis of the "fault" that supposedly makes man superior to animals—premature birth, anxiety, dread of death, and so forth—it is interesting that de Beauvoir describes women's plight as worse than that of other female animals. As we have seen, Derrida argues that in the writings of Heidegger, Levinas, and Lacan, the distinction between animal and human relies on a fault in the human. While the animal is one with his environment, the human is split from the world of being and enters the world of meaning. This distance from himself and the world causes existential alienation and leads him to compensate for his lack of animal instincts with language and tools. Derrida proposes that these faults that make man human rather than animal are reminiscent of the Fall of man from paradise described in Genesis. God expels man from Eden as punishment for his weakness and sin in eating from the tree of knowledge before he can eat from the tree of life. It is the fruit of this tree, gained through his faulty character, that enables him to see his difference from animals as well as his difference from woman. The first sign of his knowledge is that he knows he is naked and that he should cover himself—the coverings are a dead giveaway to God that man has eaten forbidden fruit. From that point on, Genesis and the Old Testament tell tales in many ways of animals and women as "forbidden fruit" by which man is continually tempted. God provides both animals and women to satisfy and control man's desires. As we know, the Fall is associated with Eve's tempting Adam, and one of her punishments is pain in childbirth. This is the apparent origin of calling menstruation "the curse," which de Beauvoir mentions as another patriarchal denigration of women's reproductive functions (1949b, 27).

It is fascinating that in de Beauvoir's analysis, it is "the curse"—the burden of woman's reproductive role—that both distinguishes her from other female animals and makes her subservient to man. Woman is unique among animals because of the pain and suffering she experiences in childbirth—both physical pain beyond that of animals and mental anguish, of which animals are supposedly incapable. De Beauvoir repeatedly describes female animals' subservience to their reproductive functions and then maintains that pregnancy and birth are even more dangerous and painful in human females: "Woman—the most individualized of females—seems to be the most fragile, most subject to this pain and danger: she who most dramatically fulfills the call of destiny and most profoundly differs from her male" (1949b, 25). Compared with mares, cows, rabbits and mice, female humans have more to fear from their reproductive function, not just because unlike other animals they are self-aware and have the potential to realize their individuality, but also because the physical activities of pregnancy, birth, and lactation are more demanding for them. De Beauvoir claims that of all the animals, the pain and danger of childbirth are greatest in woman. Moreover, she points out that while other female animals have "seasonal rhythms that assures the economizing of their strength; in women, on the contrary, between puberty and the menopause nature sets no limits to the number of pregnancies" (1949b, 117). Whether or not this is true, this is the extent of the evidence that de Beauvoir provides. Indeed as detailed as her analysis of zoology and biology is, she supports it with little evidence, presenting sweeping accounts of both biology and history without citing scientists or historians.[16] In spite of this—or maybe because of it—her account is, with some marked exceptions, compelling. De Beauvoir argues that unlike other female animals that live their destiny without resisting it, women struggle against their bodies in order not to be overtaken by the species (cf. 1949b, 27). If other females fulfill their duties to their species without question, as self-reflective human beings who add value and meaning to life, women's individuality is at odds with their duty to their species. In other words, female human beings' awareness of what Marx calls *species-being* (being part of a species) throws them into struggle against their role in the perpetuation of the species. Or as de Beauvoir might say, echoing Heidegger and early Merleau-Ponty (see chapters 8 and 9), humans exist, while animals merely live.

As a result, according to de Beauvoir, woman is more profoundly alienated by her reproductive function than is any other female animal. She describes in great detail the sacrifices that women make by gestating, lactating, and raising their young. She maintains that "the conflict between species and individual, which sometimes assumes dramatic force at childbirth, endows the feminine body with a disturbing frailty . . . and it is true that they [women] have within them a hostile element—it is the species gnawing at their vitals" (1949b, 30). Here the species is figured as some kind of gnawing animal that threatens woman's individuality and her body, particularly her vital organs. According to de Beauvoir, men (and male animals in general) have no such struggle with their duty to the species or their role in reproduction: "The male is thus permitted to express himself freely; the energy of the species is well integrated into his own living activity. On the contrary, the individuality of the female is opposed by the interest of the species; it is as if she were possessed by foreign forces—alienated" (1949b, 25). Presumably, woman's alienation is different in kind from the existential alienation that makes man aware of his freedom and distinguishes him from other animals.[17] In fact, it appears to be the alienation inherent in human self-awareness that gives rise to woman's particular kind of alienation in reproduction. As de Beauvoir insists, "Woman is of all mammalian females at once the one who is most profoundly alienated (her individuality the prey of outside forces), and the one who most violently resists this alienation; in no other is enslavement of the organism to reproduction more imperious or more unwillingly accepted" (1949b, 32). Again notice that she uses a metaphor associated with animality—prey—to describe woman's relation to her reproductive function and to her species. This passage also implies that women's resistance to their reproductive role is what makes them more alienated than other female animals. Because women are human, they are aware of their reproductive role and the way that it restricts their freedom. In addition, because human females find or create meaning through their experiences, their reproductive role has more significance than it does in other animals. As a result, women's reproductive labor is more alienating, but presumably it also can be more meaningful and creative.

As de Beauvoir describes it, man's and woman's relation to life is different because man is free and woman is enslaved. Man produces, and woman reproduces. Man creates, and woman repeats. Man opens onto the future, and woman is burdened by the past. Man escapes destiny, and woman is subject to it:

The female, to a greater extent than the male, is the prey of the species; and the human race has always sought to escape its specific destiny. The support of life became for man an activity and a project through the invention of the tool; but in maternity woman remained closely bound to her body, like an animal. It is because humanity calls itself in question in the matter of living—that is to say, values the reasons for living above mere life—that, confronting woman, man assumes mastery. Man's design is not to repeat himself in time; it is to take control of the instant and mold the future. (1949b, 65)

Although de Beauvoir is calling women to throw off their chains and transcend their destiny, this project is more difficult for women than it is for men. Because women reproduce life, which de Beauvoir views as mere repetition—rather than producing the meaning of life, which she regards as creativity—they have to engage in a sort of double transcendence in order to become men's equals. It is as if man is naturally productive and creative while woman is naturally reproductive and repetitive; it seems that woman must overcome her nature twice, once as animal and then again as female. In other words, like man, she too must overcome her animality, but unlike man, she must also overcome her femaleness. Of course, because de Beauvoir insists that femaleness is not simply a natural fact but a value or interpretation of a natural fact, the view of females as repetitive and enslaved is a product—or, should we say, by-product—of patriarchy.

Woman, then, is matchless among mammals because childbirth is more painful and dangerous for her and because she is aware of the pain and danger they inflict on her body. According to de Beauvoir, she is distinctive in that she suffers from morning sickness, which is "not observed in any female domesticated animal" and which "signalize the revolt of the organism against the invading species" (1949b, 30). Morning sickness becomes a sign of her resistance to her role in reproducing the species. (It is interesting that the English translator adds a footnote that blames poor diet for morning sickness, and H. M. Parshley felt compelled to add footnotes throughout the text with his own opinion when it differed from de Beauvoir's.) Woman is unique, too, because she "suffers" menopause, another "crisis," which de Beauvoir says makes her a kind of "third sex" (1949b, 31). In this regard, woman's reproductive physiology makes her distinctive among the animals because she is prone to more suffering and worse victimization in her relation to the species. Her fragile body both distinguishes her from other animals and makes her weaker than other animals. In addition to her weaker body that makes reproduction more alienating for her, she is aware of the "invasion" and takeover of her body by another and by the species, which makes her doubly alienated. In his reading of Lacan, Derrida diagnoses a fault at the center of man's dominion over animals, which I explore in the next chapter. In the case of de Beauvoir, it is woman's fault that makes her superior to other female animals. That is, her humanity makes her worse off than female animals that are not aware of their own plight, particularly of the restrictions on their freedom presented by reproduction. In a strange sense, woman is human because she is weaker and faulty in relation to other female animals. But if these faults raise her above animals, they also subordinate her to man.

Repeating or Creating?

De Beauvoir suggests that men originally could dominate women because women were enslaved by biology in ways that men were not. Obviously, this situation changed dramatically when women gained access to birth control, child care, and various other reproductive technologies that modulate the "facts" of biology. Still, in the history of patriarchy as she describes it, women have been associated with reproduction, which is devalued in relation to production. As we have seen, men's productive activities are seen as creative, while women's reproductive activities are seen as repetitive. De Beauvoir's text itself often uses, even embraces, such oppositions and hierarchies, particularly when she advises women to transcend reproductive labor and join men in productive labor, both physical labor or the production of goods and services and intellectual and cultural labor or the production of the Good and other values. For example, she states, "In any case giving birth and suckling are not activities, they are natural functions; no project is involved; and that is why woman found in them no reason for a lofty affirmation of her existence—she submitted passively to her biologic fate" (1949b, 63). Today, in developed Western cultures, pregnancy, childbirth, and nursing have become projects that women research, plan, and execute with the help of various products and technologies. For de Beauvoir, however, in order to gain equal status, women must make productive, creative activities associated with men's priorities over reproductive activities associated with women. Some feminist critics of de Beauvoir argue that she does not fully acknowledge the creativity and productivity of reproduction, particularly of child rearing.[18] Alison Jaggar and William McBride point out that de Beauvoir's distinction between production and reproduction is conceptually arbitrary and politically suspect. They maintain that "activities surrounding procreation . . . differ from those that Marx and Beauvoir designate as 'production' in no socially or conceptually significant way. They involve no fewer of our distinctively human capacities and they are equally susceptible to historical transformation" (1985, 264). They conclude that what has been called reproduction "is simply one form of human labor" separate from other forms of productive labor for the political purpose of devaluing women's work (264). Julia Kristeva goes so far as to argue that the women's creative role in the perpetuation of the species may be an antidote to an alienating mechanized world (cf. Kristeva 2000a). Even de Beauvoir occasionally admits that women's humanity can transform female reproduction from repetitive labor for the sake of the species into creative and meaning-making projects, especially the project of raising children. Jaggar and McBride reject even the very word *reproduction* as a label to describe women's work giving birth to and raising children because they "think that the word 'reproduction' is too strongly suggestive of the sort of ahistorical, transgenerational repetition that is more characteristic of animal than of human activity" (1985, 266). Their appeal to an opposition between animal reproduction and human procreation implies that their challenge to the opposition between reproduction and production is based on another unchallenged opposition between animal and human: that in humans, procreation is labor and creative, whereas in animals, it is merely instinctual and repetitive. Recently, however, zookeepers have noticed severe depression in some animals when their newly born babies die or are removed from their care. In several cases, zookeepers have replaced tiger cubs with piglets to alleviate the mother's depression at losing her young.[19] Although zoos are far from a "natural environment," these instances should make us wonder about what is natural in nature. If a tigress can adopt and care for piglets rather than eating them, perhaps we overestimate so-called animal instincts and the fixity of animal relationships to the environment and other species.

Whatever we think of the place of the opposition between production and reproduction in animals, given the decades of feminist scholarship on the work and creativity that goes into preparing for childbirth and child rearing (at least among women who can afford to be creative), we should agree that it is suspect in humans. As de Beauvoir points out, although women's reproductive labor often limits their choices and possibilities, it sometimes expands them. Some women even regard motherhood as one of the most meaningful aspects of their lives. Leaving aside alternative feminist valuations of the creative activities of motherhood, even in the logic of de Beauvoir's own text, the opposition between production and reproduction, figured as one of creativity versus repetition, is difficult to maintain. Above all, de Beauvoir's text deftly demonstrates that women's reproductive labor is never devoid of meaning. Therefore, because maternity is always meaningful and its meanings change across history and cultures, it is a human activity. De Beauvoir's suggestion that it wasn't always a human activity brings us back to the paradoxes of romanticism in which the origin of humanity already assumes the existence of humanity or else humanity somehow appears out of its opposite, animality. The notion that women's reproductive function once made them more like animals is also reminiscent of Freud's story of the primal horde in which, as we will see, "the father" was somehow already a father even while he was an animal, or else he was an animal even while he was also a "father." These paradoxes point to problems with the binary animal/human opposition and, in de Beauvoir's case, with the binary reproduction/production opposition. Indeed, they suggest that the two poles cannot be maintained as opposites because the relation between the two is much more complex.

The paradox of origin is less apparent in *The Coming of Age,* in which de Beauvoir observes that there was never a time when humans did not have culture and were determined entirely by nature: "However brutish it may be, there is no human community that does not possess a certain culture; the work man performs by means of tools he has made constitutes an activity upon which is based at least the beginnings of a social organization" (1972, 38). She goes on to distinguish old age in humans from old age in animals, stating that aging is more dramatic in humans:

For of all species, mankind is that in which the alterations caused by advancing years are the most striking. Animals grow thin, they become weaker; they do not undergo a total change. We do. It wounds one's heart to see a lovely young woman and then next to her her reflection in the mirror of the years to come—her mother. (1972, 5)

De Beauvoir's example of the lovely young woman growing old again implies that aging is harder on women than on men. Her example also implicates the mother in the aging process—it is her appearance that causes the "wound" when compared with that of her daughter. She also says that in some societies, old men maintain their high standing and even "monopoliz[e] the women" (1972, 40). Discussing animals, she tells a tale reminiscent of Freud's primal horde when she explains how communities of apes are dominated by one male who possesses all the females until he grows old and the younger males are able to subdue him and take his place. She also is critical of societies that "let their old people die like animals" and the scandalous way that old people are treated in contemporary Western societies (cf. 1972, 50, 216). In capitalist countries, the value of old people is defined in terms of their productivity, the same value system that de Beauvoir identifies with patriarchy and man's supposed superiority over woman.

In *The Second Sex,* it is man's ability to use tools and continue using tools that makes him dominant over woman and animals. Man becomes human by making things; he becomes *Homo faber.* The first things that he makes are tools with which to kill animals. In a sense, then, the ability to kill animals is what makes him human (never mind that animals also kill one another). De Beauvoir insists that man's productive activity is radically different from the activities of animals, because his involves tools that open up projects and projections into the future (as we will see, this view is reminiscent of that of Heidegger and of de Beauvoir's friend Merleau-Ponty in his early work). The use of tools opens up a realm beyond nature, that of meaning. De Beauvoir says,

Man's case was radically different [from woman's]; he furnished support for the group, not in the manner of worker bees by a simple vital process, through biological behavior, but by means of acts that transcended his animal nature. *Homo faber* has from the beginning of time been an inventor: the stick and the club with which he armed himself to knock down fruits and slaughter animals became forthwith instruments for enlarging his grasp on the world. (1949b, 63)

Like Heidegger and early Merleau-Ponty, de Beauvoir imagines that man's ability to physically grasp tools with his hands enabled him to mentally grasp the world in which he lives. Unlike other animals, he has the ability to shape his world and to be aware of it as a world:

He did not limit himself to bringing home the fish he caught in the sea: first he had to conquer the watery realm by means of the dugout canoe fashioned from a tree-trunk; to get at the riches of the world he annexed the world itself. . . . This is the reason why fishing and hunting expeditions had a sacred character. Their successes were celebrated with festivals and triumphs, and therein man gave recognition to his human estate. Today he still manifests this pride when he has built a dam or skyscraper or an atomic pile. He has worked not merely to conserve the world as given; he has broken through frontiers, he has laid down the foundations of a new future. (1949b, 63)

Man becomes human by conquering animals and the world, by making his mark on it.

De Beauvoir argues that "early man's activity had another dimension that gave it supreme dignity; it was often dangerous. If blood were but a nourishing fluid it would be valued no higher than milk" (1949b, 63). I will return to a discussion of blood in man's relation with animals in subsequent chapters on Freud and Kristeva. For de Beauvoir, man's bloodlust made him a brave and conquering warrior who risked his life in the hunt and in combat. He risked his life battling nature and his fellow man. According to de Beauvoir, it is his willingness to risk his life that makes him superior to animals: "For it is not in giving life but in risking life that man is raised above the animal; that is why superiority has been accorded in humanity not to the sex that brings forth but to that which kills" (1949b, 64). To de Beauvoir, one of the primary ways in which men assert their superiority over animals and nature is by conquering them and waging war against one another.

Taking life is valued more than giving life because the former involves risking one's life as well as a goal or project like hunting or war that encourages man to invent tools and "remodel the face of the earth" (cf. 1949b, 64). De Beauvoir applies Hegel's analysis of the master–slave relationship to the relation between man and woman. She maintains that because woman does not risk her life, she is not completely free, as the man is. We might wonder why de Beauvoir seems to embrace the manly occupation of war and killing, particularly in relation to transcending animality, especially since another possible interpretation of man's bloodlust and war waging is that it is a result of natural animal instincts left unchecked. Man's aggression against animals, the earth, and his fellows could be seen as a result of his inability to control his animality and not the other way around. And once psychoanalysis enters the scene—a scene also described by de Beauvoir—we could say that man's urge to master and control through violence are symptoms of the compulsion to repeat unexamined traumas or aggressions. In this framework, we cannot distinguish so easily between repetition and creativity, particularly when the highest signs of this so-called creativity are killing and warfare. Freud might interpret man's warring nature and bloodlust as manifestations of animal instincts and also the death drive, which he associates with the urge to become inert, stable, and even inorganic.

In addition, from the woman's side, de Beauvoir has already cataloged many dangers women face in pregnancy and childbirth. She claims that human females are in greater danger of dying in childbirth than other animals are, but she does not recognize childbirth as an activity through which woman also risks her life.[20] Perhaps this is because she does not recognize childbirth as an activity. If man's superiority is based on danger and risking life, it seems that woman, as de Beauvoir describes her, meets these criteria. Even if man's superiority is based on actively entering life-threatening situations, whereas woman enters hers passively, this distinction also is suspect. As feminists like Luce Irigaray have argued, there is activity in passivity, and vice versa.[21] Certainly, reproductive technologies and pressures on women to raise children following various guidelines and manuals (including those from the medical establishment, psychologists, and educational institutions), can make pregnancy and child rearing monumental projects. Conversely, man's urge to put himself in dangerous situations can be seen as a repetition of predatory animal instincts or aggressive drives to master his environment that are as unconscious as they are freely chosen projects. Again, we may wonder whether the distinctions among risking life, taking life, and giving life are as clear-cut as de Beauvoir's text makes them out to be. Finally, the valuation of taking life over giving life and the associations of the former with culture and the later with nature could be read as yet more evidence that Western values are patriarchal values; in other words, if killing is valued over giving birth, it is because men kill and women give birth.

As de Beauvoir describes it, man's superiority is based on his conquest of nature. He transcends his animality by conquering other animals. Indeed, de Beauvoir says that man "subdues Nature and Woman" using the same kind of brute physical force (1949b, 65). He establishes his "existence" against "life" through violence that changes the face of the earth and gives him control over it (cf. 65). In contrast, woman's existence has been subordinated to life, culture to nature, and therefore in her, the human being has been subordinated to its animality (1949b, 65). As man develops agriculture and domesticates animals, he also domesticates woman. De Beauvoir maintains that agriculture cruelly disadvantages and handicaps woman in several ways (1949b, 66). First, the fertility of the land becomes associated with woman's fertility, which can lead to goddess worship; and while valuing woman's reproductive role as sacred may be more desirable than debasing it, women still are excluded from the realm of the properly human and equal to men (1949b, 70). Her fertility is seen as repeating rather than creating, nourishing rather than producing. De Beauvoir concludes that "in spite of the fecund powers that pervade her, man remains woman's master as he is the master of the fertile earth; she is fated to be subjected, owned, exploited like the Nature whose magical fertility she embodies" (1949b, 73). Women, she says, are treated like cattle, owned and exchanged by men (79).

As agriculture gives rise to constructing fences to constrain domestic animals, woman goes from goddess to farm animal, still excluded from the realm of the properly human and equality with man. De Beauvoir claims that "woman was dethroned by the advent of private property," which turns woman into a beast of burden like other domestic animals. She repeatedly compares women in this period with chattel, cattle, and other domestic animals. Because man considers animals and the earth as his property, so too he takes women and children as his property. She concludes that man "could achieve his destiny only as he began by dethroning her [woman]" (1949b, 76). As my analysis has shown, however, it is also by dethroning animals and making them subservient that man achieves what de Beauvoir calls his "destiny." Recall that for Rousseau, agriculture and cultivation of grains were the true beginnings of culture and civilized man (and that he sees private property as a uniquely civilized evil). For de Beauvoir, what civilizes man enslaves woman. Even though she recognizes the association between woman's fecundity and the fertility of the crops, and even though she repeatedly compares women with animals, she does not dwell on the apparent fact that the system of private property that allows man to own the earth and women is instigated by his desire to control and domesticate animals. What her analysis overlooks is the connection between domesticating animals and domesticating women, between owning animals and owning women.

In sum, while de Beauvoir's feminist classic *The Second Sex* begins with an attempt to revalue females of all species, her vindication of woman ultimately relies on putting animals in their place. Woman is worse off than other female animals because of her double alienation, which is caused by the double whammy of more physical pain and fewer natural restrictions on her pregnancies, on the one hand, and reflective awareness of the ways that her natural reproductive role disadvantages her, on the other. Woman's "curse" is reproduction, which de Beauvoir insists is uniquely painful for women, as opposed to other female animals. It is the uniqueness of her pain and suffering, both physical and mental, that distinguishes her from other female animals. But it must be her transcendence of animality altogether that will make her free and equal to man. Even while de Beauvoir repeatedly appeals to animals and their different lifestyles to make her case against patriarchal stereotypes, in the end, she takes up the existentialist mantle that grounds the groundlessness of man on his absolute difference from animals. Animals are fixed and determined by biology; man is not. Animals are incapable of self-reflection and meaning making; man is reflective and meaning making. Animals are merely reproductive and repetitive; man is productive and creative. Woman, then, moves from man's other and the second sex only by making the animal so radically other that it cannot be even second in relation to the human because it is so different in kind.

What is striking in de Beauvoir's revaluation of woman and female is that the redemption of these terms relies on elevating them to the same status as man, both by assigning them characteristics traditionally associated with males and by accepting the patriarchal devaluation of reproduction in favor of production. In other words, following her own logic, de Beauvoir's analysis of the differences between animals and man should lead her to conclude that while reproduction is merely repetitive and replicates rather than producing anything new in animals, it is creative in humans. Her own reasoning should have led her to view human reproduction as meaningful in relation to animal reproduction. Her investigation into the effects of patriarchal values and myths on biology and history could have led her even further to question the distinctions between reproduction and production or repetition and creativity. Yet her own ambivalence about both animals and females keeps her from straying too far from the confines of patriarchal values regarding pregnancy, childbirth, and child rearing. Rather than revaluing the patriarchal preference for taking life over giving life, she seems to embrace man's aggressive and warlike nature as what allows him to conquer Nature and Woman and leads to his existential freedom. In accepting the value of existence over life, de Beauvoir does not question the ways in which "life" is value laden, not just woman's life or human life, but also all of life.[22]

Certainly, de Beauvoir's description of the supposed superiority of man and his power to conquer animals and the earth, which she sees as the activities that project him beyond animality and into transcendence and freedom, do not sound as majestic and romantic as they did fifty years ago, before widespread knowledge of global warming and the crisis of species extinction. The shrinking biodiversity resulting from man's dominion over animals and the earth endangers animals and plants and also man's ability to feed himself. Global warming was caused by man's "remodeling the face of the earth" and his lack of concern for "conserving the world as given," which threatens all life on the planet, including human life (cf. de Beauvoir 1949b, 63–64). Man's projects that create a new future—the very projects that make him human and make him radically distinct from animals— also can destroy his future. The dangerous, violent conquering impulses that de Beauvoir believes "enabled males to affirm their status as sole and sovereign subjects" and preside over animals, women, and the earth do not appear as glorious in the face of a looming environmental crisis and seemingly endless war.

CHAPTER SEVEN

Answering the Call of Nature

Lacan Walking the Dog

Duplicity: The quality of being "double" in action or conduct; the character or practice of acting in two ways at different times, or openly and secretly; deceitfulness, double-dealing.

—*OXFORD ENGLISH DICTIONARY*

But an animal does not feign feigning. . . . Speech begins only with the passage from the feint to the order of the signifier, and that the signifier requires another locus . . . for the Speech borne by the signifier to be able to lie, that is, to posit itself as Truth.

—JACQUES LACAN, *ÉCRITS*

The figure of the animal comes to the surface therefore in this difference between pretense and deception.

—JACQUES DERRIDA, "AND SAY THE ANIMAL RESPONDED?"

Once psychoanalysis enters the scene, the distinction between truth and deception becomes mired in the murky mess of the unconscious. Insofar as unconscious forces drive us beyond our control and even beyond our knowledge, we all are, and always have been, a bunch of liars. Our motives remain opaque and beyond our grasp, and our words always say more than we intend. Indeed, as Freud describes it, the human psyche revolves around deception: unconscious desires and fears sneak into consciousness; repression works to hide traumatic memories, while the repetition compulsion tricks us into reliving those traumas in new forms; dreams disguise the truth of the psyche through processes of condensation and displacement to fool the ego's censors; neuroses pass themselves off as physical ailments; and the more we deny something in the course of analysis, the more likely that it is true. Lacan takes these Freudian insights further and insists that truth is nothing more than the ability of speech to lie; in other words, speech is the process of making lies appear to be true. The capacity to make what is false appear as true is uniquely human. Even though animals can pretend and can feign, according to Lacan, they cannot make what is true appear false, which requires pretending to pretend or feigning the feint. Conversely, for Lacan, the double deception of speech constitutes man as human. It is man's duplicity, his double pretense, his double-dealing, or folding the feint back onto itself, which makes him unique among the animals.

What is this duplicity of speech that animals lack, and how can we distinguish between pretending and pretending to pretend? What are the implications of maintaining that only man can lie? In this chapter, I take up these questions in order to situate the role that animals play for Lacan and to signal the role that they play for Western thought more generally. My thesis is that Lacan uses animals to make his work appear scientific so that he can more persuasively outline the dynamics of the human psyche. That is, animals appear in his work to add rhetorical force to his descriptions of the distinctive qualities of man. We see logic familiar from the history of philosophy in which animals are used to shore up the borders of man, and are called as witnesses to man's superiority. Within this logic, animals are more than the constitutive outside of man, as they also teach man how to be human. Accordingly, man is human by virtue of animal pedagogy.

Double-Dealing Animals

While tracking animals in Lacan's work, I am struck by their various functions. In some places, Lacan points to a continuation between animals and men, but in others, he insists on a radical distinction between animals and men, and his conclusions about the divide between man and animal often are premised on the ways that animals exhibit certain characteristics usually associated with humans. His work displays ambivalence about man's relation to animals, which I link to his ambivalent relation to empirical science. On the one hand, Lacan's disdain for the empirical methods of behavioral psychology and the science envy of logical positivism in philosophy is explicit throughout this work. On the other hand, he frequently cites studies involving animals to substantiate his claims about human psychology. Here I use some of his many remarks about animals to diagnose Lacan's ambivalence toward empirical science as evidenced by his symptomatic ambivalence toward animals.

In a lecture on the state of psychoanalysis in 1956—a lecture filled with irony and biting humor, like most—Lacan observed:

I have always been struck, while taking my little dog for a walk so he could attend to his needs, by what we could glean from his activities that would help us analyze the capacities that make for man's success in society, as well as the virtues that Antiquity's thinkers meditated upon under the heading of Means-to-an-End [*Moyen-de-Parvenir*]. I hope that this digression will, at the very least, dispel the misunderstanding of attributing to me the doctrine of a discontinuity between animal psychology and human psychology, which is truly foreign to my way of thinking. (2006, 404)

Note that Lacan's insistence that his position allows for a continuity between animal and human psychology is formulated in the negative, with his use of words like *digression, dispel, misunderstanding, discontinuity,* and *foreign.* He does not assert a continuity but denies a discontinuity, and not between animals and humans but between one type of psychology and another. Even his style might be read as signaling an ambivalence about animals in relation to men. Indeed, whatever he learns from his dog has less to do with his dog than with himself (given that for Lacan, relations among human subjects always comes back to a self-relation, this should be no surprise).

The tongue-in-cheek quality of the passage is signaled in the beginning with his allusion to a little doggy-do, which perhaps reflects his opinion of behaviorist observations. In the lecture, this passage follows a suggestion that behaviorists who find the measure of man in the animal might improve their studies by considering "trace behavior" in both. It seems that behaviorists discover something about man by observing animal behavior, but the continuities may not be what they think. Instead, they may lie in what Lacan calls "trace behaviors," which cannot be observed using their crude experimental techniques (which are not even on a par with Lacan's observations while walking his dog). These trace behaviors are likely linked to imaginary formations consistent in both animals and humans and constitute perception as a sort of "residue of the real," which behaviorists ignore (cf. Lacan 1988b, 257). As such, this passage may indicate ambivalence about behaviorism as much as about animals. Indeed, at the same time that Lacan invokes their findings and cites other studies in biology, ethnology, and zoology, he jeers at their methods. Moreover, while he endorses studies that demonstrate the existence of the imaginary or the function of the imago or image in animals, he discounts conclusions that implicate what he calls the symbolic, which he reserves for man alone.

Consider another negatively worded passage which is noteworthy because in this instance, Lacan conjures continuity between the symbolic in animals and humans: "It can be seen that I do not shrink from seeking the origins of symbolic behavior outside the human sphere" (Lacan 2006, 225). This remark is sandwiched between criticisms of logical positivist attempts to catalog and thereby exhaust the meaning of speech and behaviorist attempts to excise superfluous speculations by turning to the supposed certainty of empirical experimentation on animals. Lacan goes on to describe the symbolic order as one of exchange, as in the exchange of gifts that seals a pact between individuals or tribes (see Lacan 2006, 225). Although an exchange is necessary, it is not sufficient for symbolic language. Lacan imagines that if it were, a group of sea swallows might possess a rudimentary language:

Were this the case, one would find a first approximation of language among sea swallows, for instance, during display, materialized in the fish they pass each other from beak to beak; ethnologists—if we must agree with them in seeing in this the instrument of a stirring into action of the group that is tantamount to a party—would then be altogether justified in recognizing a symbol in this activity. (2006, 225)

But Lacan insists that they are not because, as he says,

For even if there appeared among the sea swallows some kaid [sic]of the colony who, by gulping down the symbolic fish from the others' gaping beaks, were to inaugurate the exploitation of swallow by swallow—a fanciful notion I enjoyed developing one day—this would not in any way suffice to reproduce among them the fabulous history, the image of our own, whose winged epic kept us captive on Penguin Island; something else would still be needed to create a "swallowized" universe. (2006, 228)

If Lacan's flights of fancy regarding swallow slavery are indicative of his seeking the origins of the symbolic outside the human, then perhaps he is kidding us a bit when he says that he doesn't shrink from doing so.

Lacan suggests that symbolization requires exchange, exploitation, and even enslavement (he insists that only humans are capable of enslaving others), but something more also is necessary, something that animals lack. It is this "something more" that turns our world into a humanized world, something that the swallows can never do with their "world" such as it is. "This 'something else' completes the symbol, making language of it" (Lacan 2006, 228). It does so by freeing the sound or word from the here and now of experience and making it a concept that erases the thing to which it refers and makes it permanent, only now in the world of symbols. This duplicitous operation of substituting concept for thing is supposedly unique to humans in that it inherently links the imaginary and symbolic realms in ways that, at least in principle, forever cut them off from any immediate access to the real.[1] This link also means that in man, and only in man, the imaginary exists at the mercy, or might we say pleasure, of the symbolic. Presumably this is why human subjects are susceptible to analysis—the "talking cure"—and animal subjects are not.

While Lacan dispels discontinuity and denies "shrinking" in the face of the animal, at the same time he insists that only man is capable of speech. Sometimes it seems as if he is setting out criteria for speech, and thereby for human subjectivity, and then compromising them one by one in relation to animals and yet always maintaining a shifting of "something more" reserved for man alone. This something more, this trace, is what Lacan sees and behaviorists miss when they look at animals. For example, Lacan discusses experiments in which dogs are tied to tables and trained to expect meat when a bell is rung but are given apples instead, and a raccoon who is "taught, by a judicious conditioning of his reflexes, to go to his food box when he is presented with a card on which the meal is to be served is printed" and "if the service disappoints him, he comes back and tears up the card that promised too much, just as a furious woman might do with the letters of a faithless lover" (2006, 226). Lacan complains that the behaviorists conducting these experiments are tackling the problem of language by trying to "grab it by the throat," which ignores its essential imaginary dimension altogether.

Duplicity Makes the Man, or Can Animals Lie?

In his most famous essay, "The Mirror Stage," and elsewhere, Lacan invokes animals in order to document the role of the image in subject formation and ultimately in the symbolic exchange that gives way to language. In "The Mirror Stage," the pigeon and the locust are presented as evidence for the essential role of the imaginary in subject formation. Ten years later, Lacan again trotted out the pigeon and locust as witnesses to the role of the imaginary in man. Here, the role of the animal in contributing scientific credence to Lacan's theories is even more explicit:

I think, therefore, that I can designate the imago as the true object of psychology, to the exact extent that Galileo's notion of the inert mass point served as the foundation of physics. . . . Those who do not wish to understand me might object that I am begging the question and that I am gratuitously positing that the phenomenon is irreducible merely in order to foster a thoroughly metaphysical conception of man. I will thus address the deaf by offering them facts which will, I think, pique their sense of the visible, since these facts should not appear to be contaminated, in their eyes at least, by either the mind or being: for I will seek them out in the animal kingdom. (2006, 153–54)

At the same time that Lacan bats around the scientific crowd, he is playing to them by trying to make his theories interest them, by using studies of animals to prove his theses about man in a more scientific and less metaphysical or speculative way. Given the irony of his style, the duplicity of this turn to the empirical and observable in order to prove the role of the image or invisible in psychic dynamics is perhaps not lost on him.

If the imaginary doesn't separate man from animals, what does? In answering this question, to which he returns again and again, Lacan seems to taunt the animal by continually giving something and then taking it away. As we have seen, this fort-da with the animal psyche repeatedly serves as a rhetorical bolster for his theories of the human psyche. It seems that language is the main barrier between man and animal, and what is it about language that animals cannot muster? Lacan discusses various aspects of language that might qualify: the use of signs or codes, substitution or displacement, the ability to conceptualize, the ability to respond, and, more specifically, the ability to lie.

In "The Function and Field of Speech and Language in Psychoanalysis," Lacan distinguishes between language and speech based on the distinction between the use of codes by animals and the use of symbols by man. He enlists the swallows and raccoon mentioned earlier, along with bees, dogs, and other critters. He argues, again against behaviorists, that although animals can be trained to react to verbal stimulus, their reactions are never meaningful responses in accordance with the symbolic order. Although humans can also be trained to react to stimuli in similar ways, that does not prove that they are like animals. Lacan lambastes Jules Masserman's studies of animals (including the dog and raccoon) and humans in their "responses" to bells and verbal commands. He discusses a study in which humans were "trained" to contract their pupils on command by exposing them to bright light in connection with the command and then dispensing with the light. Rejecting Masserman's conclusion that these contractions were "visceral reactions to the idea-symbol 'contract,'" Lacan muses,

I would have been curious to know whether subjects trained in this way also react to the enunciation of the same term in the expressions "marriage contract," "contract bridge," and "breach of contract," and even when the term is progressively shortened to the articulation of its first syllable alone: contract, contrac, contra, contr. . . . For either the effects would no longer be produced, thus revealing that they do not even conditionally depend on the semanteme, or they would continue to be produced, raising the question of the semanteme's limits. . . . In other words, they would cause the distinction between the signifier and the signified, so blithely confounded by the author in the English term "idea-symbol." (2006, 226–27)

Lacan contends that words have meaning within symbolic systems through their relationships rather than by existing independently as idea-symbols. This distinction between idea and symbol as sign again implicates the animal.

Lacan insists that those logical positivists and behaviorists who reduce language to nothing more than signs are mistaken. Looking for evidence, like "bloodhounds on the scent," he once more turns to "the animal kingdom" to prove his point, and again with his typical irreverent reverence for empirical science, "I shall show the inadequacy of the conception of language as signs by the very manifestation that best illustrates it in the animal kingdom, a manifestation which, had it not recently been the object of an authentic discovery, would have to have been invented for this purpose" (2006, 245). Lacan gives the example of a certain bee's "wagging dance," which directs other bees to the location of food. Although the bee employs a sign as a signal or even as a code, it is not language:

We can say that it is distinguished from language precisely by the fixed correlation between its signs and the reality they signify. For, in a language, signs take on their value from their relations to each other in the lexical distribution of semantemes as much as in the positional, or even flectional, use of morphemes—in sharp contrast to the fixity of the coding used by the bees. The diversity of human languages takes on its full value viewed in this light. (2006, 245–46)

Note that it is the fixed nature of bee codes that teaches us the full value of the diversity of human languages. Although we might wonder whether all bees use the same codes, and because there are significantly many more types of insects than any other class of animal, it seems likely that there are many times more insect codes than there are human ones. In any case, the bees provide for the psychoanalyst a pedagogical lesson about human languages.

In addition to a system of signs defined by their relations to one another, what bees lack, it seems, is imagination. Indeed, it may be a lack of imagination that prevents them from relating their signs to one another rather than to the location of dinner. But Lacan has already granted imagination to animals, so it must be more than the too-direct connection between the sign and the real that is the "bee" in Lacan's bonnet. We get a sense of what this is when we return to the example of the swallows, who lack the "something more" of human language.

Recall that it is the lack of concepts that prevent swallows from "swallowizing" the universe. Even if animals have signs and imagination, they do not have "the permanence of the concept" (cf. Lacan 2006). Here Lacan concludes that animals are incapable of the generalization necessary for conceptualization.

Elsewhere, however, Lacan says in passing (again complaining about behaviorist methodology), "There are enough really rather tiresome laboratory experiments, which show that if one holds an octopus, or any other animal, with sufficient doggedness in front of a triangle, they will recognize it in the end, that is to generalize it" (1988b, 322). So if animals are capable of signs, of imagination, and even of concepts, what is lacking to make their forms of communication into language? Discussing the swallows and the bees, Lacan points to their incapacity to make the concept stand in for the thing. In other words, animals are incapable of substitution or displacement, operations necessary for meaningful speech. It is the play between presence and absence that engenders language: "Through what becomes embodied only by being the trace of a nothingness and whose medium thus cannot be altered, concepts, in preserving the duration of what passes away, engenders things. . . . It is the world of words that creates the world of things" (2006, 228–29). Other animals, then, cannot quite master the absence at the heart of representation that makes man the speaking animal.

In another lecture, however, continuing his fort-da casting and reeling back, Lacan suggests that animals are indeed capable of displacement:

Let us say that, in the animal world, the entire cycle of sexual behaviour is dominated by the imaginary. On the other hand, it is in sexual behaviour that we find the greatest possibilities of displacement occurring, even in animals. . . . The possibility of displacement, the illusory, imaginary dimension, is essential to everything pertaining to the order of sexual behaviour. (1988a, 138)

Lacan makes it clear that this imaginary function is the same in animals and man: "Is this true for man, yes or no? . . . This is nothing other than the imaginary phenomenon which I just spelt out in detail for you in the animal" (Lacan 1988a, 138). This conclusion follows a discussion of the sexual behavior of sticklebacks, which engage in a kind of zigzagging mating dance instigated by the beautiful colors on the belly and back of the male. As we will see, there is a reciprocal influence between Merleau-Ponty and Lacan, both of whom cite the example of the stickleback fish. Reminiscent of Merleau-Ponty, Lacan asks, "What comes to play in releasing the complementary behavior of the male and female sticklebacks? *Gestalten*" (1988a, 137). Merleau-Ponty also uses the example of the stickleback to make the case for the importance of mimesis in his *Nature* lectures (2003, 196). It is clear that Lacan was influenced by Merleau-Ponty's theories of perception and that Merleau-Ponty was influenced by Lacan's theories of the imaginary (e.g., see Lacan 1988a, 58).

Speaking of the stickleback, "we can," says Lacan, "quite easily make a cut-out which, even when poorly put together, will have exactly the same effect of the female" (1988a, 122). These fish are easily fooled when it comes to sex; they see what they want to see, which gives Lacan further evidence of the function of the image in both animal and human psyches, particularly when it comes to sex. He asks, "What does the development of instinctual functioning teach us in this respect? The extraordinary importance of the image" (1988a, 137). Like the pigeon and the locust before them, these stickleback fish teach us the importance of the image in the human psyche. In his discussion of the stickleback's mating rituals, Lacan applies these lessons to neurosis: "Sexual behavior is quite especially prone to the lure. This teaches us something which is important in working out the structure of the perversions and the neuroses" (1988a, 122). This raises the question of whether or not animals can be perverts and neurotics. In any case, it is once again animal pedagogy that gives Lacan evidence and insight into the psyche of man.

If animals are capable of imagination, conceptualization, and displacement, then it becomes even more puzzling how Lacan separates man from animals. What is the "something more" man has that animals don't? Throughout his work, Lacan consistently maintains that the human subject possesses a fundamental alienation or gap that necessitates the imaginary as compensation for its congenital faults, what he calls man's "prematurity" at birth. Because man's infancy and dependence are much longer than for other animals, he is incapable of the motor coordination that allows him to affect his surroundings for the first several years of life. This incapacity in turn produces imaginary, even hallucinatory, compensations for the lack of motor skills. The infant's reflection in the mirror serves as an image of wholeness and coordination that conjures what Lacan calls a misrecognition of a unified experience and agency that are not yet or truly the infant's own. This misrecognition ushers in human dependence on the image and on the Other (for both systems of meaning and human others, like the caregiver who holds an infant in front of the mirror) to mediate his experience. It is the gap between the infant's mirror image and the reality of his lack of coordination that make him unique among the animals. This is why, according to Lacan, the human infant delights in his mirror image, but the chimp supposedly finds his mirror image threatening. Lacan assumes that the chimp recognizes the image as a threat to his immediate hold on the world, whereas the human mistakes the image as the source of his own agency. It is in this gap between the image and the real that the symbolic can be inserted, which is why the gap itself makes man distinctive (cf. Lacan 1988a, 141–42). Lacan concludes:

Living animals are sensitive to the image of their own kind. This is an absolutely essential point, thanks to which the whole of living creation isn't an immense orgy. But the human being has a special relation with his own image—a relation of gap, of alienating tension. That is where the possibility of the order of presence and absence, that is of the symbolic order, comes in. (1988b, 323)

Lacan describes this gap as "a certain biological gap," which "already assumes the lack" (1988b, 323). This biological or, we might say, animal lack is what animals lack.

Lacan's idea that species stick to images of their own kind and that there is no "orgy" in nature seems conservative in view of his theory of the role of the image and the imaginary in both animals and humans. Moreover, it operates with an extremely conservative notion of sex as reproductive sex, and a conservative notion of reproductive sex at that. What about the reproductive relation between bees and flowers? What about nonreproductive sex acts of animals with inanimate objects, plants, or animals of other species? What about Derrida's monotremes? What about the way that sexual behavior in the very animals Lacan cites changes with their changing environment? Recall my "thought experiment" in chapter 5, in which I argue that attending to the hugely diverse sexualities of various animal species opens up new ways of conceiving of sex and reproduction. Think too of Deleuze and Guattari's assemblages—wasp-orchid, Hans-horse—through which "sexuality is the production of a thousand sexes," not coincidentally made possible by "the becoming-animal of the human" (1987, 278–79).

True Lies

In *The Animal,* Jacques Derrida investigates some of the animals that appear in Lacan's *Écrits,* and he challenges Lacan's desire for a fixed criterion to distinguish man from animals. As Derrida reminds us throughout this book, he is not so much concerned with giving these ethereal characteristics to animals as questioning whether or not humans possess them in the fixed way indicated by philosophers who put stock in some absolute limit between man and animal. Derrida points out that to Lacan, paradoxically, man is superior to animals because of his imperfection and lack, for which he must compensate; thus, man "received speech and technics only inasmuch as he lacks something" (2008, 122). In the words of Kalpana Seshadri-Crooks, for Lacan,

the animal's existence in the imaginary, where it merely reacts to "vital situations," also means that it cannot be conditioned by its own word—as in vouching for something or lying—which more or less expels it from time and mortality. The implication here is that the animal lacks the lack that constitutes the human subject. It is a wholly sufficient entity in that it lives in a state that is anterior to good and evil. It is neither a subject of language, nor subjected to language in the manner that the human necessarily must be because of the biological fact of his or her premature birth. Thus, as Derrida points out, the human subject in Lacan is constituted by its lack, which is what distinguished human from animal. (2003, 100)

Because the animal lacks the lack constitutive of humanity, it appears as a mythic figure of wholeness and unity; the animal comes to represent man's lost archaic ancestor, which triggers both nostalgia for its perfection and hostility toward it for man's relative fragmentation and imperfection.

Seshadri-Crooks supplements Derrida's criticisms of Lacan by suggesting that although Derrida is onto something, Lacan's works nonetheless help us challenge the fixity of the limit between man and animal. She argues that in his reading of Freud's *Totem and Taboo,* Lacan exposes the myth of the animal ancestor and animal perfection, and that by so doing, he "leads us to ask: does the animal exist?" (2003, 104). Obviously, he is not saying that animals don't exist. Rather, Lacan is challenging the general concept of *the animal,* which as Derrida so forcefully argues corrals nearly infinite numbers of diverse living beings into one general category and assigns to them one name, *animal.* More to the point, the animal's lack of lack has been associated with a lack of evil or cruelty, which are seen as the sole providence of men. Recall that Derrida says only humans can be called "beastly." Paradoxically, man is superior to the animal because he is capable of cruelty and evil and the animal is not. Man claims a privilege over the animal because while it is innocent and true, he is corrupt and duplicitous.

The centerpiece of Derrida's engagement with Lacan is the following passage from *Écrits,* which Derrida also quotes at length:

This Other, distinguished as the locus of Speech, nevertheless emerges as Truth's witness. Without the dimension it constitutes, the deceptiveness of Speech would be indistinguishable from the feint, which, in fighting or sexual display, is nevertheless quite different. Deployed in imaginary capture, the feint is integrated into the play of approach and retreat that constituted the first dance, in which these two vital situations find their scansion, and the partners who fall into step with it find which I will dare to write as their "dancity." Moreover, animals show that they are capable of such behavior when they are being hunted down; they manage to throw their pursuers off the scent by briefly going in one direction as a lure and then changing direction. This can go so far as to suggest on the part of game animals the nobility of honoring the parrying found in the hunt. But an animal does not feign feigning. It does not make tracks whose deceptiveness lies in getting them to be taken as false, when in fact they are true—that is, tracks that indicate the right trail. No more than it effaces its tracks, which would already be tantamount to making itself the subject of the signifier. (2006, 683)

In this passage, Lacan maintains that animals react to other animals (and to humans) with a "dance" that indicates relationality with others. But their very being in the world is not mediated by the dance, nor are they moved in it by the Other in the way that constitutes humanity. The human world is a world of signification through which subjects are constituted by virtue of the Other of meaning that is inherited from others on whom the fledgling subject is dependent for years. Although animals can pretend and even lure, they can neither erase their tracks nor make false tracks appear true. In other words, they cannot do what humans do when speaking, namely, make a symbol stand in for the thing. Representation erases the thing in favor of the concept that substitutes the token for reality; animals are incapable of this double operation of erasure and substitution, the inherent duplicity of speech. Speech is the human activity of putting the feint of erasure and substitution in the service of truth. That is, we use words to tell the truth about things by first erasing those very things. As Nietzsche might say, we hide truth behind a bush and then praise ourselves when we find it. The animal may deceive its predator or its prey, but it doesn't deceive itself. Animals may be capable of deception, but man is the self-deceptive animal.

Lacan insists that speech, as distinct from language, exposes the field of signification to "noise" or superfluous meanings that "speak" unconscious desire:

The antinomy immanent in the relations between speech and language thus becomes clear. The more functional language becomes, the less suited it is to speech, and when it becomes overly characteristic of me alone, it loses its function as language . . . what is redundant as far as information is concerned is precisely what plays the part of resonance in speech. . . . For the function of language in speech is not to inform but to evoke. What I seek in speech is a response from the other. (2006, 246–47)

This passage implies that animals' existence is purely utilitarian and that their reactions always function to promote life, whereas human existence is characterized by meaning in excess of use value, the chatter with which we continually and futilely try to fill the void or gap between us and the world opened by our premature birth. This superfluous stuff is the stuff of response and not of reaction, and Lacan claims that animals are incapable of any true response.[2] Because Lacan repeatedly states that there is never any real communication between human subjects and that any appearance of one is merely self-delusion, we might wonder what exactly he means by "response." Perhaps for Lacan, self-delusion is the essence of response, which becomes something like an echo chamber or hall of mirrors.

Following Derrida, we might wonder whether, particularly in light of psychoanalytic theory, we can maintain the distinction between reaction and response in human beings. Here suffice it to say that Lacan insists that "a reaction is not a response" and without evidence from the "animal kingdom" to prove it, he is left with bald assertion and his famous mathemes (cf. 2006, 247). His ambivalence toward both empirical science, especially behaviorism, evidenced by his ambivalence toward animal studies, leads him to math. It seems that as he moves closer to this "something more" that cannot be perceived in the "animal kingdom," he turns to mathemes rather than to animal studies to make his work appear more rigorous, but Lacan's math fetish is beyond the scope of this chapter, as I prefer discussing his animal thing.

In *The Animal,* Derrida "deconstructs" the distinction between reaction and response, along with the distinction between pretending and pretending to pretend, or feint and feigning the feint. After all, how can we tell the difference between pretending and pretending to pretend? How can we distinguish first-order pretense from second-order pretense? Can we so easily distinguish the two senses of duplicity, double actions from double-dealing? How can we distinguish pretending from lying? Derrida summarizes Lacan on pretense versus lie:

According to Lacan it is that type of lie, that deceit, and that pretense in the second degree of which the animal would be incapable, whereas the "subject of the signifier," within the human order, would possess such a power and, better still, would emerge as subject, instituting itself and coming to itself as subject *by virtue of this power,* a second-degree reflexive power, a power that is *conscious* of deceiving by pretending to pretend. (2008, 128, italics in original)

The animal, then, is supposedly incapable of a second-order *true* lie because although it can pretend, it is not conscious of its pretense. If Lacan has once again reduced the divide between man and animal to consciousness, then he is not only begging the question of the border between the two but also treading a precarious line given the limits of consciousness in the psychoanalytic account of the human psyche. What does it mean, post-Freud and Lacan, to say that man is conscious? And after Freud and Lacan, how can we distinguish the second-order reflexivity of consciousness from its roots in unconscious unreflexive operations "behind the scenes"? Once consciousness becomes a sleight of hand, it becomes difficult to maintain any distinction between first- and second-orders or conscious response and "unconscious" or instinctual reaction. How can we tell the difference between an animal that operates in relation to the world without the mediation of the Other and the human who operates with a mediation that he disavows?

In contrast to Lacan, Derrida argues that every seemingly simple pretense could be a pretense of pretense and every pretense of pretense could actually be simply a pretense. "As a result, the distinction between lie and pretense becomes precarious" (Derrida 2008, 133). If the animal is capable of pretense, then it has already taken the other into account. Once it does this, its pretense can become a pretense of pretense which, as Lacan describes it, always depends on the other. Once a creature starts thinking about how to deceive another and once the other creature can be deceived, it is difficult to discern the possible levels of deception, since it (deception) takes place in the relationship itself. But once deception is taken to be the essence of consciousness and speech, it becomes problematic to base any absolute border between man and animal on the truth of consciousness or speech. In addition, once Lacan takes us to the order of the "something more" beyond any observable behavior, it becomes impossible to perceive the difference between first- and second-order pretense, since the difference is really just in the mind. Lacan describes the shift from the function of the image in the animal to the function of the image in man as "imperceptible": "But what is new in man is that something is already sufficiently open, imperceptibly shifted within the imaginary coaptation, for the symbolic use of the image to be inserted into it" (1988b, 322–23). It is this imperceptible shift that opens the way to speech and language, a path closed to the animal. The difference between man and animal, therefore, is not something that can be perceived on the level of the imaginary, precisely the level on which Lacan fixes the animal.

Derrida also challenges Lacan's claim that animals cannot erase their tracks, whereas man can. Derrida reminds us that throughout his work he has shown that "the structure of the trace presupposes that *to trace* amounts to *erasing a trace* (always present-absence) as much as to imprinting it" (2008, 135, italics in original). He maintains that even a simple pretense involves some kind of erasure because it moves in a fictional direction. Even the pigeons, locusts, and stickle-backs falling in love with cardboard cutouts or their reflections in mirrors have gone some distance in changing, suspending, or erasing their relation to "reality."

Even more so, the animals who deceive their predators and their prey by playing dead or wounded or imitating someone else render "a sensible trace illegible or imperceptible" (cf. Derrida 2008, 135). When they are successful, these duplicitous beasts pass for what they are not and thereby erase their "truth."

Again following Derrida, we might wonder whether humans can ever erase their tracks, not only in the metaphorical or metaphysical senses evoked by Derrida, but also in the physical sense or, we could say, in the animal sense. As a thought experiment—and some environmental groups have tested this—try to imagine living on the earth without leaving a trace, even for one day, for one hour, for one minute. It is as impossible for man as it is for any animal to erase his tracks. But unlike most animal tracks and traces, human tracks leave irreversible damage. Even though some animals also wreak havoc on the environment, none, it seems, has done as much as man to destroy what sustains him. Can man learn to tread lightly on the earth? Given the growing concerns about the environment and the effect of human waste on it, and the dawn of the consequences of global warming caused by man's lack of concern for erasing his tracks, he might reconsider what he could learn from the animals. Perhaps they could teach us a few new steps in the dancity through which all creatures live (and die, if not lie) together.

PART FIVE

Estranged Kinship

If you're looking for a role model in a world of complexity,
you could do worse than to imitate a bee.

—*NATIONAL GEOGRAPHIC,* 2008

CHAPTER EIGHT

The Abyss Between Humans and Animals

Heidegger Puts the Bee in Being

Of all the beings that are, presumably the most difficult to think about are living creatures, because on the one hand they are in a certain way most closely akin to us, and on the other are at the same time separated from our ek-sistent essence by an abyss. However, it might also seem as though the essence of divinity is closer to us than what is so alien in other living creatures, closer, namely in an essential distance which, however distant, is nonetheless more familiar to our ek-sistent essence than is our scarcely conceivable, abyssal bodily kinship with the beast.

—HEIDEGGER, "LETTER ON HUMANISM"

Several important commentaries on Heidegger's treatment of animals explain the arguments he advances in his 1929/30 lecture course *The Fundamental Concepts of Metaphysics,* his most extensive examination of animality.[1] Therefore, I won't rehearse the entire convoluted trajectory of his analysis here. Instead, I will highlight aspects of his theory in comparing it with Merleau-Ponty's *Nature* lectures, on the one hand, and in advancing my thesis of animal pedagogy, on the other. My hope is to illuminate some of the traditional philosophical complexities of the "animal problem" and to hazard a further mutation in the evolution of philosophy's thinking of and with animals.

Heidegger begins his analysis of the animal by indicating that man is distinct from animals in his ability to become bored and melancholy. Animals cannot be bored or melancholy because they lack the ability for such attunement or mood (*Mut*). They are "deprived" of mood and thereby of world. Indeed, Heidegger characterizes the essence of animal poverty in world sometimes using the German word *Armut,* meaning "poverty" and also "a lack of spirit or cheer."[2] But the animal's lack of cheer is not to be confused with man's boredom or melancholy. In an important sense, it is through boredom and melancholy that the possibility of world opens up to man. Man's boredom and melancholy create the anxiety necessary for philosophy and creativity, which are the most appropriate responses to freedom. Animals have none of these moods, are incapable of philosophy or creativity, and therefore lack freedom. Unlike man, they are driven by instincts that hold them captive. Through his Dasein, man escapes captivity by instincts and realizes his dreadful freedom. Because the animal is captivated and does not experience the anxiety, boredom, or melancholy unique to Dasein, its privation may not be completely negative. For Heidegger, although it does not experience pleasures, at the same time it does not experience the mental anguish that comes with freedom. It is not faced with the necessity of its own resolute decisions regarding its lifestyle, since its life is predetermined. But as Derrida points out in his commentary in *The Animal,* humanity's supposed uniqueness, if not superiority over animality, is attributed to what we might consider negative qualities or defects: anxiety, dread, boredom, and melancholy (cf. Derrida 2006, chap. 4). Moreover, as we will see, despite his insistence that he is not committed to a hierarchy between man and animals, Heidegger implies one and also explicitly describes animality as the negative of humanity.

We might wonder whether before the abyss of freedom opens (signaled by anxiety and melancholy)—before Dasein—man was also captivated by instincts. Indeed, given Heidegger's insistence on moving away from a nonreflective, commonsense relationship to the world, we might wonder whether his complaint is against the ways in which man is held captive by the natural attitude. At every turn, Heidegger is adamant that whatever man does, he does in a uniquely human way, no matter how similar to the animal ways it might seem. Yet before man becomes the philosophical animal, isn't he just another animal? What are the "missing links" among the animal, the prephilosophical man, and the philosopher who brackets the natural attitude? Of course for Heidegger, the natural attitude already presupposes and presumes the essential but forgotten elements of being. To suggest a missing link is to reduce the ontological difference to which Heidegger is aiming to a merely ontic difference between beings that can be pointed to by the sharp finger of the anthropologist or paleontologist. The origin of Dasein is necessarily a missing origin that cannot be designated by any evolution of beings: "We are missing the origin that first lets these two terms (being and beings) spring forth" (1995, 362). Since it doesn't matter where science points, it can never identify being, only beings, we need the philosopher's "penetrating" gaze. It is noteworthy that Heidegger describes philosophy as circling, an activity that we normally associate with sharks or wolves rather than humans (1995, 180). Whereas in some animals, circling signifies predatory behavior, in man it signifies letting be or caring, an activity proper to the essence of Dasein who is, after all, the shepherd of being. Like a border collie, then, Dasein circles in order to guard being, to guard the being of beings or, more simply put, to guard the essence of beings by letting them be what they are in their essence. But we have to wonder whether this philosophical circling ends up merely chasing its tail.

Of course, this raises the question of whether the essence or being of beings is an essence for us or for those beings in themselves. Heidegger himself raises this question near the end of the lecture course.[3] In answer, he admits,

Our thesis that the animal is poor in world is accordingly far from being a, let alone the, fundamental metaphysical principle of the essence of animality. At best it is a proposition that follows from the essential determinations of animality and moreover one which follows only if the animal is regarded in comparison with humanity. (1995, 271)

Just paragraphs later, however, he rejects this objection and concludes that we have "no right" (*kein Recht*) (yet) to change the thesis to either deny or grant the animal access to world: "Rather we must *leave open the possibility* that the proper and explicit metaphysical understanding of the essence of world compels us to understand the animal's not-having of world as a *deprivation after all,* and to discover *poverty* in the animal's specific manner of being as such" (1983, 395; 1995, 272, italics in original). In other words, since he has not disproved the thesis, we have "no right" to reject it; this is part of the pedagogical strategy of the lecture course. It seems that we could argue that after such detailed analysis, if he has not proved the thesis, we also have no right to continue to accept it, or at least we have as much right to try out another thesis with regard to the animal. Despite Heidegger's suggestion that the entire inquiry has been about "us" all along, he concludes his investigation by insisting that this *animal pedagogy* teaches us something about the essence of world and humanity, as well as the essence of animal and animality as such. Heidegger is dogged in his circling of the animal in an attempt to determine the essence of world, and he claims the "right" to continue to examine the animal and animality for the sake of "asking about ourselves" in the "correct" or "right" way (1995, 281). Not by turning our attention to subjects rather than objects like animals and stones, says Heidegger, but by using the investigation of the animal as an instrument with which to pry open the essence of man (cf. 1995, 281). Man gives himself the right to use animals (or, in this case, denies himself the right not to use animals) as he sees fit and for his own purposes.[4]

Early in his analysis of the animal, Heidegger tells us that insight into the essence of the animal is "indispensable if we are to accomplish our task," which is determining the essence of world, particularly as it pertains to man's world forming. He refers to the analysis of the animal as background for the analysis of man:

"In the end our earlier analysis of captivation as the essence of animality provides as it were a suitable background against which the essence of humanity can now be set off, and indeed precisely in respect of what concerns us here: world and world-formation" (1995, 282). Heidegger uses his analysis of animals to offset the world of Dasein. Animals and the analysis of their nature are heuristics for our insights into humanity. Animals can teach us something about ourselves.

This animal pedagogy is further evidenced when Heidegger begins his discussion of animality with his famous three theses: (1) the stone is worldless; (2) the animal is poor in world; and (3) man is world forming. He then anchors the discussion of all three theses on the second, the animal. The animal's captivation is used to disarticulate the difference between not having a world and having a world. Heidegger makes explicit the pedagogical stakes of the lecture course: comparative analysis is pedagogically valuable because it can help us ascertain the essence of world, finitude, and solitude, the subtitle of the lectures. At one point, Heidegger asks whether the animal falls on the side of the stone or stands with man and concludes that the animal is in between (in its own strange way) and therefore gives meaning to both poles. In regard to world formation, however, it turns out that the animal stands in for the negative pole to man's positive. In discussing the animal, Heidegger concludes,

We have merely acquainted ourselves with the negative side of the matter. And we should consider the fact that we ourselves are the positive side, that we ourselves exist in the having of world. That is why, through the apparently purely negative characterization of world in our examination of the animal's not-having of world, our own proper essence has constantly emerged in contrast, even if not in any explicit interpretation. (1995, 272)

The animal's privation of world turns out to be the negative side of man's having world after all.

Although Heidegger rejects the notion of hierarchy, the animal appears as the negative of the human. Moreover, in its essence it is deprived of the world as it is opened to man. If we look more closely at the passages in which Heidegger mentions hierarchy, they are more ambiguous than some of his commentators suggest. Indeed, it is unclear whether or not he is actually denying a hierarchy between the worlds of animals and humans.[5] For example, in a section of the lecture course entitled "The relationship between poverty in world and world-formation does not entail hierarchical assessment. Poverty in world as deprivation of world," Heidegger claims that although he is trying to compare an analysis of the essences of animals and humans, no such comparison is possible, since they have radically different ways of being. In other words, on an ontological level, animals and humans have nothing in common and therefore cannot be evaluated in relation to each other. This strange defense against hierarchies insists that because animals are radically deprived of something open to man, the relative terms *poor* and *rich* (as they are employed by Heidegger) should not be interpreted as signs of hierarchical value judgments. But this is only because of the animal's complete deprivation, which—whatever Heidegger says to the contrary—makes sense only in relation to man's way of being. Animals are not the negation of man (even if their privation of world is the negation of man's having world) because they are of a radically different order that cannot be compared with man. In the end, one main lesson of Heidegger's pedagogical comparison is that any true comparison is impossible.

Later in the lecture, Heidegger states, "Thus nature, whether it is lifeless nature or indeed living nature, is in no way to be regarded as the plank or lowest rung of the ladder which the human being would ascend, thus to assert his strange essence" (1995, 278). This passage also implies that there is no hierarchical value judgment between animal life and human life. On closer examination of this passage, however, it becomes apparent that again Heidegger is denying hierarchy only because it would mean that humans and animals had enough in common to be compared. Hierarchy would mean that they differed in degrees, although he insists that they differ in kind of being. To him, the environments of man and animals "are not remotely comparable" because animals live under the influence of nature, whereas "man exists . . . out of our own essence and not from nature's influence" (1995, 278). With the ladder metaphor, Heidegger is not saying that there is no hierarchy between animals and humans but is denying the evolution of the human way of being from the animal way of being. In other words, at least on an ontological level, we aren't related to animals. Heidegger compares us with animals to teach us that in any essential sense, we cannot be compared to animals. We are the shepherds and they are the sheep.

For Heidegger, the investigations of the animal and the essence of animality are primarily pedagogical insofar as they teach us something about man's world. Heidegger uses animals in the service of his insights into man. Moreover, when he does mention individual animals or specific types of animals rather than *the animal* or *animality* in general, he cites the most probing and invasive types of biological and zoological studies in which they are removed from their homes and dismembered. The centerpiece of his analysis is the example of a bee whose abdomen was removed while it was eating honey and who continues eating anyway, the honey spilling out of its amputated torso. This is supposed to prove that the bee is simply driven by instinct and does not have any relation to its food as food (or to its own abdomen as such). In fact, insects are Heidegger's prime examples.

Rarely does he mention animals that we might consider closer to our own way of being.[6] In the lecture course, the closest he comes is perhaps the dog, whom he says "does not exist but merely lives" (1995, 210). Because his aim throughout the course is to show a radical rupture or abyss between animals and Dasein, it should be no surprise that he chooses only desiccated insects as his interlocutors.

Although Heidegger insists that animals and all living beings are not merely ready-to-hand, like stones or inanimate objects, because they are mobile and, to a limited extent, self-moving, he treats his animal examples as ready-to-use in his analysis of world. He employs an instrumental relationship to them that throughout his work he cautions us to avoid.[7] In the name of guarding and protecting the being of beings, he endorses dismembering them. Their bodies are sacrificed to their essence; more specifically, their bodies are sacrificed so that we might discern their essence not only as it appears to us but also as it serves our interests in ourselves and our own self-knowledge. So that we can avoid treating ourselves as objects, as mere standing reserve, we treat laboratory animals as such. In order to move beyond a subject-centered ontology in which man presides over all other creatures on earth, Heidegger implicitly endorses domination over these animals as mere objects under the microscope of man's penetrating gaze. In fact, he repeatedly uses the metaphor of "penetration" both to prescribe what his philosophical investigation should do to the essence of animality and to describe the limits of animality in terms of the inability of anything to penetrate what he calls their "disinhibiting ring," or the limited environment that their instinctual being opens up to them (e.g., 1995, 232, 254). In his analysis, however, the animal is figuratively and literally penetrated (e.g., the dissected bee) for the sake of both science and philosophy. The philosopher gives himself the right to penetrate beings in order to access their being and, in a generous if strangely perverse reading, all this in order to guard or shepherd with his powerful circling gaze. Man is the philosophical watchdog of being.

For Heidegger, of course, this activity is evidence of the abyss between animals and humans. Animals are not able to philosophize; and while they may be able to penetrate other beings, they can never penetrate being—that toothsome activity is reserved for man. In his attempt to penetrate the essence of world and world formation, Heidegger goes back and forth on the question of whether or not animals have world, and he asserts the abyss between animals and humans, at least insofar as we are Dasein. Given Heidegger's analysis, we might imagine that in a sense, animals are, by definition, creatures without a conception of world; that humans are, by definition, creatures with a conception of the world; and that these definitions refer more to how we use the terms *animal*, *human*, and *world*— to our concepts and language—than they do to the creatures themselves. They are, to use Heidegger's terminology, ontological rather than ontic distinctions. It is through language that we have access to the being of beings, the world of essence, that is, world formation itself. If language is the house of being and the home of man, then Heidegger's analysis of animals has everything to do with the fact that according to him, they are not linguistic creatures and we are; and as a result he leaves animals with neither house nor home.

We have access to *logos* and they do not. But it is our access to *logos* that enables us to deceive one another. For Heidegger, as for Lacan, it is man's duplicity that separates him from the animals. In his lectures, Heidegger maintains that the essence of *logos* includes the possibility of deception:

That *logos* to whose essence there belongs (among other things) the ability to be deceptive is a pointing out. To deceive means: to pretend something, to present something as something it is not, or to present something that is not such and such as being such and such. This deception, this being deceptive that belongs to the essence of *logos* . . . is a concealing. (1995, 310)

The *logos,* to which man has unique access, has deception as its heart. Throughout his writings, Heidegger emphasizes the concealing nature of language/*logos*. In this passage, it becomes clear that the possibility of deception presupposes making something present, even as concealed, even as pretense.

In *The Animal,* Derrida discusses this passage in which *logos* and the uniquely human revolve around deception (2008, 142). He argues that once again man's humanity is defined as a lack or defect and that once again man's humanity is defined as the ability to deceive. Only man can lie or pretend that something is the case when it is not. We might even say that man's humanity is defined as a privation, now a privation of truth. In this regard, how is the privation that constitutes man's humanity different from the privation that Heidegger attributes to animals? Indeed, doesn't the animal's privation that Heidegger cites eliminate the constitutive privation that makes man Dasein? According to Heidegger, the pretense that marks man as such already assumes the *logos* as monstration:

For precisely whenever I want to pretend something to someone else, I must first already be in a position to want to point something out to him. The other person in general must in advance take my discourse as having this tendency to point out; only in this way can I deceive him about something. (1995, 310–11).

As he did in regard to Lacan's analysis, Derrida believes that in Heidegger's analysis, because animals pretend in order to fool their predators, their prey, or their mates, they engage in pretense that presupposes *logos*. In other words, if animals can pretend, then they too must be capable of monstration directed toward another. They too must be pointing something out to someone. Resonant with Lacan's formulation of the impossibility of an animal's covering its tracks or engaging in second-order pretense, that is, pretense directed toward an other, Heidegger's allows for the possibility of animal monstration directed toward others, which in his analysis (as well as Lacan's) is supposedly reserved for humans. Recall that Derrida takes his analysis in the opposite direction as well, arguing the humans are not capable of truly covering their tracks or discerning first-order from second-order pretense. Their monstration never shows what it intends to show, which is precisely Heidegger's point in insisting on the concealing dimension of *logos*. Once we add the psychoanalytic notion of the unconscious, however, the orders of concealment and deception become complicated and virtually impossible to distinguish from each other. In other words, we cannot distinguish human pretense from animal pretense or human monstration from animal monstration, although this is not to say that animals and humans have the same capacities. Rather, it is that we are not reliable witnesses to our own capacities or to theirs.

If animals have access to *logos,* might they also have access to language? Or if they ever acquired access to language, would they become Dasein? Heidegger's view seems to leave open the possibility that if an animal developed the capacity for language and thus for world formation, it would cease being animal and leap over the abyss into the category Dasein. Although Heidegger doesn't entertain this possibility—focused as he is on insects rather than language-using apes—it does not seem inconsistent with his analysis. In contrast, Heidegger's commitment to the absolute separation between animal and human suggests a conceptual and linguistic rigidity that has implications for how we imagine other creatures as well as how we treat them. Heidegger's humble shepherd may not be Descartes' sovereign subject, but in relation to his flock, that is, all other creatures of the earth, he still wields the staff.

Heidegger's notion of Dasein as *ek-stasis* and rupture leads him to the absolute abyss between animal and humans. Dasein *ek-stasis* is his escape from captivation, which is dependent on his entrance into language. Heidegger cannot abide by evolutionary theory that makes man a mutation of animal. Language is not something merely added to the body or to animality. Rather, language is a way of being in the world and a way of having access to it. Again, Heidegger is not denying evolution on an ontic level, the level of biologists, so much as on a conceptual level, the level of philosophers. It may seem ironic, then, when in the lecture course he turns to biology and zoology to prove his thesis about animal poverty.[8] In *The Fundamental Concepts of Metaphysics,* with its comparative animal pedagogy, Heidegger uses life sciences to make his analysis more convincing. As Lacan's does, his ambivalence toward animals (in terms of their in-between status, between humans and stones) signals, at least in this text, an ambivalence toward science itself. Of course, Heidegger's criticisms of technology and technoscience are well known, which makes even stranger his use of high-tech experiments in zoology and biology to prove his point.

Heidegger singles out two biologists whose discoveries he finds helpful: Driesch and Uexküll. According to Heidegger, Driesch addresses the animal in a holistic way and Uexküll shows how the animal is bound to its environment (1995, 261). Heidegger is especially fond of Uexküll (who, as we will see, was a favorite of Merleau-Ponty as well) because "amongst the biologists Uexküll is the one who has repeatedly pointed out with the greatest emphasis that what the animal stands in relation to is given for it in a different way than it is for the human being" (1995, 263–64). Even so, Uexküll doesn't go far enough in separating man and animal—in that his term *Umwelt,* which refers to the animal environment—is too suggestive of a world (*Welt*), and he goes so far as to name an "inner world" of the animal, which Heidegger rejects as anthropomorphism (1995, 263). Despite these shortcomings, Heidegger thinks that Uexküll's observations can be useful to philosophy, particularly in overcoming the Darwinian view of the ascent of man from animals. On the one hand, Uexküll's research undermines any neat subject/object dichotomy by defining the organism in relationship with its environment. The organism is not merely adapting or reacting to outside stimuli; rather, its relationship with its environment is dynamic. On the other hand, the organism is englobed by its environment in a way determined by its instinctual body, which Dasein supposedly escapes in its access to beings as such. Heidegger finds in Uexküll both an anti-Darwinian sentiment that goes along with his anti-Cartesian one while at the same time maintains the absolute separation between human and animal. Heidegger decides that the difference between animals and man, between poor in world and world formation, is not one of degree or quantity but of quality (1995, 195; cf. 350). He contends that "the world of the animal . . . is not simply a degree or species of the world of man" (1995, 200), and he repeatedly says that "the animal is separated from man by an abyss" (e.g., 1993, 230; 1995, 264).[9]

In *The Fundamental Concepts,* this abyss is that between behavior (*Benehmen*) and comportment (*Sichverhalten*). Animals behave, whereas humans engage in the self-reflexive activity of comporting themselves. Animal behavior is locked into its instinctual ring, whereas human comportment is intentional and free. Heidegger likens animal behavior to physiological processes in the animal's body:

It is not as if the beating of the animal's heart were a process different from the animal's seizing and seeing, the one analogous to the case of human beings, the other to a chemical process. Rather the entirety of its being, the being as a whole in its unity, must be comprehended as behavior. (1995, 239)

Heidegger concludes that captivation does not merely accompany animal behavior but defines it. Animals are captivated by their instincts and therefore have no true or conscious relationships with others or their environment, while humans comport themselves toward others and their environment in a conscious way, that is, a world-forming way (cf. 1995, 237).

Heidegger gives the example of a lizard lying on a rock sunning itself. He claims that the rock and sun are given to the lizard in a lizardlike way defined by the lizard's way of being, "which we call 'life'" but not existence. To exist is to have access to the environment and others as beings, which animals do not have. Heidegger observes that "when we say that the lizard is lying on the rock, we ought to cross out the word 'rock' in order to indicate that whatever the lizard is lying on is certainly given *in some way* for the lizard, and yet is not known to the lizard *as* a rock" (1995, 198, italics in original). Yet as Derrida reminds us, this "as structure" of being is inherently deceptive. Can we ever be certain that a rock is given to us *as* a rock qua rock? Derrida suggests that Heidegger's inclination here to erase all relationships between animals and their fellow beings erases the animal being itself and risks the letting be of their being toward which Heidegger aims (2008, 159–60). This leads Derrida to ask once again about the ability of man to erase his tracks. In other words, can man perform this erasure of animal relationships that Heidegger's text requires? On the one hand, given the deceptive nature of *logos,* is man any more certain of his access to beings in themselves than other animals can be? On the other hand, is man any more capable of erasing his tracks or the tracks of other animals than any animal is of erasing its own tracks?

Derrida also challenges Heidegger's claims that humans are capable of *Mitsein* and animals are not. Heidegger maintains that dogs live but do not exist; and to be with another being requires that one exist, and vice versa. He says that domestic animals "belong to the house," but not like the roof belongs to the house. They live with us but don't exist with us; they feed while we eat and therefore are there with us but not truly with us. In other words, an encounter with an animal, even one with whom we share our home, is not possible. We cannot know their world and they cannot know ours, and therefore any transposition between the two is severely limited if not impossible. Indeed, for the animal, transposition is foreclosed from the beginning. For Heidegger, animals are not capable of the *Mitsein* that is characteristic of Dasein. Derrida's analysis should lead us to ask whether human beings are capable of *Mitsein* in this essential and unlimited sense.

Heidegger maintains that

the Dasein of man, the Da-sein in man means, not exclusively but amongst other things, being transposed into other human beings. The ability to transpose oneself into others and go along with them, with the Dasein in them, always already happens on the basis of man's Dasein, and happens as Dasein. For the being-there of Da-sein means *being with others,* precisely in the manner of Dasein, i.e., existing with others. (1995, 205, italics in original)

He argues that Husserl's theory of empathy between humans presupposes an illusory gap between them that must be bridged. Heidegger insists, though, that there is no gap and therefore no bridge is necessary. In an important sense, the unbridgeable gap between man and animals guarantees the essential transposability of humans. Heidegger's comparative pedagogy enables us to be with other human beings by limiting the ways in which we can be with nonhuman beings. In turn, the uniqueness of Dasein's ability to transpose himself into others is ascertained by comparing it with the animal's absolute inability to do so.

Again we can challenge Heidegger's analysis from several directions. First, are human beings truly capable of the kind of unlimited transposition that he imagines? Second, are animals incapable of any transposition whatsoever? In other words, is the limit between humans and animals as absolute as Heidegger's ontology requires? Third, if we are capable of having only true encounters with other human beings, aren't we, as John Berger might say, as a species alone in the world? (Berger 1980). Can we, then, encounter only what is like us and never any creature unlike us? If so, how can we encounter one another in our difference and uniqueness as human beings? These questions about the possibility of relationships between animals and humans take us back to Derrida's discussion of Heidegger's *Geschlecht* and the possibility of kinship between man and animals.

From chapter 5, recall that Derrida examined Heidegger's ontological difference in his use of the word *Geschlecht*. Specifically, he argues that this word—meaning "kinship," "family," "species," "mark," "stamp," "humankind," and "sexual difference," among other things—signals an inherent connection in Heidegger's thought between sexual difference and animal difference. Derrida's conclusion is that Heidegger replaces one form of dogmatic humanism with another by setting up an absolute limit between humanity and animality (cf. 1987a, 173–74). By identifying man's hand as unique, singular, and proper to man in its ability both to grasp and to give, Heidegger draws a definitive line between man and animals that cannot be crossed in either direction. Derrida says of this distinction: "Man's hand then will be a thing apart not as a separable organ but because it is different, dissimilar (*verschieden*) from all prehensile organs (paws, claws, talons); man's hand is far from these in an infinite way (*unendlich*) through the abyss of its being" [*durch einen Abgrund des Wesens*] (1987a, 174; Derrida is quoting Heidegger's *Was heisst Denken*).

Heidegger's privileging of the human hand over all other appendages becomes more "proof" of the abyss between man and animal. To imagine any kinship between man and animal thus becomes a monstrous experiment (which is perhaps why, as we will see in chapter 10, Agamben is drawn to Heidegger's analysis of animality). Derrida plays with the word *monstrous* in relation to *monstration*, which, according to Heidegger, is unique to man: "The hand is monstrosity [*monstrosité*], the proper of man as the being of monstration. This distinguishes him from every other *Geschlecht*, and above all from the ape" (1987a, 169). Because animals are incapable of monstration, they are not like man. In Derrida's analysis, this monstration makes man akin to the monstrous and therefore to what has been associated with animality. He contends that in Heidegger's analysis, the very names "man" or "human" or "Dasein" become problematic because of his dogmatic insistence on the abyss between man and animal:

What Heidegger says of the ape without hand—and then, as we are going to see, without thinking, language, gift—is not only dogmatic in its form because Heidegger knows nothing about this and wants to know nothing, has no doubt studied neither the zoologists (even were it to criticize them) not the apes in the Black Forest. [Are there apes in the Black Forest?] It is serious because what he says traces a system of limits within which everything he says of man's hand takes on sense and value. Since such a delimitation is problematic, the name of man, his *Geschlecht*, becomes problematic itself. (1987a 174, bracketed question is mine)

Man's *Geschlecht*, his difference, kinship, and family, become problematic. How can he maintain his kinship with and within the family of man? Only as cut off from the family of animal? Is there no kinship between man and animal? And if not, how can there be any kinship among men?

As we have seen, the distinction between human and animal *Geschlecht* does not merely point to (or demonstrate) a difference or differences. Instead, it sets up an opposition, perhaps even a war, and at least a violent marking of the territory of man against that of the animal. Man marks his territory by naming and thereby distinguishing one species, one family, from another. But in order to maintain man's territory as separate and singular, Heidegger creates an abyss around it that no other creature can cross. The distinction becomes more than mere difference; now it is absolute limit or opposition. Humanity and Dasein are set up and maintained through the absolute denial of kinship between man and animals. According to Heidegger, though, the human would not show through without animal difference. Demonstration of the humanity of Dasein necessitates closing off the animal to any possibility of monstration. Heidegger's most sustained analysis of animality in *The Fundamental Concepts of Metaphysics* announces the presence of an abyss between animals and man but demonstrates man's dependence on animals. He maintains that animals are necessary to demonstrate what it means to have a world. In an important sense, it is what animals themselves demonstrate in their inability to monstrate that opens up the possibility of man's own monstration.

Heidegger's thought sees the kinship of man or humankind as possible only through the impossibility of kinship with animals. In addition, it is possible only by insisting on the kinship of animal kind, despite the infinite number of differences among species of animals. What Agamben might call Heidegger's *anthropological machine* produces a homogeneous family of man set against a homogeneous family of animals. In this regard, his famous ontological difference disregards any ontic differences that might introduce the possibility of relationships across differences or even by virtue of differences rather than limit contact by erecting absolute borders that protect us from any true encounter with others. It is telling that in his analysis of the impossibility of kinship (or even true companionship) with animals, Heidegger insists on dispelling the illusion of the gap between individual humans that some philosophers have imagined constitutes the radical difficulty, if not impossibility, of true relationships between people (or consciousnesses—the problem of other minds—as philosophers may say). He says,

This theory emerges from the view that in his relationship to other human beings, man is first of all an isolated being existing for himself. We would therefore in principle initially have to seek a bridge from one human being to another and vice-versa. But the illusion of such isolation arises from the circumstance that human beings factically move around in a peculiar form of being transposed into one another, one which is characterized by an indifferent going alongside one another. This illusion of a prior separation between one human being and another is reinforced by philosophical dogma that man is initially to be understood as subject and as consciousness, that he is primarily and most indubitably given to himself as consciousness for a subject. (1995, 208)

Based on Heidegger's analysis, can't we extend this reasoning to the gap between humans and animals? In other words, could we be suffering under an illusion that humans and animals live in isolation from each other because our being with them appears to us as merely being alongside them based on the further illusion that we are primarily conscious and subjects and they are not? Furthermore, if we consider human beings as a species, as Heidegger most certainly does, and if we do not share our world with other living creatures, then aren't we therefore isolated? If an abyss separates us from other living creatures, then as a species we are isolated and alone in the world. But given man's factical dependence on animals for as far back as we can imagine and continuing today, and given the conceptual dependence of the notion of humanity on the notion of animality, it seems that humans are, in both essence and fact, related to animals. The abyss between humans and animals may be another philosophical illusion based on privileging consciousness that leads to bridge building where none is needed.

Implicitly criticizing Husserl's theory of empathy as what bridges the gap between human consciousnesses, Heidegger compares our ability to "transpose" ourselves into other humans, into animals, and into stones.[10] He argues that it doesn't make sense even to ask about transposition or empathy between people, since our being with others is a given in our experience, which means that empathy is either unnecessary or presupposed by our being with. Although to a limited extend we can talk about empathy with animals, we cannot empathize with stones. This analysis again shows the ambiguous and in-between status of animals, but only in our experience of them. Heidegger is quick to point out that while we have access to animals as beings, and therefore can exist with them (in a limited way), they do not have access to us as beings and therefore can never exist with us. We could say that in Heidegger's analysis, humans' ability to be together is dependent on the inability of animals to be with us. The dogmatism of the illusion that there is a gap between isolated human beings that necessitates philosophical bridge building is displaced onto the dogmatism that there is a gap between humans and animals that necessitates philosophical bridge building (or not, if the abyss cannot be crossed). The absence of any gap between humans is dependent on the abyss between us and animals.

Despite his philosophical circling (or tail chasing, depending on what you think of his methodology) and his pedagogical roundup of the concepts of humanity, animality, and world, he may have too quickly concluded that human beings are, in essence, being with one another and not merely being alongside one another. And he may have concluded too quickly that animal beings are separated from human beings by an abyss that limits them to merely being alongside rather than being with. For in an important sense, being with may be an ideal to which we aspire but can never achieve, like Derrida's notions of gift, hospitality, or forgiveness. As we will see, being with in the sense of kinship may also be an ideal that we cannot assume based on generation, descent, or blood, or on *Geschlecht* in terms of being the same species. Kinship, too, may be an ideal to which we aspire. The so-called brotherhood of man in no way ensures that human beings treat one another as brothers. Despite Heidegger's "scarcely conceivable, abyssal bodily kinship with the beast," perhaps animals can be dear friends, even family.

CHAPTER NINE

"Strange Kinship"

Merleau-Ponty's Sensuous Stickleback

What the meditation of our "strange kinship" with the animals (and thus
with the theory of evolution) teaches pertaining to the human body. It
is to be understood as our projection-introjection, our Ineinander with
Sensible Being and with other corporeities.

—MERLEAU-PONTY, *NATURE: COURSE NOTES*

If Heidegger objects to Uexküll's anthropomorphic use of *Umwelt* to describe the
animal environment because it attributes too much world to animals, Merleau-
Ponty objects to Uexküll's "humanism" because it doesn't make the animal's *Umwelt* rich enough.[1] Like Heidegger, Merleau-Ponty looks to Uexküll because his
theories can be used to denounce the Cartesian dichotomy between subject and
object (cf. 2003, 168). Unlike Heidegger, who sees in Uexküll biology's most radical separation between man and animal, Merleau-Ponty uses Uexküll to argue
for continuity between man and animal. As we will see, this is not evolutionary
continuity but a "strange kinship" based on embodiment and resulting styles of
life. Merleau-Ponty endorses the biologist's research insofar as

Uexküll denounces the Cartesian dichotomy, which joins an extremely mechanistic way
of thinking to an extremely subjective way of thinking. Descartes is in effect antimecha-
nist to the extent that he posits consciousness as universe entirely different from that of
mechanism. Uexküll himself posits the *Umwelt* as a type of which the organization, the
consciousness, and the machine are only variations. (2003, 168)

Like Merleau-Ponty, Heidegger argues against a mechanistic view of nature but
asserts the ontological difference between human Dasein and animals, despite any
ontic similarities biologists or zoologists may find. Merleau-Ponty, in contrast,
uses Uexküll to demonstrate that human consciousness is just one type, theme,
or style of behavior among others.

Although Merleau-Ponty insists on a "strange" continuity between animals and man, like that of most philosophers, his use of animals serves to enlighten us about man. His investigations into animal behavior, perception, and culture are motivated by his hypotheses about human behavior, perception, and culture. In both his earlier and later work, he uses animal examples and illustrations to prove his theories of human consciousness. In his attempts to ground consciousness in the body through his theories of perception and behavior, he turns to the natural world and especially animals to make his arguments more vivid. In this regard, like Heidegger, he enlists animals in a form of animal pedagogy. In his work, the concept of animality and examples of individual animals serve to reinforce his notions about the role of perception and behavior in man. By identifying the prefiguration of language and culture in animal behavior, Merleau-Ponty's thesis that human language and culture are grounded in perception and behavior becomes more compelling. If our consciousness is linked to our embodiment and if Merleau-Ponty can demonstrate that the precursors to this form or style of consciousness already operate in an animal embodiment, he can further justify his turn to the body. Moreover, as Heidegger does, Merleau-Ponty pokes and prods laboratory animals in the name of science.[2] In addition, the zoological or biological experiments he cites are more often than not designed to teach us something about humans rather than the animals who are under the microscope. Although he explicitly rejects reductionistic versions of the theory of evolution, his *Nature* lectures describe a progression from lower to higher forms of animals and finally to human embodiment and behavior. Still, Merleau-Ponty could be interpreted as providing an alternative conception of evolution, one that allows for kinship between lower and higher life-forms, not as antecedents and descendents but as sharing similar bodily structures, functions, or behaviors. Instead of emergence and generation, he talks of a lateral relationship and different styles of being.

Throughout his work, Merleau-Ponty reconsiders behavior along with perception as the ground of his phenomenology. He starts with animal embodiment in order to prove his theses about human embodiment. Heidegger, on the contrary, distinguishes between behavior, which he attributes to animals, and comportment, which he maintains is unique to man. By so doing, however, Heidegger reinscribes the split between body and consciousness integral to the split between subject and object that he rejects. Merleau-Ponty addresses the subject/object split at the levels of behavior and perception, where body and consciousness cannot be distinguished so easily. Leaving aside for the moment Merleau-Ponty's distinctions between behavior and perception, it is his theory of behavior that brings humans and animals into thematic harmony with each other. Following his metaphor of melody, we could say that man and animal are different, even dissonant, parts of the same tune.[3] In contrast to Heidegger, who maintains that attunement is what separates the two by an abyss, Merleau-Ponty finds a resonance between them. Heidegger's insistence on rupture and abyss versus Merleau-Ponty's insistence on continuity and kinship turns on their radically different conceptions of behavior.

As we have seen, for Heidegger, behavior signals captivation by instinct, as opposed to intentional comportment. Although Merleau-Ponty's assessment of animal behavior in his early work is like Heidegger's, in his later *Nature* lectures it becomes more complex.[4] In *The Structure of Behavior,* for example, Merleau-Ponty concludes that

the gestures of behavior, the intentions which it traces in the space around the animal, are not directed to the true world or pure being, but to being-for-the-animal, that is, to a certain milieu characteristic of the species; they do not allow the showing through of a consciousness, that is, a being whose whole essence is to know, but rather a certain manner of treating the world, of "being-in-the-world" or of "existing." (1983, 125–26)

Here, although he rejects mechanism and behaviorism even to describe animals, unlike Heidegger he already attributes meaning to their behavior:

Like that of stimulus, the notion of response separates into "geographical behavior"—the sum of the movements actually executed by the animal in their objective relation with the physical world; and behavior properly so called—these same movements considered in their internal articulation and as a kinetic melody gifted with a meaning. (1983, 130)

At this point, Merleau-Ponty is already quite taken with Uexküll's metaphor of the relationship between organism and its environment as a melody singing itself (see 1983, 159).

In *The Structure of Behavior,* Merleau-Ponty distinguishes, as Heidegger does, between man and animals in terms of temporality and the ability to project oneself into different possible futures. Whereas man can relate to various possibilities, the animal can relate to only what is actual. Merleau-Ponty gives the example of monkeys who use sticks as tools to get food but cannot imagine the sticks in what we can see as their various purposes and instantiations: as part of a tree, as a tool, as a walking stick, as kindling, and so on. For the monkey, the stick is nothing more than what it uses to eat ants (1983, 175). Thus Merleau-Ponty concludes:

This power of choosing and varying points of view permits man to create instruments, not under the pressure of a *de facto* situation, but for a virtual use and especially in order to fabricate others. . . . These acts of the human dialectic all reveal the same essence: the capacity of orienting oneself in relation to the possible, the mediate, and not in relation to a limited milieu. (175)

In *The Structure of Behavior*, faithfully following Uexküll, Merleau-Ponty holds a view of animals very similar to Heidegger's: Animals are locked into limiting environments cut off from imagining other possibilities, whereas man in his essence is open to possibilities and futural projections. Moreover, the monkeys in this text serve to better illuminate the behavior of man rather than to garner attention in their own right. They are, then, primarily examples of animal pedagogy.

Here Merleau-Ponty's monkeys are not so different from Heidegger's in that neither of them can grasp the meaning of their actions or relate to objects as beings apart from their immediate utility. Heidegger invokes the ape in order to distinguish the hand of man from all other creatures' claws and paws. Only human beings have hands, which signals their ontological difference from animals. It is not just that humans have a different kind of appendage from other animals that allows them the dexterity of an opposable thumb but that they can grasp things and point to things on the level of concepts and speech. The hand becomes a sign of the abyss between man and animals. Recall my remarks in chapter 5 about Heidegger's hand and Derrida's analysis of it. Here, suffice it to say that for Heidegger and for the early Merleau-Ponty, monkeys can never grasp what man can because they have no access to the world of meaning and futurity.

Decades later, however, in the *Nature* lectures, Merleau-Ponty takes the theories of Uexküll in another direction and concentrates on the meaning of animal behavior.[5] Now animal behavior and animal environments, along with human behaviors and human consciousness, become different *themes* or *styles* of behavior, consciousness being only one type of behavior among others (2003, 166). Perhaps it is telling that Merleau-Ponty concludes his 1958/59 lecture course on Heidegger, which otherwise does not mention animals, with the problem of kinship with them. In his conclusion, he cites a passage from "Letter on Humanism," in which Heidegger claims that our kinship with animals is both more proximal and more distant than our kinship with divinity, in that we are separated from them by an abyss. Heidegger calls this "our scarcely conceivable, abyssal bodily kinship with the beast" [*die kaum auszudenkende abründige leibliche Verwandtschaft mit dem Tier*] (Heidegger 1993,, 230). Merleau-Ponty relates Heidegger's remarks about our "kinship" with animals to Husserl's notions of *Ineinander* (intertwined) and

Einfülung (empathy), notions that play a major role in Merleau-Ponty's *Nature* lectures and later in *The Visible and the Invisible*. In the last line of Merleau-Ponty's lecture on Heidegger, he refers us to his course on Nature, where he takes up this problem of our strange kinship with animals (1958, 148). Merleau-Ponty's interpretation of Heidegger's "strange" or "abyssal" kinship with animals, however, seems far from Heidegger's own remarks. As we have seen, Heidegger makes a point of describing the paradox of our "strange kinship" as that while we may seem close to animals in terms of world formation we couldn't be further from them if we were gods. For Heidegger, an investigation into the world of animals reveals that there can be no intertwining between man and animal, since man is self-reflective Dasein and animals merely exist. If there is any empathy between them, it is entirely on the side of the human. Certainly, for Heidegger, *ineinander verliebt sein,* or "being in love," is completely out of the question for animals and unthinkable between animals and humans.

For Heidegger, if language is essentially what separates man and animal and opens the human to Dasein, then Merleau-Ponty locates the fundamental dynamics of meaning on the levels of perception and behavior. Language and culture are not cut off from the animal body but resonate with it in a formal or figurative sense. For Merleau-Ponty, behavior becomes richer and acquires meanings that set up and prefigure linguistic meaning. Already in behavior we find futural projections, responsivity, interrogative gestures, imitation, imagination, interpretation, expression, pleasure, and ultimately even *logos* and culture. Merleau-Ponty's analysis of behavior also points to a transformation in what we might consider access to world and world formation. As Merleau-Ponty maintains, if once we study behavior we no longer see where behavior ends and consciousness begins, then unlike Heidegger we can no longer use the distinction between behavior and consciousness to separate having or not having access to world (cf. 2003, 178). We thus could say that when Merleau-Ponty turns to nature in his later work, he finds world prior to consciousness.[6]

Merleau-Ponty calls animality the *logos* of the sensible world (2003, 166). Even Uexküll's *Umwelt* takes on greater significance; it is not just the container of instincts à la Heidegger but also the possibility of the "interpretation of symbols" (2003, 176). The sense in which we might say that the animal is captivated by its environment changes dramatically. The animal is no longer held captive by its milieu as a prisoner but now as a fascinated participant-spectator whose imagination is gripped by its surroundings and fellow beings. Merleau-Ponty describes imagination displayed in behavior as dreamlike and repeatedly mentions the oneiric quality of behavior in both animals and humans (e.g., 2003, 178, 188, 193). Moreover, the level of the imaginary or of the image prefigures *logos* and symbolic languages. In this regard, along with Lacan, Merleau-Ponty emphasizes the relation between the imaginary and the symbolic.

Unlike Heidegger, Merleau-Ponty sees behavior as like language in that it is meaningful and expressive (2003, 146, 188). It does not aim so much at objects as at communication through symbols. Merleau-Ponty claims that gestures are to actions what words are to sentences (2003, 155). Behavior possesses its own *logos,* and animality is the *logos* of the natural world. As such, language is not a rupture from the natural world but a continuation of it. For Merleau-Ponty, life is meaningful and there is meaning only in the living. Machines occupy a similar place in his comparative analysis as animals do in Heidegger's; Merleau-Ponty says that machines function while animals live. Unlike Heidegger, he does not distinguish between merely living and existing; rather, living beings exhibit different styles of existing. If meaning, style, expression, and *logos* are already exhibited in behavior, then animals also are intentional beings oriented to their environments and others. Life itself is richer in Merleau-Ponty's account than in Heidegger's, for whom life alone is poor in world compared with Dasein's world formation.[7]

Merleau-Ponty also describes a connection between instinct and the image that casts instincts in a very different light from Heidegger's instincts. Perhaps the most fundamental difference is that for Merleau-Ponty, instincts are aimed toward pleasure, whereas for Heidegger, they are aimed toward self-preservation. Whereas Heidegger describes animals as encircled by rings of instinct from which they cannot escape, Merleau-Ponty describes instincts as themes or styles of behavior oriented to pleasure. Since animals act on instincts, Heidegger concludes that they are not aware of objects or of themselves but merely are caught up in their behavior, like the bee who does not recognize its food or its own abdomen. For Heidegger, animal behavior is not intentional in that it cannot be truly said to be oriented to anything at all. Merleau-Ponty would agree that behavior is not object oriented, but not because behavior is not intentional. On the contrary, it is not that animals are not aware enough to take objects. Rather, it is that perception and behavior are so thoroughly relational that ultimately it becomes artificial to separate subjects from objects. Moreover, instinctual behavior is oriented to pleasure and communion with fellow creatures, which also defy neat categorization into subjects and objects. As Merleau-Ponty says, "Instinct is before all else a theme, a style that meets up with that which evokes it in the milieu, but which does not have goals: it is an activity for pleasure" (2003, 193). It becomes obvious that Merleau-Ponty and Heidegger have vastly different conceptions of instinct. Whereas Heidegger insists that animal behavior is not object oriented because animals are incapable of recognizing objects, Merleau-Ponty maintains that it is not object oriented because it goes beyond any such mechanistic causal relationships toward richer relationships between responsive beings. In this regard, Merleau-Ponty also differs from Lacan, who claims that animals cannot respond but merely react to stimuli.

In the *Nature* lectures, Merleau-Ponty begins to depart from Uexküll, who sees the animal locked into its symbiosis with its environment. Uexküll's tick, a favorite of Giorgio Agamben, makes clear Merleau-Ponty's departure. Not without irony, Agamben calls Uexküll's description of the tick's *Umwelt* a "high point of modern antihumanism," in that it gives the tick's-eye view of life (2004, 45). According to Uexküll, the tick is plugged into a circuit, sensitive only to the smell of butyric acid, the temperature of mammalian bodies, and the texture of skin, all of which are necessary for nourishing itself with the blood of mammals. Agamben imagines that the tick might relish the taste of blood or enjoy sucking it but finds in Uexküll the opposite conclusion: the tick automatically absorbs any liquid at the right temperature (37 degrees) (2004, 46). Deleuze and Guattari also admire Uexküll's tick, in which they find a quintessential ethical relationship beyond the three affects identified by Uexküll:

It will be said that the tick's three affects assume generic and specific characteristics, organs and functions, legs and snout. This is true from the standpoint of physiology, but not from the standpoint of Ethics. Quite the contrary, in Ethics the organic characteristics derive from longitude and its relations . . . we know nothing about a body until we know what it can do . . . with the affects of another body. (1987, 257)

Like Merleau-Ponty, what Deleuze and Guattari find remarkable about Uexküll's tick is not the way in which it is chained to its narrow environment but rather the complexity and power of its relationships with others, relationships by virtue of which it exists.

Uexküll also cites a laboratory experiment in which a tick was kept alive for eighteen years waiting for nourishment, which prompts Agamben to ask: How this animal can "wait" when it has neither sense of time nor world? And how can it live in a laboratory cut off from its environment if it is nothing more than part of a circuit plugged into its *Umwelt* like, as Merleau-Ponty says, a key in a lock? Merleau-Ponty mentions the same laboratory experiment and concludes from it that space and time are relative. Perhaps eighteen years is the time after which the tick no longer has a sense of time (something like moments smaller than one-eighteenth of a second in humans). Merleau-Ponty is critical of Uexküll because he still dissects the tick's environment into three compartments chained together rather than interpreting its meaning as a whole. Merleau-Ponty would not accept Uexküll's tick as the high point of antihumanism because Uexküll limits truly meaningful experiences in relation to environment to humans alone, whereas for Merleau-Ponty, animal behavior is full of meaning too. The continued privilege of the human *Umwelt* in relation to animals' and his suggestion that Nature is unknowable to us (outside our own *Umwelt*), leads Merleau-Ponty to call Uexküll a Kantian humanist (2003, 177). Taking up Uexküll's metaphor of melody but leaving behind that of chains and adding an analogy to dreams, Merleau-Ponty insists:

The notion of *Umwelt* no longer allows us to consider the organism in its relation to the exterior world, as an effect of the exterior world, or as a cause. The *Umwelt* is not present in front of the animal like a goal; it is not present like an idea, but as a *theme that haunts consciousness*. If we wanted to use an analogy with human life, we would have to understand the orientation of this behavior as something similar to the orientation of our oneiric consciousness toward certain poles that are never elements of a dream. Such a mode of knowledge is applicable to the relations between them and the parts of the organism, to the relations of the organism to its territory, and to the relations of animals among themselves, so well that *we no longer see where behavior begins and where mind ends*. (2003, 178; italics added)

For Merleau-Ponty, the *Umwelt* is not a narrow band chained around the organism but a melody that haunts it. Animals, like humans, are haunted and fascinated by their environments and fellow beings, making their captivation more awestruck than mechanical.

In Heidegger's analysis, in contrast, animals are incapable of recognizing other animals or objects in their midst, let alone responding to them or taking pleasure in them. Everything is part of the closed circuit open only to instinctual demands for food and sex and the like. He gives the example of the preying mantis that eats her mate after sex: "The one animal is never there for the other simply as a living creature, but is only there for it either as sexual partner or as prey" (1995, 250). For Heidegger, animals do not have any true relationships with their environment or to their fellow animals. Compare this with Merleau-Ponty's analysis of the mating displays of stickleback fish. In contrast to biologists who are perplexed by the "dance" of the male stickleback when it sees a female and zigzags forward and back and who conclude that the male alternates between taking the female as a sexual partner or as a rival, Merleau-Ponty argues that the stickleback's dance is not a contradiction between treating the female as a mate and as a rival but is treating the female as a fellow being. He maintains that "sexual behavior is more than simple copulation—it is monstration, a ceremony in which the animals give themselves to each other" (2003, 196). Throughout the *Nature* lectures,

Merleau-Ponty emphasizes the demonstrative and communicative aspects of animal behaviors. Whereas the biologists, like Heidegger, speculate that the female stickleback is either sexual partner or rival, Merleau-Ponty argues that they see each other as more than just partners or rivals but also as fellow creatures. The demonstrative aspect of the "dance" is not a "failure of instinct" but indicates a "natural duplicity of instinct" insofar as it also involves rituals that evoke sociality and symbolism (2003, 196–97). The natural duplicity of instinct is related to its imaginary component, which also inaugurates its symbolic and social aspects.

Merleau-Ponty calls instinct a type of fetish because the animal both knows and doesn't know what it wants and because instinct does not aim at the real but at the image for the sake of pleasure (2003, 193). The stickleback is just one example of an animal (fish) that can be fooled into its mating dance by the image of its partner. Other animals, objects, and images can be substituted for the sexual partner. Recall that Lacan also gives examples of animals, including the stickleback, who are susceptible to the image. Whereas Lacan is ambivalent about whether or not animals have an active imaginary that goes beyond mere stimulus/response, Merleau-Ponty interprets the primacy of images in animal society as being like those in human society because they create the possibility of displacements as protosymbolic exchanges in rituals of communication.

Merleau-Ponty describes the substitution of image for real partner as a type of displacement that signals the protosymbolic nature of animal rituals and ceremonies. The imaginary dimension of animal behavior also indicates that the relation between the environment and the animal is not one of strict cause and effect insofar as various objects or images can evoke the same responses. For example, the butterfly may react in the same way to another butterfly or to a stick covered with the secretion of another butterfly, or the bird may react in the same way to the red throat of its mate or to another red object (cf. 2003,193). From these examples, Merleau-Ponty concludes that instinct is useful or functional in a Darwinian evolution of adaptation to outside circumstances as well as in the meeting of inside and outside that takes us beyond any mechanistic explanations of behavior and toward the excess of symbolic meaning. The rituals and ceremonies of sexuality and of taking nourishment exceed what is merely necessary for survival. In fact, in some cases they may be detrimental to survival. Animals, like humans, live for more than mere survival; they also live for pleasure and their own forms of social interaction, what Merleau-Ponty calls "animal culture" (2003, 198).

In addition, man is not the only being who interrogates being. For Merleau-Ponty, behavior itself is a form of interrogation. He describes movement as a way of questioning and responding in relation to the environment and others and the body: "An organ of the mobile sense (the eye, the hand) is already a language because it is an interrogation (movement) and a response (perception as Erfühlung of a project), speaking and understanding. It is a tacit language" (2003, 211; cf. 156, 219). Behavior both addresses itself to the world and others and responds to them. Action, says Merleau-Ponty, is an interrogative style of being (2003, 156). If behavior is a style of questioning, then asking and answering questions is no longer the privilege of man, à la Descartes. What appears to Lacan as mere reaction becomes a style of response. Heidegger's disinhibiting ring that captivates the animal becomes instead a medium of communication. Heidegger's animals are reduced to using one another without any relationships, whereas Merleau-Ponty's fellow creatures give themselves to one another. Questioning does not have to be conceptual or linguistic to count as a form of interrogation; rather, metaphysical interrogation begins in the body.

For Heidegger, man's everyday, unreflective ways of being in the world presuppose metaphysical interrogation, but animal ways of being in the world are closed to such interrogation, which is the difference between world formation and world poverty. As Derrida so powerfully argues, Heidegger derails metaphysical humanism, but only by opening the throttle on a man/animal dichotomy that takes humanism down another track. The world may no longer revolve around man's reason as its agent and telos, but it does depend on an absolute distinction between man and animal that having a world at all is to be human. Derrida contends that in an important sense, Heidegger, Lacan, and Levinas all import another type of humanism (the human against the animal) in their attempts to overcome metaphysical humanism (see, e.g., 2006, 197).

Like his contemporaries, Merleau-Ponty rejects metaphysical humanism. Overall, though, in certain ways his work continues to privilege human perception and behavior. In the *Nature* lectures in particular, Merleau-Ponty attempts to take us beyond both a subject-centered ontology and a human-centered one. He does so by invoking the common figure of the body, as different as their configurations and styles may be, in thinking through the relationship among perception, behavior, culture, and world. In an important sense, the whole of Merleau-Ponty's project is an attempt to show that metaphysical interrogation is already operating at the bodily level of perception and behavior. Because behavior itself is a form of interrogation, relationships among beings are possible not just for man but also for animals. Animals have their own styles of culture and *logos*.

Merleau-Ponty disagrees with the botanist Linnaeus that he "hardly knows a single distinguishing mark which separates man from the apes, save for the fact that the latter have an empty space between their canines and their other teeth" (Linnaeus 1995, 4–5).[8] Rather than some mark on the body that may distinguish or identify them, the stuff of taxonomy, Merleau-Ponty is concerned with embodiment itself and what it entails. In this regard, like Derrida, Merleau-Ponty wants to find a way of marking differences that is not reduced to counting or numbers. Embodiment entails perception and behavior, sensation and movement, and although they may be radically different in man and apes, both share in having them, which for Merleau-Ponty also means having world.

Merleau-Ponty identifies a type of continuity between animals and humans with shared embodiment, which entails perception and behavior or movement. It is crucial to note from the outset that this continuity or kinship is "strange" in that it contains a discontinuity at its heart. For Merleau-Ponty, this is not a body in repose or dissected by biologists. Instead, it is the living body, dynamic and full of movement. In different ways, living bodies perceive and act, sense and move, in reversible relations with their environments and other beings. Merleau-Ponty describes the differences between bodies and behaviors as differences in styles or themes. He finds no abyss separating the bodies of animals and the bodies of humans. Because human consciousness always and necessarily embodies consciousness, it resonates with animal consciousness.[9] Human desire also resonates with animal desire: "Already in the animal, in the ceremony of love, desire is not mechanical functioning, but an opening to an *Umwelt* of fellow creatures (possibility fixation on others), communication" (2003, 225). Merleau-Ponty describes a configuration of animal and human embodiment. He is more concerned with what embodiment entails than he is with the space between the canines and other teeth.

This configuration between animals and humans, however, is not adaptation or hierarchy, emergence or generation, but a *lateral relationship*.[10] Animal bodies and cultures emerge concurrent with human bodies and cultures because there is continuity among the physical world, biological life, behavior, and consciousness.[11] There is a fundamental kinship among all living beings through our shared embodiment, which includes both reflective and unreflective consciousness (2003, 251). Consciousness for Merleau-Ponty is the body folding over onto itself, touching itself, seeing itself, and therefore it is not separated from the body. Once consciousness is radically embodied in this way, it cannot be denied to other forms of embodied life. The differences become differences of styles or, we could say, differences of lifestyles. In Merleau-Ponty's metaphor of melody, we could describe these differences in style or theme as different ways of "singing the world," as he says in *Phenomenology of Perception* (2002, 217).[12]

It is important to note that like Heidegger, Merleau-Ponty attempts to navigate between the poles of vitalism and mechanism. As he says, consciousness is not in atoms. Consciousness is not *in* matter or *in* the body per se. Consciousness is the "other side" of the body. So, too, the world is the other side of the body: "We understand better that the human body is, for the human, not the stand-in for or lining of his 'reflection' but rather reflection in figural form (the body touching itself, seeing itself), nor is the world an inaccessible in-itself, but 'the other side' of his body" (2003, 268). This "other side" is both inseparable and distinct; the two cannot be separated and yet they are different. Life cannot be reduced to the mechanistic explanations of the biological sciences; but neither is it some transcendent vital force hiding in the physical. It is an "unfurling," as are processes that cannot be reduced to either mechanism or viatlism.[13] Merleau-Ponty is describing the human body as well as bodies and embodiment in all animal forms. He sees his *Nature* lectures as developing an "archeology of the body, and especially the human body," but not exclusively the human body. What is true of other bodies qua bodies is also true of human bodies, and vice versa. As bodies, they exist in a "relation of intercorporeity in the biosphere with all animality." Human bodies become "properly human" through a "reinvestment" of the body in itself, "reflection as the coming-to-self of Being" without any addition of transcendental subject (2003, 268).

In the *Nature* lectures, Merleau-Ponty describes consciousness as one side of a leaf, as in a leaf in a book or a sheet of paper. This course also leads him away from the dichotomous opposition between activity and passivity in which one element or subject is the cause and the other is its effect. Neither the organism nor its environment has sole causal power. Neither the body in its materiality nor some transcendent consciousness is the causal agent of animal or human behavior. Instead, organism and environment are in a relationship, which engenders activity (and passivity) on both sides. The notion that the organism is a melody singing itself undermines any neat dichotomy between active and passive.[14] As we know, for Merleau-Ponty, the notes and melody are not in a relation of cause and effect, even though they are intimately related. Metaphors of melody and of folds or leaves figure the body and consciousness as inseparable yet distinct. Merleau-Ponty describes the relationship between notes in a melody and parts of a melody as inseparable; the notes are not the melody but there is no melody without them. So too, the notes do not cause the melody, or vice versa; the metaphor of melody circumvents the dichotomy between cause and effect: "Just as we cannot say that the last note is the end of the melody and that the first is the effect of it, neither can we distinguish the meaning apart from the meaning where it is experienced" (2003, 174). Following Uexküll, Merleau-Ponty observes that the reversible relation between the organism or animal and its milieu is like a melody singing itself, so we cannot separate activity from passivity. Indeed, for Merleau-Ponty, passivity becomes an essential aspect of activity. In turn, life itself is defined in terms of activity: "We must understand life as the opening of a field of action" (2003, 172). But his notion of action cannot be reduced to traditional distinctions between cause and effect, subject and object, or inside and outside. The agency of this action lies in the field or space between the organism and its environment and others: "Each part of the situation acts only as part of a whole situation; no element of action has a separate utility in fact. Between the situation and the movement of the animal, there is a relation of meaning which is what the expression *Umwelt* conveys" (2003, 175). Merleau-Ponty interprets Uexküll's *Umwelt* in terms of Gestalt theory of figure and ground or part and whole. The double configuration of part and whole makes activity possible, and what is active from one perspective or from one side might be seen as passive from the other. The metaphors of leaves and folds convey this sense of sides or perspectives. What is seen as body or visible is just one perspective on what from another angle is mind or invisible.

Merleau-Ponty's thesis that the mind and body are inseparable yet distinct has implications for thinking about the relation between man and animals. He says that because "mind is incredibly penetrated by its corporeal structure," "the relation of the human and animality is not a hierarchical relation but a lateral, a surpassing (*dépassement*) that does not abolish kinship" (2003, 268, translation modified; see original, 1994, 335). He insists on the "lateral union of animality and humanity" insofar as they are necessarily given together (2003, 271). In Derridian terms, we might say that they are inseparable yet distinct, what Leonard Lawlor points to as Derrida's "staggered analogy." Even the notion of a staggered analogy, however, risks privileging the human if the place of the animal is known or determined or even supposed in relation to the human as a starting point. In other words, if the analogy starts with one and moves to the other as analogous in time or space or both, then it risks reinstating a hierarchy. While the stagger may protect one from falling into the other, it also reopens the possibility of one taking priority (in time and space) over the other. The figure of lateral union, however, does not privilege one over the other but suggests that they come at the same time and in the same space. If humans and animals are kin through a lateral relationship, then humanity does not emerge from animality, nor is it radically separated from animality.

In his later work, Merleau-Ponty attempts to navigate between biological continuism and metaphysical separationism (to use Leonard Lawlor's terminology). He attempts to think outside what he sees as a classical dilemma:

Either the being that stands before us may be likened to a human being, in which case it can be given, by analogy, the usual human attributes of the healthy adult. Alternatively, it is no more than a blind mechanism—living chaos—in which case meaning cannot possibly be ascribed to its behaviour. (2004b, 71)

He objects to the views that animals are either prototypes of human beings or machines (2004b, 70). As we have seen, he proposes an alternative to the either/or of humanlike or machine by focusing on styles of behavior and relationships between beings and their environments. It is noteworthy that in his 1948 radio lectures, Merleau-Ponty implicitly criticizes his earlier use of animal studies, particularly those of chimpanzees, to show that animals are incapable of projecting themselves into the future and therefore are incapable of higher thought processes. In these lectures, he rejects animal studies that use human intelligence and human reason as a standard by setting the animal "tasks that are not its own" (2004b, 75). Rather than judge the animal world according to human standards, he proposes that we "live alongside the world of animals instead of rashly denying it any kind of interiority" (2004b, 75). His notion of "living alongside" means that we can both live with and exist with animals, which disagrees with Heidegger and also gives a richer significance to what he calls the "lateral relationship" between humans and animals.

For Merleau-Ponty, as for Heidegger, it is not a question of a missing link between man and animals. Recall that to Heidegger, the very distinction between them bespeaks the ontological difference that cannot be reduced to some (ontic) being between the two because that difference is the difference between beings and access to Being, which is the difference that makes man human, as opposed to animal. For Merleau-Ponty, however, the ontic and ontological are two sides of the same body, which is not a thing but a relationship (in both animals and humans) (cf. 2003, 209). There is not an abyss between the ontic and ontological. Instead, they are two sides of a leaf or sheet, two sides of a fold in nature. Whereas Heidegger sees an infinite and unbridgeable gap between beings and the question of Being, Merleau-Ponty sees two sides of the same living being. Developing his use of Gestalt theory, Merleau-Ponty describes the difference as a matter of perspective determined by the shifting configuration of foreground and background. The difference between ontic differences between beings and ontological difference (the difference between beings and Being) is a difference of configuration. We could say that metaphysics is the other side of the natural world and that all behavior is a metaphysical interrogation of that world.

Robert Vallier concludes that in the *Nature* lectures, Merleau-Ponty develops an "ontology of difference" "by attending to the way in which the manifest activity of a living body differentiates itself from the world, and thus signifies" (Vallier

2001, 203). Vallier argues that Merleau-Ponty uses animal studies to show that embodied life is a process of self-differentiation in relation to others and environment. He interprets Merleau-Ponty's lateral relationship or lateral kinship as a differentiating principle and the most fundamental characteristic of embodied life. The living body of all creatures is constantly differentiating itself from its environment. It is this structure of differentiation, or differential relations, that embodied life shares. In Vallier's words, "by attending to the differentiation of materiality existence, the studies on animality thus disclose a principle of difference that would have to be at the basis of [what Merleau-Ponty calls] a 'different ontology' or an ontology of difference" that would be built on differentiations of the flesh (see Vallier 2001, 205; I will return to the notion of the flesh later). Strange kinship, then, comes through shared differentiation.

The "strange kinship" (*étrange parenté*) between humans and animals results from the lateral relation of animality and humanity. It cannot be reduced to classical theories of evolution in which humanity is the telos of animality, on the one hand, or to an abyss between body and consciousness (or animal and Dasein), on the other (Merleau-Ponty 1994, 339). This kinship neither erases all differences between animals and humans, thereby making them identical, nor erases any similarities between them, thereby making them radically separate. Instead, strange kinship allows for an intimate relation based on shared embodiment without denying differences between lifestyles or styles of being. Merleau-Ponty's theory of stylistic differences maintains difference without allowing it to become the grounds for ethical or epistemological hierarchies of beings. Human beings have a style of behavior peculiar to them. Various animals have their own styles of behaviors. One type of being is not the ascent or descent of the other. Neither is one separated from the other; they are inseparable yet distinct. This strange kinship is not based on descendants or on generation but on a shared embodiment in a shared world, even if the style of body and the style of inhabiting that world are radically different.

At this point, it is important to consider that in his later work, Merleau-Ponty advances a peculiar notion of world as flesh.[15] His descriptions of the flesh of the world, with both skin or pellicle and thickness, change the Heideggerian landscape in which Dasein is world forming and animals are poor in world. If world is conceived in terms of flesh, how does that change what it means to have or not to have world, to make or not to make world? Indeed, Merleau-Ponty invokes the image of flesh in order to navigate between biological continuism and metaphysical separationism by giving us a figure in between the two. In other words, flesh both connects and separates us from the rest of the world and its other inhabitants. Merleau-Ponty explains:

The flesh is not matter, is not mind, is not substance. To designate it, we should need the old term "element," in the sense it was used to speak of water, air, earth and fire, that is, in the sense of a general thing, midway between the spatio-temporal individual and the idea, a sort of incarnate principle that brings a style of being wherever there is a fragment of being. (1968, 139)

As he does throughout his work, Merleau-Ponty steers between idealism and empiricism, between mechanism and vitalism, by postulating this in-between element. But he is clear that this element is not the combination of mind and matter or some hybrid of the two (1968, 140). It is primary in the sense that the in-between is primary, that is, in the sense that there is no *one* that is primary. Indeed, he says that there is a dehiscence or fission at the heart of this elemental flesh (1968, 146). The flesh is both passive and active, mass and gesture, interior and exterior—both animal and human (1968, 271); it cannot be reduced to one or the other.

Like Derrida's logic of both-and, Merleau-Ponty embraces the inseparability of what the history of philosophy has too often seen as contradictory elements. He criticizes philosophy for being "flattened to the sole plane of ideality or the sole plane of existence" (1968, 127) when it would be more accurate to describe our being *in* the world as a being *of* the world in which and through which I am both distinct and inseparable because, like the world, I am flesh. The space between me and the world, between me and other beings, is not an empty void but is filled with flesh; flesh engenders both the divergence (*écart*) and the connection of beings (1968, 272). More precisely, it is the thickness of the flesh (*épaisseur de chair*) that both connects me to and makes me distinct from the world (1968, 127). Derrida's call to "thicken" (*épaissir*) the limit between man and animal resonates with Merleau-Ponty's thickening of the world. In a sense, Merleau-Ponty thickens the borders between human beings and all other beings, between us and our environment, with the thickness of flesh. What Merleau-Ponty calls the thin pellicle or skin of the world and its beings is always accompanied by a thickness. Moreover, the porous and pliable nature of the skin never makes it a firm boundary. Things get under the skin and through it; indeed, the skin alternately breathes and suffocates if the fluidity of the relation between the inside and outside is cut off. Ultimately this fluidity separates the inside from the outside even if they remain, in an important sense, distinct.

Merleau-Ponty sometimes describes this fleshy relationship as a "kinship" (*parenté*) (1968, 133, 138): the flesh as an in-between element, the flesh through which we are kin, the flesh through which we are at the same time strangers (*étrangers*) because of its elemental dehiscence, the flesh that engenders the chiasm, the crossing or intertwining. Flesh opens the possibility of strange kinship. Ted Toadvine put it nicely:

It is precisely this "strange kinship" that the notion of the flesh is intended to make cogent, since it provides a means for understanding the visibility of the invisible, that is, the vital inherence of spirit, in a way that treats the two as obverse and reverse or as part of a single ontological circulation. Just as the dual aspect of my body, splitting into sensible and sentient, figures being's dual aspect of visibility and invisibility, so life diverges along multiple lines, both human and nonhuman, neither remaining simply one nor becoming entirely multiple. Thus, we can neither draw a sharp ontological boundary between human and nonhuman animals nor arrange their relations hierarchically. (Toadvine 2007a, 51)

Whereas Toadvine emphasizes the continuity between animals and humans and the emergence of the human out of the animal (especially in other passages not cited here), I want to emphasize kinship as well as the strangeness evoked by Merleau-Ponty.[16] The relation between human and animal is both kinship or intertwining and chiasm or divergence. We are neither the same nor radically different. More accurately perhaps, following Derrida, we could say that we are *both* the same *and* different and that both our sameness and our differences are ultimately undecidable, even though we are forced to decide everyday as a matter of practical relationship and ethical obligation. One point of Derridian ethics is to subject our practical decisions or the must of everyday life to the must of ethical obligation.

How might Merleau-Ponty's notion of strange kinship change our notion of kinship and thereby our notion of ethical obligations? Strange kinship is based on neither generation nor descent but on figuration. How can we imagine a kinship that is based on embodiment and not generation? And if we can, does this mean that animals can be our brothers and sisters or even our parents and children? How can animals be or become our kin? Reconceiving of kinship outside generation or blood ties also brings up questions about kinship between humans: How do we become kin if not through descent? What does our shared embodiment mean to our kinship? Who is this "we," and how is it determined by changing notions of kinship? Rethinking what we mean by kinship certainly has implications for both ethics and politics.

In *Antigone's Claim,* Judith Butler argues that kinship is based on repeated proclamations of kinship through actions, gestures, and claims or words. In her analysis, kinship is not determined by natural generation, descent, or bloodlines but by the repetition of performative utterances that become social norms. In her reading of Sophocles' play *Antigone,* she elaborates "the socially contingent character of kinship" (2000, 6). Butler sees Antigone's relationships and thereby her identity formed through her deeds and claims about those deeds. Her "freedom" to choose her fate comes through her own actions as the result of her decisions, which of course are always made in a network of socially prescribed norms and always exceed her sovereign control. She is spoken by language and culture as much as she speaks them. Butler believes it crucial to note that norms function only when they fail; they are social ideals whose embodiment or instantiation always falls short. Butler describes the operation of norms as a constant tension between the impossible ideal and the failures through which it is constituted. In a sense, then, kinship is a goal rather than a given.

Merleau-Ponty's suggestions about kinship in the *Nature* lectures resonate with some aspects of Butler's analysis. For instance, his "strange kinship" is based on neither generation nor descent. It is a shifting notion that changes with our perspective, which is mobilized by whether we are considering a part or whole, figure or ground. Merleau-Ponty identifies kinship with embodiment, which also is important to Butler's theory. For Butler, however, the body itself and bodily identities are the result of performance. Although Merleau-Ponty does not use the language of performance, like Butler, he emphasizes action. One central characteristic that bodies share by being bodies is the ability to move or act, what he calls *behavior*. The freedom of this action, however, does not come from decisions or deeds (whether they issue from an autonomous subject or are the result of repetitive performances or speech acts). Merleau-Ponty instead describes human freedom as the result of the human *Umwelt* as an "open field" of relationships:

The human universe is not the product of freedom in the Kantian sense, that is, event based freedom which is attested to in a decision; it is, rather, a structural freedom. In brief, it is the theme of a melody, much more than the idea of a nature-subject or of a supersensible thing, that best expresses the intuition of the animal according to Uexküll. The animal subject is its realization, transspatial and transtemporal. The theme of the animal melody is not outside its manifest realization; it is a variable thematizatism that haunts its particular realizations, without these themes being the goal of the organism. (2003, 178)

It is difficult to compare Merleau-Ponty's language of haunting and melody with Butler's language of performance. But it is clear that for Merleau-Ponty, human freedom and man's kinship with animals are not the results of deeds or decisions but are the results of the structure or form of embodiment. One characteristic of embodiment that Merleau-Ponty emphasizes in *Phenomenology of Perception* is the anonymity of perception. At some level, all embodied creatures share this anonymity of subjectless perceptions and sensations that have neither authorship nor names.[17] Both animal and human behavior are intimately related to this anonymous level of perception, which Merleau-Ponty describes as dreamlike or haunted.

Perhaps we could say that social norms haunt human behavior like a melody that both changes and repeats the same refrain. Human and animal behavior share this haunting. We even can imagine the *Umwelten* of humans and animals, or at least of some humans and some animals, overlapping to share an environment. Whereas in Butler's account (as in Heidegger's), linguistic performance determines kinship, in Merleau-Ponty's account, a *logos* of the natural world operates on a perceptual and behavioral level in tandem with language. For Merleau-Ponty, this is the basis of our strange kinship with animals. One implication would seem to be that for Butler and Heidegger, while we can exist with animals, they cannot exist with us. We might include them in our performances of kinship, but they can never perform their kinship with us unless, perhaps, we extend our notion of utterance or deed beyond where Butler takes us. Butler concludes her meditation on Antigone by suggesting that the very notions of the human and humanity are founded on notions of kinship and that it is through kinship norms that some "humans" are excluded from humanity proper:

And in acting, as one who has no right to act, she [Antigone] upsets the vocabulary of kinship that is a precondition of the human, implicitly raising the question for us of what those preconditions really must be. . . . If she is human, then the human has entered into catachresis: we no longer know its proper usage. . . . If kinship is the precondition of the human, then Antigone is the occasion for a new field of the human, achieved through political catachresis, the one that happens when the less than human speaks as human, when gender is displaced, and kinship founders on its own founding laws. (2000, 82)

Butler evokes a crisis in kinship that opens the category human onto the "less than human," but in her deed- and claim-centered discourse, the new kinship that she imagines still excludes animals. According to her analysis, the "less than human" is always still human, and it is on the basis of its estranged kinship with humanity that it makes its claim. Taken to its limits, Butler's provocative analysis should imply that both *kinship* and *human* are socially contingent, normalizing institutions that operate through a logic of exclusion or abjection of their own constitutive outside, which as we have seen throughout this book, continues at a primary level to take us back to the animal and animality.

In thinking about the kinship between animals and humans, however, it may be more effective in undermining the man/animal divide to question the possibility of kinship among humans than to insist on the possibility of our kinship with animals. Can we assert that there *is not* kinship with animal beings if we cannot at the same time assert that there *is* kinship with other human beings? In other words, isn't the determination that animals are not our kin—that they cannot be our brothers, sisters, parents, or children—based on the assumption that human beings can have those relationships to us? If neither humans nor animals can have such relations, then the absolute limit between man and animal again begins to crack. Recall that this is the tack Derrida takes in regard to Lacan's separation between response and reaction. Derrida argues that human beings are not capable of the kind of response that Lacan imagines in opposition to reaction. Even if not all reactions are responses (which they very well may be), all responses are also, at some level, reactions. In other words, there is not a pure response, particularly after psychoanalysis and the unconscious enter the scene.

So too, we could argue that there is no pure kinship. Like response (or justice, hospitality, forgiveness, democracy), kinship is an ideal that is never fully realized in actual experience. Derrida argues in *The Politics of Friendship* that fraternity is always precarious; furthermore, instantiations of brotherhood can be exclusionary or used to justify violence. As I observed in the last chapter, in regard to animals, the kinship of humankind may be such a brotherhood. There we saw some of the ways that the notion of kinship among humans is based on the impossibility of kinship with animals (in Heidegger's analysis). We also began to question the assumption that kinship among humans is given. With Merleau-Ponty's suggestion that kinship is not a result of generation or descent, and with Butler's notion of kinship as the result of performance, we ask again, can animals be our kin? Or perhaps it would more appropriate to ask whether they can be our kin any more or less than we can be kin to one another? This, in turn, may lead us to ask how we can be so sure that we are kin to one another.

Although she does not discuss animals, Mary Beth Mader's diagnosis of Sophocles' *Antigone* can help elucidate the stakes of these questions for kinship. In reference to the play, she asks, "What is a brother?" which should be, but is not always, an obvious question, since Oedipus is both Antigone's brother and her father, and Polynices is at once her brother, uncle, and nephew. I won't rehearse Mader's subtle analysis here but instead turn to her conclusions. She states that the drama of *Antigone* revolves around human generation and kinship: "It is precisely the precarious status of this generational order that is the source of the deep distress and anguish that fuels Antigone's determined course and the dramatic line of the play" (Mader 2005, 16). What is at stake in the play, she argues, is whether kin or brothers are the result of a natural order or whether they can be formed by human actions. The play displays some ways in which the natural order of kinship can be confounded to the point that it is impossible to disambiguate those relations. In a sense, the Oedipus drama makes a mockery of ideal family relations and any assumptions about natural generation or descent. Mader argues that norms of kinship have clouded critical commentaries on the play to the extent that one scholar claims that "there is no closer relationship imaginable than that between the mother and the children of her own body" which, Mader says, sounds "like a joke when pronounced about the Oedipal family!" (2005, 25). She concludes "that any one of us could read over the remark in seriousness as a demonstration of the persistent unthinkability of the everyday tangle of kinship" (2005, 26).

If ideals of kinship make it profoundly "unthinkable" between human beings, then what does it mean to insist that kinship between humans and animals is unthinkable? Is it any more unthinkable than the reality of failure that haunts our ideals of human kinship? Butler's and Mader's readings of *Antigone* show the limits of thinking of kinship in terms of blood relations or human generation. Once we recognize that kinship is an impossible ideal, and a violent bloody ideal at that, we may be open to the possibility of "strange kinship" based not on blood or on generation but on a shared embodiment and the gestures of love and friendship among living creatures made possible by bodies coexisting in a world on which we all depend.[18]

CHAPTER TEN

Stopping the Anthropological Machine

Agamben's Ticktocking Tick

> To render inoperative the machine that governs our conception of man
> will therefore mean . . . to risk ourselves in this emptiness: the suspension
> of suspension, Shabbat of both animal and man.
>
> —AGAMBEN, *THE OPEN*

In *The Open,* Giorgio Agamben diagnoses the history of both science and philosophy as part of what he calls the "anthropological machine" through which the human is created with and against the animal. In his analysis, early forms of this "machine" were operated by humanizing animals, thereby making some "men" considered to be animals in human form, for example, barbarians and slaves. Modern versions of the machine operate by animalizing humans, making some "people" considered to be less than human, for example, Jews during the Holocaust and, more recently perhaps, Iraqi detainees. Agamben describes both sides of the anthropological machine:

If, in the machine of the moderns, the outside is produced through the exclusion of an inside and the inhuman produced by animalizing the human, here [the machine of earlier times] the inside is obtained through the inclusion of an outside, and the non-man is produced by the humanization of an animal: the man-ape, the *enfant sauvage* or *Homo ferus,* but also and above all the slave, the barbarian, and the foreigner, as figures of an animal in human form. (2004, 37)

The divide between human and animal is also political and sets up the very possibility of politics. Who is included in human society, and who is not is a consequence of the politics of "humanity," which creates the polis itself. In this regard, politics itself is the product of the anthropological machine, which is inherently lethal to some forms of (human) life. Although Agamben's analysis could be extended to include a diagnosis of the dangers to animal life, in *The Open* he is concerned primarily with the dangers to human life.[1]

In this chapter, I examine Agamben's analysis of the man/animal dichotomy and the anthropological machine that produces it. In the first sections, I delineate the ways in which Agamben moves with and against Heidegger. Agamben maintains that Heidegger's comparative pedagogy in his lecture course *The Fundamental Concepts of Metaphysics* continues the work of the anthropological machine by defining Dasein as uniquely open to the closedness of the animal. Even so, Agamben's own thinking does not so much open up the concept of *animal* or even open up man to the possibility of encountering animals as it attempts to save humanity from the anthropological machine that always produces the animal as the constitutive outside within the human itself. It is the space of the animal or not-quite-human in the concept of humanity that for Agamben presents the greatest danger. Agamben believes that the only way to stop the anthropological machine is through a "Shabbat" of both man and animal. Here I argue that Agamben's return to religious metaphors and the discourse of religion as a supposed counterbalance to the science and philosophy through which the machine operates at best displaces the binary man/animal with the binary religion/science and at worst returns us to a discourse at least as violent as the one from which he is trying to escape.[2] As an alternative, I look to Merleau-Ponty's reanimation of science in his *Nature* lectures. In the conclusion, I suggest that perhaps we need both Agamben's diagnosis of the politics of science and Merleau-Ponty's creative reenactment of science if there is any hope of stopping the anthropological machine.

As a prelude, I would like to consider two central problems with Agamben's analysis of the man/animal dichotomy: First, he does not consider the function of woman in that binary, and second, he does not consider violence to animals. The place of animals in the anthropological machine is central to my analysis throughout the chapter. Agamben argues that the dichotomy between man and animal is a division within the category of human itself. In both the earlier and modern versions, humanity is divided into more and less human types, which justifies slavery and genocide. For Agamben, the question is not human rights but how the category of human is produced and maintained against the animal, which functions as both constitutive outside and inside, rendering some "men" either nonhuman or subhuman.

Some commentators have criticized Agamben for not considering how the binary of man and woman operates in relation to that of man and animal.[3] As we have seen in our discussion of Derrida and sexual difference, these two binaries are virtually inseparable in the history of Western thought. In the words of Emma

Jones, the anthropological machine also is an "andrological machine" (2007, 36). Jones argues that in order to stop the anthropological machine, we also have to stop the andrological machine. She concludes that "the deep complicity of this division [male/female] with the logic of the anthropological machine requires that we begin from a destabilization of these sexed unities, in order to free the life of the body from the management of ontology, which, Agamben suggests, is our most pressing task" (2007, 39). Certainly, if the two oppositional binaries are as closely linked as feminist philosophers insist, then stopping one will throw a wrench into the other. Agamben's apparent blindness to the operations of woman in the anthropological machine point to the ways in which the distinction between man and human, one that he sometimes attempts to draw, continually risks falling back into the distinction between man and woman.[4] Agamben's concern is with why some men are treated like animals or subhumans. That is, in the category of human, there is a split between man and his others. We could add that within the category of human there also is a split between man and woman that makes woman continue to operate as subhuman. It is not just the figure of the refugee or the concentration camp victim that occupies what Agamben calls the "no-man's land" between proper citizen and animal. Traditionally woman has played, and continues to play, this role. Agamben's question, which he associates with modernity, is why some men or some people come to be treated like animals or as in between human and animal. This question could first and foremost be asked of female human beings: How did women come to be treated as in between man and beast?

Extending the scope of Agamben's interrogation, we might ask the question from the other side: Why do we treat animals like animals? Or how does animality justify enslavement and cruelty? In addition to Agamben's investigation into how the category of humanity is produced through the anthropological machine, we must also investigate how the category of animality becomes beholden and subservient to humanity. In the words of Dinesh Wadiwel,

Human violence represents not only a capacity for dehumanization alone, but is tied closely to the justification of violence against the non-human. This reflects not only the capacity for humans to harm each other, but draws attention to the sustained incarceration, torture and violence that is directed towards animals in slaughterhouses, experimental laboratories and factory farms. (Wadiwel 2004, par. 2)

This raises the question of whether the concentration camps that become, for Agamben, emblematic of our age were modeled on factory farms, slaughterhouses, and animal experimentation, or the other way around. Throughout his work, if Agamben is concerned with "machines" that produce the human or humanity through violence, can mechanized slaughter and the literal machines used to tag, milk, butcher, and package animals for human consumption be far from our thoughts? As Wadiwel observes, "The spiritual home of biopolitics is not the concentration camp but the slaughterhouse" (2004, par. 33). In regard to animals, Agamben's metaphor of the anthropological machine becomes eerily real. And for all his faults in considering animals, even Immanuel Kant recognizes that how we treat animals is an indication of how we treat one another. Moreover, we can become accustomed to killing and abusing people by "practicing" on animals. Perhaps, then, as some provocateurs suggest, the concentration camp and the slaughterhouse are of a piece when it comes to biopolitics.[5]

Agamben's "Deconstruction" of Heidegger

Although Agamben begins and ends his diagnosis of the anthropological machine in *The Open* with invocations of a messianic banquet, the centerpiece of his analysis is Heidegger. In a sense, Agamben follows Heidegger in challenging Darwinian theories of evolution in regard to the concepts of human and animal (by insisting that biology cannot be separated from the language we use to describe it). Even while challenging Heidegger's distinction between animality and humanity or Dasein, Agamben embraces Heidegger's insistence on animality as what is concealed about and from humanity. In some passages in *The Open,* Agamben seems to accept a Heideggerian abyss between man and animal, an abyss that Agamben suggests is not wide enough in Heidegger's thought.[6] As we know, Heidegger says that even our beloved dogs and cats live with us but don't truly exist with us in the sense of encountering us. Dasein is open to Being and thereby to other beings as such, but animals are not.

Agamben's relation to Heidegger is complicated in that he takes over the language of concealment and unconcealment at the same time that he "deconstructs" it.[7] He takes it over in his own criticisms of technoscience, while in his critical engagement with Heidegger's lectures, he maintains that the unique unconcealment at the heart of the clearing opened to Dasein turns out to be none other than the captivation of the animal. In other words, the animal is revealed to man as concealed; more precisely, it is man's own animality that is revealed to him as concealed. Animality is the concealed within the unconcealment of Dasein. According to Agamben, the struggle between concealment and unconcealment is the struggle between man and animal itself (cf. 2004, 69–70). Man's humanity is dependent on remaining open to the closedness of animality (particularly man's own animality). In Agamben's terminology, man suspends his animality in a zone of exception (2004, 79), and by effacing his own animality, he retains his privileged position in the dichotomy of man/animal. By closing himself to the closed environment of the animal, he opens himself to the world of the properly human. Humanity, then, is dependent on the exclusion of animality, which all the while operates as its constitutive outside (or, more accurately, outside within). Agamben describes the definitive boredom that Heidegger attributes to Dasein as an awakening *from* captivation *to* captivation so that Dasein sees itself as open to its own non-openness. "This resolute and anxious opening to a not-open, is the human" (Agamben 2004, 70). Following Agamben, we could say that animality with its world poverty is the mysterious beating heart concealed and revealed at the center of humanity with its world formation. Because of the structural connection between animality and humanity, Agamben contends that in the case of animals, it is impossible for Dasein to perform the activity essential to it, which is to leave beings alone. Man cannot let animals be (themselves), because as a human he depends on seeing animals as closed systems from whom he differs in his openness (as opposed to their closedness) (cf. 2004, 91).[8]

To Agamben, Heidegger's comparative analysis of man and animal is another example of the anthropological machine in action: humanity is produced by excluding animality, against which it defines the human as precisely not-animal. In this way, the human becomes the exception, the exceptional animal who is not really an animal after all. In a sense, then, the human is both the telos and the missing link between animal and man. Agamben points out that both versions of the anthropological machine

> are able to function only by establishing a zone of indifference at their centers, within which—like a "missing link" which is always lacking because it is already virtually present—the articulation between human and animal, man and non-man, speaking being and living being, must take place. Like every state of exception, this zone is, in truth, perfectly empty, and the truly human being who should occur there is only the place of a ceaselessly updated decision in which the caesurae and their rearticulation are always dislocated and displaced anew. (2004, 37–38)

We could say that the notion of the human acts as a transcendental signifier produced through the various and multifarious instances of its own failure.[9] The truly human is an empty ideal produced through the continual disavowal of the failure of *Homo sapiens* to escape its animality. The so-called abyss between man and animal is produced by abjecting animality from the concept of humanity. This way of thinking resonates with Agamben's argument that the category *human* is ultimately empty because it is continually shifting. Agamben insists, however, that the "missing link" between animal and man has always been filled by either exotic ape-men and wolf-children or slaves and victims of genocide considered to be subhuman animals.

In *The Open*, even while Agamben points to the shifting and unstable significations of the term *human*, he is more concerned with the ways in which we do and do not maintain the space between animal and human, the so-called missing link. The greatest danger of the anthropological machine is that along with the categories *human* and *animal*, it produces a phantom third category between the two, which both connects and separates them and thereby constitutes and sustains them:

> What would thus be obtained, however, is neither an animal life nor a human life, but only a life that is separated and excluded from itself—only a *bare life*. And faced with this extreme figure of the human and the inhuman, it is not so much a matter of asking which of the two machine (or of the two variants of the same machine) is better or more effective—or, rather, less lethal and bloody—as it is of understanding how they work so that we might, eventually, be able to stop them. (2004, 37–38, italics in original)

A bare life is one produced by biological and medical science as a living body separated from its social, political, and even ecological context. It is an exceptional body (monstrous or sacred) whose fate can be determined outside systems of law or reason (see Agamben 1998). As such, the deadly killing power that it provokes seems virtually unstoppable. Thus, Agamben maintains that only by understanding how this logic works, that is, how the anthropological machine creates *Homo sapiens*, who are considered less than human, can we hope to stop it.[10]

The Ghost in the Machine

The philosophical inquiry that can break the machine is opposed to the scientific inquiry that fuels it. Agamben suggests that science collapses the distinction between man and animal in dangerous ways by reducing humanity to biology. By so doing, man is reduced to an animal determined by his own disinhibiting ring; his freedom becomes merely one effect of various physical causes revealed by biological and medical science to be predetermined after all. The mystery of the universe and life evaporates under the searing gaze of the scientist. Agamben seems nostalgic for a philosophical gaze that invests meaning in rather than disinvesting it from life. He claims that today philosophy has lost its relevance because it has become merely spectacle or a private affair, without relevance to public life and history. Even philosophy is becoming more scientific in its mode of inquiry, and so instead of enhancing the mystery of life through multiple interpretations, it tries to reveal all its secrets, thereby signaling the end of interpretation and the end of both philosophy and science.

Agamben's criticisms of science and our technoscientific age revolve around the disappearance of the mysteries of biological life under the gaze of ever more powerful instruments. He argues that by closing ourselves to the mysteries of animality, we become like Heidegger's animals caught in a disinhibiting ring of cause and effect or stimulus/response determined by our physiology (2004, 77). We are no longer open to the mysteries of life but instead toil under the impulse to disclose all of life's secrets. Medical science and biology attempt to reveal human life to be determined by our DNA or chemical reactions in our brains, making us no different from other animals. If science succeeds in turning man into an animal whose every desire can be determined by chemical processes in his brain, then "neither man nor animal—and perhaps, not even the divine—would any longer be thinkable" (Agamben 2004, 22). When human life becomes just another form of animal life, we are in danger, Agamben warns us, of collapsing a distinction on which the very categories of ethics and politics are based:

When the difference vanished and the two terms collapse upon each other—as seems to be happening today—the difference between being and the nothing, licit and illicit, divine and demonic also fades away, and in its place something appears for which we seem to lack even a name. Perhaps concentration and extermination camps are also an experiment of this sort, an extreme and monstrous attempt to decide between the human and the inhuman, which has ended up dragging the very possibility of the distinction to its ruin. (2004, 22)

Agamben argues that what was merely an "innocuous paleontological find," the ape-man, becomes the Jew or others deemed subhuman (2004, 37). Given the oppositional and hierarchical nature of the man/animal dichotomy, however, in what sense is paleontology, or zoology or biology for that matter, ever innocuous? Although it may be harmless (even beneficial to man), is the subordination of animality to humanity ever innocuous to animals? In fact, doesn't the animalization of man work to enslave or justify "extermination" only when animals are imagined as abject and disposable creatures subjected to the whims of man? The anthropological machine produces the human and the dangerous in-between space of sub- or nonhuman *Homo sapiens* only by producing the animal as deprived intellectually, morally, and politically. The machine must be stopped not only for the sake of man but also for the sake of animals. A possible wrench in the works could be to revalue animals and animality rather than accept and thereby perpetuate their status as denigrated. Justifying abusing or killing some "people" by arguing that they are animals or like animals is compelling only if we assume that animals deserve, or even require, abuse and slaughter. Using the argument that people are animals or like animals in order to treat them as inferiors likewise assumes that animals are inferior. A Nietzschean revaluation of the animal and animality may be one strategy to address the animalization of man as justifying slavery and genocide.

Another strategy would be to follow Derrida in trying to render obsolete the categories of man and animal by opening ourselves to diversities of both animal species and individual animals (Derrida 2008). As I contended earlier, following Derrida and examining how the anthropological machine produces humanity, we need to begin to see how it also produces the monstrous category *animal,* which erases the nearly infinite differences among species and herds them all into the same abject and inferior pen. The machine produces subhuman *Homo sapiens,* who supposedly therefore deserve their exploitation and enslavement, as well as other subhuman species, who therefore deserve their exploitation and enslavement. Furthermore, unlike the other subhumans, they can never appeal to human rights, and given the dichotomy that produces the categories *human* and *animal,* animal rights operate as an oxymoron. The anthropological machine may produce the human and the subhuman within the human, but it also produces a world filled with other living creatures and other "resources" that "exist" only for man. In this light, Heidegger's insistence that animals live but do not exist (except *for* man), takes on a new twist.

The metaphor of *machine*—as in the anthropological machine—is central to Agamben's analysis of the dependence of the category of human on the category of animal in the production of the very notion of humanity. Yet the category or notion of machine (in relation to the other two categories) is never questioned in *The Open,* which seems odd in an era dominated by technologies that simulate intelligence and life. How does the binary man/animal change when machines are thrown into the mix? Isn't medical science replete with machine and computer metaphors to describe the human body, particularly the brain? Perhaps Agamben would see this as a continuation of Descartes' conclusion that animals are types of machines. Still, in the computer age, it seems as urgent to investigate our investments in androids and bionic men as subcategories of man as it does to interrogate the man/animal divide as it creates the category *human.* At present, the category of the human is at the same time set off against the cyborg and also imagined as functioning like a machine. Like the animalization of humanity, the mechanization of life also can lead to the loss of meaning and the valorization not of bare life but of the efficiency, along with the exchangeability and disposability of the machine: the body as machine that can be turned on or off at will, the body as machine that can be assembled or disassembled. Since the advent of factory farming, mechanized slaughter, and meatpacking, animals have been subjected to automated processing; Agamben's worry is that the human genome project, cloning, and transplantation will do the same to human bodies. It is significant that Agamben's metaphors of machines of production are conceptually and literally assembling and dissembling animal bodies. Along with science and medicine, machine metaphors are seeping into philosophy, as evidenced by Agamben's discourse of the anthropological machine and by that of Foucault, Deleuze, and others. Perhaps what Agamben prescribes as a "Shabbat" of the categories man and animal could be the awakening of an analysis of the categories *living* and *machine*.

What happens if we add the machine to the man/animal dichotomy? Perhaps we merely end up with Descartes' machine-animal. Or perhaps we open the man/animal dualism to a third that transforms our thinking about both. For example, Adèle Thorens argues that Heidegger and Merleau-Ponty come to radically different conclusions in their discussions of man and animal because whereas the third term in Heidegger's comparative analysis is the stone (an inanimate object), the third term in Merleau-Ponty's comparison is the machine and the science of cybernetics. By comparing both humans and animals to machines, Merleau-Ponty finds similarities because unlike machines, both man and animals have living bodies. Considering man in relation to machine forges an alliance between humans and animals as creatures, who, in Merleau-Ponty's words, live rather than function: "the machine functions, the animal lives" (2003, 162). Moreover, perhaps reflecting on the metaphors of machinery that inflect our articulations of the man/animal binary also will help defuse "the anthropological machine." Following Agamben's example, we could diagnose the role of machine metaphors in creating the opposition between man and animal and/or in producing the notion of humanity. The most striking example might be Descartes' animal-machines against which he defines man's freedom and man's soul. We could extend Agamben's discursive analysis to the category *machine* as essential to the division between man and animal. This investigation might include the various transformations that the machine age, industrialization, and now artificial intelligence have produced in the philosophies of man versus animal. Within the confines of this chapter, I can only point in that direction.

The "Shabbat" of Man and Animal

Although Agamben says that a new mythology of man or animal will not stop the anthropological machine, in an odd turn he embraces religious discourse as an alternative to science (cf. 2004, 92). In a strange echo of Heidegger's famous "only a God can save us now," Agamben observes:

To render inoperative the machine that governs our conception of man will therefore mean no longer to seek new—more effective or more authentic—articulations, but rather to show the central emptiness, the hiatus that—within man—separates man and animal, and to risk ourselves in this emptiness: the suspension of the suspension, Shabbat of both animal and man. . . . Perhaps there is still a way in which living beings can sit at the messianic banquet of the righteous without taking on a historical task and without setting the anthropological machine into action. (2004, 92)

For Agamben, both man and animal can be "outside of being" as more than bare life or biological automatons. As bare life, all creatures are unsavable (i.e., mortal and finite), unknowable, and without meaning, that is, uninterpretable. Agamben's messianism, then, is perhaps more reminiscent of Derrida's than Heidegger's, particularly when he says that both man and animal might be "saved precisely in their being unsavable" (2004, 92).

Following Derrida, Leonard Lawlor describes an "irreligious" religion that replaces rather than sacrifices. He maintains that by naming the animals, we can save them: "Because of the emphasis on singularity, this structure is not a structure of sacrifice but a structure of saving by means of replacement" (2007, 111). He suggests that through the name, we can welcome animals and others by eating them symbolically rather than literally:

Only in this way, through the name, can we welcome, make a place for the animals, internalize them, even eat them. . . . But this replacement, which does not sacrifice, would be a way of eating the animals well. Here, through the specific internalization of the name (and not the flesh of the animals), we are able . . . to advocate a kind of vegetarianism that is compatible with a minimal carnivorism, but what I am really advocating is a kind of asceticism. (2007, 105)

This method of saving, however, seems to be the one that Agamben is opposing because it is a continuation of the urge to assimilate everything, to know everything, to bring everything under the auspices of either philosophy or science by naming. Naming as a way of respecting singularity and replacing literal sacrifice with symbolic sacrifice—and, it seems, literal saving with symbolic saving—is not the radical letting be of beings that Agamben proposes. We might say, so much the worse for Agamben. Although I am sympathetic to the sublimatory power of naming as a way to substitute symbolic violence for real violence, what attracts me to Derrida's formulations of hyperbolic ethics is that as Agamben maintains, although not all can be saved, we nonetheless have an obligation to try to save them anyway. Although not all can be welcomed, we must decide to welcome strangers, even though this decision flies in the face of what protects us from the worst, which is the radical (metaphysical) undecidability of each singular being. We don't know who or how to welcome and yet we must do so anyway. Even though we cannot name them, because in their singularity they are beyond the name, we must name them anyway. We must name and rename them in our attempts to let them speak or sign in their own names, as Derrida might say. In other words, we can hope for saving grace or forgiveness only by acknowledging that all cannot be saved without allowing this acknowledgment to become a justification for quietism or inaction.

Agamben discusses the etymology of the Latin verb *ignoscere*, which means "to forgive," and not, as we might expect, "to not know" or "to be ignorant" (*ignorare*) (2004, 91). He suggests that not forgiving by not knowing is to leave something alone, "to render it unsavable" (91). Here he follows Heidegger in embracing a letting alone of beings so that their being might show through. Nonetheless, he criticizes Heidegger for describing Dasein in terms of its opposition to animality, which makes Dasein dependent on animality and prevents letting animals be in their own animality rather than in their animality as it exists for us.

There seems to be a tension, however, in Agamben's insistence on the role of philosophical inquiry in stopping the machine, on the one hand, and the letting beings be "outside of being," on the other. Is philosophical inquiry any less invasive and penetrating than science? (Heidegger, among others, repeatedly uses metaphors of penetration.) How does philosophical interpretation preserve the mystery of life any more than science does? Agamben's turn to religious discourse appears to be an attempt to allow for mystery rather than to endorse the violent penetration of nature, especially of the human body, by science and medicine. Where does this Shabbat leave philosophy, and where does it leave science? Moreover, haven't religion and religious discourse caused as much or more violence, enslavement, and genocide than science has? Indeed, haven't philosophy, religion, and science all been put into the service of justifying the inhumane treatment of some subset of humanity? In the end, doesn't Agamben's own discourse replace the opposition between man and animal with the opposition between religion and science?

Judeo-Christian religion could be said to represent the view that man and animals are separated by an abyss, that the divine providence of man is guaranteed only by his metaphysical separation from animals. This is the older version of the anthropological machine as producing the human by extracting the animal. Western science, however, insists on the biological continuity between humans and animals, which Agamben identifies as the modern version of the anthropological machine that reduces humans to animals (or bare life) and thereby leaves them open to dissection and disposal. As we have seen, however, metaphysical separationism and biological continuism are two sides of the same coin or, in Agamben's parlance, two versions of the anthropological machine.[11] Given the influence of religion on philosophy and science, we might discover that the opposition between science and religion has been behind the opposition between animal and man all along. In this case, revaluing religion over science may not give the binary a rest, after all. Is there a way to navigate between the extremes of religion and science?

Demystifying and Remystifying Science

As an alternative to reinstating religious discourse, consider reanimating and revitalizing science by recalling the wonder, even admiration, that motivates both science and philosophy at their best. Perhaps this wonder or mystery is also what motivates religion at its best. Indeed, the wonder that motivates the best of both religion and science is also the birth of philosophy. Agamben diagnoses one of the central problems with scientific discourse as the tendency to reduce life to bare life by emptying it of all mystery and therefore its meaning. Without mystery, life is more like a functioning machine than an assembly of living creatures. Without mystery, the meaning of life is reduced to determining which stimulus causes which reaction. Given the realities of our dependence on technoscience, rather than return to religion we might do better to look for the mysteries in science itself. In this section, I propose that reanimating and reinterpreting science are parts of Merleau-Ponty's project in the *Nature* lectures.

Like Agamben, Merleau-Ponty injects meaning into every experiment from biology, zoology, or psychology that he discusses. Like Agamben, Merleau-Ponty criticizes natural sciences that treat living bodies as objects or specimens to be parsed into ever smaller units.[12] Unlike Agamben, Merleau-Ponty offers another conception of nature as dynamic and of all bodies as living responsive bodies rather than bare life or mere materiality. Against the tendency toward extolling bare life or the body in itself as evidenced in contemporary biological sciences,

Merleau-Ponty proposes a philosophy of life that revitalizes phenomenology and science. The body at the center of Merleau-Ponty's phenomenology is not an object but dynamic life that cannot be understood through the lens of a microscope. Merleau-Ponty goes further by suggesting that science is always motivated by a mystery that exceeds it, the mystery of life. For example, in discussing the twenty-seven species of crab in the Barbave Islands and their twenty-seven different types of sexual display, Merleau-Ponty insists that we cannot reduce their behavior to the utility of reproduction because that would ignore the richness of their expression as "the mystery of life in the way that animals show themselves to each other" (2003, 188). He also states that "there is a mystery of the sensible . . . which entirely grounds our Einfühlung (empathy) with the world and the animals, and gives depth to Being" (2003, 312). In these passages, it is the relationships among animals and between human animals and other animals that spark the mystery of life. Merleau-Ponty goes so far as to assert that there is a natural magic that attracts scientists to the study of nature: "If these facts retain so much attention from scientists, it's because something is in question with the observer, or because the facts seem to realize a natural magic," which is the animal's "mysterious" relationship with its milieu (2003, 185). By bringing up magic and mystery, Merleau-Ponty makes clear that he does not mean some type of vitalism or magical life force operating within organisms. Instead, he is referring to a scientific curiosity about life that always exceeds the mechanistic tendencies of the scientific method. By rediscovering that aspect of science, we can regain its mystery and even its magic.

Merleau-Ponty describes as the heart of science the interplay between mystery and fact, extraordinary and ordinary, sensible and miracle, visible and invisible. Through his creative and philosophical interpretations of science and specifically biology, unlike Heidegger and Agamben, Merleau-Ponty refuses to merely dismiss science and technology as dangerous. Rather, he attempts a reanimation and reinterpretation of science by continually navigating between vitalism and mechanism without giving up on the meaningfulness of science. For Merleau-Ponty, science is not simply or in principle opposed to philosophy; science and philosophy can engage in a reciprocal exchange that enlivens both. If empirical science needs an infusion of philosophy, perhaps philosophy too needs an injection of empirical life. Meaning lies somewhere between abstract philosophical categories and the so-called brute facts of empirical observation.

In a section of the *Nature* lectures entitled "The Phenomena of Mimicry: Living Beings and Magic," Merleau-Ponty says, "To admit the existence of a sense organ is to allow for a miracle just as remarkable as allowing for a resemblance between the butterfly and its milieu" (2003, 186). He sees his discussion of mimicry and his attempts to reconcile inner agency with outer agency, and activity with passivity, as efforts "to make the ordinary and the extra ordinary communicate," because "on the one hand there is a frenzied freedom of life, and on the other, an economy of life" (2003, 186). By choosing one pole over the other, scientists and philosophers find themselves caught up in classical binary oppositions that force us to choose between sides of life, between inner and outer, mind and body, activity and passivity, proximity and distance, identity and difference, continuity and separation, and animal and man.

Let's return to Merleau-Ponty's notion of "strange kinship," which brings these two sides together. "Strange kinship" allows us to be together with other embodied beings, not because we share an origin and evolution or a language and culture, but because our bodies relate to their environments and other bodies. He insists on the "lateral union of animality and humanity" insofar as they are necessarily given together (2003, 271). If humans and animals are laterally related as kin, then humanity neither emerges from animality nor is forever cut off from animality. The question of the origin of man or the origin of language cannot be answered in terms of evolution but remains a mystery because, according to Merleau-Ponty, quoting de Chardin, "man came silently into the world" (2003, 267).

Humans are not the ascent or descent of apes or other animal beings in the sense of a hierarchy of being. Instead, we are kin through the lateral relation of shared embodiment and the structures of perception and behavior accompanying it. This notion of kinship is not based on blood or generation but on what we might call the alternating dissonance and harmony of lifestyles on this planet that we share. We are alike through our embodiment, but we are strangers through the differences in our lifestyles. For Merleau-Ponty, what Agamben calls the hiatus between man and animal is not filled with some ape-man or missing link or is it empty and void. Rather, it is the space of the fold between two sides of the natural world or, as he says, the relationship between notes and melody. Although the notes and the melody are not identical, there would be no song without them; they are related but not the same.

What in the *Nature* lectures Merleau-Ponty calls the "intertwining" of animality and humanity becomes in *The Visible and the Invisible* (1968) the "intertwining" between the visible and the invisible, body and mind. As we saw in the previous chapter, what Merleau-Ponty calls in the later work the "thickness of flesh" and the permeability of skin makes "intercorporeity" possible (1968, 141). Both the thickness of the flesh and the permeability of the skin enable communication with the world and others (1968, 135). The thickness of the flesh guarantees relations, and the skin ensures that we can distinguish our experience from the other's. Since the flesh and skin are not objects but are synergetic, we are never cut off from the other. The skin is a boundary but a permeable boundary. Flesh makes communication possible because as Merleau-Ponty says, it is the "reversible." By reversible, he means that we are both sensing and sensible, both subject and object:

The body is both subject and object because a sort of dehiscence opens my body in two, and because between my body looked at and my body looking, my body touched and my body touching, there is overlapping encroachment, so that we must say that the things pass into us as well as we into the things. (1968, 123)

By virtue of the flesh, which we share with other living beings and the world, we can sense and be sensed by others and by ourselves. The reversibility of the tangible opens up an "intercorporeal being" which extends further than any one individual and forms the "transitivity from one body to another" (1968, 143). This transitivity extends between humans and animals because they also have flesh that connects them and skin that keeps them separate. Both connection and separation are necessary for relationships, and both are entailed by embodiment itself.

As we have seen, the continuity that Merleau-Ponty describes between animals and man is not that of Darwinian evolutionary science but that of configurations and styles of behavior repeated throughout the natural world. To continue the musical metaphor, they are a type of leitmotif. Or perhaps we should say styles of style that are repeated, in that all living creatures have lifestyles that resonate with their environment and their fellows.[13] Both dissonance and harmony are parts of the melody of life. To emphasize one over the other, as Heidegger and Agamben do when they insist on separation over continuity, is to risk losing the richness of life that brings with it the mysteries that they also cherish. To "let beings be," in Agamben's sense of the unsaved and the unforgiven and of what we are ignorant, is not the same as celebrating the mysteries of life or the mysteries of philosophy and science. Returning philosophy to religion, as Agamben does, seems like a step backward on the journey away from scientific demystification and technological management of life, particularly in regard to the hierarchy between man and animal that produces the human at the center of God's creation and justifies man's inhumanity to man. Another tack might be to follow Merleau-Ponty's revisioning of science as a creative endeavor motivated by the infinite mysteries of life and fulfilled by ongoing interpretations of the between, the chiasmus, and kinship that signal both the gap and intertwining between living creatures as a fold in life itself that is part of the mystery of life.

In conclusion, Agamben may be right that we need to suspend the animal within man. And we certainly need to break the anthropological machine that creates subhuman "peoples" who are enslaved, tortured, and murdered. But we also need to consider how this machine affects nonhuman animals and investigate the man/animal dichotomy from both sides and not just the side of humanity. Even in Agamben's critical analysis of the man/animal split, he engages the category of animal from within the category of human in order to diagnose the ways in which some humans are exploited by others. With this complex form of what I am calling "animal pedagogy," we learn something about the category *human* by exploiting its relation with the category *animal.* And with the exception of the tick whose pleasures and mysteries Agamben imagines, animals themselves are irrelevant to this analysis.

Still, Agamben's final prescription of a Shabbat of both animal and man has profound consequences for animals as well as humans. If the category of the human has been used to justify all sorts of atrocities inflicted on humans by humans, it also has been used to justify all sorts of atrocities inflicted on animals by humans. Perhaps demonstrating, as Agamben does, the violence at the heart of the concept of humanity that justifies man's inhumanity to man in terms of the exclusion of his own animality can also highlight the violence of considering animality a characteristic in need of exclusion. Moreover, Agamben's insistence on framing the philosophies of humanity and the perpetuation of the man/animal dichotomy in terms of the politics of power shows how what appears to be "innocuous" scientific discovery becomes, or is part of, deadly political maneuvering.

PART SIX

Psychoanalysis and the Science of Kinship

CHAPTER ELEVEN

Psychoanalysis as Animal By-product

Freud's Zoophilia

> Man has not all that much reason to be proud at being the last to appear
> in creation, the one who was made out of mud, something no other be-
> ing was worthy of, and so he searches for honorable ancestors, and that is
> where we still are—as evolutionists, we need an animal ancestor.

> —JACQUES LACAN, "NAMES OF THE FATHER SEMINAR"

In nearly every essay he wrote, Freud mentions animals: animal examples, animal
anecdotes, animal metaphors, animal idioms, and, of course, animal phobias.[1]
Cataloging the animals that appear in his texts begins to look like a zoological
compendium of species running from apes to wolves and at least (by my count)
eighty other animals in between, including beetles, caterpillars, crayfish, don-
keys, emus, fox, frogs, giraffes, gnats, herring, jaguars, kangaroos, lizards, moths,
opossum, oysters, porcupines, ravens, snails, starfish, tigers, toads, wasps, and
whales. Animals play a central part in the imaginary of the father of psychoanalysis. Moreover, animals are the beating heart that pumps blood into the body of
Freud's most important psychoanalytic concepts, including the primary processes
of displacement and condensation, the castration complex, the Oedipal complex, anxiety, neurosis, and the family romance.[2] My thesis in this chapter is that
Freud's use of animals both sets up and undermines his Oedipal story and family
romance. At almost every level, animals are involved in defining the uniquely
human psyche and creating its dynamics through the "science" of psychoanalysis. Both the nuclear family that serves as the milieu for the psychosexual drama
acted out by human beings and the "family of man" are drawn from these various
uses of animals, as examples, metaphors, and central players in phobia. At the
same time, however, the relationship between humans and animals articulated by
Freud, particularly in *Totem and Taboo,* undermines what he calls there the "real
family" with its Oedipal drama. At the very least, his analysis of kinship, which
comes through anthropology, is in tension with the psychoanalytic family, and

Freud goes to great lengths at the end of that text to try to explain how we get from primary kinship with animals to the family of man, specifically the patriarchal family, which grounds psychoanalytic theory. Furthermore, in the narrative of *Totem and Taboo* (and the science of kinship on which it is based), the notion of kinship based on shared blood is born from sharing the flesh and blood of animals ritualistically sacrificed. The notion of human kinship is based on a fundamental sacrifice of animal kinship at both the literal and symbolic levels. As the menagerie of animals in Freud's writings make evident, these sacrificial lambs and scapegoats reappear to haunt the imaginary of the father of psychoanalysis and of humankind more generally.

It becomes clear when examining the work of Freud, Lacan, and Kristeva that the animal is reduced to the natural world, which is imagined as being opposed to the world of culture or language, the symbolic realm, which is definitive of humanity. As psychoanalysis teaches us, however, the distinctions and exclusions that we take to be essential to our identities are always retroactively constituted as original.[3] That is, the circular and repetitive temporality of the primary processes of the unconscious creates our psychic reality in relation to complex relations with the world and others which are always infused by imaginary and symbolic operations. Just as a cigar is never just a cigar, the animal is never just an animal. The very conceptions of animality and the natural world against which psychoanalysis defines the uniquely human world of the psyche and symbols are—if we apply the psychoanalytic logic to its own discourse—fantasies, even if foundational fantasies. Animal difference and sexual difference, both cornerstones of psychoanalysis, are themselves constructs already steeped in imaginary and symbolic operations retroactively placed at the origin of psychic life. What we take to be original to the imaginary and symbolic operations of the psyche turn out to be products of them. My aim in this and the next chapter is to show how close readings of the discourses of psychoanalysis reveal textual sore spots where the animal or feminine figures escape from their natural enclosures and bite back.

Which Comes First, the Father or the Animal?

Although animals show up throughout Freud's *Interpretation of Dreams* (the text in which he introduces the concepts of condensation and displacement), it is in *Totem and Taboo* that we learn that the very operations of condensation and displacement central to the human psyche develop through our relation with animals.[4] Specifically, totemism involving animal totems and the taboos they engender give rise to substitution and representation, the operations defining humanity.

The move from "savages" to civilization is the result of a literal sacrifice of the father-animal by the brothers in the primal horde, which involves a symbolic sacrifice of the animal and the substitution of "father," followed by the literal killing of animals in rituals that turn that primal murder into sacrifice. In this complicated movement, it becomes clear that a substitution of animal and father is at the heart of totemism as well as Freud's analysis of totem and taboo. Moreover, implicitly at least, the sacrifice of animals—or we could say the exclusion of animals from those who can be murdered—guarantees and reaffirms the brothers' commitment not to murder one another. In other words, killing animals prevents us from killing humans, but only after the father displaces the animal (or, the animal becomes the father).[5] The logic of this "after," however, like the logic or temporality of psychoanalysis itself, is repetitive and circular.[6] As we will see, Freud uses the animal phobias in his discussion of animal totemism in order to domesticate the animal and thereby turn it into a father. Elissa Marder describes how the substitution of the father with an animal that figures so prominently in Freud's conclusion has been prefigured by Freud's invocation of the animal phobias to make his case:

It is important to point out that Freud invokes the existence of the animal phobia as proof and symptom of the fear of the father well before he presents the famous narrative of the primal murder at the end of the text. . . . More specifically, at the level of his argument, the introduction of "animal phobias" creates a textual divide, or threshold, between what he designates as pre-historical and/or primitive culture . . . and the infamous derivation of the murderous foundation of patriarchal "civilization" with which the text ends. (Marder 2009b)

The human comes into being only by making a father out of the primal animal (totemism), which is possible only because the taboo against murder makes him into a father, which in turn is the result of the animal's displacement by a father. So the "father" in this primal scene, the father on whom the Oedipal situation, the laws of civilization, and the possibility of representation that makes us human are founded was "originally" an animal. As Kalpana Seshadri-Crooks points out, the murder of the father is "the moment not only of the institution of the prohibitions against murder and incest, but of the very notion of the human, of the separation between human and animal, of their interrelation" (2003, 102). This separation is dependent, however, on the substitutability of man and animal.

In his reading of *Totem and Taboo,* Lacan suggests that the primal father "originally" must have been an animal, since before the band of brothers' murder, they were "cannibal savages" operating without guilt, society, or any prohibitions, because these were instituted through the original murder and ensuing festival (cf. Freud 1913, 140). In reference to Lacan's reading of Freud's *Totem and Taboo*, Kalpana Seshadri-Crooks maintains:

Lacan's assertion that the primal father must have been an animal, insofar as the so-called animal is characterized by a satisfaction that knows no bounds, also raises the question of the animal as such as a mythic creature, a grammatical function that must be posited to grasp the organization of (sexual) meaning . . . given the implications of thinking through the primal father as an animal for the institution and significance of the moral law, the question of the existence of the animal as an ontic category becomes impossible. (2003, 104)

Seshadri-Crooks's argument is that Lacan's reading can help us see how the animal functions as a transcendental signifier to produce the law. In this way, the animal as a mythical being who does not and cannot exist—the being whose satisfaction knows no bounds—structures meaning systems, including kinship relations, that constitute both civil society and the notion of humanity. She also points out that Lacan is critical of Freud because this myth of the primal animal cannot in itself explain the displacement of animal for father because it is a prerequisite for the very category *father* and all other denotations of kinship. Lacan contends that "the primordial father is the father from before the incest taboo, before the appearance of law, of the structures of marriage and kinship, in a word, of culture" (Lacan 1987, 88). In other words, what could it possibly mean to talk about a *father* before kinship relations as we know them? This question is relevant to Freud's analysis, since early in *Totem and Taboo* he repeatedly claims that "savages" did not have a concept of kinship through blood relations but through clan relations mediated by their identification with totem animals. If early kinship is defined as identification with a totem animal, as Freud maintains, then that is more evidence that the so-called primal father must have been an animal (symbolically or literally, which may amount to the same thing). Lacan insists that patriarchal kinship relations and the ensuing incest taboo and Oedipal complex cannot be explained by the primal horde and its murderous act. Only the names or designations "father," "mother," "brother," "sister" can make sense of the incest taboo with which Freud concludes his text. The incest prohibition is meaningless without some such kinship relations, on the one hand, and the incest taboo institutes a particular form of kinship, on the other. In Freud's analysis, patriarchal kinship is the result of the primal horde and the subsequent substitution of an animal for the father in rituals designed to both renounce and repeat his murder.

The substitution of the father for an animal is part of repeated displacements going from animal to father and back to animal in Freud's text. Indeed, Freud's theory of the foundational role of the taboos against incest and patricide—prohibitions that correspond to the Oedipal complex—depends on the substitution or displacement of animal for father, and vice versa. The series of displacements is complicated. Crucial to Freud's analysis is his identification of children, "savages," and neurotics, which at critical points in his argument becomes a substitution of one for the other. Although in a very few passages Freud qualifies his comparison of these three groups, overall his entire thesis and conclusion depend on it (see, e.g., 1913, 31, 66, 99). Like psychoanalytic temporality, Freud's explanation of the onset of civilization and the Oedipal prohibitions moves back and forth among primitive men, children, and neurotics without regard for linear time or history (despite Freud's remarks that suggest a history with an origin and our links to primitive ancestors). Freud makes several moves in this series of displacements, one of which is to propose that "savages" are *contemporary ancestors* from whom we can learn something about our own psychic dynamics. This move follows an analysis drawn from anthropology, especially the work of G. J. Frazer and William Robertson Smith, which tells Freud that primitive men regarded animals as their contemporary ancestors.[7] Quoting Frazer that "the totem animal is also usually regarded as the ancestral animal of the group," Freud observes that "originally, all totems were animals, and were regarded as the ancestors of the different clans" (1913, 106, 107). He argues further that "totemism constitutes a regular phase in all culture" (108). He agrees with the anthropologists that primitive men regarded themselves as the same species as their animal ancestors; that like children (and neurotics, particularly phobics), they did not distinguish between humans and animals. Along with the claim that early clans did not distinguish themselves from animals, what is striking about Freud's analysis is that it seems to follow the same logic as the totemism he describes. Only now, instead of animals as contemporary ancestors, we have the savage clansmen as contemporary ancestors. In Freud's theory, the savage man who takes an animal as his ancestor takes the place of the animal. In other words, still existent tribal cultures are contemporary ancestors who are exempt from history and continue to represent for us our own prehistoric form and from whom we can learn about our past and our present. The first paragraph of *Totem and Taboo* explains the notion of contemporary ancestors as well as the correlation between primitives and neurotics:

Prehistoric man, in the various stages of his development, is known to us through the inanimate monuments and implements which he has left behind . . . and through the relics of his mode of thought which survive in our own manners and customs. But apart from this, in a certain sense he is still our contemporary. There are men still living who, as we believe, stand very near to primitive man, far nearer than we do, and whom we therefore regard as his direct heirs and representatives. Such is our view of those whom we describe as savages or half-savages; and their mental life must have a peculiar interest for us if we are right in seeing in it a well-preserved picture of an early stage of our own development.

If that supposition is correct, a comparison between the psychology of primitive peoples, as it is taught by social anthropology, and the psychology of neurotics, as it has been revealed by psycho-analysis, will be bound to show numerous points of agreement and will throw new light upon familiar facts in both sciences. (1913, 1)

Freud imagines a contemporary ancestor who provides a "well-preserved picture" of our own early development and from whom we not only learn about ourselves but also develop the sciences of man. What we might call the "myth" of this contemporary ancestor is identified with both children and neurotics and acquires an explanatory power that becomes a cornerstone of the human sciences that concern Freud. Much like the mythical power of the totemic animals of primitive men, Freud's mythical contemporary ancestor gives us insight into the contemporary psyche and haunts the imaginary of the sciences of man. Moreover, this mythic ancestor who represents a kind of living fossil through which we see ourselves "proves" both that we are civilized because we are not primitives and that this animalistic and animistic past lingers at our most vulnerable spots, namely, children and neurotics. This analysis raises the specter of our animal past while reassuring us that we have evolved beyond it. It also implicitly posits our civilization as the telos of those primitives (and animals), even if they are our contemporaries. To see other contemporary (or past), but less technologically advanced, cultures as examples of our own past, contemporary ancestors, or living fossils is extremely problematic in that it assumes that all cultures should be measured in terms of Western culture, that all cultures have Western culture as their telos, and that our notions of progress and futurity should be shared by all.[8] These assumptions engage in pernicious types of displacement that substitutes us for them, and vice versa, and erases differences by reducing all cultures to our standards. What becomes clear is that Freud is arguing that the contemporary psyche resembles the totemic psyche of primitive man as its telos and that our civilization resembles totemic social organizations as their telos and also that Freud's own analysis follows a sort of totemic logic by which mythic contemporary ancestors become powerful harbingers of our own destiny.

Along with the problematic implicit substitution of savage ancestors for animal ancestors, many explicit substitutions are at work in Freud's text. Freud moves easily between children's attitudes toward and relationships with animals and those of primitive man. For example, in analyzing what he calls the "return of totemism in childhood," Freud remarks:

There is a great deal of resemblance between the relations of children and primitive men towards animals. Children show no trace of the arrogance which urges adult civilized men to draw a hard-and-fast line between their own nature and that of all other animals. Children have no scruples over allowing animals to rank as their full equals. Uninhibited as they are in the avowal of their bodily needs, they no doubt feel themselves more akin to animals than to their elders, who may well be a puzzle to them. (1913, 126–27)

This passage suggests that the hard-and-fast line between humans and other animals is drawn through socialization, especially through the taboos that separate us from animals. But it should also make us wonder whether the kinship relations that structure psychoanalysis—father, mother, child—haven't already effaced "earlier" kinship relations with animals, a kinship that children still keenly feel.

Throughout *Totem and Taboo* and his later essays on anxiety, Freud slips between totemism and childhood animal phobias. For example, in a central passage from *Totem and Taboo* in which he is trying to ground the Oedipal complex by combining anthropology and psychoanalysis, he moves from discussing the case of a little boy's fascination with fowl back to the anthropological discussion of totemism, all while trying to establish the "return of totemism in childhood." First, Freud mentions one of his own cases, that of "Little Hans" whose horse phobia Freud diagnoses as a fear of castration at the hand of his father. Freud maintains that the displacement of the fear of the father onto the horse allows the boy to cope with his ambivalent relation with his father by splitting his father into what we could call a good father and a bad father, the horse substitute. In some sense, Freud observes, this is a case of "reverse totemism" because the little boy fears the horse and only later comes to admire and identify with it. In the second case, that of "Little Árpád," a patient of Ferenczi's, the boy has an ambivalent attitude toward chickens: he identifies with the cock, wants to marry the hens, enjoys their slaughter, and dreams of a "fricassee of mother" (1913, 130–31). Freud sees in this fowl phobia a clear-cut Oedipal wish accompanied by ambivalence toward both parents. Even though in this "positive" case of totemism, the boy wants to kill and eat his mother and not his father, Freud concludes without doubt that "these observations justify us, in my opinion, in substituting the father for the totem animal in the formula for totemism" (1913, 131). He justifies psychoanalysis through which he has shown that animal phobias are motivated by castration fear that makes it expedient for the male child to substitute a fierce animal for his beloved (yet hated and feared) father, on the one hand, and evidence from anthropology that primitive men describe their totem animals as substitute fathers, on the other (1913, 131). He describes the substitution of a large animal for father as a "natural" one even as he himself substitutes humans for wolves in the primal scene of the Wolf-Man's fantasy and thereby domesticates the wolves.

Freud's refusal to accept the wolves as wild animals and his insistence that what the patient actually saw was either sheepdogs or his parents having sex domesticate the Wolf-Man's fantasies and the so-called primal scene. Deleuze and Guattari claim that "the wolves never had a chance to get away and save their pack; it was already decided from the very beginning that animals could serve only to represent coitus between parents, or, conversely, be represented by coitus between parents" (1987, 28). Freud turns the wild wolves into domestic dogs or humans, just as he does with the Rat-Man's rats, and even with Little Hans's horses which become even more domesticated in the figure of the father. Furthermore, Freud reverses the gaze of the wolves from the Wolf-Man's dream and maintains that the child is looking at the wolves (sheepdogs or doggie-style parental surrogates) rather than the other way around (cf. Deleuze and Guattari 1987, 28). The wildness of the wolves indicated by their hungry gaze is replaced by a child's look that reduces the wolves to storybook characters or zoo animals. Following Deleuze and Guattari, Gary Genosko concludes:

In breaking the eye contact between the child and the wolves of his dream through the reversal of positions and the associative shift onto dogs, Freud accomplished a full-blown domestication of the scene. The gaze of the other is emptied, symbolically of course, becoming an unseeing look like that of zoo animals, objects for our inspection. (1993, 614)

Much like the Wolf-Man's wild dreams and fantasies, wild animals become domesticated so that they can be put into the service of psychoanalytic interpretation and psychoanalytic theory. Or conversely, psychoanalysis domesticates wild fantasies just as its own fantasies and discourse domesticate wild animals. Freud's development of psychoanalysis is built on hundreds of examples of domesticated animals; Lacan's theories are often based on animal studies that cage and experiment with animals; and the power of Kristeva's notion of abjection comes from domesticating and domesticated animals. Indeed, for Freud, the contemporary Oedipal family is born out of the concurrent domestication of animals and the father. Freud even compares human civilization to the "domestication of certain species of animals" (see "Why War," 1933).

Gary Genosko points out that on several occasions Freud invokes the image of a "nature reserve" to describe the realm of fantasy. The "nature reserve," or preserve, of fantasy is a place where the imagination can run wild even in the context of civilized society. Genosko states that the image of the nature preserve allows for a wild space within the domesticating tendencies of psychoanalysis:

Freud suggests to us that fantasies that are informed by wildness and wilderness, especially the experience (contextual and textual) of nature reserves, produce a crack in the near-ubiquitous domestication of life, and thus provide for the child's and adult's enchantment of their relations with animals, some of whom were never desacralized or remained "wild." As much as psychoanalysis shows signs of domestication, it also leaves room for potential escape routes into the paradomestic. (1993, 629–30)

We could say that Freud's "invention" of psychoanalysis with its unconscious is itself the production of a "nature reserve" where desires and images run wild within the larger confines of the psyche. Despite the best efforts of psychoanalysis to tame this region of the psyche, at the same time psychoanalysis operates on the principle that the unconscious necessarily remains inaccessible to consciousness; that there is always something that remains unconscious and thereby undomesticated and wild. But it is illuminating to consider the tension between the fundamental undomesticatability of the unconscious and the ways that Freud's texts (and his practice) attempt domestication, particularly for our purposes here, through the domestication of animals and the substitution of tame animals for wild ones, especially the substitution of the most domestic of animals (the human-animal, the father), for other animals such as horses or wolves.

Perhaps what is most striking in Freud's series of substitutions is that he is "surprised" when he "discovers" that the father is behind both children's animal phobias and primitive totems (1913, 156). Freud maintains that just as the substitution of animal for father is "natural" for children, so too it is natural for primitive men: "Indeed, primitive men say the very same thing themselves, and, where the totemic system is still in force to-day, they describe the totem as their common ancestor and primal father" (1913, 131). Here we see how quickly Freud moves from ancestor to father, even though as he has already argued, primitive men have a radically different conception of kinship, which includes all members of their clan and their totem animals. Freud justifies applying the logic of totemism to animal phobia by claiming that what remained in the background of anthropology—that primitive men describe their totem animals as ancestors—takes the foreground in psychoanalysis. In a footnote, he says that he arrived at this idea after Otto Rank mentioned a dog phobia in a young man who acquired his illness after "he thought he had heard from his father that his mother had had a severe fright from a dog during her pregnancy" (1913, 132). Earlier in the text, quoting Frazer, Freud described one theory of totemism based on the attribution of paternity to an animal by a pregnant woman who does not make the causal connection between sex with a man and the birth of a child: "Thus totemism would be a creation of the feminine rather than of the masculine mind: its roots would lie in 'the sick fancies of pregnant women.'. . . Such maternal fancies, so natural and seemingly so universal, appear to be the root of totemism" (1913, 118). Freud sees the dog that frightens the young phobic's mother during her pregnancy as analogous to the animals to whom primitive women attributed paternity. In the imaginary of the young phobic, the dog takes the place of his father, and therefore Freud finds reasonable the fluid movement from animal totem to animal phobia. He takes the attribution of paternity as the starting point of totemism and animal phobias.

At this point, however, it may surprise Freud's readers that the easy substitution of one for the other leads him to what he suggests is a startling realization:

The first consequence of our substitution is most remarkable. If the totem animal is the father, then the two principal ordinances of totemism, the two taboo prohibitions which constitute its core—not to kill the totem and not to have sexual relations with a woman of the same totem—coincide in their content with the two crimes of Oedipus, who killed his father and married his mother, as well as with the two primal wishes of children, the insufficient repression or the re-awakening of which forms the nucleus of perhaps every psychoneurosis. (1913, 132)

The substitution of animal phobia for animal totemism, and of neurotics for savages, leads to the "remarkable" discovery that Oedipal desire is what drives both. After moving back and forth between these two, interpreting both the animal ancestor of totemism and the phobic's terrifying animal as a displaced father and using one interpretation to shore up the other, it is indeed remarkable that Freud begins the last section of *Totem and Taboo* as follows:

At the conclusion, then, of this exceedingly condensed inquiry, I should like to insist that its outcome shows that the beginnings of religion, morals, society and art converge in the Oedipus complex. This is in complete agreement with the psycho-analytic finding that the same complex constitutes the nucleus of all neuroses, so far as our present knowledge goes. It seems to me a most *surprising* discovery that the problems of social psychology, too, should prove soluble on the basis of one single concrete point—man's relation to his father. (1913, 156, italics added)

What about man's relation to animals, the relation that led to this mythical father? Readers of Freud's *Totem and Taboo* will not be surprised that he finds the father behind both totemism and phobia, since throughout the text his series of substitutions guarantees that he will find what he is looking for in the end (and in the beginning). What might be more surprising is that the reader doesn't have to look far to see behind this father the repeated appearance of animals. Animals serve a definitive role in the theory of substitution or displacement and in the theory of the Oedipal complex with its family romance and blood kinship. They also put the teeth in Freud's theory of the castration complex.[9]

Eat or Be Eaten

In the major cases of animal phobia that Freud analyzes and repeatedly invokes throughout his writings, from the "Analysis of Phobia in a Five Year-Old Boy" (1909a) on, he identifies the threat posed by the animal with the father's castration threats, and the boy-child's fear of being bitten by the animal in question is interpreted as a fear of castration.[10] For example, in his analysis of Little Hans (the Five Year-Old Boy), Hans is afraid that a horse will bite him. Likewise, both the Rat-Man and the Wolf-Man get their names from the animals that they fear will bite or devour them.

The Rat-Man is named for his famous story of an "Eastern" punishment in which rats used their teeth to bore into the anus of the victim (1909b, 166). It doesn't take long for Freud to discover that one of the imagined victims of this punishment is the patient's father. The rest of the analysis turns on the patient's relationship with his father, his father's disapproval of his sexual relations, and the patient's imagined punishment associated with sex. Later in his analysis, Freud links the rat phobia to anal eroticism associated with the patient's childhood plagued by worms. The rats come to represent many things, including money, disease, the penis, and children. The association between rats and children involves, among other things, the fact that when he was a child, the patient liked to bite people. In developing this interpretation, Freud identifies the turning point in the analysis when the patient recounted a visit to his father's grave:

Once when the patient was visiting his father's grave he had seen a big beast, which he had taken to be a rat, gliding long over the grave. He assumed that it had actually come out of his father's grave, and had just been having a meal off his corpse. The notion of a rat is inseparably bound up with the fact that it has sharp teeth with which it bites and gnaws . . . he himself has been just such a nasty, dirty little wretch, who was apt to bite people when he was in a rage, and had been fearfully punished for doing so. (1909b, 215–16)

This scene of that rat/child feasting on the body of the father prefigures Freud's primal horde, which feasts on the body of the father, first literally when the "brothers" were still animals and then figuratively when they become human and their meal becomes another sort of animal. The Rat-Man's phobic fantasies involve being devoured by rats or his father being devoured by rats as a sort of punishment levied for his father's cruelty and the patient's own sexual indiscretions.

The Wolf-Man also is afraid of being devoured by animals. Although the fear of being devoured or bitten by wolves is central to Freud's analysis, the patient reports other animal phobias—butterflies, caterpillars, swine—with some involving similar fears.[11] In the case of the Wolf-Man, Freud interprets the dreaded wolf as a father substitute that threatens to devour the patient, just as he had seen a wolf devour seven little goats in a fairy-tale book with which his sister used to torment him as a child: "Whenever he caught sight of this picture [of a wolf] he began to scream like a lunatic that he was afraid of the wolf coming and eating him up. His sister, however, always succeeded in arranging that he see this picture, and was delighted at his terror" (1918, 16). Freud surmised that in the cases of the Wolf-Man and Little Hans, their father used to pretend to want to gobble them up (1926, 104). He likens this to another case of a young American whose father read him stories about

an Arab chief who pursued a "ginger-bread man" so as to eat him up. He [the patient] identified himself with this edible person, and the Arab chief was easily recognized as a father-substitute. . . . The idea of being devoured by the father is typical age-old childhood material. It has familiar parallels in mythology (e.g. the myth of Kronos) and in the animal kingdom. (1926, 105)

Freud's allusion to the animal kingdom suggests that children see animals eating one another and become afraid that they, too, might be eaten by an animal.

We might also wonder whether children see themselves eating animals and become afraid that the animals may bite back, that they fear that they too might be edible. It seems that this may follow from Freud's remarks about children's identification with animals. In some of his most famous case studies involving the fear of being bitten or eaten by animals, the patient, like the Rat-Man, is identified specifically with animals' biting. Recall Freud's conclusion that "children have no scruples over allowing animals to rank as their full equals. Uninhibited as they are in the avowal of their bodily needs, they no doubt feel themselves more akin to animals than to their elders, who may well be a puzzle to them" (1913, 127).[12] Children's tendency to bite one another is presumably one of the bodily impulses they share with animals. This equality between children and animals makes them (like Freud's savages), cannibals, at least in their imaginaries. They eat their own kind and easily become afraid of being eaten by them. In a certain sense, all fear is linked to the fear of being eaten, the fear of becoming the eaten rather than the eater, becoming passive rather than active.

The opposition between eating and being eaten operates throughout Freud's metapsychology under the guise of the opposition between activity and passivity. As we know, for Freud, activity is associated with masculinity, and passivity is associated with femininity. In the case of the animal phobias and the fear of being devoured by the father, Freud sees a hidden wish: the desire to be in the feminine or passive position in relation to the father in a sexual way. Extrapolating from the cases of Little Hans and the Wolf-Man, in his later work on anxiety Freud concludes that "it shows that the idea of being devoured by the father gives expression, in a form that has undergone regressive degradation, to a passive, tender impulse to be loved by him in a genital-erotic sense" (1926, 105). In his earlier analysis of the Wolf-Man case, he argues that the patient witnessed animal coitus, performed by either his parents having sex "doggie" style or sheepdogs having sex.[13] A central factor in Freud's supposition is that the patient must have seen his mother's genitals (or some version of female genitals) and his father's (or the animal's) "violent" movements in relation to them. The young patient saw this scene as both threatening and exciting. (As we know from Freud's writings on fetishism and elsewhere, the "castrated" female genitals make the threat of castration seem real.) According to Freud, the Wolf dream suggests that the patient wanted to submit to his father's violence/passion in the way that his mother had.[14] In other words, he wanted to adopt the passive position in relation to his father. Freud makes explicit the connection between the wolf phobia, the fear of being eaten, and the passive position of the mother in relation to the father:

His relation to his father might have been expected to proceed from the sexual aim of being beaten by him to the next aim, namely, that of being copulated with by him like a woman; but in fact, owing to the opposition of his narcissistic masculinity, this relation was thrown back to an even more primitive stage. It was displaced on to a father-surrogate, and at the same time split off in the shape of a fear of being eaten by the wolf. (1918, 64)

Freud goes on to describe three simultaneous sexual trends in the Wolf-Man's relation with his father:

From the time of the dream [about the wolves] onwards, in his unconscious he was homosexual, and in his neurosis he was at the level of cannibalism; while the earlier masochistic attitude remained the dominant one. All three currents had passive sexual aims; there was the same object, and the same sexual impulse, but that impulse had become split up along three different levels. (1918, 64)

In sum, the Wolf-Man had adopted a passive feminine position in relation to his father by splitting his father in the figure of the wolf, which he feared would eat him. Yet at some level, he wanted to be eaten by his father and thereby adopt the passive feminine position in relation to him.

Throughout his discussion of animal phobias, Freud's analysis suggests a strong association between cannibalism and sex, an association that he does not explore, however.[15] In his discussions of Little Hans, the Rat-Man, and the Wolf-Man, the fear of being eaten or devoured accompanies sexual desire. In the case of Little Hans, the patient is afraid of being bitten by the horse/father as punishment for his desire for his mother. In the case of the Rat-Man, the patient fantasizes rats/himself eating his father and identifies with biting rats. In the case of the Wolf-Man, the patient is afraid of being devoured by wolves, which he also identifies with his father, but at the same time he associates the wolves with sex and a desire for his father. In each of these cases, biting or being bitten, eating or being eaten, is linked to repressed sexual desires. Freud specifically identifies the fear of being bitten with a castration threat, proposing that the fear is one of cannibalism by the father, who, like Kronos, threatens to eat his young. The association between cannibalism and sex in the animal phobias suggests an alternative primal scene in which the young patient—the Wolf-Man in particular—may have seen or imagined his parent's oral sex act as an act of cannibalism. The mother's "castration" could be imagined to be the result of the father's cannibalism, which is in keeping with the link between the father and biting, gnawing, or devouring animals. The boy's ambivalence comes from fearing yet desiring "castration" from his father, who threatens to bite or eat his penis. In an important sense, then, it is the fantasy of cannibalism or the dog-eat-dog world of animals—recall that children don't distinguish between humans and animals—that gives the castration threat its teeth. Recall, too, that for Freud, cannibalism is an essential element of the totemic meal that inaugurates humanity and human civilization defined against animality and animal nature. I will return to the role of cannibalism and the totemic feast later in this and the next chapter.

Trotting Out the Animal Phobias

As we have seen, biting, eating, and devouring anchor Freud's theories of both the castration and Oedipal complexes. They also are central to the dynamic theory of anxiety he develops midcareer, which turns on the reactivation of passivity or, in terms of the animal phobias, a reversal between biting and being bitten, or eating and being eaten. In "Inhibitions, Symptoms and Anxiety" (1926), Freud claims that his new theory of anxiety, which he now sees as the result not of repression but of the return of the repressed, puts "neurosis *on all fours* with phobias" (1926,

127, italics added). Throughout this lengthy examination of inhibitions and anxiety, and his other work from this period on anxiety, Freud repeatedly returns to animal phobia in order make his case. Little Hans, the Wolf-Man, and the Rat-Man, along with Little Árpád (who suffers from a chicken phobia—the fear that he will be bitten by a cock—guess where), take center stage in Freud's later theory of energetics. It seems that whenever Freud needs an example to prove his point, he trots out the animal phobias.

The 1926 essay "Inhibitions, Symptoms and Anxiety" is exemplary of how Freud uses animal phobias to prove his theories. He begins the essay with the theoretical overview of his new "economic" theory of anxiety: "Anxiety is not newly created in repression; it is reproduced as an affective state in accordance with an already existing mnemic image" (1926, 93). So it is not repression per se but the return of the repressed that causes anxiety. Freud trots out Little Hans's horse phobia to prove his point: "Let us start with an infantile hysterical phobia of animals, for instance, the case of 'Little Hans,' whose phobia of horses was undoubtedly typical in all its main features" (1926, 101). As we know, Freud interprets Little Hans's fear that the horse will bite him as the fear of castration from his father. Freud's "unexpected" finding is that in both Hans and the Wolf-Man,

the motive force of the repression was fear of castration. The ideas contained in their anxiety—being bitten by a horse and being devoured by a wolf—were substitutes by distortion for the idea of being castrated by their father. . . . But the affect of anxiety, which was the essence of the phobia, came not from the process of repression, not from the libidinal cathexes of the repressed impulses, but from the repressing agency itself. The anxiety belonging to the animal phobias was an untransformed fear of castration. It was therefore a realistic fear, a fear of danger which was actually impending or was judged to be a real one. It was anxiety which produced repression and not, as I formerly believed, repression which produced anxiety. (1926, 108; cf. 1932, 86)

The animal phobias "prove" that the fear of castration is fundamental to masculine anxiety and leads to both repression and regression in the form of the phobia in which the castration threat becomes the threat of being bitten and the father is replaced by an animal.

In the next section of the essay, Freud begins by saying that the choice of the animal phobia may have been "unlucky" because not all neuroses carry with them anxiety (1926, 111). But it isn't long until Freud again returns to the animal phobias: "Let us go back again to infantile phobias of animals; for, when all is said and done, we understand them better than any other cases" (1926, 124). What Freud then describes is the temporality of anxiety as one of both expectation and repetition (a repetition that he later identifies with animal instinct, see 1932, 106). More than the "danger situation," what causes anxiety is the expectation of danger, specifically the "helplessness" experienced while waiting for it (1926, 166). This helplessness or passivity leads to the compulsion to repeat as a way of trying to master the situation through an active reenactment:

A danger-situation is a recognized, remembered, expected situation of helplessness. Anxiety is the original reaction to helplessness in the trauma and is reproduced later on in the danger-situation as a signal for help. The ego, which experienced the trauma passively, now repeats it actively in a weakened version, in the hope of being able itself to direct its course. It is certain that children behave in this fashion towards every distressing impression they receive, by reproducing it in their play. In thus changing from passivity to activity they attempt to master their experiences psychically. (1926, 166)

Anxiety and the compulsion to repeat that anxiety are the result of an interplay between activity and passivity. Freud's energetic theory is based on this movement between masculine and feminine, active and passive, eating and being eaten. Freud concludes his own later summary of the theory of anxiety in "Anxiety and Instinctual Life," but now discussing the relationship between aggressive instincts (e.g., the boy's Oedipal hatred of his father) and sexual instincts (e.g., the boy's Oedipal desire for his mother): "It is like a prolongation in the mental sphere of the dilemma of 'eat or be eaten' which dominates the organic animate world. Luckily the aggressive instincts are never alone but always alloyed with the erotic ones" (1932, 111). This passage suggests that "eat or be eaten" applies to both aggressive and sexual instincts and, furthermore, that the two are essentially linked by the formula "eat or be eaten." The animal phobias with little boys both fearing and desiring to eat and be eaten, as they have seen animals (and perhaps their parents) doing, makes this clear. The mental, like the physical, world is a doggie-eat-doggie world.

She's Some Kind of Animal!

At this point, it seems that there is a tension between the active and passive roles of father and mother in Freud's account of the animal phobias and his account of totemism. As we know, Freud compares animal phobias to totemism and throughout his writings compares primitive men and children, especially in their proximity to animals. In the animal phobias, however, if the mother is in the position of being eaten, so to speak, and the father is in the position of eating, how does that jibe with Freud's story of the primal horde of brothers eating their father? In *Totem and Taboo*, the father is put in the position of the eaten (the passive feminine position), and the son is in the active masculine position of eating. Of course, in both totemism and animal phobia, the animal takes the place of the father, or vice versa. Although the mother remains closely associated with the animal (both in the Wolf-Man's primal scene as Freud imagines it and throughout Freud's writings on the mother), it is the father who is replaced by a specific animal: horse, rat, wolf. As we learn in *Totem and Taboo*, this primal substitution of an animal for the father is the inauguration of society and representation, but the mother is no more than a possession of the father and then subsequently of the brothers. In the case of the father, then, the substitution is made explicit and is therefore a sign of civilization (or, we might say, the difference between the savage and the neurotic), but in the case of the mother, the identification with animality remains implicit, unsublimated, and beyond either representation or the social.[16] In the terms of *Totem and Taboo*, the father/animal substitution is the result of the activity of the brothers and not of the mothers or sisters, even though Freud speculates that it has its origins in the "sick fancies" of pregnant women who imagine they were impregnated by animals—a fantasy in which the father/brother plays no part at all (1913, 118).

The seemingly contradictory role of women/animals is particularly interesting in that what is uncanny about the animal phobias seems to be the reactivation of the passive position rather than the activity itself. Freud's analysis of the uncanny helps elucidate the connection between the uncanny and the reactivation of the passive or feminine position (and its link to the reactivation of the animal). In his essay "The Uncanny," Freud discusses the uncanny effect of Hoffmann's Sand-man story as revolving around a fear of castration. In the story, a student named Nathaniel has a fear of having his eyes ripped out by the "Sand-man," a figure with whom his childhood nurse threatened him if he didn't go to bed. According to the nurse, this wicked man throws sand into naughty children's eyes so that their eyes jump out of their heads and he can carry them back to his own children, who "sit up there in their nest, and their beaks are hooked like owl's beaks, and they use them to peck up naughty boys' and girls' eyes with" (1919, 228). Although Nathaniel's phobia is not explicitly identified as an animal phobia, there is an obvious connection to the fear of birds pecking out his eyes. Later we learn of Nathaniel's terror at finding out that the "girl," Olympia, whom he sees through his window, is actually an automaton with empty eye sockets, which are about to be filled with real human eyes. It is seeing Olympia's missing eyes (like seeing the "castrated" female sex) that has the uncanny effect on Nathaniel, who realizes that his love object is actually an object. Freud suggests that what is truly uncanny about Olympia is the reactivation of passivity, that a passive or dead object appears alive. Witnessing the return to life of the lifeless doll is terrifying and yet compelling. Freud interprets the effect of this reactivation of the passive feminine as reactivating Nathaniel's passive feminine attitude toward his father: "This automatic doll can be nothing else than a materialization of Nathaniel's feminine attitude towards his father in his infancy" (1919, 232). An uncanny sensation is produced when something that should be passive becomes active or something domesticated becomes wild, whether that something is a girl or an animal.

It is telling that in the etymology of the German word *Heimlich* (which means "home," or the opposite of *Unheimlich,* "uncanny") with which Freud begins his essay on the uncanny, we learn that *Heimlich* denotes "tame," as in tame animals versus wild animals (1919, 222). The appearance of wild animals in the midst of domestic ones can produce an uncanny effect, particularly if the animal in question is a tame or domestic animal become wild, a passive animal become active, like Little Hans's horse. The same holds true for girls and women; they are expected to be passive, so when they are not, their unexpected activity produces an uncanny effect. We are surprised when domestic girls or animals become wild and bite back. For the male child, according to Freud, the threat of biting is always directed at the penis and brings with it the castration complex. Interestingly, he describes the function of the castration complex as inhibiting and limiting masculinity and encouraging femininity (see Freud 1926; cf. 1915, 134). Earlier, in "Instincts and Their Vicissitudes," Freud described how the drives can pass from active to passive in terms of both their aims and their objects, and loving becomes being loved, biting becomes being bitten, and eating becomes being eaten. It is as if the subject's own activity is projected outward and now, instead of assuming an active position in relation to the world, the subject assumes a passive position. The castration complex, which Freud often associates with the fear of being bitten or devoured, encourages passivity or the feminine position. The subject's assumption of the passive feminine position is correlative with imagining another in the position of the active masculine position, as if the threats of punishment or feelings of ambivalence lead the subject to imagine his own urges to bite or to eat turning on him from the outside. Since the infant's first relationship with eating comes through the maternal breast or mother's milk, we might wonder why the fantasies of being bitten, eaten, or devoured (which Freud interprets as castration threats) don't come from the mother. I will discuss Melanie Klein and Julia Kristeva's theories of the devouring and abject mother in the next chapter. For now, I want to consider two other distinguishing features of the animal phobias as Freud explains them.

First, in his interpretations of Little Hans, the Rat-Man and the Wolf-Man, Freud finds that in each case, the animal phobia is linked not only to fear of castration from the father, or a desire to take the mother's place in copulation, but more specifically to the wish to have children. If they want to take their mother's place in the sexual relation to their father, they also want to take her place as a mother. In a sense, they want to give birth to themselves. In this regard, Freud's analysis implies that these boys imagine doing away with their mother (not—or in addition to—their father) and mothering themselves. They want babies from their father, and they appear to identify with babies from their father. These babies are abject offspring, which, as we will see, Kristeva reinterprets as jettisoned from an abject mother. Freud, however, returns the wish for a child back to the father and the boy's incestuous desire for him.

In the case of the Wolf-Man, Freud interprets an episode with an enema as follows:

The necessary condition of his re-birth was that he should have an enema administered to him by a man. (It was not until later on that he was driven by necessity to take this man's place himself.) This can only have meant that he had identified himself with his mother, that the man was acting as his father, and that the enema was repeating the act of copulation, as the fruit of which the excrement-baby (which was once again himself) would be born. The phantasy of re-birth was therefore bound up closely with the necessary condition of sexual satisfaction from a man. So that the translation now runs to this effect: only on the condition that he took the woman's place and substituted himself for his mother, and thus let himself be sexually satisfied by his father and bore him a child—only on that condition would his illness leave him. Here, therefore, the phantasy of re-birth was simply a mutilated and censored version of the homosexual wishful phantasy. (1918, 100)

Freud interprets the patient's fantasies about being back in the womb and identifying with his mother as about the father's and the patient's homosexual desires for him. Notice that the mother assumes the passive posture of being satisfied by the father and that the boy imagines himself submitting to the father in the same way. Freud goes on to say that whether the neurotic's incestuous desires are directed at his mother or his father is correlated with whether the "subject's attitude is feminine or masculine" (1918, 102). Even what seems to be the boy's fantasy of giving birth to a child—to himself—is reinterpreted by Freud as passive, perhaps because the "act" of giving birth is feminine and therefore, by nature, passive. In his writings on anxiety, using the animal phobias as his proof, Freud goes to great lengths to discount Rank's thesis that the castration fear is founded on the primal separation from the maternal body through the trauma of birth. Freud insists that castration is primary—even more so than birth trauma—and that even the fear of death and war trauma take us back to the threat of castration as the first cause of anxiety (cf. 1918, 129–30). The fears or traumas of birth, death, war, and loss of love (this is how Freud translates the castration threat in females) all are reduced to the castration complex. Freud's arguments to this effect continually return him to the animal phobias.

As the preceding passage indicates, the Wolf-Man has fantasies of having abject children or excrement babies. In the case of the Rat-Man, Freud discovers that one of the main reasons his patient does not marry "his lady" is that she cannot have children and that he was "extraordinarily fond of children" (1909b, 216–17). The Rat-Man also refers to psychoanalysis as "the child" who would solve his problems but whom he also imagines kicking (1909b, 311, 313). In Freud's theories of female sexuality, according to which most "female troubles" can be cured by having a child, the Rat-Man could again be interpreted as preferring a feminine position. Freud discusses the Rat-Man's attachment to children in the context of interpreting the rats as children. The rats of his obsessional fantasy are identified with himself as a biting child and the children that he wishes he could have. Here again, children (and the patient as a child) are identified with something dirty or disgusting. In the case of the Wolf-Man, it was excrement, and in this case, it is dirty rats. The Rat-Man also has a fantasy of shitting into other children's mouths and copulating with an excrement penis (see 1909b, 286, 287). Many of the Rat-Man's fantasies and obsessions involve abjection—for example, one of his recurring obsessions and wishes is not to wash, which of course would make him rattier.

The desire for children is even more central to the case of Little Hans, who is "mummy" to his imaginary children until he is convinced that boys can't have babies, and consequently he becomes their father (e.g., 1909a, 96). He insists that he will have a baby girl like his sister Hanna, but he doesn't want his mother to have any more babies and wishes his sister were dead (1909a, 87, 72). His father repeatedly tells him that babies are delivered by the stork. (Note that Little Hans was most afraid of horses with carts, which his father called "stork boxes" and which Freud associated with Han's mother's pregnant belly.)[17] At one point, Hans claims that he laid an egg and out of it came a little Hans, whereupon he asked his father, "Daddy, when does a chicken grow out of an egg? When it is left alone? Must it be eaten?" (1909a, 85). Little Hans imagines giving birth to himself by laying an egg, but he also seems worried that in order to give birth, one may have to eat the egg. He wants to have his mother to himself, but he also wants to be his own mother or mother to his own children. Like the Wolf-Man and the Rat-Man, Little Hans imagines shit babies, which leads Freud to suggest that there is a symbolic equivalence between shit babies/penises (money, rats, etc.). It is noteworthy that this equation supports his theory that having a child resolves penis envy in women. Discussing Hans, Freud concludes:

The arrival of his sister brought into Han's life many new elements, which from that time on gave him no rest. . . . He rejected the proffered solution [to the question of where babies come from] of the stork having brought Hanna [his baby sister]. For he has noticed that months before the baby's birth his mother's body had grown big, that then she had gone to bed, and had groaned while the birth was taking place, and that when she got up she was thin again. He therefore inferred that Hanna had been inside his mother's body, and had then come out like a "lumf" [Han's word for turd]. He was able to imagine the act of giving birth as a pleasurable one by relating it to his own first feelings of pleasure in passing stool; and he was thus able to find a double motive for wishing to have children of his own: the pleasure of giving birth to them and the pleasure (the compensatory pleasure, as it were) of looking after them. (1909a, 133)

Freud comments that this wish to give birth to a baby/turd is not in itself what causes Han's phobia; rather, Hans suspects that his father had something to do with conception, knows that his father comes between him and his mother (especially in terms of whether or not he gets to sleep in bed with her), and hates him for it. According to Freud, Hans's ambivalent feelings for his father are displaced onto the horse—more precisely, the hatred is placed there so that the love can be reserved for his real father. But because his fear of horses is triggered by the birth of his sister and his fear seems mostly directed toward the "stork box" that delivers the dreaded sister, both mothers and sisters may be at least as important, if not more important, than the father in explaining Han's phobia.[18]

Sadistic and Seductive Sisters

Through the birth of Little Hans's sister, we have moved from Freud's images of Kronos eating his babies and the phobic's fear of being eaten by his father to the phobic's fantasy of shitting babies and thereby taking the place of his mother and giving birth to himself (and to his sister). For Hans, his sister seems to be the ultimate little shit baby. The Rat-Man, too, has frequent associations between his sisters and excrement, rats, filth, lice, disease, and so on. In association with his excrement-eating dream, which I mentioned earlier, he says to his sister Julie, "Nothing about you would be disgusting to me" (1909b, 287). It becomes clear in Freud's analysis, however, that his patient's phobias and fantasies are as much connected to his two sisters as they are to his mother and father. The Rat-Man seems caught between his incestuous desire for his younger sister Julie and his guilt over the death of his older sister Katherine. In addition, it is the Wolf-Man's sadistic sister who torments him with frightening storybook pictures of wolves that send him into screaming fits.

Discussing the Wolf-Man, Nicholas Abraham and Maria Torok suggest that in Russian, his mother tongue, the word for six (Shiest)—as in six wolves—is closely related to the word for sister (Siestra) (1986, 17). They claim that the Wolf-Man's wolf dream includes a "sixter" of wolves that indicates that his phobia is directly related to his sister, whom they maintain he has incorporated into his own identity (1986, esp. 75). They maintain that what the Wolf-Man witnesses as Freud's so-called primal scene is not intercourse between his parents but incestuous relations between his father and his sister and that this is the traumatic sight causing his phobia (1986, esp. 76).[19] Like Hans and the Rat-Man, the Wolf-Man too has fantasies of debasing his sister and usurping her dominant position. The incestuous scene is traumatic in part because he is left out of it: he is not the object of his father's desire. It is noteworthy that Freud does not consider that his Russian patient had seen and recounted seeing real wolves and not just storybook wolves, domestic sheepdogs, or his parents having sex "doggie style," as Freud surmises (see Genosko 1993). In other words, while debating the status of the Wolf-Man's witnessing the primal scene, Freud considers the reality of the sex act in humans behaving like animals, domesticated dogs and sheep, but he does not consider the reality of the wolf in the life of his patient, even though the patient saw wolves and wolf carcasses shot by his father (Genosko 1993, 613). Gary Genosko also points out that the patient had seen Anna Freud's dog while visiting Freud and that he remarked that the dog resembled a wolf and that the dog was named "Wulf," or Wolf (1993, 611–12).

Returning to Freud's analysis of the Wolf-Man's sister, we see that his patient's sexual development, fantasies, and phobias are directly linked with her. Freud describes how after their rivalry in early childhood—and his sister's seductions of her young brother—when reaching puberty, the patient and his sister became "like the best of friends" (1918, 22). After the patient made a pass at his sister and she rejected him, Freud recounts that he subsequently seduced a house servant with the same name as his sister and that all his love objects were substitutes for his beloved sister (1918, 22). He continued to choose servant girls, however, according to Freud, because at the same time he wanted to debase his sister. Immediately following his analysis of his patient's sister substitutes, Freud discusses the patient's reaction to his sister's death, which Freud says was surprising, given how much he loved his sister and how little he grieved for her. Freud discovers, however, that the patient weeps at a poet's grave, a poet whom his father associated with the patient's sister. Freud concludes that the patient's grief is displaced because of his ambivalent relation to his sister, which is characterized by both unconscious incestuous love and jealousy. It also is noteworthy that in Freud's account, it is after the young patient's rejected sexual advances toward his "Nanya," or nanny, that he becomes cruel to animals. As Freud describes it, even his sexual curiosity about Nanya is piqued by his sister; and through them both he "learns" about both castration and sexual desire. In addition to his concern with castration, which became associated with animals in fairy tales, he became occupied with where children came from, particularly in relation to a story in which children were taken out of the body of a (male) wolf (1918, 25). Like Little Hans, the Wolf-Man's phobias are linked both to a wish that males could have babies and to his sister. Like the Rat-Man, his sexuality is shaped in relation to his animal phobias as well as his desire for his sister(s) and their deaths. Freud diagnoses the Wolf-Man's cruelty to animals as a result of his rejected sexual advances and his budding awareness of castration, which Freud reasons is linked to his regression and his "anal impulses" (1918, 26). These impulses lead him to "be cruel to small animals, to catch flies and pull off their wings, to crush beetles underfoot; in his imagination he liked beating large animals (horses) as well" (1918, 26). Although Freud's final message about this case returns us to castration threats levied by the father against the son, threats that lead to ambivalence and the displacement of hatred onto animals, lurking behind these animal totems we once again find a sadistic, seductive, and eventually dead sister.

Although these sisters repeatedly show up in his patient's dreams, fantasies, and stories, their central part in the familial drama drops out of Freud's conclusions about his animal phobics, which continue to revolve around the Oedipal family romance. Moreover, the role of the sister disrupts Freud's easy slippage between animal phobia and totemism, characteristic of both his work on the animal phobias and his account of the origin of civilization in *Totem and Taboo*. Although all of Freud's phobics' animal fears are intimately linked to their sisters, the sisters have no role in the story of the primal horde—the band of brothers—who kill their father and "marry" their mother, thus fulfilling the Oedipal prophecy of psychoanalysis. Here, too, the kinship relations that interest Freud are those among brother, son, and father, determined by their struggles to sexually possess women, usually figured as mothers rather than sisters. Freud's interpretation of totemism shares with his phobics' fantasies an implicit concern for paternity. By seeing all women in terms of motherhood and associating sexual desires for women by men with desires for their mothers, Freud repeats the phobics' concern with where babies come from. Women as mothers, birth givers, and possessors of children are desired by brothers/sons in order to substitute themselves for the father and, as we have seen, not only father themselves but also give birth to themselves. The death of the sister provides fuel for the phobic fantasy of taking her place as the one who can identify with the mother as the birth giver and possessor of children. In Freud's descriptions of animal phobia, we might say that the sisters bite back and disrupt Freud's neat analyses of castration and oedipal complexes.

Really Strange Kinship or the Oedipal Family as "Real" Family

It is not just in the animal phobias, however, that the sisters bite back. In *Totem and Taboo*, Freud's notion of kinship has as its telos the Oedipal family which is undermined by the anthropological accounts of the history of kinship that he uses to produce it. As we know, Freud's psychoanalysis revolves around the Oedipal family with its family romance, in which the children have and repress desires for their parents, desires/repressions that can lead to neurosis. We also discover in *Totem and Taboo*, however, that the nuclear family with one mother, one father, and one or more children was not the original organization of the family. Rather, as Freud makes sure to point out several times, the primitive peoples discussed by the anthropologists on whose work he draws, defined their kinship relationships not in terms of family but rather in terms of their totem animal. The relations between children and their parents were radically different from the ideal of the nuclear family. Instead, children were raised by groups of adults who identified themselves as kin. Sometimes Freud suggests that all the adult women were viewed as mother and all the adult men as father, and all the children in the group were viewed as siblings (e.g., 1913, 6–7). Recall that Freud quotes Frazer: "The totem bond is stronger than the bond of blood or family in the modern sense" (1913, 3). Later, he repeats the sentiment without quoting him: "The totem bond is stronger than that of the family in our sense" (1913, 105). In the first few pages of the text, Freud poses the "riddle" of the family: "The riddle of how it came about that the *real family* [*wirklichen Familie*] was replaced by the totem clan must perhaps remain unsolved till the nature of the totem can be explained . . . replacing real blood-relationship [*reale Blutsverwandtschaft*] by totem kinship" (1913, 6, italics added; see also 1940, 12). By "real family" Freud means blood relations defined as the nuclear family. Because most of *Totem and Taboo* offers various anthropological accounts of group marriage, totem clans, and forms of kinship not linked to consanguinity, the riddle is not how the real family became a totem clan but how the totem clan became the so-called real family. In an important sense, the text is Freud's attempt to explain the domestication of the family, especially the father, through the domestication and sacrifice of animals.

According to the logic of the text, the domestication of the family that engenders kinship through blood requires both the literal and symbolic sacrifice of animals. Kinship with animals once stronger than consanguinity in defining the family is sacrificed for the sake of human kinship, and this symbolic sacrifice of animal kinship for human kinship is performed through ritual and ceremonial sacrifices of animals. It seems that animal blood must be shed so that human blood can create the bond of kinship. As we have seen, in the totem clan, the totem animal is viewed as an ancestor, and the border between humans and animals, if there is one, is porous. Freud quotes Frazer: "The farther we go back, the more we should find that the clansman regards himself and his totem as being of the same species, and the less he distinguishes between conduct towards his totem and towards his fellow-clansmen" (1913, 104). Indeed, the clan shares in its relation with the totem animal the kinship among humans created through kinship with the animal, and the clan "believe themselves to be of *one blood,* descendents of a common ancestor" through their totem animal (1913, 103, italics added). In addition, the family is coextensive with the clan, which includes animals. The totem animal in particular holds a special place in the clan, insofar as like other members of the clan, he cannot be killed or eaten because killing and/or eating these animal ancestors is akin to murdering or cannibalizing other members of the clan. The tension in Freud's analysis becomes apparent when he introduces the fable of the primal horde or band of brothers.[20] As we have seen, the designations "brother," "father," and "mother" carried radically different denotations and connotations before the rebellion of the primal horde against the primal "father." In addition, the substitution of the father for an animal in the totemic festival that Freud identifies with the onset of totemism does not, as he implies, initiate the "real family" or kinship through consanguinity. Rather, an animal is substituted for the primal father, and in subsequent festivals the ritualistic sacrifice of an animal takes the place of the sacrifice of the father. But if this celebration that creates the kinship bond in the clan comes through identification with, and substitution of, the totem animal, then this onset of totemism works against Freud's notion of brothers, fathers, mothers, or the so-called real family defined in terms of blood and the Oedipal myth.

Perhaps this is why, as we have seen, in his conclusion, Freud claims to be "surprised" to find the Oedipal complex at the beginnings of humanity (1913, 157). Freud's surprise is uncanny, if not disingenuous, in that the Oedipal complex with its patricidal tendency is, again as Nietzsche might say, the truth that Freud continually hides behind a bush and praises himself when he finds it. But it is surprising that Freud can find the "real" Oedipal family by tracing the outlines of the history of the family in the clan. If anything, this history demonstrates that the modern notion of the family is just one of the many possibilities for conceiving of kinship. Certainly, Freud's "discovery" that the Oedipal family is the real family or that the real family is an Oedipal family unsettles the anthropological research on which he bases his case that the incest prohibition is definitive of kinship. It is uncanny that the Oedipal family relations are entirely incestuous to the point that the father is simultaneously a brother, an uncle, and a nephew. If the Oedipal family is the real family, then the categories that sustain that family, particularly the notion of father, become inherently unstable. Another of Freud's most important discoveries is the operation of the primary processes of the unconscious that enable, even require, displacements and condensations like this, especially when the father is concerned. As we have seen, these operations separate humans from animals only insofar as humans identify with animals. Humans are unique, then, owing to their ability to substitute animals for themselves, and vice versa. In this sense, we could say that humans become human only by virtue of their relationships, even identification, with animals.

At the end of *Totem and Taboo*, Freud struggles with the problem of how the patriarchal family reappears out of totemism. After all, the primal horde does away with the authoritarian father figure and redistributes his authority to all the brothers as the inauguration of civil society. How, then, does the authoritarian father, necessary to the patriarchal and the Oedipal family, reappear? The text suggests that it comes through the domestication of the father resulting from the domestication of animals. The very notion of god, which transforms totemism into theistic religion, is a domestication of animality. The animal is a father surrogate who is replaced by a "superior" father surrogate, the god, as the totemic feast becomes "a simple offering to the deity, an act of renunciation in favour of the god" (1913, 150). The god becomes the agent of the sacrifice:

This is the phase in which we find myths showing the god himself killing the animal which is sacred to him and which is in fact himself. . . . At this point the psycho-analytic interpretation of the scene coincides approximately with the allegorical, surface translation of it, which represents the god as overcoming the animal side of his own nature. (1913, 150).

The separation of god, animal, and man, which had not existed before or during totemism, appears alongside the domestication of animals. Freud repeatedly remarks on the blood kinship of god, animal, and man. For example, he points out, "The sacrificial animal was treated as a member of the tribe; the sacrificing community, the god and the sacrificial animal were of the same blood and members of one clan" (1913, 136). The blood bond affirmed through totemism becomes associated with a much narrower conception of kinship. In Christian religious rituals, it is celebrated through the Eucharist, in which the "blood of the grape," wine, is substituted for the blood of Christ. Animals lose their sacred character as they become yoked to the plow and put into the service of man. As the dominion of man over animals increases, they no longer appear worthy of reverence or identification with the god. Now man himself must replace animals in the process of substitution that produces religion, culture, and art. Freud describes Christianity as the culmination of this process, in that the animal that was once substituted for the father becomes again substituted by man, the son of God: "The original animal sacrifice was already a substitute for a human sacrifice—for the ceremonial killing of the father; so that, when the father-surrogate once more resumed its human shape, the animal sacrifice too could be changed back into a human sacrifice" (1913, 151). The father "has regained his human shape" through totemism's connection between animal and father, one consequence of which is that the changing conceptions of animals change the conception of the father (see Freud 1913, 136–37, 147–51). Still, for Freud, vestiges of primal totemism can be found in Christianity's Eucharist, which is a ritualistic and symbolic consumption of Christ's body and blood, recalling the totemic feast:

The ancient totem meal was revived in the form of communion, in which the company of brothers consumed the flesh and blood of the son. . . . Thus we can trace through the ages the identity of the totem meal with animal sacrifice, with the anthropic human sacrifice and with the Christian Eucharist. (1913, 154)

The flesh and blood of an animal are replaced with that of the god (god become flesh and blood).

There Will Be Blood

In this history of animal sacrifice and meals made of animal flesh, the phrase "flesh and blood" that marks our modern sense of kinship harks back to animals, as they are the original flesh and blood. Certainly, in *Totem and Taboo,* the role of flesh, and, perhaps most remarkably, of blood is at every turn taken by animals in the construction of human kinship and the human sciences that analyze it. We could surmise from Freud's analysis of totemism that blood relations were originally relations with animals and that the bonds of blood kinship were originally formed by consuming or assimilating the flesh and blood of an animal. Discussing the nature of sacrifice, Freud says that

whenever food is eaten in common, the participation in the same substance establishes a sacred bond between those who consume it when it has entered their bodies. . . . This bond is nothing else than the life of the sacrificial animal, which resides in its flesh and in its blood and is distributed among all the participants in the sacrificial meal. A notion of this kind lies at the root of all the blood covenants. . . . This completely literal way of regarding blood-kinship as identity of substance makes it easy to understand the necessity for renewing it from time to time by the physical process of the sacrificial meal. (1913, 137–38)

The group shares in the flesh and blood and thereby is identified with that blood but also becomes complicit in the shared act of killing and eating. Blood relations assume this double meaning of sharing in, or eating, the body of the animal and in the acts of sacrificing it and consuming it, acts akin to murder and cannibalism if performed outside ritualized ceremonies. As Freud describes it, with the primal horde and band of brothers, this sacrifice becomes the crime of patricide, and so from that time forward, murder, incest, cannibalism, and bestiality are prohibited.[21] Freud quotes anthropologist Robertson Smith, who calls these crimes "offenses against the sacred laws of *blood*," and "in primitive society the only crimes of which the community as such takes cognizance" (1913, 143, italics added). To renew their bond, the brothers repeat the murderous act now domesticated through ritual animal sacrifice. Under any other circumstances, however, killing and eating the totem animal is a crime. It must be a communal act so that no one individual is responsible and every member of the tribe shares responsibility: "The rule that every participant at the sacrificial meal must eat a share of the flesh of the victim has the same meaning as the provision that the execution of a guilty tribesman must be carried out by the tribe as a whole" (1913, 136; cf. 146). If all eat the flesh, the act is a sacrifice and not a crime. The blood tie, then, is established not only by consuming the flesh and blood of the animal but also by sharing in the spilling of its blood and tearing of its flesh.

Citing Robertson Smith, Freud argues that "there is no gathering of a clan without an animal sacrifice" and that "the sacrificial meal, then, was originally a feast of kinsmen, in accordance with the law that only kinsmen eat together" (1913, 135). Only kinsmen eat together, and they become kin through that act. Moreover, they come together as a clan, as kin, only by sacrificing an animal. In this sense, human kinship is dependent on the sacrifice of animal kin and eventually the sacrifice of animal kinship altogether. The developmental and anthropological accounts of the origins of humanity and civilization that Freud presents in *Totem and Taboo* can be read as a lesson in the foreclosure of animal kinship for the sake of human kinship, specifically the form of human kinship that we recognize as the family. Of course, our views of animals (and humans) continue to evolve, and the family may come to include beloved family pets and companion animals, which, if Freud is right, should also change our conceptions of paternity and maternity. Our notions of kinship and the familial relations among brother, sister, father, and mother are historical concepts open to continued transformations.

Certainly the importance of sharing a meal together as a central ritual of establishing family and community continues. In many regions of the world, especially the United States, sharing animal flesh is traditionally part of family and community rituals, which include Memorial Day or Labor Day barbecues, eating turkey at Thanksgiving or Christmas, and eating ham at Easter. Meat eating continues to be identified with particular (Christian) celebrations that bring people together as kin. Freud points out that "in our own society the members of family have their meals in common," but he is quick to add, "The sacrificial meal bears no relation to the family. Kinship is an older thing than family life" (1913, 135). Freud emphasizes the distinction between kinship and the family as part of his argument that the Oedipal family with its strong father figure is a return of the pretotemic cultures and the dominant primal father who is killed and eaten with the onset of totemism and whose power is distributed to the brothers: that is, patriarchy becomes a fraternity.

Kinship defined through blood relations becomes more limited, and eventually animals and neighbors are excluded. Kinship is still described in terms of blood, but no longer as literally ingesting flesh and blood. The blood of the totem animal is considered sacred, which has the double sense of holy and unclean. The blood of this animal is not to be spilled or consumed outside the communal festival and ritual sacrifice. Furthermore, taboos on blood initiate the incest taboo that Freud identifies with the onset of totemism. Sex and mating must be between members of different tribes or different animal totem clans. Freud explains: "The totem is of the same blood as the man and consequently the ban upon shedding blood (in connection with defloration and menstruation) prohibits him from sexual relations with a woman belonging to his totem" (1913, 120; cf. Freud's discussion of restrictions on blood in relation to gods, 1913, 133–34). Freud does not elaborate on the connection between the taboo against killing the totem and the taboos associated with defloration and menstruation, but this passage suggests that when blood is or becomes associated with women, it is or becomes taboo. As Freud describes it, the incest taboo originally was a blood taboo related to prohibitions against sex between blood kin and also to prohibitions related to women's blood. At this point, we might say that the connection among animals, women, and blood thickens. I will return to the relation among taboo, animal, women, and blood in the next chapter, when I discuss Kristeva's notion of abjection.

In *Moses and Monotheism*, Freud suggests that the power of women increased after the totemic overthrow of the primal father and thus began an era of matriarchy (1939, 131). In part, that text is Freud's attempt to explain how matriarchy gave way to patriarchy and the return of the autocratic father. This later description of totemism makes it clear that the ceremonial meal substituting the totem animal for the murder and cannibalism of the primal father is attended by only male clan members. Although he maintains that totemism and the death of the primal father bring with them matriarchy and fraternity, women are still absent from the ritualized remembrance of the distribution and assimilation of power by the brothers: "Once a year the whole male community came together to a ceremonial meal at which the totem animal (worshipped at all other times) was torn to pieces and devoured in common" (1939, 131). While the brothers gain their power by consuming the flesh and blood of their father/totem, the women's power in this story remains a mystery (see also the next chapter). In sum, all these arguments point to the historical and contingent nature of kinship and family relations.

In our everyday parlance, we are accustomed to thinking of our kin as our "flesh and blood." Reflecting on the literal meaning of "flesh and blood," which is tied to animal flesh, we realize that in terms of kinship, "flesh and blood" is a metaphor. After all, members of the same family have different types of blood and, we might say, different types of flesh; they do not literally share flesh and blood. Furthermore, the ways in which we think that family members share flesh and blood is linked to an association between the maternal body and animality: In and through the maternal body, flesh and blood are generated and transmitted to future kin (I will return to this connection in the next chapter). It is only in the maternal body that kin literally share blood, and even then, the circulation of blood, often of different types, is negotiated by the placenta, which acts as a sort of third party (see Oliver 1995). The adage "blood is thicker than water" suggests that we have greater ethical obligation—or at least more intense emotional bonds—to those with whom we share blood than to those with whom we share water, which may be read a metaphor for food. Sharing blood is more binding than sharing food. But as we have seen, in Freud's account based on nineteenth-century anthropology, the idea of sharing blood originated in the literal sharing of the flesh and blood of animals. Sharing the flesh and blood of an animal in the totemic feast cemented the bond of kinship among members of the clan. Shedding and consuming animal blood both signaled and produced identifications with the blood of the totem animal, which became the first form of kinship. We don't have to go far in our reflection on the metaphor of "flesh and blood" to see animal kin as the tain in the mirror of the "brotherhood of man" and human kinship.

CHAPTER TWELVE

Animal Abjects, Maternal Abjects

Kristeva's Strays

A strange metaphor of contagion runs through Freud's *Totem and Taboo,* as if breaking taboos is a communicable disease. Animals and women are associated with this form of infection that threatens the community from inside. Freud describes a magical power attributed by primitive peoples to animals, objects, and persons, which can be contagious if not properly controlled through prohibitions. Since prohibitions correspond to desires that still exist in the unconscious, this magical power is, in effect, the power of temptation: "The magical power that is attributed to taboo is based on the capacity for arousing temptation; and it acts like a contagion because examples are contagious and because the prohibited desire in the unconscious shifts from one thing to another" (Freud 1913, 35). Like the totem animal and the taboos linked to it, the magical power is seen as sacred and threatening, holy and unclean. Freud identifies the magical power with what he calls "special individuals," "exceptional states," and "uncanny things," including priests and babies, menstruation, puberty and birth, and sickness and death, or anything associated with infection and contagion (1913, 22).[1] It is this exceptional quality that makes these beings, states, and events "'sacred' and 'above the ordinary' as well as 'dangerous,' 'unclean' and 'uncanny'" (Freud 1913, 22). Freud observes that something about the power of both women and animals is uncanny, specifically the dangerous power of animals and women to tempt men. It is the power of these "temptations of the flesh" to spread throughout the community that makes them contagious. Moreover, the infectious power of women and animals threatens what Freud describes as the brotherhood of man with a fall from civilization back into animality. The temptations that Freud mentions involve breaking the taboos that separate man from animals, including those against incest, cannibalism, and bestiality.

The uncanny effect that Freud describes in relation to animals and women becomes explicit in the work of Julia Kristeva, whose notion of abjection and analysis of cultural prohibitions or taboos help elucidate the psychic stakes in identifying women with animals and both with contagion.[2] Kristeva's *Powers of Horror* returns us to the fantasies of eating and devouring associated with both animals and women, particularly mothers. Her analysis enacts and reveals a slippage between maternity/femininity and animality on which psychoanalysis is based and is at the heart of the "sciences of man." In this chapter, I explore Kristeva's interpretation of the role of the mother in Freud's animal phobias and in the primal feast central to his *Totem and Taboo.* Throughout her discussions of Freud, Kristeva restores the figure of a powerful maternal authority, which she sees as remaining repressed in Freud's theories and in our culture more generally. As we will see, however, in uncovering this repressed maternal authority, Kristeva repeats the identification of mother and animal. Indeed, the force of her theory of abjection relies on the power over the human psyche held by animals and animality. Furthermore, because animals and animality in her texts are reduced to stand-ins for the mother and the maternal body, she erases animals as they exist outside human imaginary or symbolic systems. In Kristeva's writings, animals are symbols through which humans become speaking beings. In this regard, we could say that in psychoanalysis, animals become nothing more than human by-products. The ambivalence toward animals and animality in the history of Western thought is evidenced in Kristeva's work by her attempts to return our own animality to theories of language. She does this by turning animals into symbolic substitutes for the very kinship relations that our relations to them engender. In other words, as with Freud, for Kristeva animals are significant as substitutes for, and constitutive of, human kinship relations. In her case, they mark the territory of the relation between mother and child.

Adding Women to the Science of Man

As Freud does, Kristeva relies on evidence from anthropology to make her case in terms of collectivities and individual psychology. And she too easily moves back and forth between the social and the psychological, social science and psychoanalysis. She uses the "sciences of man," particularly anthropology, to diagnose the human psyche, now figured in terms of sexual difference rather than the generic man. In her early work, anthropology appears as a description of "facts" on which she bases her own theories (cf. 1982, 65, 78). But as she assimilates "data" from anthropology into her own psychoanalytic and social theories, Kristeva criticizes anthropologist Mary Douglas for integrating "Freudian data" while "naively" rejecting Freudian premises (1982, 66). This discourse of facts and data is in tension with Kristeva's account of the role of the imaginary and symbolic processes in psychic life. What she takes as "fact" or "data" obviously must be interpreted by her and the anthropologists whom she cites. Her acceptance of these supposed brute facts, however, is at odds with her later theory of narrativity and the role of fantasy in psychoanalysis and life. Like Freud and Lacan before her, Kristeva has an ambivalent relation to science. Sometimes she insists that facts are facts and that the analyst can discern universal truths from them, but at other times, she insists that all theory, including both science and psychoanalysis, are imbued with imaginary and symbolic constructs that depend on cultural valuation and ultimately on fiction (cf. 1982, 68).

Kristeva constantly interjects a personal discourse using the pronoun "I" at the same time that "I" appears as universal. But unlike Freud, she rarely explicitly discusses herself or her own dreams or fantasies. The following passage is an interesting example of Kristeva's ambivalence—or perhaps disavowal—of the status of the personal in her work, which despite its deeply personal tone claims to be universal:

My reflections will make their way through anthropological domains and analyses in order to aim at a deep psycho-symbolic economy: the general, logical determination that underlies anthropological variants (social structures, marriage rules, religious rites) and evinces a specific economy of the speaking subject, no matter what its historical manifestations may be. In short, an economy that analytic listening and semanalytic [*sic*] deciphering discover in our contemporaries. Such a procedure seems to me to be directly in keeping with Freudian utilization of anthropological data. It inevitably entails a share of *disappointment* for the empirically minded ethnologist. It does not unfold without a share of *fiction,* the nucleus of which, drawn from actuality and the subjective experience of the one who writes, is projected upon data collected from the life of other cultures, less to justify than to throw light on them by means of an interpretation to which they obviously offer resistance. (1982, 68, italics in original).

Note that Kristeva says "one who writes" to designate the universal writer rather than herself personally. Also, she claims that unlike the anthropologists who conduct empirical research on specific cultures and histories, she will be making universal claims that aim at the "deep" economy that crosses cultures and eras. The notion that ethnographic research gives us access only to a surface and contingent economy but that psychoanalysis gives us access to a deep and universal economy is, of course, suspect. It is noteworthy, however, that unlike Freud, Kristeva explicitly identifies the role of fiction in her use of anthropological data. So although she accepts the empirical research as fact, she simultaneously challenges anthropological interpretations of those facts and suggests that a deeper more universal interpretation requires "a share of fiction."

Inspired by Freud, and yet perhaps moving away from his commitment to the scientific status of psychoanalysis, Kristeva constantly turns to literature for evidence of her theories. Whereas Freud, and even more so Lacan, frequently uses examples of animals from biological or zoological sciences, Kristeva prefers literary texts. Aside from *Powers of Horror* with its reliance on anthropology, Kristeva rarely uses examples from either biological or social science. Indeed, her argument in *Powers of Horror* is that art and literature have taken the place of religion in the production of cultural meanings. What counts as *evidence* or *proof* changes dramatically with this move from science to literature, from empirical studies to fiction. Freud gives the first hints of this shift when late in his work, he calls instincts or drives the "mythology" of psychoanalysis:[3] "The theory of the instincts is so to say our mythology. Instincts are mythical entities, magnificent in their indefiniteness" (1932, 95). In this same text, "Anxiety and Instinctual Life," Freud justifies turning to philosophy (even while taking jabs at it) rather than science to develop the "science" of psychoanalysis (cf. 1932, 107). Freud himself often gives examples from literature, particularly Goethe and Shakespeare. And of course, the notion of the Oedipal complex, on which his theory is founded, is based on literature.

The movement from anthropology to literature is just as dramatic in Kristeva's *Powers of Horror* as it is in any of Freud's writings. For example, in just a few paragraphs, she goes from discussing religious rituals in India to Sophocles and Oedipus (cf. 1982, 81, 84–85). Without any regard for differences among cultures or religions, she moves easily between ancient Greek literature and contemporary ethnographic social science focused on South Asia. In this regard, Kristeva is right in saying that her work is in keeping with Freud's use of anthropological research, which he employs in conjunction with references to Goethe and other literature, his case studies, and his own personal experiences and cultural observations. In fact, in an important sense, *Powers of Horror* can be read as Kristeva's attempt to rewrite Freud's account of the emergence and significance of religion using current anthropological data. She continues Freud's "deep" research into the psychic economy underlying economies of exchange and kinship studied by contemporary anthropology. Focusing on the fear of contagion and defilement invoked by Freud in relation to both totemic religions and childhood animal phobias, Kristeva reinterprets this fear as a general one associated with abjection and its source in the maternal body.

Animal Phobia as Fear of the Unnamable

The first half of *Powers of Horror,* which sets out the theory of abjection, could be read as an account of the essential link between animal and mother in the constitution of the human psyche. In the first chapter, which begins with an epigraph from Victor Hugo about "beasts," Kristeva describes the abject as what challenges borders, whether they are the borders of the individual or the social. On the level of the individual, the primary frontier is the border with the maternal body, and on the level of the social, the primary frontier is the border with the animal:

The abject confronts us, on the one hand, with those fragile states where man strays on the territories of *animal.* Thus, by way of abjection, primitive societies have marked out a precise area of their culture in order to remove it from the threatening world of animals or animalism, which were imagined as representatives of sex and murder. The abject confronts us, on the other hand, and this time within our personal archeology, with our earliest attempts to release the hold of *maternal* entity even before existing outside of her, thanks to the autonomy of language. It is a violent, clumsy breaking away, with the constant risk of falling back under the sway of a power as securing as it is stifling. (Kristeva 1982, 12–13, italics in original)

As Kristeva describes it, abjection is the result of the return of repressed ambiguity or ambivalence inherent in these "fragile" boundaries, which are as precarious as they are necessary. We all are "strays" in that because we straddle borders, we do not entirely belong to one side or the other.[4] The abject is neither fish nor fowl so to speak, but the in-between that resists categorization. It is a separation within the inseparable, a division before there is one . . . or two. It is the first stirrings of the human psyche, or what Kristeva calls the "speaking being" and sometimes the "speaking animal" (e.g., 1982, 15).

She describes the abject as the most fragile and most archaic sublimation of "an 'object' still inseparable from drives" (1982, 12). This not-yet-object still inseparable from the fledgling subject becomes the "object" of primal repression, which is aimed at a "something else" against which the being struggles to become human. Kristeva says that "in this struggle, which fashions the human being, the *mimesis,* by means of which he becomes homologous to another in order to become himself, is in short logically and chronologically secondary. Even before being like, 'I' am not but do separate, reject, abject" (1982, 13). In regard to Freud's concern with the mimetic power of temptation, specifically the temptation to act like an animal, we might read Kristeva as pointing to a separation prior to imitation but one that still depends on the animal. Freud says, "What is in question is fear of an infectious example, of the temptation to imitate—that is, the contagious character of the taboo" (1913, 71–72). It is noteworthy in regard to the role of imitating animals that in Freud's account of animal phobia, particularly in the case of the Wolf-Man, the primal scene is characterized by the imitation of animal sex.[5] The temptation is not just to eat animals but to act like them, which includes eating other animals.

Kristeva's analysis suggests that human beings separate themselves from animal beings so that they can imitate those beings in order to become human. Imitation requires prior separation. This circular logic of separation and imitation takes us back not only to Freud's analysis of animal totems in *Totem and Taboo* but also to Rousseau's concern with the power of imitation in the origin of language and in education and to Derrida's deconstruction of the role of imitation in Rousseau's theory of nature, all of which involve animals and what I am calling *animal pedagogy*. Recall that Derrida argues that imitation turns out to be originary in Rousseau's account of language. In my earlier analysis, Rousseau's theory of language relies on animal pedagogy that links imitation to animals as our first teachers. Kristeva, however, identifies a relation with animals prior to this imitation, a relation characterized by abjection. She points to a separation from animals before the symbolic separation that results from imitation and our dependence on animals to learn language. As Derrida does, Kristeva finds another animal lurking behind the origins of humanity, a darker, more frightening beast, our dependence on which we disavow and abject. This abjection is the constant attempt, and constant failure, to separate from the primary "object," which is the (or an) animal on the level of society and the (or a) mother on the level of personal archaeology. In other words, abjection is a disavowal of the essential dependence on animals (or mothers) that enables separation and autonomy, which in turn enables imitation and through which we become speaking beings, human beings. Kristeva's theory of abjection can be read as an account of the primary disavowal that erases our dependence on animals from our psyches and discounts their roles in teaching us to be human. Abjection, then, is a disavowal of the animal pedagogy at the heart of humanity, or at least at the center of the human sciences, including psychoanalysis.

The second chapter of *Powers of Horror* explores the connection between abjection and animals by returning to Freud's discussion of animal phobias. Kristeva begins this chapter with an epigraph from Lautréamont that could serve as an example of how animals are used to delineate the outlines of man on the frontier of the animal: "A regal soul, inadvertently surrendering to the crab of lust, the octopus of weakmindness, the shark of individual abjection, the boa of absent morality, and the monstrous snail of idiocracy!" (Kristeva 1982, 32). Kristeva does not comment on this passage, which she presumably invokes because it explicitly mentions abjection. As we will see, however, it is indicative of a tension between her analysis of Freud's animal phobias and the role of what she calls the unnamable in that dynamic. It becomes obvious in passages like this one from Lautréamont that not only are animals given names but also those names are used to define the human soul against animal nature. This does not mean that these names do justice to, or even sublimate, those animal natures or animality itself, if there is such a thing; but that naming (as Derrida points out) can be another way of possessing animals, presiding over them, and disavowing our dependence on them, disavowing animal pedagogy. Conversely, as we will see, the "unnamable" and the "timeless" are names that Kristeva gives to animals and animality. Animals and nature are designated as being outside both name and time, as the constitutive outside that enables both; and animals and animality are associated with the intractability of the bodily drives that exceeds and yet necessitates the symbolic in human beings. This theoretical dependence on the animal and animality that gives force to the theory of the drives and the theory of abjection remains implicit, if not entirely erased, in Kristeva's writings.

Kristeva's theory of abjection, however, can help explain how this process of disavowal works. In her discussion of animal phobia, for example, she identifies powers of mimesis, introjection, and projection that operate as psychic motors for what Freud interprets as fear of castration from the father. In her metapsychoanalytic moves, Kristeva makes explicit the role of representation and semiotics that remain implicit in Freud's theory of animal phobia (and totemism) and also their theoretical underpinnings. In *Powers of Horror*, Kristeva argues that Freud's analysis of phobia gives us his clearest description of "the relation to the object, which is crucial for the constitution of the subject" (1982, 33). She examines the connection between fear and object suggested by animal phobia and concludes that the discovery of the object and the onset of language are plagued by fear, which she calls "the *upsetting* of a bio-drive balance" (1982, 33, italics in original). The infant comes in contact with the world and others and experiences its first wants in relation to them. These primary wants are not yet either desires or namable but instead fall under the general category of "fear." In the case of animal phobia, specifically that of Little Hans, Kristeva maintains that the animal—a horse— stands in for a general fear that cannot be reduced to the fear of castration:

The phobia of horses becomes a hieroglyph that condenses all fears, from unnamable to namable. From archaic fears to those that accompany language learning, at the same time as familiarization with the body, the street, animals, people. The statement "to be afraid of horses," is a hieroglyph having the logic of metaphor and hallucination. By means of the signifier of the phobic object, the "horse," it calls attention to the drive economy in want of an object—that conglomerate of fear, deprivation, and nameless frustration, which properly speaking, belongs to the unnamable. (1982, 33)[6]

According to this account, the phobic object stands in for the nameless and general fears associated with the infant's first sense of wanting, its first sense of its own separation from the world and from others, and its first recognition of objects. In other words, the phobic object represents the bodily drives themselves and the infant's frustrated and frustrating attempts to master them through language. Kristeva remarks that Little Hans has "stupendous verbal skill." He is so "eager to name everything that he runs into the unnamable" and is left with the impression of meaningful experiences for which he has no language; or in Kristeva's terminology, he has sense without significance (1982, 34). It is in this sense that she describes the horse as hieroglyph, as a living symbol of what is most pressing to Hans but also what he cannot name. Unlike Freud, for Kristeva the horse is neither a substitute for the father nor a symbol of the boy's fear of castration (although castration fear can evolve out of more primordial feelings of want).[7] Rather, the horse is a symptom of the weakness of the paternal function and the inability of the father to protect the boy from the outside world.[8] The horse shows up because the paternal function necessary for language acquisition cannot keep up with the boy's wants. We might say that the meaning or sense of his experience outstrips his ability to express it in words. Because the symbolic level of Hans's experience is inadequate to the affective level, he adopts hieroglyphic symbols into which many different affects are condensed. Following Lacan, Kristeva identifies language and the symbolic level of experience with the paternal function and identifies wants or needs with the maternal function. We could say, then, that in phobia the paternal function does not adequately counterbalance what Kristeva calls the *abject mother*. Words act like temporary "life preservers" on the uncharted and dangerous waters of bodily drives, which for the infant are anchored to the maternal body in ways that are pleasurable but also threatening (cf. Kristeva 1982, 37). This double aspect of being simultaneously threatening and compelling, fascinating or alluring, is characteristic of abjection.

Kristeva describes the acquisition of language as a foundational fetishism through which words are substituted for things. On the deepest psychic levels, words are compensations for the loss of the maternal body and the want of bodily needs that first signal to the infant its separation from its mother, its primary "object." Kristeva complicates any form of object-relations theory by insisting that before the maternal body can become an object, it must become an abject. She also maintains that the maternal body is a primal thing that remains locked in the "crypt of the psyche" of the child unless or until language can counterbalance or compensate for it (cf. 1989). She says, "The fetish becomes a life preserver, temporary and slippery, but nonetheless indispensable. . . . Because of its founding status, the fetishism of 'language' is perhaps the only one that is unanalyzable" (1982, 37). If we take her analysis back to Freud's theory of fetishism, we realize that the foundational fetish is a substitute for the missing maternal phallus, which, following Lacan, Kristeva interprets as the sense of wanting and satisfaction associated with bodily drives in relation to the mother. In this reading, castration becomes an existential lack associated with feelings of unsatisfied want that, through language, give way to desire. If phobia revolves around castration fears, these are not so much specific fears about losing the penis as they are general fears about losing the means of satisfying one's bodily drives; they are fears that one is separated from the world and others on whom one's satisfaction or happiness depends. Words help reconnect us to the world and others and compensate for this fundamental separation. In regard to animal phobia, Kristeva observes that Little Hans is caught between maternal anguish and the inadequacy of paternal words.[9]

Eat and Be Eaten

In light of my analysis of the relationship among biting, eating, and devouring in all of Freud's cases of animal phobia, it is illuminating to turn to Kristeva's account of that relationship. Kristeva argues that fear hides an aggression, which at the earliest stages is an oral aggression related to both food and speech: "From the deprivation felt by the child because of the mother's absence to the paternal prohibitions that institute symbolism, that relation [the symbolic language relation] accompanies, forms, and elaborates the aggressivity of drives . . . want and aggressivity are chronologically separable but logically coextensive" (1982, 39). The child feels aggression in response to its fear of the loss of both maternal satisfaction and paternal prohibition. Whereas Freud identifies this aggressivity as one directed at the father through its substitute, the phobic animal, Kristeva sees a preobjectal aggression that comes from bodily drive force and latches onto the animal as a symbol for everything threatening and scary in the child's young life: "Fear and the aggressivity intended to protect me from some not yet localizable cause are projected and come back to me from the outside: 'I am threatened'"

(1982, 39). She contends that the child responds to both deprivation and prohibition with aggressive impulses, which in the case of the maternal body may literally include the urge to bite or devour, to incorporate the maternal body in order to hold onto it (cf. 1982, 39). The child's own aggressivity is projected onto something outside itself, an animal, as a shield against the deprivation and prohibition exercised toward it by its parents as well as against its own violent impulses. At this stage, these impulses revolve around incorporation as an attempt to devour and thereby possess the parental love (not-yet) object. As Freud also argued, the phobic animal symbol becomes a way for the child to negotiate its ambivalent feelings toward its parents.

At the same time that the child is learning language and incorporating the words of its parents, it is trying to incorporate them. For the infant, the mouth is the first center of bodily cathexis associated with pleasure, deprivation, and language acquisition. Words, like breast milk and food, pass through its mouth. Kristeva interprets the phobic's fantasies of being bitten, eaten, or devoured by a scary animal as a projection of its own aggressive drives, particularly the urge to bite, eat, or devour the maternal body. Along with Melanie Klein, we might imagine that the infant's earliest desires to bite, eat, or devour are in relation to the mother rather than the father. Furthermore, that ambivalence is originally directed toward her. In Kleinian terminology, the mother's breast is split into the good and the bad breast. The bad breast, like Freud's uncanny reactivation of feminine passivity, threatens to turn on the infant and bite or devour him: the maternal breast bites back. Kristeva extends this Kleinian thesis with her theory of the abject mother, who appears as both fascinating and threatening to her child.[10] The child's own active aggressive impulses are projected onto the devouring creature—animal or mother—who threatens it from the outside rather than from inside. The phobic creature acts as a sort of defense, since we *can* run away from threats from the outside—horses, wolves, dogs—but we *cannot* run away from threats from the inside, like ambivalence. As Freud also points out, this reactivation of the outside threat serves to pacify the child, who can adopt a subject position (albeit passive) in relation to an object (albeit condensed and threatening). Kristeva describes the process:

In parallel fashion to the setting up of the signifying function, phobia, which also functions under the aegis of censorship and representation, *displaces* by *inverting* the sign (the active becomes passive) before *metaphorizing*. Only after such an inversion can the "horse" or the "dog" become the metaphor of my empty and incorporating mouth, which watches me, threatening from the outside. (1982, 39–40, italics in original)

The biting and devouring mouth of the child is projected onto the biting and devouring mouth of the animal; the child becomes passive, no longer the agent of aggression, while the animal (mother) becomes active, now the agent of aggression.

For Kristeva, phobia represents the failure of introjection of what is incorporated through the mouth, both maternal breast and paternal words (1982, 40). The precocious child does not yet have the linguistic or symbolic competence to properly displace the thing by substituting words, so it displaces it by inverting its own impulses onto a telegraphic symbol like the phobic animal. This child may have a facility with, and fascination for, words, but its logorrhea does not effectively stop-up the empty mouth deprived of the maternal breast. Unlike Freud who understands both the totem animal and the phobic animal as substitutes that represent the father, Kristeva believes that the phobic animal does not represent but merely stands in for. She maintains that lurking behind the relation between the father and the animal is the maternal body and all the sensations associated with separation from it, that is, all the sensations associated with becoming a subject over and against the world and others as objects. For Freud, totem and phobic animals are the harbingers of language and the psychic process of displacement that allows words to compensate for, if not completely replace, things. For Kristeva, however, not yet counterphobic, language or words are not up to the task of counterbalancing the abject mother; words are not adequate substitutes for things, particularly what she calls "the maternal thing" (1989).[11] Therefore, the child finds another thing (the horse or wolf) to stand in for the many things that it cannot represent in words: its wants, the desires of its parents, and the sounds, sights, smells, and textures of its world. In this sense, for Kristeva, phobia is not so much a displacement as a condensation. Since we all ultimately are in the position of the phobic unable to find the right words to adequately capture our experience or compensate for the nostalgic longing for (imagined) unity with the world and others, we continue to speak, write, and search for words with which to describe what remains unnamable.[12] In this context, Kristeva says, "phobia literally stages the instability of object relation" (1982, 43). Phobia shows us how and why the subject/object split is a precarious fantasy, necessary and yet illusory. As much as we try, the thing cannot be completely incorporated and thereby possessed through language. At the same time, as much as we try, the thing cannot be completely expelled or abjected because it always returns. But words can act as go-betweens or messengers between fragile, always precarious, porous not-yet or not-quite subjects and fragile, always precarious, porous not-yet or not-quite objects.

Shit Babies

Kristeva's theory of abjection sheds new light on Freud's cases of phobic boys. As we saw in the last chapter, Little Hans, the Wolf-Man, and the Rat-Man all imagine giving birth to themselves and taking the place of their mother. In their fantasies, this maternal position is associated with excrement, filth, and abjection. They become members of what Kristeva calls the "erotic cult of the abject," which, approaching perversion, does not manage to "dodge" castration because the sense of wanting or longing is not yet identified with an object like that precious bodily member. Rather, the phobic lives by finding a symbol for all frustration, deprivation, and want—an abject symbol like rats gnawing at an anus—to stand in for but still not represent "his whole life" and the flows of his experience (Kristeva 1982, 55). It is as if abject bodily fluids associated with phobic fantasies are leaking out of a hole in the psyche itself: "To preserve himself from severance, he is ready for more—flow, discharge, hemorrhage. . . . The erotization of abjection, and perhaps any abjection to the extent that it is already eroticized, is an attempt at stopping the hemorrhage" (Kristeva 1982, 55). The fledgling subject's erotic life becomes tinged with abjection and represented by the hieroglyphic logic of phobia characterized by frightening yet fascinating animal symbols.

Kristeva reinterprets phobia as a form of abjection. The phobic "subject" incorporates a devouring abject mother with whom he cannot quite identify and yet carries around as so much psychic baggage. This phobic subject's sense of self becomes constituted by abjection so that he identifies with the abject rather than with the mother herself. In other words, the phobic identifies with the preobjectal maternal abject rather than with the mother as object. Through this incorporation of abjection, the phobic "subject" tries to give birth to his abject self by shitting (or splitting) himself, among other forms of expulsion (cf. Kristeva 1982, 54). In a sense, the abject phobic is leaking himself from his various bodily orifices, much as he imagines he was leaked from parental orifices. He is especially fascinated with where babies come from, and as we have seen, this question is inspired by births of siblings, particularly sisters. The role of the father in this process seems suspect to the young phobic, for whom the paternal function is flimsy protection from the power of maternal abjection (cf. 1982, 72).

For Kristeva, phobia and abjection are firmly anchored to the maternal body. In *Powers of Horror,* she describes maternal authority as earlier than, and a prerequisite for, paternal authority, especially in terms of individual development but also in social development. She identifies two main polluting or abject objects that fall from the body, which she contends are related to the maternal and/or the feminine: excrement and menstrual blood. As we have seen, Freud's phobic boys all are fascinated with excrement. And Freud himself repeatedly returns us to blood in *Totem and Taboo,* where he explicitly connects blood in general to menstrual blood in particular. Kristeva maintains that excrement represents danger from the outside and menstrual blood represents danger from the inside, either the borders of the "clean and proper" self or within the borders of the group:

Excrement and its equivalents (decay, infection, disease, corpse, etc.) stand for danger to identity that comes from without: the ego threatened by the non-ego, society threatened by its outside, life by death. Menstrual blood, on the contrary, stands for the danger issuing from within the identity (social or sexual); it threatens the relationship between the sexes within a social aggregate and, through internalization, the identity of each sex in face of sexual difference. (1982, 71)

Kristeva maintains that the association between menstrual blood and the maternal or feminine is obviously connected to sexual difference. As for excrement, first, she claims that the child imagines that the mother has an "anal penis," perhaps like the excrement penis imagined by the Rat-Man; and second, she claims that the mother and maternal authority become associated with sphincteral training, which is a frustration that follows the maternal deprivation of the breast. Through these bodily frustrations, deprivations, and disciplinary actions, the maternal authority appears "chronologically and logically immediate" in early childhood experience (1982, 71). These unspoken regulations—not quite prohibitions—set up proper social (paternal) prohibitions.

Through its first interactions with the body of the infant, the maternal body maps out the boundaries of the "clean and proper" self for the child. According to Kristeva,

Maternal authority is the trustee of that mapping of the self's clean and proper body; it is distinguished from paternal laws within which, with the phallic phase and acquisition of language, the destiny of man will take shape. If language, like culture, sets up a separation and, starting with discrete elements, concatenates an order, it does so precisely by repressing maternal authority and the corporeal mapping that abuts against them. (1982, 72)

Note that she says the "destiny of man," suggesting that the notion of man and humanity take shape in relation to repression of maternal authority. Throughout *Powers of Horror,* Kristeva repeatedly says, "Abjection is coextensive with social and symbolic order, on the individual as well as on the collective level" (1982, 68).

Both the individual and the collectivity of man or human acquire their identities as such through separation from both maternal and animal, which, in Kristeva's account, are intimately connected.

Mother Phobia

For Kristeva, the fear of animals correlates with the fear of maternity. She sees the totem animal or the phobic animal as symbols of the fear of the maternal body. Behind what Freud identifies as fear of the father or fear of castration are more primal and abyssal fears connected to bodily animal drives in relation to the maternal body. Kristeva diagnoses the cultural link between the maternal body and animality that gives maternity its "magical" and "fearsome" power (as Freud might say). On the level of the social, this power is the mother's generative power (1982, 77), and on the level of the individual, this power is the mother's authority over the infant's body and its satisfaction. Both collectively and individually, we depend on the maternal body (and animals and our own animality) for continued life, and this dependence is repressed through a process of abjection in order for the group or individual to assert its independence and fortify the boundaries of its identity. Kristeva interprets the prohibitions against incest and contact with mothers or women, particularly during menses—symbol of women's fertility and generative powers—as attempts to regulate their power, what she calls "a loathing of defilement as protection against the poorly controlled power of mothers" (1982, 77).

Reminiscent of Freud's *Totem and Taboo,* the association between women and blood (particularly menstrual blood and the afterbirth or ejection of the placenta after birth) is seen as a sign of the contaminating power of the maternal body. Women's blood is considered polluting in a way that threatens to spread like disease or infection if not kept in check (see Kristeva 1982, 77–78). Kristeva argues that prohibitions against contact with maternal bodies are more prevalent in areas where overpopulation is a danger. This suggests that as in the Freudian account in which contagion spreads via temptation and imitation, here too the female body and the signs of its fertility are temptations that must be controlled. Kristeva discusses various rituals surrounding defilement, all of which, she says, revolve around the mother: "Defilement is the translinguistic spoor of the most archaic boundaries of the self's clean and proper body. In that sense, if it is a jettisoned object, it is so from the mother" (1982, 73). She argues that purification rituals use symbols and language to reach back to this archaic boundary associated with the mother (and the animal) in order to inscribe this abject preobjectal "spoor" within a signifying system. She maintains that the inscription at stake here is one of "limits, an emphasis placed not on the (paternal) Law but on (maternal) Authority through the very signifying order" (1982, 73). In this regard, she describes these rituals as acts rather than symbols. Again, as with the phobic animal, the inscription does not so much represent as stand in for the abject maternal body. Because the totem animal is involved in a ritual of purification of this type, it also is a stand-in rather than a representation or symbol proper. Like the phobic animal, it operates as a sort of hieroglyph that condenses an amorphous group of experiences and fears into one location. Again, Kristeva emphasizes the unnamable out of reach of the paternal symbolic that motivates these rituals. In her account, unlike Freud's, they are not motivated by fear of the father and castration but by fear of the mother and the loss of her body or by fear of the loss of the body itself. Because all bodies become reminders of the abject maternal body, their animality must be repressed in favor of an abstract untouchable body, a sacred body excluded from the realm of flesh and blood. Whether it is fear of the mother or the father, the animals in animal phobias are either representatives of or stand-ins for, parental threats.

French psychoanalyst Annie Birraux, one of the few scholars to discuss the animals in animal phobias, concludes that children's fear of animals is a result of their similarity to humans and the easy imaginary displacement of human attributes onto animals, and vice versa, especially the child's images of its parents (2007). Birraux argues that a fear of animals is natural and is produced, or at least used, in cultural deployments of animals in children's literature, fairy tales, television, and films. For my purposes, what is interesting about her assessment of the role of animals in animal phobias is that she links them to what she calls "parental pedagogy of fear" (*pédagogie parentale de la peur*) (2007, 13). Birraux maintains that this parental pedagogy can be found in children's literature that uses animals to construct moral tales and is a means of helping children negotiate anxiety and fear in general. Taking a more Freudian (or even Foucaultian) turn, we could view this parental pedagogy of fear as a way of using animals to discipline their children by instilling fear into them. Through tales involving animals, they learn how to behave as humans in socially acceptable ways. Like Kristeva, Birraux suggests that the fear of animals signals general anxiety and fear. Kristeva's theory of abjection, however, complicates the notion that the fear of animals is natural and that in children's fantasies they are like us. Although in Kristeva's theory, abjection is the process through which we assure ourselves that we are not like them precisely because at some level we know, or fear, that we are indeed like them. Also, for Kristeva, as we have seen, this general fear or anxiety always takes us back to the maternal body.

Returning to anthropological literature, Kristeva maintains that in cultures needing population growth for survival, prohibitions against contact with the maternal body, namely, incest and cannibalism, are relaxed (1982, 78). These anthropological accounts lead her to ask:

Is that parallel [to concerns for overpopulation and prohibitions] suffcient to suggest that defilement reveals, at the same time as an attempt to throttle matrilineality, an attempt at separating the speaking being from his body in order that the latter accede to the status of clean and proper body, that is to say, non-assimilable, uneatable, abject? (1982, 78)

She goes on to propose that fear of the mother's generative power makes her body abject and uneatable and also all bodies abject and uneatable: "I give up cannibalism because abjection (of the mother) leads me toward respect for the body of the other, my fellow man, my brother" (1982, 79, parentheses in original). The body becomes inedible, not literal flesh and blood that, like animals', can be consumed, but metaphorical flesh and blood, which is to say, kin—fellow man, brother. In other words, giving up the literal consumption of flesh and blood produces and is produced by the metaphorical notion of flesh and blood as kinship. We don't eat our kin. In regard to animals, the circular logic runs as follows: if we eat animals, they are not our kin; animals are not our kin, so we eat them. Because we literally consume their flesh and blood, they are not our metaphorical flesh and blood, and vice versa. Because they are not our metaphorical flesh and blood, they can be our literal flesh and blood in terms of what we eat.

Kinship by Marriage or Meals?

Kristeva's analysis of the structural relation between the mother and the animal in the process of abjection and identity formation prompts us to ask why the taboo against eating the abject maternal body does not also apply to eating the abject animal body. To Kristeva, the social struggle against the abject is a battle of the sexes over whether paternal or maternal power will triumph; it is a battle between patriarchal and matriarchal social formations. Behind these struggles are the animals. Even while discussing the power struggle between masculine and feminine or paternal and maternal, Kristeva takes us back to the animal. She asks whether food loathing or prohibitions against certain foods, particularly animal flesh and animal products, is a matter of marriage or of meals.[13] Following this line of thought (from the anthropologist Célestin Bouglé, now combined with theories of Louis Dumont and Mary Douglas), Kristeva argues that loathing or revulsion must be explained in terms of an opposition between pure and impure, which is imposed on or displaces sexual difference. The opposition between pure and impure allows for the substitution of rituals of purification for sacrifice. Both rituals of sacrifice and rituals of purification, however, revolve around killing and eating animals. Using recent anthropological research in *Powers of Horror*, Kristeva updates Freud's *Totem and Taboo*. There she traces the origins of religion, particularly religious taboos, but unlike Freud, she finds the mother and maternal body rather than the father behind all such taboos.[14] In the transition from rituals of sacrifice to rituals of purification, one thing remains the same, the abjection of the maternal body or of animal. Whereas for Kristeva the maternal body is essentially linked to animality and animal bodies, her analysis trades on that animality and animal bodies in order to give the abject mother her power. We could say that despite her departure from Freud in regard to the priority of the mother over the father, it is still the animal that puts the teeth into her notion of the abject-devouring mother.

The role of the maternal body in relation to the animal is particularly poignant in Kristeva's analysis of what she calls the "semiotics of biblical abomination," or the food prohibitions of the Old Testament (see 1982, chap. 4).[15] There, she argues that fear of the maternal body, its generative power, and its authority over the bodily functions of children gives rise to food taboos involving mixing her body (or its symbolic equivalents) with the bodies of her children (or their symbolic equivalents). On the symbolic and imaginary levels, she interprets these food prohibitions as again revolving around the abjection of the maternal body. Literally, however, this abjection is played out on the bodies of animals and regulations concerning what parts of those creatures can and cannot be eaten and how. In this regard, all animal bodies become symbols for the maternal body and its relation to the bodies of children (i.e., all of us, since we all are born from a maternal body). Animal bodies become symbols for human bodies, and both our rituals of animal sacrifice and of purification involving eating only certain animals or animal parts take us back to our relationships with our mothers. Insofar as they become symbols for human bodies and human relations, we could argue that animals themselves do not exist in Kristeva's text.

Although Kristeva identifies food prohibitions with the border between human and animals, she continually fastens that border to the maternal body:

When food appears as a polluting object, it does so as oral object only to the extent that orality signifies a boundary of the self's clean and proper body. Food becomes abject only if it is a border between two distinct entities or territories. A boundary between nature and culture, between the human and the non-human. (1982, 75)

This passage suggests that the boundary with nonhuman animals "pollutes" the clean and proper borders of the human. To Kristeva, however, this pollution turns out to be just another form of maternal contaminant. Her thesis is that

biblical impurity is permeated with the tradition of defilement; in that sense, it *points to* but does not *signify* an autonomous force that *can* be threatening for divine agency. I shall suggest that such a force is rooted, historically (in the history of religions) and subjectively (in the structuration of the subject's identity), in the cathexis of maternal function—mother, women, reproduction. (1982, 90–91, italics in original)

She argues that dietary prohibitions are aimed at the mother as the first source of nourishment and milk. These taboos are attempts to fortify precarious boundaries between the maternal body and the social and individual subject because they are directed toward "intermixure, erasing of differences, threat to identity" (1982, 101). Biblical food prohibitions are aimed at separation and distinctions that avoid the ambiguity and mixing threatened by the maternal body. All food prohibitions, then, according to Kristeva, are symbolic regulations of the power of the maternal.

For example, she maintains that the biblical command "Thou shalt not seethe a kid in his mother's milk" is a metaphorical prohibition against incest between mother and child symbolized by mixing its flesh with her milk (1982, 105). She concludes that biblical dietary prohibitions are *based upon the prohibition of incest* (1982, 105, italics in original). On the symbolic level, all food taboos involving animals are really prohibitions against contact with the maternal body. Kristeva even interprets the Eucharist in terms of the maternal body. Unlike Freud, who describes the Eucharist as another ritualistic repetition of the totemic celebration of eating the father, Kristeva sees it as both a repetition and a disavowal of the mother, the primal "object" of the urge to devour. She regards cannibalistic urges to eat the body of another as always disguised (or not so disguised) wishes to eat the mother. According to her, every body recalls the maternal body, the first body encountered by the infant. The Eucharist brings together food and body in a ritualistic way that harks back to cannibalism, symbolically repeating it as a way of preventing actual eating of bodies—except, as we have seen, the bodies of animals. Kristeva maintains that by bringing together body and bread, the Eucharist tames cannibalism: "By surreptitiously mingling the theme of 'devouring' with that of 'satiating,' that narrative [the Eucharist] is a way of taming cannibalism. It invites a removal of guilt from the archaic relation to the first pre-object (ab-ject) of need: the mother" (1982, 118). In this passage Kristeva speaks of "taming" cannibalism as if it is an animal instinct that must be domesticated. Furthermore, she identifies both the urge to devour and satiation with the maternal body by insisting that the Eucharist is a purification ritual aimed at curbing and regulating incestuous and cannibalistic desires for the mother and the maternal body.

While opening psychoanalysis to its maternal and feminine other—which should not be underestimated or undervalued—Kristeva ultimately forecloses the possibility of animal others.[16] In her analysis of biblical dietary restrictions, she discusses at length taboos on various animals and animal parts but continually insists that these animals are stand-ins for the mother, much as Freud insists that the animals in animal phobias are representatives for the father. The process that Kristeva describes, however, is the metonymic slippage from milk and blood to maternal body rather than the metaphorical substitution of horse or wolf for paternal threats. Kristeva is concerned about distinguishing the process of substitution or sacrifice identified by Freud in *Totem and Taboo* from the process of ritual purification involving dietary restrictions rather than killing and eating per se. In other words, dietary restrictions prevent the kind of murderous sacrifice of the primal horde in which the animal becomes the father, and vice versa. What Kristeva does not acknowledge is that animals are still killed and eaten even when purification rituals regulate that activity. The difference is one of emphasis. In purification rituals, killing animals is no longer a necessary part of the ritual (with some exceptions, e.g., Jewish kosher regulations for the bleeding of animals, which Kristeva interprets as again signaling the threat of blood, a metonym for menstrual blood). In all cases, however, animals are killed; only now their killing is not part of a ritual sacrifice but a regular part of domestic culinary practices, which involve various restrictions on how the animal flesh is prepared. In other words, killing animals has become domesticated.

Kristeva sees the progression from ritual sacrifice to rituals of purification as a move away from violence and toward more sublimatory and therefore more humane forms of regulation. Her analysis sees ritual sacrifice as glorifying the violence of killing, whereas the rituals of purification sublimate it. Yet in contrast to Kristeva, we could argue that rituals of purification merely domesticate the killing of animals and allow for a radical disavowal of their slaughter to the point that we end up with factory farming and mass killing hidden away from view rather than the ritualized but extremely limited killing celebrated as animal sacrifice. Animals are no longer sacrificed because neither their lives nor their deaths have the symbolic value they did before factory farming. In psychoanalytic theory, their only symbolic value is either as a substitute for the father à la Freud or as a stand-in for the mother à la Kristeva. Moreover, the psychoanalytic domestication of animals itself forecloses the possibilities of either their wildness or their kinship with humans. They cannot be our mother or father or sisters or brothers, but they must represent them or stand in for them. They must be sacrificed instead of them—that is, killed in their stead. Or they must be regulated as a means of regulating ourselves. In either case, their value is defined entirely in terms of human relations and human exchange. Whether sacrificed or regulated, animals are killed or exchanged so that human society and human kinship is possible, and all these accounts are based on, or presuppose, killing and eating animals. In this case, we are *not* what we eat, and eating animals proves that we are not like them. Rather, we become fathers, mothers, sisters, and brothers on the basis of killing and eating animals. Symbolically, they bind us together as kin through the flesh and blood of their bodies. At the same time, animals reassure us that if we can eat them, we are human and not animals. That is, they die like animals so that we can live as humans.

Kristeva also describes the distinction between man and God as a dietary distinction. Man is not God because unlike God, he is prohibited from eating certain foods. For example, in Genesis, God expels Adam and Eve from the Garden of Eden for eating from the tree of knowledge, but he does so before they can eat from the tree of life, which would make them immortal (cf. Kristeva 1982, 95). Kristeva points out that Adam's temptation is both a feminine and an animal temptation: Eve is tempted by the serpent and Adam is tempted by Eve to eat forbidden fruit. Following J. Soler, Kristeva interprets Genesis as reserving dominion over living beings for God and giving man the right to eat animals only after the Flood; and only then as an acknowledgment of his essential evil (1982, 96). At this point, temptations of the flesh become associated with both women and food, particularly meat eating. Temptations of the flesh can be interpreted as temptations arising from the flesh, from our so-called animal nature, or as temptations for flesh, as in the temptation to get "a piece of tail," in the sense of either women's flesh or a rump roast. Kristeva reads this urge to kill and eat flesh as recognition of the death drive in its most primordial form, as the urge to devour (1982, 96). The prohibition against murder is no longer extended to killing and eating animals but becomes displaced onto dietary prohibitions that prohibit eating carnivorous animals. Man can eat only herbivorous animals and cannot eat or assimilate/incorporate rapacious animals or predatory animals that kill. Our own murderous nature is displaced onto those animals that we are not allowed to consume (cf. Kristeva 1982, 98).

Although her analysis of the death drive and the urge to devour in relation to killing and eating animals is an explicit acknowledgment of the violence done to animals in order to reinforce the boundaries of the notion of the human and ourselves as nonanimals, again Kristeva presents it as more evidence that animals are stand-ins for the maternal body. Immediately following her discussion of the death drive in relation to devouring animals, she claims that biblical dietary prohibitions are paralleled and founded in "the abomination provoked by the fertilizable or fertile feminine body (menses, childbirth)" (1982, 100). Kristeva's analysis not only makes explicit that abjection of the feminine and maternal body on which the Western imaginary thrives and on which man defines himself as clean and proper but also points to the inherent connection in this imaginary of animals and women, especially mothers. What animals and mothers supposedly share is their connection to nature, and as Kristeva says, "The body must bear no trace of its debt to nature: it must be clean and proper in order to be fully symbolic" (1982, 102). Acknowledging this debt is not only breaking the incest taboo by speaking of connectedness to the maternal (animal) body but also staging the return of the repressed maternal, animal, body.

As many feminists have pointed out, in the Western imaginary, man constitutes himself as properly man against both the feminine and the animal. Kristeva's analysis makes a crucial contribution to psychoanalysis by revealing man's indebtedness and subsequent disavowal of both. She does so in part by complicating the maternal function, which she imbues with speech, law, and authority, attributes traditionally reserved for the paternal function and required for autonomy from the maternal body. What Kristeva's theory of abjection itself disavows, even while describing it, is our indebtedness to animals, who metaphorically and literally nourish our sense of ourselves as human and as kin. The very notions of maternity or paternity, mother or father, that drive psychoanalytic theory are based on the displacement or condensation of these figures and animals. Whether it is Freud's father totem phobia or Kristeva's mother meal abject, the slippage between animals—specifically dead ones—and our closest and most influential kin contributes to both our social identity and individual identity.

Feasting on the Maternal Body (Again)

As we have seen, in *Powers of Horror*, Kristeva, unlike Freud, emphasizes the prohibition against incest with the mother rather than the prohibition against murder of the father in her account of the origin of civilization. More than a decade later, in *The Sense and Nonsense of Revolt* (2000b), Kristeva returns to Freud's *Totem and Taboo* and again emphasizes regulations aimed at relations with the maternal body, through both the incest taboo and now the totemic feast. There she reads Freud's story of the primal horde of brothers who overthrow, kill, and eat their father as a tale of revolt and feast (2000b, 12). The celebration that follows the murder cements the social bond through shared food (even if in this case, it is the body of the murdered father). Kristeva dwells on both the negativity and creativity in revolt, which produce the subject as "I" (2000b, 14). In her analysis, subjective agency is produced through a revolt against traditional order that allows the assimilation of that order, thereby authorizing the self. In other words, revolt is necessary for both social order and individual subjectivity. At the same time, it undermines all order, whether social or individual. As she describes it, revolt or rebellion is a necessary part of the process of becoming a subject, a process that is always precarious and never finished. Kristeva argues that revolt (which is a negative moment) and the celebration that follows (which is a positive moment) are moments of *jouissance* or pleasure, including pleasure in violence and destruction. Again, she sees Freud's account as repressing the feminine, both the feminine of women as objects of desire and the feminine position or passive position of the brothers in relation to the overpowering father (2000b, 13). The revolt is a way of reactivating that passivity, but as a result, it is also a guilty act—even uncanny act—that requires recompense and atonement. Conversely, the celebration of the feast is a ritual that can be repeated, only now without the murder of the father, in order to regulate and contain murderous impulses. This is the way that Freud describes the totemic meal, as a repetition of, and ritualistic celebration that replaces, the murder. Kristeva emphasizes the sense of renewal and joy that comes through both revolt and feast. She also points to what Freud calls "the cherished fruit of the crime" as the appropriation of authority that is ritualistically reproduced in the assimilation of his body by eating and then subsequently the assimilation of his substitute in the form of the animal. As we have seen, even while describing the substitution of animals for human bodies, neither Kristeva nor Freud diagnoses the disavowal of animal killing, assimilation, and kinship in the formation of human society. This is even more apparent in *The Sense and Nonsense of Revolt* than it was in *Powers of Horror*, as animals have almost entirely disappeared from the story of the primal feast.

In *The Sense and Nonsense of Revolt* Kristeva acknowledges that in Freud's account the totemic feast signals the onset of religion, along with substitution, representation, and displacement. She nonetheless is concerned with what happens when religion loses its value and asks whether revolt (and therefore the authorization of subjectivity) is still possible. She maintains that revolt is connected to a time before time or the timelessness of the unconscious, which is associated with both the maternal body and animality. Whereas Freud is interested in the operations of representation foundational to religion, Kristeva is interested in what makes those very operations possible. As usual, Kristeva looks for the law before the law, the authority before authority, the time before time, and so on;

and as usual, she finds the maternal body and maternal function behind symbolic systems (which Freud and Lacan associated with the paternal function). In her retelling of Freud's *Totem and Taboo,* she focuses on the return of an archaic timelessness, of "pure embodied time," that enabled Freud's Oedipal revolt (2000b, 16). She proposes that access to this timelessness is regenerating and gives rise to all forms of creativity, which authorize the subject. As she describes it, creativity requires revolt and rebellion, and the meaning of life depends on creativity.[17] Life has meaning only in that we can creatively authorize ourselves by revolting against and then assimilating the power of our symbolic systems, especially language. Kristeva describes this process as one of making the clichés of language one's own: "'I' will express my specificity by distorting the nevertheless necessary clichés of the codes of communication and by constantly deconstructing ideas/concepts/ideologies/philosophies that 'I' have inherited" (2000b, 19).

Kristeva's appeal to timelessness presents another facet of the assimilation of the primal father's authority. The feast celebrating the death of the father is not just a repetition of the crime or a reminder of the guilt that binds the brothers or even of the mobility of power as it now moves from the father to the brothers. Rather, Kristeva's account suggests that the ritual feast puts us in touch with a "lost time," a time of want and satiation, an archaic time associated with the maternal body as the first "object" of want and satiation and with animality as the primal state of human existence. In a sense, with the feast we are repeating and recalling the timelessness of the infantile state, which may very well be an imaginary time. For that reason, it becomes associated in Kristeva's thought with the imaginary father as the figure through whom the timelessness of the maternal body moves into the sequential time of paternal language. We *imagine* that before language, we existed in a purely embodied state, as animals did. We long for this timelessness, for pure bodily experience, for the absolute unity of being and meaning, what Freud might call the "death drive." Sublimation, for Kristeva, becomes a process of articulating this death drive rather than acting on it. It is the process of assimilating the timelessness of the drives or unconscious (of the animal) into time (the temporality of the human), what Kristeva calls a "timeless temporality" (2000b, 16). We come in contact with our own animality only by sublimating timelessness and unconscious drives into time, by bringing them into temporality. (Elsewhere I discuss the promise of this proposal for social theory; see Oliver 2004.)

Kristeva proposes renewed humanism that comes through rediscovery of the timelessness of revolt figured as a return of our own repressed and abjected maternal and animal bodies. In criticizing what she calls "our culture of distraction" for "flattening psychic space," she insists that creative revolt is still possible:

Revolt has taken place, it has not been erased, it can be read, and it offers itself to a rootless humanity now governed by the relativism of images as well as monetary and humanitarian indifference. Nonetheless the capacity for enthusiasm, doubt, and the pleasure of inquiry has perhaps not been entirely lost. This is the heart of the ultimate defense of human life; the meaning of language and the architecture of the idea in the human mind. (2000b, 19)

Kristeva's work itself can be read as a defense of human life and human meaning. My question here is whether or not that life and meaning are bought at the expense of animal life and animal meaning. On this question, Kristeva's work, like Freud's and Lacan's before her, is ambivalent.

Considering the status of animals in Kristeva's texts, it is noteworthy that in *The Sense and Nonsense of Revolt,* immediately following her engagement with Freud's *Totem and Taboo,* she introduces the figures of horse-man and horse-boy. Following anthropologist Georges Dumézil, Kristeva discusses what he calls "turbulent boys" as those "who represent the jouissance, rupture, displacement, and revolt underlying purity, repentance, and the renewal of the pact" (2000b, 25–26). In particular, she examines the Mithraic religious priest figured as Gandharva, half-horse and half-man (2000b, 26). She argues that this

dual human and animal nature . . . seems to indicate, as though by metaphor, ardor and violence, a force difficult for anthropology to contemplate, a "going to the limit," the metaphor of the horse suggesting the vigor of the drive and a psychical and extrapsychical setting-into-motion that we have difficulty symbolizing. (2000b, 26)

What exceeds symbolization—or, at least, is difficult to symbolize—is the animal or animality, especially because it is part of human nature. This human/animal figure represents for Kristeva the possibility of renewal and *jouissance* that motivates rituals of purity—the celebratory aspect or feast before the disciplinary aspects of such rituals. Following Dumézil, she says that "the 'turbulent boys' are destructive but that they also promote fertility and joy during feasts" (2000b, 26). In this reading, rituals of purity become spaces where "man brushes up against his animality" (2000b, 27). The pleasure in revolt, then, is figured by these horse-boys, whose horsing around may be destructive as well as creative.

Returning to the question of whether or not Kristeva disavows the central role of animals and animality in the constitution of the human and humanity in her texts, my analysis suggests that the answer is an ambivalent yes and no. On the one hand, Kristeva talks of a *lost* time and a time before time that suggests something like Freud's problematic notion of animal ancestors, the idea that we were once animals but have progressed beyond them, that humanity is the telos of animality, that animal timelessness gives birth to human temporality. She goes so far as to suggest that the time before time is the time between birth and the acquisition of language, the time when the infant is an animal who does not speak. To illustrate, she gives the example of the feral child raised by wolves who never speaks (2000b, 37, cf. 33). On the other hand, Kristeva insists that this so-called lost time returns, that we have access to it through the semiotic dimension of language, and that our own animality is the return of the repressed. She repeatedly refers to humans as "speaking animals" to emphasize that we, too, are animals no matter how much we "progress" or, more accurately, no matter how much we protest (cf. 1982, 15). At the same time, however, she maintains that the abjection of both the maternal body and our own animality is necessary to identifying as groups or individuals. So even though we can never rid ourselves completely of our connection to the maternal body or our connection to our own animality or to animals, our ability to enter human culture demands that we try. Kristeva proposes a dynamic and fluid movement between repression and the return of the repressed, between what she calls the symbolic and the semiotic elements of signification, between meaning and being or human and animal, that gives rise to the "speaking animal." In this regard, ambivalence is part and parcel of the human condition and of Kristeva's theory. Indeed, her theory of abjection is a theory of ambivalence: we abject ambivalence and ambiguity in favor of fixed identities; yet those fixed identities are always constituted and supported by abjection, which also threatens to undo them.

In regard to animals and animality, Kristeva moves back and forth between suggesting, on the one hand, that they are linked to a lost time and lost experience associated with "pure embodiment," and that they are part of the metonymy animal-maternal-body-food on which patriarchal symbolic systems are based, on the other hand. In other words, according to her theory, animals and animality stand in for the materiality of the body itself before signification and for the metonymical slippage between maternal bodies and animal bodies. Yet Kristeva constantly risks erasing animals by making them into nothing more than stand-ins for the maternal body (cf. 2000b, 20–21). Even in her discussions of the violence of sacrifice and her implication that rituals of purification are more civilized or humane, she neglects to consider that in both, animals are killed and eaten. In sum, even while she opens psychoanalysis onto its feminine and maternal others, she forecloses its animal others. Moreover, the force of her theories of abjection and maternity comes from animals and animality in ways that point to her movements toward the feminine and the maternal as based on movements away from consideration for the role of animals and animal pedagogy. Like Freud's theories of paternity and castration, Kristeva constructs theories of maternity and abjection by disavowing or ignoring the animals and animality at their heart. Even as she attempts to bring the dynamic, living, speaking animal body back into the human sciences, she does so by sacrificing—or, at least, purifying—animals and animality for the sake of the human and humanity. In this regard, like that of so many thinkers before her, Kristeva's humanism is built on the metaphorical and literal backs of animals. Her theory of human speech and signification disavows the animal pedagogy lurking in the shadows. Her notion of sublimation comes at the cost of not only replacing real animals with symbolic or metaphorical animals but also reducing animals to mere stand-ins for human kinship relations. For Kristeva, as for so many thinkers before her, human kinship is bought at the expense of animal kinship.

Sustainable Ethics

This project started as a work of mourning for my beloved companion of eighteen years, Kaos. Friends sometimes warned me that I should stop thanking Kaos and Wizard in the acknowledgments of my books, that scholars would not take my writing seriously if I continued to thank my cats. Now they are probably convinced that I have gone to the dogs (except for those who know that I am a cat person). Recently, at small symposium where I presented some ideas for the first chapter, friends and strangers alike challenged my turn to animals. Some of them even said that although they had followed my work up to this point, they could not follow the animals. Certainly, in the face of domestic violence, endless war, genocide, ethnic cleansing, racism, sexism, and all the other forms of violence that humans inflict on one another, the ethical treatment of animals seems secondary. Indeed, focusing on animals in this context may seem unethical, a way of displacing the injustices inflicted on human beings and distracting us from the history of oppression, slavery, and torture whose bloody reach continues to mar what we call humanity. It is legitimate to ask why I would turn to animals at a time when our "inhumanity to man" continues unabated. But following animals through the history of philosophy, particularly recent philosophies of alterity, has shown me that the practices of oppression, slavery, and torture are historically inseparable from the question of the animal. Tracking the animals through the writings of more than three centuries of philosophers has taught me that our concepts of man, humanity, and inhumanity are inherently bound up with the concepts of the animal, animality, and animals. The man/animal binary is not just any opposition; it is the one used most often to justify violence, not only man's violence to animals, but also man's violence to other people deemed to be like animals.

Until we interrogate the history of this opposition with its exclusionary values, considering animals (or particular animals) to be like us, or recognizing that we are also a species of animal, does very little to change "how we eat the other," as Derrida might say. Even if moving people or animals from one side of the man/animal divide to the other may change our attitudes toward them, it does not necessarily transform the oppositional logic that pits *us* against *them* and justifies our enslaving, imprisoning, or torturing (not to mention eating) *them*. This project, then, is not just about animals. It concerns whether or not we can conceive of ethical relationships beyond either continuism or separatism, beyond identity politics or abyssal alterity. In other words, can we find a way of relating to others, whether or not they are like us, without excluding them on the basis of what makes them different or unique? What we learn from following the animals as they track and are tracked through the history of philosophy is that neither sameness nor otherness alone can be the basis of ethics. Rather, we must consider the relationship between sameness and otherness, identity and difference, man and animal. We must attend to the relationships that nourish and sustain us, to the relationships that we disavow and to the relationships in whose name we kill. The problem for ethics, and more particularly for politics, is that we cannot be certain that our justice or love does not end up harming others. The more certain we are about what is right and just, the more we risk following moral rules and laws like automatons without thinking, and the more we risk becoming reactionaries fighting for just ends by any means possible. When we become self-righteous about our morals or ideals, we no longer respond to, or encounter, others. Instead, like Don Quixote, we see only projections of our own fantasies about them and ourselves. What Derrida calls hyperbolic ethics demands that we never give up exploring our own fantasies, especially those in which we are the heroes, the good guys, the just and true, fighting against the forces of evil and darkness—the fantasies in which we are humane and the others behave like animals.

Throughout its history, Western philosophy has tried to answer the fundamental existential questions of human life, to paraphrase Kant: Who am I? What should I do? What can I hope for? Tracking the animals as they run through this history demonstrates that the answers to these questions are intimately bound up with our relationships to the animal, animality, and animals. When we ask who we are in relation to the philosophers' animals, we may come up with different answers to questions about the meaning of life, not just human life, but all of life. I have called on philosophy's animals to witness to the ways in which the various animal examples, animal metaphors, and animal studies that populate the history of Western philosophy bear the burden of instructing and supporting the conceptions of man, human, and kinship central to that thought. I hope that doing so tears down fences and also reveals how and why those fences were constructed. Can we imagine a "free-range" ethics that breaks out of the self-centered, exclusionary, and domineering notions of individuality, identity, and sovereignty? Throughout this book, I have tried to suggest that considering animals necessarily transforms how we consider ourselves and that reconsidering both *other* or animal and *self* or human and acknowledging the intimate conceptual and practical relation between them have implications for thinking about our obligations to others and to ourselves.

In this era of global warming, species extinction and shrinking biodiversity, endless war, military occupation and expanded torture, record wealth for the few and poverty for the rest, and gated communities and record incarceration, we need, more than ever, a sustainable ethics. We need an ethics born from, and nurturing, a transformation from the traditional image of man as conquering nature to one of human beings nourishing it. Although we can never be certain of the difference between conquering and nourishing, between trophy and trophe, we have an ethical obligation to continue to try to foster nourishing relationships with others, with ourselves, and with the earth. Indeed, because it is impossible to know, to be certain, and to succeed once and for all, we have an obligation to tirelessly attend to our own limitations and the needs of others. In the words of John Llewelyn, we need to acknowledge that the needs of others obligate us to do something, that they make a claim on us "to revise our idea of what it means for something to make a claim, a claim that puts us under a direct responsibility toward it and under a responsibility to review our idea of neighbourhood and responsibility" (1991, 277). This ecological conscience, as he labels it, calls us to a responsibility for others, including other animals, and the earth.

Our ethical responsibility comes not from what *we* can do or what *we* can master but from what we cannot do and what we cannot master. It comes not from what *they* can do or what *they* can master. Our ethical responsibility comes not from our sovereignty or our autonomy but from our interdependence and our dependence on the earth and its creatures. As Cora Diamond might say, we all are in the same boat (cf. 1978). Accordingly, rather than imagine how many dogs we need to throw overboard in order to save ourselves, as the calculators of animal rights are fond of doing, we need to learn to share. We need to learn to sacrifice our own greed and gluttony rather than to sacrifice others for the sake of our own wealth. Capitalist individualism and the freedom of the market are threatening the lives and welfare of animals everywhere, including *Homo erectus,* whose upright posture doesn't do him much good if he keeps burying his head in the sand.

Can we imagine an ecological subjectivity acknowledging that it exists through its relationships with its environment and those around it? Can we imagine that this acknowledgment brings with it an obligation to nourish and nurture those others on whom this ecological subjectivity relies for its vitality? Can we imagine sharing the earth with all its inhabitants, not just in terms of occupying the same planet, but also in terms of caring for one another? Can we imagine a sustainable ethics that obligates us to sustain both ourselves and the others through which we both live and exist? Sustainable ethics is a virtuous ethics if we return *virtue* to its roots in plants and animals that have a beneficial effect on the human body. We learn from *Animal Lessons,* however, that we disavow precisely this form of virtue in our relationships with animals and the earth. Rather than acknowledge the ways in which we benefit from animal pedagogy and animal kinship, we exclude the animal, animality, and animals so that we can fence off what is properly human. In Kristeva's terms, we abject the animal and expel it from the realm of humanity in order to ensure ourselves of our own clean and proper boundaries. Once we begin to follow the animals in the history of philosophy, however, we cannot continue to maintain those boundaries, because there are infinite varieties of animals, some of whom will jump over whatever fences we may set for them and because we ourselves do not fully possess and control what is "proper to man." Like Roy's trained tiger Montecore, philosophy's animals bite back. And when they do, they expose philosophy's own limits and the limits of the human, which is to say, its illusion that it can master the impossible.

Instead, a sustainable ethics would have to be an ethics of limits, an ethics of conservation. Rather than assert our dominion over the earth and its creatures, this ethics would oblige us to acknowledge our dependence on them. It would require us to attend to our response-ability by virtue of that dependence. Again, it would challenge us to witness to what is beyond recognition, beyond rights, but not beyond responsibility, namely, what sustains us (even if it is nameless). It would be an ethics born from an acknowledgment of sustaining relationships. Sustainable ethics is an ethics of the responsibility to enable response, not as it has been defined as the exclusive property of man (man responds, animals react), but as it exists all around us. All living creatures are responsive. All of us belong to the earth, not in the sense of property, but as inhabitants of a shared planet. A sustainable ethics would be an ethics circumscribed by the circumference of the globe, which, if we pulled our heads out of the sand, would compel us to avow our own limitations and obligate us to relearn our primary-school lesson, that we need to share. Given the environmental urgency, generosity has become a virtue that we cannot afford to live, or exist, without.

Introduction

1. Catharine MacKinnon (2004) discusses the relation between loving and killing in terms of both women and animals.

2. Derrida's title, *L'animal que donc je suis,* can also mean "The Animal That I Follow."

3. In his eulogy for Emmanuel Levinas, *Adieu* (1997a), Derrida discusses the difficulty of "properly thanking" our teachers.

4. Donna Haraway suggests (esp. 2004) some alternative ways of thinking about kinship that open kin beyond the human and beyond blood. Feminist anthropology and recent work on gay marriage also challenge traditional notions of kinship in interesting ways, some of which could be provocatively extended to animals. For example, see Collier and Yanagisako 1987 and Weston 1991. Beth Conklin's work on cannibalism (2001) also challenges Western notions of kinship, particularly our relationships to animals and what we eat.

5. For a criticism of the notion of fraternity, see Derrida 1997b.

6. The survey was conducted by the American Kennel Club and reported in the March 28, 2008, issue of *Mother Jones Magazine.* The parrot and tiger examples come from this same article (Gettelman and Gilson 2008).

7. See Gettelman and Gilson 2008. It is noteworthy that Deleuze and Guattari associate becoming-animal with becoming-woman (1987).

8. In chapter 10, I discuss Agamben's analysis of the nonhuman within the human in relation to animals.

9. Deleuze and Guattari also focus on relationships. Their notion of becoming-animal in particular imagines differently the relation between man and animal. Although I

mention Deleuze and Guattari in passing, I do not include a sustained analysis of their texts. My reasons are varied. Foremost among them are, first, in the Continental tradition their work has already been widely employed in discussions of animals and animality (e.g., see Baker 2002; Birke and Parisi 1999; Brown 2007; and Lorraine 1999). Second, their relational conception of becoming-animal is in some ways an exception to the historical trajectory I trace. Third, limitations of time and space prevent me from entering their texts in ways that I have not heretofore done in order to do justice to either the novelty or the limitations of their texts. Fourth, although I am sympathetic to their criticisms of "pets," I do not agree that "anyone who likes cats or dogs is a fool" (Deleuze and Guattari 1987, 240). Finally, I am more interested in exploring relations in terms of responsivity rather than machine metaphors such as assemblage, geographical metaphors such as deterritorialization, geometric metaphors such as lines of flight, or biological metaphors such as rhizomes, all of which sound too deterministic for my tastes.

10. Donna Haraway discusses (2003) some of the historical and social ways in which humans and animals developed together as what she calls "companion species." Her work indicates that the symbiotic relation between animals and humans is not just conceptual. She also discusses (2004) animals in terms of kinship.

1. The Right to Remain Silent

1. Some notable exceptions are Donna Haraway and philosophers working in the "Continental" tradition: Giorgio Agamben, Gilles Deleuze and Félix Guattari, David Wood, Jacques Derrida, Len Lawlor, Cary Wolfe, and Matthew Calarco. Notable examples of those who engage in the "animal rights" or "animal welfare" debates in these, or similar, terms are Peter Singer, Tom Regan, John Rawls, Robert Nozick, Richard Posner, Cora Diamond, and Martha Nussbaum (not coincidentally, all working in the "analytic" tradition). Daniel Dennett, among other philosophers of mind, regularly discusses the relation between animal intelligence and human intelligence.

2. Matthew Calarco suggests that women's rights and animal rights, among others, are related "if only for contingent historical reasons" (2008, 8). He identifies two problems with the current debates in animal rights philosophy: (1) adopting the language of identity politics pits animal rights against women's rights and other rights; and (2) these discourses continue to "determine animality and animal identity according to anthropocentric norms and ideals" (2008, 8).

3. For a discussion of some of the problems of drawing lines, particularly in terms of public policy, see Rachel 2004.

4. Making fun of such list drawing, Daniel Dennett refers to them as "scorecards" and quotes Leiber:

Montaigne is ecumenical in this respect, claiming consciousness for spiders and ants, and even writing of our duties to trees and plants. Singer and Clarke agree in denying consciousness to sponges. Singer locates the distinction somewhere between the shrimp and the oyster. He, with rather considerable convenience for one who is thundering hard accusations at others, slides by the case of insects and spiders and bacteria; they, pace Montaigne, apparently and rather conveniently do not feel pain. The intrepid Midgley, on the other hand, seems willing to speculate about the subjective experience of tapeworms. . . . Nagel appears to draw the line at flounders and wasps, though more recently he speaks of the inner life of cockroaches. (Dennett 1998, 343)

5. Discussing Confucianism, Henry Rosemont argues that a majority of the world live in cultures without notions of individuals as rights-bearing persons because they have no conception of rights (1991, 73).

6. Hooks (2007) was echoing Sojourner Truth's speech, "Ain't I a Woman?" at the Women's Rights Convention, Akron, Ohio, May 29, 1851.

7. Henry Rosemont argues that the majority of the world's population live in cultures that do not have a concept of rights (1991).

8. According to Brown,

Women's struggle for rights occurs in the context of a specifically masculinist discourse of rights, a discourse that presumes an ontologically autonomous, self-sufficient, unencumbered subject . . . rights in liberalism also tend to depoliticize the conditions they articulate. . . . Thus rights for the systematically subordinated tend to rewrite injuries, inequalities, and impediments to freedom that are consequent to social stratification as matters of individual violations and rarely articulate or address the conditions producing or fomenting that violation. Yet the absence of rights in these domains leaves fully intact these same conditions. (2002, 432–33)

9. In terms of women's rights, Wendy Brown discusses some of the ways in which rights entail regulations and disciplinary techniques, particularly because they are rights of protection rather than positive rights, which currently are the only type of rights afforded to animals. For women, Brown argues,

To have a right as a woman is not to be free of being designated and subordinated by gender. Rather, though it may entail some protection from the most immobilizing features of that designation, it reinscribes the designation as it protects us, and thus enables further regulation through that designation. (2002, 422)

10. Wendy Brown discusses (2002) the paradox of basing rights claims on identity politics.

11. As we will see, the ability to "sign in one's own name" comes under attack by Derrida, who argues that we cannot be so certain that humans can sign in their own names, which further complicates the issue of considering whether or not animals can do so.

12. See O'Neill 2008, 24.

13. Duncan Kennedy discusses the move from interests to rights as a rhetorical gesture that turns preferences into rules (2002, 188).

14. Regan gives his famous lifeboat example (1983). Gary Francione and Alan Watson (2000) like the fire example. In response to the criticism that she is a killjoy because she doesn't want people to enjoy their steaks, Brigid Brody argues that killing one of their joys is nothing compared with killing the animal and all its joy; she also says that in principle, she is not against eating animals (or humans) that died of natural causes if they could be made tender and hygienic, even though in practice she says she might choke on said casserole made of Great-Aunt Emily (Brody 1989). Peter Singer compares dogs to soy milk and his daughter to Kahlúa when discussing which one he would save in a fire (Singer 1999).

15. Kennedy also argues,

Rights are a key element in the universalization projects of ideological intelligentsias of all stripes. A universalization project takes an interpretation of the interests of some group, less than the whole polity, and argues that it corresponds to the interests or ideals of the whole. Rights arguments do this: they restate the interests of the group as characteristic of all people. (2002, 188)

16. Spain is on the verge of approving rights for great apes to comply with the Great Apes Project. Headlines in *The Guardian* and the *Christian Science Monitor* read, "Spanish Parliament Approves 'Human Rights' for Apes" and "Spain to Grant Some Human Rights to Apes" (Glendinning 2008 and O'Carroll 2008). Catharine MacKinnon argues, "Like women's rights, animal rights are poised to develop first for a tiny elite, the direction in which the 'like us' analysis tends" (2004, 271).

17. Derrida says,

On the one hand, casting doubt on responsibility, on decision, on one's own being-ethical, seems to me to be—and is perhaps what should forever remain—the unrescindable essence of ethics: decision and responsibility. Every firm knowledge, certainty, and assurance on this subject would suffice, precisely, to confirm the very thing one wishes to disavow, namely the reactionality in the response. I indeed said "to disavow" [*denier*], and it is for that reason that I situate disavowal at the heart of all these discourses on the animal. (2003, 128)

I discuss this passage in chapters 4 and 5.

Literary theorist and philosopher Cary Wolfe develops a brilliant comparison between Derrida and Cora Diamond on the issue of rights versus justice. Wolfe says,

For both, the question of the animal requires an alternative conception of ethics to what we find in the liberal justice and rights tradition of analytical philosophy as it manifests itself in work such as Singer's. For Singer, as we have seen, ethics means the application of what Derrida will elsewhere characterize as a "calculable process"—in Singer's case, it is quite literally the utilitarian calculus that would tally up the "interests" of the particular beings in question in a given situation, regardless of their species, and would determine what counts as a just act by calculating which action maximizes the greatest good for the greatest number. In doing so, however, Singer would reduce ethics to the very antithesis of ethics in Diamond's and Derrida's terms because he would overleap what Derrida calls "the ordeal of the undecidable," which "must be gone through by any decision worthy of the name." For Derrida, "A decision that didn't go through the ordeal of the undecidable would not be a free decision, it would be the programmable application or unfolding of a calculable process. It might be legal; it would not be just." "Ordeal" is indeed the word we want here, which is one reason Diamond rivets our attention more than once on Elizabeth Coetzee's [*sic*] "rawness" of nerves, her sufferance of a responsibility that is both undeniable and unappeasable. (Wolfe 2008, 19)

18. For an insightful discussion of the connection between rights and private property (and Marx's criticisms of private property in terms of rights) see legal theorist Duncan Kennedy's "The Critique of Rights in Critical Legal Studies" (2002). He discusses Marx's criticisms that voting rights and rights to free speech also guarantee rights to private property. For another discussion of the relationship between the Western notion of rights and capitalism, see Rosemont 1991, in which he concludes,

To be sure, that model [individuals as purely rational, self-seeking, autonomous individuals] especially as it has been taken to imply human rights—has advanced significantly the cause of human dignity, especially in the Western democracies, but it also has a strong self-fulfilling prophetic nature, which is strengthened further by the demands of capitalist economies; and I believe that model is now much more of a conceptual liability than an asset as we approach the twenty-first century, continuing our search for how to live, and how best to live together on this increasingly fragile planet. (1991, 89)

19. Giorgio Agamben argues that we cannot separate human rights from the rights of citizens. Instead, the limit-case is the refugee, who should have human rights even without rights of citizenship, but who in practice does not. He maintains that the concept of citizen is outmoded for dealing with contemporary politics (see esp. Agamben 1996).

20. For a fascinating history of relationships between humans and animals from predomesticity through present-day factory farming, see Bulliet 2005, in which he discusses the connection between the notion of private property and owning animals.

21. Feminist theorist Catharine MacKinnon discusses (2004) the association between women and animals, particularly in terms of considering animal rights and the issue of names. See also Adams and Donovan 1990, 1995; and Dunayer 1995.

22. For a sustained analysis of the interconnections between the exploitation of animals and of women, see Adams and Donovan 1990. In the introduction to his recent book on animals in Continental philosophy, Matthew Calarco describes the problem of treating animal rights as analogous to, but distinct from, other rights struggles: "Animal rights are seen as floating in an empty space distinct from political concerns about, for example,

women's rights, environmental justice, or worker's rights (all of which are, on my understanding of the question of the animal, intimately related to animal rights, even if only for
contingent historical reasons)" (Calarco 2008, 7–8). As he points out, this pits one group
against another in the fight over whose rights are more important while ignoring the ways
in which systems of oppression have historically been interconnected.

23. See Diamond 2001 and 2008. Cary Wolfe makes a similar argument in his introduction to *Philosophy and Animals* (2008), in which he compares Diamond's and Derrida's
views of animal suffering and the capacity to suffer or bodily vulnerability as what we share
with animals. As Wolfe points out, Diamond's rejection of animal rights is still based on
taking the human as the standard, even of experiences that we do not properly "experience" such as death (2008, 21–22). Furthermore, whereas Diamond talks about suffering
as a capacity, Derrida analyzes how it is a strange capacity in that it is an incapacity, an
inability to avoid suffering (cf. Wolfe 2008, 25–26). In this regard, we could say that Diamond's analysis still holds onto the sovereignty of the Cartesian subject.

24. Philosopher Ann Murphy is developing an analysis of the concepts of violence and
vulnerability in Continental philosophy.

25. For a discussion of the use of the term *vulnerability* in the news media following the
terrorist attacks, see Oliver 2007.

26. Similarly, some philosophers, particularly feminists (including Iris Young, Gail
Weiss, and Shannon Sullivan) have developed ethical theories using Merleau-Ponty's notions of shared embodiment. For example, at a conference, I heard a young philosopher from France using Merleau-Ponty's analysis of shared embodiment to develop an
ethical theory. Like other recent attempts (including my own) to bring out the ethical
implications of Merleau-Ponty's phenomenology of embodiment, she argued that the
structures of perception and behavior inherent in embodiment bring with them implicit
obligations. Again, part of the argument is that our radical dependence on the world and
others—what Merleau-Ponty calls the reversibility of the flesh—obligates us to them,
that is, obligates us to that by virtue of which we exist at all. During the Q&A after her
engaging presentation, given that animals have been on my mind recently, I asked the
speaker about nonhuman creatures with whom we share embodiment; I asked whether
her Merleau-Pontyan analysis applies to them as well. She seemed surprised, even shocked,
by the question. She hadn't considered that animals, too, have bodies.

27. For a provocative application of Butler's notion of vulnerability to animals, see
Taylor 2008, in which she argues, "Butler's account of an ethics of interdependence, embodiment, vulnerability, and mourning is a compelling incentive for thinking about the
lives not only of humans, but of animals more generally, and that there is nothing about
Butler's ethics that would justify an exclusion of non-human animals" (2008, 61).

28. For a discussion of the limits of politics of recognition, see Oliver 2001.

29. I argue elsewhere that

philosophically, it is crucial to question the notion that vulnerability is constitutive
of humanity, not just because we share vulnerability with all creatures but more par-

ticularly because it is not our vulnerability per se that distinguishes humans from other creatures; and most especially because the very notion of vulnerability is inherently linked to violence. The word vulnerable comes from the Latin word *vulnerabilis* which means *wounding*. The first definition of *vulnerable* in the Oxford English Dictionary is "Having power to wound; wounding"; the second is "That may be wounded; susceptible of receiving wounds or physical injury." *Vulnerable* means both the power to wound or wounding and the capacity to receive wounds or wounded. (2007, 137)

That we are both violent and vulnerable may have particular significance in our relation to animals, particularly because our violence toward and domination over animals has helped secure our identity as properly human.

30. For a defense of Butler's ethics in relation to animals, see Taylor 2008.

31. For a philosophy of dependence, see esp. Kittay 1995, 1996, 1998, 1999.

32. Dennett argues that

snakes (or parts of snakes!) may feel pain—depending on how we choose to define that term—but the evidence mounts that snakes lack the sort of overarching, long-term organization that leaves room for significant suffering. That doesn't mean that we ought to treat snakes the way we treat worn out tires, but just that concern for their suffering should be tempered by an appreciation of how modest their capacities for suffering are. (1998, 351)

He concludes that we cannot compare human and animal suffering.

33. Daniel Dennett argues that animals (at least the lower ones) feel pain but that they do not suffer. Suffering, he maintains, is based on having a memory of experiences and a sense of the future, which he claims animals do not have. He does not, however, see this as a reason not to consider our ethical obligations to avoid causing animals pain (1998).

34. For discussions of Derrida's deconstruction of Bentham's "Can they Suffer," see Calarco 2008; Lawlor 2007; and Wolfe 2008.

35. For a discussion of the reasons why I do not consider Deleuze and Guattari at greater length, see n. 9 of my introduction.

36. Donna Haraway discusses "companion species" and details some of the ways in which dogs in particular have developed in symbiotic relation with humans (2003, 2004). Cora Diamond rejects animal rights discourse in favor of a notion of fellow creatures that would respect animals in their differences from man (1978, 2001, 2008). Cary Wolfe (2008) extends Diamond's and Derrida's discussion of fellow creatures. John Berger (1980) provocatively suggests that without animals, man would be lonely as a species.

37. Kant imagines a "cosmopolitan constitution" of continents engaged in peaceful mutual relations that bring the entire human race under the same universal laws of hospitality. He contrasts this ideal with the "inhospitable conduct of the civilized states," "especially the commercial states, the injustice of which they display in *visiting* foreign

countries and peoples (which in their case is the same as *conquering* them) seems appallingly great" (1970, 106, italics added or in original). Kant's 1795 description of European interests in the Caribbean is chilling in light of current U.S. interests in Iraq and our economic woes:

> The worst (or from the point of view of moral judgments, the best) thing about all this is that the commercial states do not benefit by their violence, for all their trading companies are on the point of collapse. The Sugar Islands, that stronghold of the cruelest and most calculated slavery, do not yield any real profit; they serve only the indirect (and not entirely laudable) purpose of training sailors for warships, thereby aiding the prosecution of wars in Europe. And all this is the work of powers who make endless ado about their piety, and who wish to be considered as chosen believers while they live on the *fruits* of iniquity. (1970, 107, italics added)

2. You Are What You Eat

1. The exact date of "On the Origin of Languages" is unknown; Catherine Kintzler (1993) puts it between 1756 and 1761. Thanks to Benigno Trigo and Kalpana Seshdri-Crooks (who also suggested the notion of animal pedagogy) for extremely helpful suggestions on this chapter.

3. Say the Human Responded

1. Herder's view of evolution is ambivalent. He frequently insists that man is radically distinct from animals and that his reason and language do not have animal origins. Yet, in his *Ideen zur Philosophie der Geschichte der Menschheit,* he allows for a limited notion of evolution. While Kant agrees with Herder when he disclaims evolution, Kant's criticisms of Herder stem from the places in which Herder imagines humans in proximity to animals (see Wilson 2006 and Zammito 2006).

2. This remark is from the student minutes of Heidegger's seminar on Herder. *On the Essence of Language* (1939) includes Heidegger's lecture notes followed by seminar minutes taken by his students.

3. In a discussion of Kant's response to Herder, Catherine Wilson argues, "Herder said not only that culture was zoologically and geographically determined but that men had learned almost everything worth knowing from animals" (2006, 391). Kant, she claims, rejected this idea as monstrous as it would lead to "any sort of grotesquerie" (Wilson 2006, 392).

4. Heidegger compares Herder's view with that of biologist Uexküll, whose theories are central to Heidegger's comparative analysis of humans and animals in *The Fundamental Concepts of Metaphysics* (see 1999, 137). See Chapter 8 for a discussion of Heidegger's use of Uexküll.

4. "Hair of the Dog"

1. For a discussion of Rousseau's animal examples in relation to diet, see Yousef 2000.

2. Rousseau uses the same word, *goût,* for taste in both the physical and the moral sense.

3. For insightful readings of this text, see Calarco 2008; Lawlor 2007; Wolfe 2008.

4. Derrida coins the term *differánce,* with *á* instead of *e* in order to highlight the double meaning of the Latin verb *differre,* which means both "to defer" and "to differ." In *Of Grammatology,* he defines *differánce* as "An economic concept designating the production of differing/deferring" (1967, 23). In the essay "Differánce" in *Margins of Philosophy* (1968), he associates *differánce* with the play of signification and the dynamic relationship between words or concepts that constitutes both difference and identity.

5. As we have seen, Rousseau is not consistent on the issue of whether man evolves slowly or erupts suddenly from Nature or animal existence. As we know, Derrida exploits this ambiguity in his reading of Rousseau in *Of Grammatology;* while Paul de Man challenges Derrida's interpretation of Rousseau, arguing that Derrida frames Rousseau by skewing textual evidence away from what de Man sees as Rousseau's commitment to an evolutionary view. See de Man 1983 and Derrida 1967; also Rousseau 1966, 1984.

6. Thanks to Kyoo Lee for pointing out the logical sense of the word *follow.*

7. For provocative discussions of the ramifications of Derrida's work for thinking about vegetarianism, see Calarco 2004a and Wood 1999.

8. In the United States, we might ask whether a head of state could gain office without declaring himself a hunter, along with television ads featuring rifles and retrievers. Sara Guyer discusses the paradoxical position of what she identifies as Derrida's cannibalism: "Calling the very possibility of the Good (du Bien) into questions, while at the same time insisting upon its necessity, an ethics of cannibalism recognizes the status of the other and then compels us to eat him" (1995, 63–80).

9. Given that farmers regularly name their prized heifers and bulls and then send them to slaughter, and given that certain proper names incite us to kill (admittedly perhaps because they function as more than names)—Sadaam Hussein, Osama bin Laden—I am not entirely convinced that Lawlor's recipe, as tempting as it may be, will lead to less violent ways of eating, although in time and numbers of names involved, it may put a dent in factory farming and slaughter. Lawlor's recipe also supposes that we can draw a line between naming and counting so that a number cannot function as a proper name. Certainly, even factory-farmed animals are tagged, numbered, and accounted for on an invoice. Couldn't any proper name degenerate into something like an ID tag? My point is that naming does not prevent counting, which may be why Derrida keeps asking whether animals (including humans) can "answer in their own names"—names that are not assigned to them by another, that is, an impossible name. At least all our names come from some sort of shared language, from something social that transcends any individual. Lawlor does observe that naming is necessary but not sufficient. Indeed, all the prescriptions he lists are necessary but not sufficient, thus the title of his book, *This Is Not Sufficient.* The kind of sublimation of our violent impulses into names and words that Lawlor's theory

implies does seem promising. Later I will return to Derrida's repeated use of the phrase "worthy of its name" and Kristeva's notion of abjection in relation to animals.

10. Julie Klein puts it nicely:

> In all of its implications, then, eating exhibits the intersection of natural necessity and human convention, or culture. This is perhaps the richest, and consequently most difficult to digest, food for thought in "Eating Well.". . . In this sense, while eating is necessary, there is not a single or intrinsic pattern of alimentation that obtains in all cases. Appetite appears in differing modalities and configurations, and satisfaction takes many forms. (2003, 198)

Klein concludes from this that Derrida's analysis has the potential to open up material, historical, and political factors involved in taste. She argues, however, that Derrida stops short of embracing the possibility of infinite variations in taste, because to do so would be "abandoning a natural ground for ethics." Unlike Klein, I read Derrida as ungrounding ethics in the name of ethics. His insistence on pure unconditional hospitality is intended to throw ethics into the aporia of adherence to its own most rigorous imperative of infinite undecidability that can never appeal to a "natural ground."

11. Matthew Calarco (2004a) brings this charge against David Wood.

12. In *Émile,* Rousseau distinguishes the way that children learn by imitation from the way that monkeys imitate, insisting that humans don't ape when they imitate. But he also insists that children must develop good habits through imitation and then go on to learn the lesson by heart, in the sense of feeling and understanding whether or not an action is good rather than just miming others (2003, 81). As we have seen, Derrida exploits this tension on the issue of mimesis in Rousseau's work, whereas Paul de Man defends Rousseau against Derrida's charge that despite his intentions, Rousseau makes imitation primary (see de Man 1983; Derrida 1967).

13. In *The Animal,* Derrida maintains that we give ourselves the right to dominate the animals and argues that man's sovereignty is self-sustaining and self-given because it has no foundation outside itself (see 2008, 89). In *Rogues* (2005), Derrida gives a more developed and sustained version of the same argument.

14. One can own a house, but can one ever own a home? Space and the ethos connected with it are not within the control of anyone as absolute sovereign. David Carroll nicely described the problematic, which he associates with a kind of nomadic character in Derrida's work:

> What is original, what makes hospitality in its most radical, implacable sense, therefore, possible is not possession but a "radical dispossession." In this sense no one is really ever originally or completely master of his/her house or truly at home in his/her home(land). The law of hospitality is rooted in this original displacement or deferment of the "natural right" to possess and along with it the right to sovereignty—over either oneself or others. (Carroll 2006, 822)

15. Analyzing Derrida's remarks on the impossibility of the gift, Maria Margaroni persuasively argues that "the theorist of differ*á*nce performs what I consider a strategic 'forgetting' of the differantial [*sic*] spacing entailed in the movement of giving, the spatio-temporal *écart* that defers the return of the gift, ensuring that on its return the given will be altered" (Margaroni 2004, 49).

16. In his essay "Perpetual Peace," in the section on universal hospitality, Kant says,

> The stranger cannot claim the right of a guest to be entertained, for this would require a special friendly agreement whereby he might become a member of the native household for a certain time. He may only claim of right of resort, for all men are entitled to present themselves in the society of others by virtue of their right to communal possession of the earth's surface. Since the earth is a globe, they cannot disperse over an infinite area, but must necessarily tolerate one another's company. (1970, 106)

17. For an interesting and instructive debate over the role of the impossibility of pure forgiveness in Derrida's analysis, see Milbank (2001) and Dooley (2001). Milbank maintains that Derrida's insistence on absolute or pure forgiveness undermines any possibility of an ethics of forgiveness and sacrifices the self to the other. Dooley argues that Milbank misreads Derrida's use of the impossible in hyperbolic ethics:

> The whole point of Derrida's discourse is to suggest that "pure absolute self-sacrifice" is impossible, that no matter how hard I try I can never abandon my heritage, my language, or my tradition. But I can, by keeping the impossible dream alive, prevent this law from becoming an obstacle to those who do not come under its jurisdiction. (Dooley 2001, 145)

18. In *Rogues*, Derrida describes the event as the arrival of the singular, other, or, we could say, new:

> A calculable event, one that falls, like a case, like the object of some knowledge, under the generality of a law, norm, determinative judgment, or technoscience, and thus of a power-knowledge and a knowledge-power, is not *at least in this measure*, an event. Without the absolute singularity of the incalculable and the exceptional, no thing and no one, nothing *other* and thus *nothing*, arrive or happen. (2005, 148, italics in original).

19. Elsewhere I question this strategy, if that is what it is, of using one discourse of purity against another. There I argue that hyperbolic ethics requires us to investigate our investment in even this "higher" or conceptual form of purity. See Oliver 2004, especially the last chapter and the conclusion, and also Oliver 2003.

20. For a helpful discussion of Derrida on the impossibility of secrets, see Lawlor 2007, esp. 46–47.

21. Derrida plays off the notion that only humans dream, by suggesting that his might be the dream of an animal, in the double sense in which an animal is the subject who is dreaming and an animal is the one dreamed about, only now an animal capable of speaking, or singing, in a new language (see 2008, 62–64).

22. For a sustained analysis of the role of blood in Derrida's "Circumfession," see Oliver 1997, 53–68.

23. Throughout *The Animal,* Derrida plays with the idiomatic use of the word *animal* in describing an individual as a *political animal* or a *competitive animal.* This use of animal connotes talent and passion as well as an instinct for politics of competition. Derrida turns the phrase into the "autobiographical animal" to indicate the animal, man, who has a taste or instinct for autobiography, for saying "I am" (see, e.g., 2002, 416). It is noteworthy that he begins *Monolingualism of the Other* with "I am some allegorical figure of this animal," referring to a monolinguistic animal (1998, 1).

24. Derrida seems to talk about philosophers in general and the entire history of philosophy in a sort of tongue-in-cheek gesture to highlight the ways that animals have been totalized into one group without distinctions. He often uses the term *man* in the same general way. In the end, he seems to imply that only by deconstructing the binary opposition man/animal can we recognize difference among not only animals but also humans.

25. In *The Animal,* Derrida argues that only man can act beastly but that animals or beasts cannot behave beastly (see 2008, 64). He also plays with the word *bête,* which means "beast" or "stupid."

26. He also says:

> It is *not just* a matter of asking whether one has the right to refuse the animal such and such a power. . . . It *also* means asking whether what calls itself human has the right rigorously to attribute to man, which means therefore to attribute to himself, what he refuses the animals, and whether he can ever possess the *pure, rigorous, indivisible* concept, as such, of that attribution. (2008, 135, italics in original; see also 2008, 72, where he challenges Descartes' "thinking purity")

27. Here I have a slightly different interpretation from Matthew Calarco (2008), who seems to suggest that Derrida wants to keep the human/animal binary and merely add to it.

28. In his latest work on hospitality, forgiveness, and democracy, Derrida repeatedly uses this phrase, "worthy of its name" (*digne de ce nom*). I continue to analyze this phrase in the next chapter.

29. In *This Is Not Sufficient,* Lawlor does not problematize Derrida's discourse of purity; rather, throughout that text he suggests that Derrida gives us a discourse of contamination and not one of purity. But in the end, even Lawlor returns us to a discourse of purity when, with Cixous, he calls Derrida, Foucault, and Deleuze part of a generation of incorruptibles. He concludes, "This generation will remain pure" (2007, 117).

30. Derrida continues to discuss forgiveness and the gift:

Another example would be the unconditionality of the *gift* or of *forgiveness*. I have tried to show elsewhere exactly where the unconditionality required by the purity of such concepts leads us. A gift without calculable exchange, a gift worthy of its name, would not even appear *as such* to the donor or donee without the risk of reconstituting, through phenomenality and thus through its phenomenology, a circle of economic reappropriation that would just as soon annual its event. Similarly, forgiveness can be given *to* the other or come *from* the other only beyond calculation, beyond apologies, amnesia, or amnesty, beyond acquittal or prescription, even beyond any asking for forgiveness, and thus beyond any transformative repentance, which is most often the stipulated condition for forgiveness, at least in what is the most *predominant* in the tradition of the Abrahamic religions. (2005, 149, italics added).

31. See Oliver 2001 and 2004.

32. Leonard Lawlor mentions Derrida's thickening of limits in several places in passing in *This Is Not Sufficient* (2007).

33. In *Of Grammatology*, Derrida calls his project "radically empiricist" in that it looks to the material of language, in which "the very concept of empiricism destroys itself" (1974, 162). This passage appears in the same section as Derrida's famous claim "There is nothing outside of the text" (158).

34. Rousseau also distinguishes between eating plants and collecting plants for display, associating the latter with greed and the corruption of nature. Alexander Cook analyzes Rousseau's criticisms of what Cook calls "exotic botany" in relation to his views of "nature versus property" (see Cook 2002). Jean Starobinski, in contrast, gives a more romantic account of Rousseau's own interest in botany, associating plants with innocence: plants "bestow their innocence on the person contemplating them" (1988, 236).

35. As we have seen in the conclusion of chapter 4, an alternative to contemporary ideas of "manly virtue" is the archaic notion of virtue as the healing power of certain plants and animals. This older sense of virtue suggests a beneficial nourishing relationship between humans and their environment and earthly companions. This form of virtue stands in contrast to manly virtues as conquering others in the same way that trophe differs from trophy. Trophe can humble us in the face of the earth and others upon whom we depend, while trophy fills us with pride over our conquest of them.

36. In his recent book, Matthew Calarco argues that we need to get rid of the human/animal distinction altogether (2008).

37. Anne O'Byrne (2002) provocatively and productively reads Derrida's notion of autoimmunity in relation to the maternal body's acceptance of the DNA of the other body/fetus.

38. For an excellent discussion of Derrida's notion of autoimmunity in terms of suicidal tendencies in recent war and terrorism, see Lawlor 2007. We could apply Lawlor's analysis to factory farming and recent moves to cloning that drastically deplete biodiversity and

invite the possibility of deadly autoimmune responses in the form of viruses and bacteria that could wipe out entire species.

39. I am echoing Leonard Lawlor (2007, 15) when he says that fundamentalist religions today are forms of autoimmunity that secrete their own poison.

40. See Oliver 2004.

5. Sexual Difference, Animal Difference

1. In her introduction to *Glas,* Peggy Kamuf summarizes Derrida's strategy:

That is, displacing the familial moment, the point at which sexual difference is determined in oppositional terms and then reduced, negated, relieved (*aufgehoben*) to permit passage to the next moment, had to shake up the whole structure. In effect, by reading this moment as the strangle-point of the vast dialectical architecture, Derrida "sexualizes" that structure throughout. (Kamuf 1991, 317)

For an insightful analysis of Derrida's reading of Hegel on the question of woman, see Rawlinson 1997, and for a provocative engagement with Derrida's *Glas,* see Spivak 1977, 2005.

2. For provocative discussions of Derrida's criticisms of Heidegger and Levinas, see Chanter 1997 and Grosz 1997. See also Nancy Holland's introduction to *Feminist Interpretations of Derrida,* 1997.

3. Elizabeth Grosz describes the significance of Derrida's thinking of difference beyond binary opposition:

In short, the debate on the status and nature of difference has tended to see it as a struggle of two entities, two terms, pairs; a struggle to equalize two terms in one case, and a struggle to render the two terms reciprocally in the second case. The concept of difference has been historically linked to the functioning of various dualisms. It is Derrida who demonstrated that difference exceeds opposition, dichotomy, or dualism and can never be adequately captured in any notion of identity or diversity (which is the proliferation of sameness or identity and by no means its overcoming or difference). Derrida understood that difference is not only at the heart of philosophy . . . but more significantly, for his work was never simply with texts, terms, or concepts alone, that difference is the methodology of life and, indeed, of the universe itself. (Grosz 2005, 90)

4. In "Dreaming of the Innumerable," John Caputo explores the connection between undecidablity and multiplicity in terms of justice and ethics. He argues that "for Derrida, dissemination and undecidability are the conditions, the 'quasi-transcendental' conditions, of justice—for women, for men (for animals, for everybody)—conditions of the

dream of justice, which is also, when it comes to sexual difference, a dream of the innumerable" (Caputo 1997, 141).

5. Elsewhere (1995), I discuss the ways that Derrida's insistence that concepts of woman, the feminine, and femininity are undecidable and should not become objects of knowledge possibly undermine the project of feminism.

6. For a helpful discussion of Derrida's notion of the gift, see Cheah 2005.

7. Elsewhere (2004, esp. chap. 4 and conclusion) I discuss several problems with this discourse of purity and contamination, particularly as Derrida uses it as an intervention into other discourses of purity and contamination, namely, the Holocaust and apartheid with their discourses of ethnic or racial purity and contamination.

8. In this regard, the notion of purity and "worthy of its name" might conjure the concept of *différance* from Derrida's earlier work. If Derrida wishes to maintain with that notion both the sense of deferral and differing in the word *difference,* the qualification *pure* could perform the deferring function, while the idiom "worthy of its name" could perform the differing function. Now, however, both connote the realm of ethics, which the earlier term *différance* did not. Given that Derrida is fond of multiplying the meaning of words, demonstrating their heterogeneous etymologies, and exploiting meanings that seem at odds with one another, this idiomatic expression—"worthy of its name"—casts a strange shadow on his hyperbolic ethics. The French *digne* means "worthy," "proper," "fitting," so that Derrida's phrase "worthy of its name" (*digne de ce nom*) implies an economy of property, since he is discussing what is proper to the concepts of gift, forgiveness, hospitality, and so forth.

9. Derrida would probably reject my characterization of his position as "radical idealism." In *Of Grammatology,* Derrida calls his project "radically empiricist" in that it looks to the material of language, in which "the very concept of empiricism destroys itself" (1974, 162). This passage appears in the same section as Derrida's famous claim "There is nothing outside of the text" (158).

10. Ellen Armour (1997) argues that Derrida provides a necessary supplement to Irigaray's notion of the divine in relation to the feminine.

11. Feminist philosopher Lisa Guenther is currently developing a notion of ethical indifference that might resonate with what I am calling *unremarked difference.* In her theory, the notion of indifference can prevent difference from becoming oppositional or hierarchical.

12. For a more in-depth discussion of Derrida's hyperbolic ethics, see Oliver 2004, chap. 4, in which I argue that even our ethical ideals must be subject to the vigilant self-interrogation of hyperbolic ethics.

13. See Judith Butler's pioneering work reconceptualizing gender in *Gender Trouble* (1990) and *Undoing Gender* (2004b). See also the work of Anne Fausto-Sterling (1979).

14. Ellen Armour made this point in a presentation at Vanderbilt University in December 2006.

15. For discussions of this passage in Derrida's text, see Calarco 2008; Lawlor 2007; and Wolfe 2008. Lawlor creatively uses Derrida's cat to point to what he calls, following

Derrida, the "staggered analogy" between man and animals (2007, 77). In one of my favorite passages, Lawlor describes the analogy between Derrida and his cat:

> In other words, we have a comparison between two things that are not completely visible, between two things that are concealed or covered up. So we have to say, then that Derrida resembles his cat less when he is uncovered and naked; he is most like a cat when he is fully clothed, when he is most uncatlike and most different from a cat. When Derrida is most human, most technological, most concealed, he is most indeterminate, and when he is most indeterminate, when he is only appresented, when he is imperceptible and clandestine, he most resembles a cat. In still other words, Derrida is most catlike when he is most human; when he is writing aporias, he most resembles a cat pacing back and forth before a door, waiting to be let out or to be let in. (2007, 78)

Calarco reads the cat example as showing the "singular event" of each particular animal subject (2008, 121–22). Wolfe discusses the cat example in terms of an exposure to the other that brings forth the ethical call (2008, 36–37). For a discussion of Derrida's use of cats in his earlier work, see Wood 2004. It is striking that none of these accounts of Derrida's cat discusses the sex of the cat, about which Derrida is adamant. He insists that it is a female cat looking at his sex, and sexual difference comes to play in his embarrassment. But none of these (male) theorists sees her sex. Perhaps ashamed of Derrida's mention of the sex of his pussycat, they avert their eyes.

16. For an excellent analysis of Derrida's "answer" to the question of which comes first, sexual difference or difference in general, see Berger 2005.

17. For a discussion of scientific evidence that by the end of the century half of all life on earth will be extinct, see Whitty 2007. It is telling that progressive discourses revolving around racial and ethnic diversity come at a time of drastically dwindling biodiversity, a coincidence worth further analysis.

6. The Beaver's Struggle with Species-Being

1. Jean-Paul Sartre's nickname for Simone de Beauvoir, his lover, was *El Castor,* the Beaver. I would like to thank Gaile Poulhaus for suggesting that I write a chapter on de Beauvoir's use of animals in *The Second Sex.*

2. De Beauvoir uses the singular term *woman* throughout her text to designate the category assigned to women by patriarchal values. Her notion that women are born female but not born woman indicates the distinction between sex and gender that has been identified by feminist scholars as one of the fundamental lessons of *The Second Sex.* Her inclusion of female animals in her assessment of how patriarchal values debase females, however, challenges interpretations of *The Second Sex* as simply enforcing a distinction between sex and gender. My use of "woman" instead of "women" in this chapter is merely meant to mirror de Beauvoir rather than to endorse the use of the singular and universal

category. For a different take on the complexities of de Beauvoir's commitment to any sex/
gender distinction, see Gatens 2003; and for insightful discussions of de Beauvoir's sex/
gender distinction, see Butler 1986a and b, 1989c; Kruks 1992; and Wittig 1992.

3. For discussions of de Beauvoir's ambivalence toward woman, feminine sexuality,
and motherhood, see Allen 1995; Andrew 2003; Arp 1995; Bergoffen 1997, 2000; Brison
2003; Chaperon 1995; Deutscher 1997, 2003; Gatens 2003; Greene 1980; Seigfried 1985;
Klaw 1995; Leighton 1975; Léon 1995; Simons 2006; Vintges 1996; and Ward 1995, among
others.

4. Ibid.

5. Recent feminist commentaries on this section have come to mixed conclusions. For
more critical accounts, see Moi 1986 and Seigfried 1985; and for a more sympathetic reading of this section, see Fallaize 2001; Bauer 2001; and Vintges 1996.

6. For a revelatory study of the inaccuracies, deletions, and biases in zoologist Howard
Parshley's translation of *The Second Sex,* see Simons 1999 and 2006, esp. chap. 5. For a
detailed account of the history of Parshley's translation, see Patterson 1992; Bauer 2001;
and esp. Moi 2004.

7. Charlene Haddock Seigfried criticizes (1985) de Beauvoir for accepting the facts of
biology as value free and not extending her criticisms of patriarchal myths far enough,
arguing that there must be a more interactive relationship between facts and myths than
de Beauvoir allows (1985, esp. 220–21 and 227). Elizabeth Fallaize contends (2001) that
the main point of the first section of *The Second Sex* is to challenge the neutrality of all
facts and to suggest that facts are always interpreted; that is, they always are imbued
with myth.

8. For a helpful discussion of de Beauvoir's use of the word *saraband* to describe the
imagery of zoology, see Fallaize 2001. In a footnote, Fallaize points out that the Robert
French dictionary defines *sarabande* as a lively and lascivious Spanish dance and indicates
an idiomatic use of saraband—*danser, faire la sarabande,* which means "to run amok." The
saraband of imagery in biology, then, could be interpreted as a lascivious dance between
fact and myth, run amok.

9. In a compelling essay, Donna Haraway argues, "Primatology is politics by other
means" (1984, 489 and 515). Her detailed account of the field suggests that research on
primates is fueled by desires to locate the origins of human behavior, particularly human
sexuality. Her analysis suggests that de Beauvoir is not alone in using animal studies to
draw conclusions about woman or gender. Indeed, her thesis is that primatology (and
perhaps much of zoology) is about gender politics in one sense or another.

10. Elizabeth Fallaize comments on de Beauvoir's value-laden interpretations of the so-
called biological facts: "Far from deconstructing images, Beauvoir is here building images
of her own, and with gay abandon. However, the difference is that she does not imagine
these images to be in danger of fanning the flames of male hostility against women"
(2001, 78).

11. Charlene Haddock Seigfried discusses the conclusions of primatologist Sarah Blaffer
Hrdy to show that the so-called biological facts can be interpreted in different ways. She
argues that Hrdy's studies suggest that females are dominant and sexually aggressive in

order to ensure reproductive success. Seigfried concludes: "Beauvoir's and Hrdy's biological female are diametrically opposed. The weak, unstable, passive, female animal, overwhelmed by pregnancy has been replaced by the assertive, lusty, dominance-oriented female who revels in reproductive success" (1985, 226).

12. In *The Second Sex,* she mentions the praying mantis several times (see 1949b, 18, 200, 254, 260, 467, 640, 716).

13. For discussions of de Beauvoir's views of motherhood and pregnancy, see Arp 2001; Bauer 2001; Bergoffen 1997; Fallaize 2001; Lázaro 1986; O'Brien 1981; Okely 1998; Patterson 1989; Pilardi 1991; Rich 1977; Simons 1999; Smith 1986; Ward 1995; and Zerilli 1992, among others. For a helpful criticism of de Beauvoir's distinction between reproduction and production, see Jaggar and McBride 1985; and Vintges 1996.

14. Ibid.

15. For discussions of de Beauvoir's relation to existentialism and particularly to Sartre's philosophy, see Fullbrook and Fullbrook 1994, 1995; Greene 1980; Holveck 1995; Kruks 1995; O'Brien and Embree 2001; Simons 1995, 1999, 2001; Singer 1985; and Vintges 1995, among others.

16. For a discussion of de Beauvoir's use of anthropology in relation to contemporary studies, see Sanday and Goodenough 1990; also Lundgren-Gothlin 1996; Mahon 1997; and Vintges 1996.

17. For discussions of de Beauvoir's notion of freedom, especially in relation to Sartre's, see Arp 2001; Bauer 2001; Bergoffen 1995; Kruks 1987, 1995; Linsenbard 1999; Marks 1987; Pilardi 1993; Simons 1995, 1999, 2006; Singer 1985; and Vintges 1996, among others.

18. See n. 6.

19. The Sriracha Tiger Zoo in Thailand reportedly regularly has tigers nursing piglets and sows nursing tiger cubs when necessary (Roberts 2005).

20. Fredrika Scarth argues that de Beauvoir's account suggests that pregnancy is a form of risk that enables Hegelian subject formation. She concludes: "Beauvoir isn't valorizing a masculine model of subjectivity. Rather, in the process of shifting subjectivity from a masculine preserve to a human capacity she in fact alters the meaning of subjectivity and the project and the relationship of risking subjectivity" (2004, 155). According to Scarth, because it is the relation to otherness and even the other within that gives rise to subjectivity, pregnancy should be the ultimate risk of the other within.

21. See Irigaray 1974, 1985, 1992, 1993.

22. For fascinating recent discussion of the valuation of "life," see Agamben 1996 and Lawlor 2007.

7. Answering the Call of Nature

1. Henry Sullivan defends Lacan's insistence on the uniqueness of human language in terms of desire, which is unique to humans: "Language and technology mark the point where material conditions cease to impinge on anatomy, and the homization of the planet begins" (1991, 46). As Lacan does, even while Sullivan criticizes evolutionary biology,

he falls back on it in his conclusion about the evolutionary power of language (see Sullivan 1991).

2. For a provocative argument in favor of animal responsiveness, see Marjolein Oele 2007. See also Ted Toadvine 2007a, who argues that phenomenology makes it possible to see that animals not only react but also respond.

8. The Abyss Between Humans and Animals

1. For excellent exegetical essays on this text (which also offer critical remarks), see Calarco 2004b (this is the most critical of these five) and 2008; Franck 1991; Kuperus 2007; and McNeill 1999. For even more creative readings of this text and others on Heidegger's animal, see Agamben 2004; Derrida 1987a and b, 1991b and c, 2006 (chap. 4); and Lacove-Labarthe and Nancy 1997. For another reading of this text in relation to Merleau-Ponty's *Nature* lectures, see Thorens 2005. For a discussion of Heidegger's views on animals in relation to Wittgenstein, see Glendinning 1996. For a fascinating critical extension of Heidegger's views on animals and his philosophy of Being that makes them more useful for thinking about our ethical obligations to animals and the environment, see Llewelyn 1991, in which Llewelyn moves from the standard animal rights arguments that we have ethical obligations to animals because they are rational or suffer or have interests, to the argument that we have ethical obligations to all beings in need. Buchanan (2007) also critically extends Heidegger's analysis of animals to make it more useful for thinking of reciprocity with animals.

2. See, e.g., Heidegger 1983, 307. Heidegger variously uses the words *Armut* and *Weltarm* to refer to the animal's poverty in the world, whereas McNeill translates *Armut* as "poverty" and *Weltarm* as "poor in world" (1999, 236).

3. For a discussion of the strengths and weakness of Heidegger's comparative approach, see Calarco 2004b, 2008; also Derrida 2006, chap. 4.

4. Derrida discusses (2008) sovereignty and right in relation to the question of animals and the use of animals in the history of philosophy.

5. For example, Matthew Calarco says,

Of greater importance to Heidegger than answering the skeptical question concerning circularity is to ensure that his thesis—"the animal is poor in world"—not be understood in terms of a hierarchical value judgment. He insists repeatedly throughout the lecture course that the thesis "the animal is poor in world" does not mean to say that the animal is "poor" in comparison with, and by the measure of, man who is "rich" in having world. (2004b, 21)

Later Calarco defends Heidegger against charges of humanism but levels his own charge of anthropocentrism (2004b, 29). In a more sympathetic reading (1999, 198) , McNeill argues that Heidegger is neither essentialist nor humanist in his analysis of animals. He maintains that Heidegger avoids hierarchical value judgments by consistently insisting that he is describing ontological rather than ontic differences. This reading allows that in terms of ontic differences between beings, some may perform certain tasks better than others, but in terms of ontological difference, there is no comparison and therefore no value judgment. Moreover, McNeill concludes that it is precisely the ontological difference between man and animals that opens up man to his infinite responsibility for other beings (cf. 1999, 246).

6. See Calarco 2004b, 2008.

7. Calarco nicely formulates the tension between citing animal experiments and Heidegger's criticisms of technoscience:

> It is highly revealing in the context that Heidegger has nothing to say about the domination of life in these experiments, particularly the experiment where a bee's abdomen is cut away, and this despite his railings against the techno-scientific domination of nature which is prevalent throughout several of his texts. One perhaps wonders why the double sacrifice of this bee—sacrificed once (literally) in the name of scientific knowledge and a second time (symbolically) in the name of the ontological difference—even if it does not touch the bee at a cognitive level, does not "touch" *thought* more closely. (2004b, 25–26, italics in original).

Discussing Heidegger's mutilated-bee example, David Morris argues that

> we could say instead that a mutilated bee is a bee only for the experimenter who "prepares" it, that is it no longer really a bee, that is cannot behave toward the bowl in a bee-like manner because it has lost its belly. We might also say that the full belly of the (unmutilated) bee flying away from the scent of the bowl is an animal recognition of surplus honey. Instead of manifesting recognition in language or individual behaviour, this is a recognition of surplus in a kind of movement to be read against the overall movements of the hive. A mutilated bee cannot show this kind of recognition. But then again, a human who has lost the feeling of pain may lose the ability to show, in individual behavior, recognition of dangerous things in hand, yet recognition of danger can nonetheless be read in the individual's behaviour in virtue of fellows alongside who help point out the danger. (2005, 59–60)

Morris criticizes Heidegger's conclusions drawn from laboratory experiments instead of fieldwork, as well as conclusions drawn from observing individual or "lone" animals instead of groups.

8. Derrida suggests that Heidegger's analysis in *The Fundamental Concepts of Metaphysics* risks biological determinism insofar as it seems to ground metaphysics in biology (cf. Derrida 2008, 144). He even says that this latent biologism signals a latent politics. Is Derrida suggesting that Heidegger's latent biologism shares the same political impulses as eugenics?

9. McNeill provides an insightful interpretation of Heidegger's insistence on abyss, arguing that for Heidegger it is not the case that animals and humans are separated by an

abyss and therefore we become linguistic beings or Dasein. Rather, our becoming Dasein opens the abyss. In other words, the abyss does not refer to the ontic level of beings but to the ontological level of being. Indeed, it is the ontological difference that opens the abyss, and not vice versa. McNeill asserts, "The Augenblick thus shows itself as the veritable abyss of world, an abyss that does not lie between different entities as beings present at hand, but that is the finite opening enabling and calling for attentiveness to Others—to all Others—in the context of their worldly presence" (1999, 246). The essential rupture between man and animals is what opens up the possibility of ethical responsibility and, more specifically, man's responsibility toward other beings, including animals.

10. Compare this passage from Heidegger's *The Fundamental Concepts of Metaphysics:*

It is precisely this inconspicuous and self-evident going alongside one another, as a particular way of being with one another and being transposed into one another, that creates the illusion that in this being alongside one another there is initially a gap that needs to be bridged, as though human beings were not transposed into one another at all here, as though one human being would first have to empathize their way into the other in order to reach them. For a long time now this illusion has also led philosophy astray and has done so to an extent one would hardly credit. Philosophy has reinforced this illusion even further by propounding the dogma that the individual human being exists for him- or herself as an individual and that it is the individual ego with its ego-sphere which is initially and primarily given to itself as what is most certain. This has merely given philosophical sanction to the view that some kind of being with one another must first be produced out of this solipsistic isolation. (1995, 206).

9. "Strange Kinship"

1. Adèle Thorens argues that Merleau-Ponty's alternative interpretation of Uexküll's *Umwelten* allows us to answer Heidegger's question of whether animals have world in the affirmative: "To the initial question posed by Heidegger, Merleau-Ponty responds positively. Yes, animals, principally higher animals, have a world. Yes, there is in life an unbelievable potential of creation and from this [*inépuissable emergent*] dynamic entities [*qui sont bein des mondes*]" (2005, 239). Thorens also argues that one reason why Heidegger's and Merleau-Ponty's comparative analyses of animals and humans yield such different conclusions is that while the third term in Heidegger's comparative analysis is inanimate objects such as stones, in Merleau-Ponty's it is machines, particularly cybernetics. Merleau-Ponty finds more in common between man and animals by comparing them to machines: whereas machines function, both humans and animals live. Unlike Thoren, who attributes the differences between Heidegger and Merleau-Ponty on the question of animals to the difference between Heidegger's *Umring* and Uexküll's *Umwelten,* I believe that Merleau-Ponty goes beyond Uexküll and also that the difference in their answer to the question of having world comes back to the radical difference in their notions of behavior and instinct.

2. Elizabeth Behnke argues that when he turns to science, Merleau-Ponty looks in the wrong place for the kinship between animals and humans. That is, by considering only animal experiments and overlooking our everyday relationships with animals, Merleau-Ponty takes a "frontal" view of animals and thereby treats them as mere objects. She concludes:

> Similarly, the question of the human–animal "relation" is treated only ontologically, and there is only fleeting reference to human–animal sociality. More seriously, however, the unthematized relation between human beings and animals that undergrids many pages of this volume is a frontal relation of contemplation, objectification, intervention, and domination; the animals are not only observed from the outside and theorized about, but interfered with—removed from their native *Umwelt*, experimented upon, severed, grafted, dissected, etc. (1999, 99)

I agree with Behnke that this aspect of Merleau-Ponty's thought is in tension with his overall conclusions about behavior and the relational nature of human subjectivity. In addition, I agree that his conclusions about the "strange kinship" between humans and animals might have been different had he considered our animal companions.

Discussing Merleau-Ponty's comparative analysis of monkeys and humans in *The Structure of Behavior*, David Morris (2005) criticizes him for drawing his conclusions from individual or "lone" animals rather than from groups of animals. His analysis of Merleau-Ponty on animals might have been different if he had considered Merleau-Ponty's *Nature* lectures, in which his examination of animal behavior is significantly expanded and has evolved with the rest of his thought. For example, unlike Merleau-Ponty, Morris concludes that an individual animal is like one note in a melody, which should not be analyzed in isolation. Yet he seems unaware of both Uexküll's use of the metaphor of melody to describe the animal's relation to its environment and of Merleau-Ponty's extension and development of that metaphor in relation to animal and human behavior.

3. In the *Nature* lectures, Merleau-Ponty takes over the metaphor of melody from Uexküll. Ted Toadvine points out that in his earlier work, especially *The Structure of Behavior*, Merleau-Ponty takes musical metaphors from Bergson. Toadvine says that

> Merleau-Ponty appropriates Bergson's metaphor of musical structure to characterize the contrast between animal and human consciousness. Throughout *Structure*, Merleau-Ponty characterizes animal behavior as a "melodic unity" or a "kinetic melody," but only at the symbolic level of behavior characteristic of humanity do we find an orientation toward the theme as such. (Toadvine 2007b, 20)

Toadvine's essay presents a detailed analysis of the changing metaphors of melody and music in relation to the distinction between human and animal in Merleau-Ponty's thought. Toadvine traces the metaphor of melody from *The Structure of Behavior* through the *Nature* lectures and articulates the difference between the early and later work:

"Whereas Merleau-Ponty's earlier use of the musical metaphor had emphasized the fixity of the organism's melody by the prior structures of vital need, here [*Nature* lectures] the accent is on the ecological relationships formed between organism, other creatures, and their milieu" (Toadvine 2007b, 27).

4. For an excellent account of the development of Merleau-Ponty's thought on animals and animality, see Toadvine 2007b. Unfortunately, this essay had not been published when I wrote this chapter, but fortunately I found it as I was revising the book. Robert Vallier (2001) gives a detailed account of Merleau-Ponty's philosophy of animality in the *Nature* lectures and how it relates to his project as a whole.

5. For an excellent analysis of Merleau-Ponty's relation to Uexküll in the *Nature* lectures, see Vallier 2001. There, in a footnote, Vallier says that Merleau-Ponty's use of Uexküll is similar to Heidegger's, although he wasn't aware of Heidegger's writings when he gave his *Nature* lectures (Vallier 2001, 208). I disagree. As I argue in this chapter, Merleau-Ponty's interpretation of Uexküll takes him in a very different direction than Heidegger's.

6. Renaud Barbaras makes a similar argument in his interpretation of Merleau-Ponty's theory of nature (2001). Quoting Merleau-Ponty's *Nature* lectures on the formless world already apparent in living bodies prior to consciousness, he argues that once Merleau-Ponty begins his analysis with Nature, the world is no longer constituted by consciousness but is instituted through embodiment: "Thus the Merleau-Pontian reduction, in its original form, is understood as reduction to the incarnate subject; by means of Gestalt psychology and physiology, the perceived world is then attained as world, no longer constituted by, but correlative of or inhabited by this incarnate subject" (2001, 25, cf. 29). Given that Heidegger, like Merleau-Ponty, rejects the Husserlian reduction that yields the disembodied transcendental ego and that he, too, formulates an ontology that is not subject centered, his version of world formation should not be seen as constituted by consciousness but perhaps as a correlate of or inhabited by it. In a later article, however, Barbaras criticizes Merleau-Ponty's philosophy of life because it is still grounded in consciousness (see Barbaras 2003).

7. As Robert Vallier points out (2001, 198), already in *The Structure of Behavior*, Merleau-Ponty maintains that signification in the sense of being oriented to gives us the category of life without relying on vitalism.

8. Agamben quotes this passage from Linnaeus in chapter 7 of *The Open*, entitled "Taxonomies." Agamben identifies Linnaeus with an "optical machine" for recognizing man mirrored in the ape (2004, 27). Linnaeus refuses to describe *Homo* but offers the philosophical adage "know thyself." Agamben interprets this "know thyself" as an imperative for recognition that sets in motion the anthropological machine with which man identifies (produces) himself as human by distinguishing himself from animals:

Homo sapiens, then, is neither a clearly defined species nor a substance; it is, rather, a machine or device for producing the recognition of the human. . . . It is an optical machine constructed of a series of mirrors in which man, looking at himself, sees his own image always already deformed in the features of an ape. (Agamben 2004, 26–27)

It is noteworthy that Linnaeus put *Homo* in the general category of Anthropomorpha or "manlike" animals. Apes, lemurs, and bats also are part of this manlike category. Agamben suggests that identity as a struggle for recognition in some sense begins with this "know thyself." However, the irony of Linnaeus's "know thyself" is that his taxonomy would be read only by humans and that he need not describe them, since they were already well known to themselves.

9. Ted Toadvine delineates the difference between human consciousness and human language and animal signification (2007b). Obviously, I take Merleau-Ponty's analysis in a different direction, endorsing a type of continuity that allows for differences. For a discussion of why Merleau-Ponty's remarks on language in the *Nature* lectures are not meant to suggest that animals have language, see Vallier 2001, esp. 210.

10. For a discussion of what Merleau-Ponty means by lateral relation, see Vallier 2001.

11. Discussing Merleau-Ponty's philosophy of science, Nancy Holland describes what she calls the emergence of consciousness from nature:

Consciousness "emerges" seamlessly from biological life, just as the biological emerges from the physico-chemical. The perceptual/behavioral nexus from which they both arise takes the form of fields that give us a world meaningfully organized in terms of biological salience and solicitations of action, as well as in terms of cultural significances and possibilities of behavior. (2002, 31)

I would diverge from Holland's account in that the notion of lateral relationship implies that there is not an emergence or any kind of hierarchy but that life and consciousness arrive together. In this, I also diverge from Ted Toadvine's conclusions about the *Nature* lectures and the emergence of human consciousness from animal life (see Toadvine 2007a, esp. 50; 2007b, esp. 29–30). Although Toadvine quotes Merleau-Ponty ("Animality and human being are given only together"), he concludes that human life emerges from animal life (Merleau-Ponty 2003, 217; Toadvine 2007b, 30). In addition, Toadvine interprets Merleau-Ponty's remarks on the intertwining between animal and human as "entailing no fundamental ontological discontinuity" between them (2007a, 50), but I emphasize that strange kinship entails both continuity and discontinuity and that Merleau-Ponty's notion of intertwining as developed in his later work is intimately bound to his notion of chiasm, gap, or *écart,* which signals difference at the heart of this ontological continuity.

12. Ted Toadvine comments (2007b) on this passage in relation to Merleau-Ponty's metaphor of melody. He concludes his essay: "But perhaps an ontology of life cannot avoid listening more carefully to the upheavals and turbulence of Being, to the contrapuntal refrains that constitute each organism's characteristic style of 'singing the world'" (Toadvine 2007b, 30–31). I would add that perhaps an ontology of life *should* listen more carefully to the dissonances and contrapuntals that disrupt the harmony of the world.

13. Robert Vallier describes the subtleties of Merleau-Ponty's attempts to navigate between mechanism and vitalism in the *Nature* lectures in his excellent essay "The Indiscernible Joining" (2001).

14. Mauro Carbone interprets Merleau-Ponty's metaphor (following Uexküll) of a melody singing itself as a way of avoiding both mechanism and vitalism. Moreover, he says that this metaphor captures a relationship before the distinction between activity and passivity that inhabits the dualism of subject and object (2004, 30). Carbone concludes that Merleau-Ponty presents a notion of the "listening eye"—what he calls *voyance*—that rejects the separation between the activity of seeing and the passivity of listening (38). Many of the ways in which Merleau-Ponty mixes the senses and makes all sense perception dependent on relationships among the various senses and between organisms and their environments undermine the traditional oppositions between activity and passivity.

15. Robert Vallier points out that Merleau-Ponty's notion of the flesh (*la chair*) is a translation of Husserl's *Leib,* or "life." Vallier concludes that regarding Merleau-Ponty: "In that this ontology [of difference] would thus also be *of the flesh,* then the principle of difference on which it is grounded would also be a principle of life" (2001, 205, italics in original). Renaud Barbaras and Ted Toadvine also describe Merleau-Ponty's philosophy as a philosophy of life (see Barbaras 2003; Toadvine 2007a).

16. See n. 11.

17. In *Phenomenology of Perception,* Merleau-Ponty says, "Toute perception a lieu dans une atmosphère de généralité et se donne à nous comme anonyme" (1945, 249; 2002, 249–51).

18. Donna Haraway criticizes (e.g., 2004) the bloody and violent nature of traditional notions of kinship and suggests the ways in which we must reconceive of kinship to include all sorts of families and critters. Deleuze and Guattari describe an alternative to Oedipal kinship relations using their concept "becoming-animal" (1987). Emphasizing becoming over being, they say that becoming-animal "is not an evolution, at least not an evolution by descent and filiation. Becoming produces nothing by filiation; all filiation is imaginary" (1987, 238). Although I do not engage in a sustained analysis of Haraway or of Deleuze and Guattari, I am sympathetic to their attempts to reconceive of kinship relations.

10. Stopping the Anthropological Machine

1. Matthew Calarco makes a similar argument in relation to Agamben's earlier work (Calarco 2000, 2008), and he also discusses (2008) the relation of *The Open* to Agamben's earlier work.

2. For a discussion of Agamben's religious imagery in *The Open,* see Mendieta forthcoming.

3. For example, Dinesh Wadiwel asks why Agamben does not consider the role of women in the anthropological machine, particularly in light of feminist criticism that demonstrates the "symbolic links between animality and femininity, either through an association of woman with nature, the body and the passions [e.g., Luce Irigaray and Genevive Lloyd] or a direct connection between violence against women and violence against animals [e.g., Carol Adams]" (Wadiwel 2004, par. 32).

4. For a discussion of Agamben's distinction between man and human, see Wadiwel 2004.

5. See, e.g., J. M. Coetzee's *The Lives of Animals* (1999), in which Elizabeth Costello, the main character, argues that slaughterhouses are a form of animal Holocaust that rivals the Nazis' attempts to exterminate Jews. See also Charles Patterson's *Eternal Treblinka* (2002), in which he says that in relation to animals, all of us are Nazis; see also Wadiwel's commentary on Patterson (2004).

6. Dinesh Wadiwel also worries that sometimes Agamben sounds as if he is arguing for a more absolute separation between man and animal (Wadiwel 2004). But he finds reassurance in Agamben's concluding remarks on Titian's lovers, which, he believes, indicates that Agamben is proposing a philosophy of love as a way out of biopower and a way to stop the anthropological machine (see Wadiwel 2004).

7. Matthew Calarco gives an excellent analysis (2001) of Agamben's earlier work, before *The Open,* in relation to Heidegger, particularly on the question of the animal. It is almost as if Agamben's *The Open* is a response to Calarco's earlier challenge. See also Calarco 2008.

8. Following Derrida, we might also ask what kind of power the passive "letting be" is that is definitive of Dasein. Is it that animals cannot be passive enough? That they lack the "ability" or "power" of passivity, the ability or power to "let it be"? Derrida takes this tack in relation to the possibility of animal suffering. If humans are distinct from animals in their capacity to suffer pain—or, in Heidegger's discourse, melancholy—then what kind of strange power is this power to suffer? (see Derrida 2008).

9. Here I am applying Kalpana Seshadri-Crooks's analysis (2000) of whiteness as a transcendental signifier to the notion of humanness.

10. Wadiwel (2002) develops a persuasive account of how we might apply Agamben's notion of bare life to animals and concludes that for Agamben it is not a matter of reinstituting a gap between humans and nonhuman animals but of eliminating the gap. Only by eliminating the gap will the zone of indetermination and the risks of the in-between category be eliminated. I am more sympathetic to Wadiwel's interpretation of Agamben than to Agamben's explicit discussions of animals and the risks of treating humans like them.

11. The distinction between metaphysical separationism and biological continuism comes from Leonard Lawlor's book on Derrida's animals (2007).

12. For a helpful discussion of Merleau-Ponty's phenomenology as a philosophy of life, see Vallier 2001, in which Vallier says that

the focus on behavior allows us to say that the motif in the name of which Merleau-Ponty engages this critique is that of *life* or the *living; it is *life* that escapes from biological discourse when it views the organism as a collection of parts, and no catalogue of parts will disclose the life of the whole. (2001, 190, italics in original)

13. I recently heard a report on National Public Radio that even plants recognize their kin. When neighboring plants are related to them, they are not as aggressive in taking

water and nutrients from the soil as they are when their neighbors are not relatives. See "Researchers Find Discriminating Plants," June 10, 2008.

11. Psychoanalysis as Animal By-product

1. In an essay on Freud's preference for single-celled organisms, Judith Roof claims that there are "sparse" references to animals in Freud's work. I disagree. Animals are everywhere in Freud's work, although they may not be the stuff of biological science preferred by Roof. Roof's analysis of the role of single-celled organisms in what she calls Freud's "Cellular Romance" is provocative and insightful:

> Occupying a large share of Freud's sparse references to animals, the single-celled organism both is and is not "human"; its difference from humanity both is and is not a positive feature. This ambivalent status makes the example of the protista valuable as a link between the human and the animal, as well as between the animate and the inanimate, the simple and the complex, the mortal and the immortal, its dual position guaranteeing the commonality of fundamental processes throughout a range of species. At the same time, the protist is the anthropomorphized subject of a psychoanalysis as Freud interprets its impulses, demonstrating how even the microbiological is ultimately a mirror for the human. (2003, 102)

2. Although she did not have time to elaborate her claim in the context of her conference presentation at the Society for Phenomenology and Existential Philosophy in 2007, Elissa Marder argued, "As it happens, throughout Freud's work, animals do the lion's share of the theoretical work in the meta-psychology for the conceptual foundation of the idea of death, castration, and consequently the difference between the sexes" (see 2009b). Her formation of the role of animals in Freud's work helped me clarify my thesis as I was revising this chapter. Marder draws these conclusions in the context of thinking about the relation between maternity and death in Freud's writings.

3. My thanks to Elaine Miller for articulating the problematic in these terms and for discussing this chapter with me. Her comments, along with those of a group of faculty and graduate students at Miami University of Ohio, were helpful in revising this chapter.

4. For an interesting discussion of how Freud develops the theory of displacement in *Totem and Taboo,* see DiCenso 1999, esp. chap. 4.

5. Kalpana Seshadri-Crooks (2003) discusses the distinction between killing and murder instituted by the primal murder.

6. Gary Genosko discusses the circular reasoning of Freud's substitution of the animal for father, and vice versa (1993, esp. 627).

7. Edwin Wallace (Wallace 1983), among others, has shown how Freud's theories and the anthropological theories on which his theories are based have been discredited. See also Barnes 1959; DiCenso 1999; and Lewis 1988.

8. For a discussion and criticism of the notion of contemporary ancestors, see Oliver 2001.

9. Elissa Marder describes the circular reasoning of Freud's theory of castration in relation to animals and animal phobia:

> Sometimes he seems to *prove* the theory of castration anxiety based on his analysis of the clinical example, and sometimes he posits castration and then *explains* the phobia on the basis of the theory. . . . But the argument that the animal phobia is *both* a function of pre-historic knowledge of castration *and* a specific response to childhood events depends, once again, on the presumption of an ambiguous "special proximity" between boy children and large animals, and the specific psychic malleability of the figure of the animal itself. (2009a, forthcoming, italics in original)

10. For general discussions of Freud's theory of phobia, see Compton 1992; Lewis 1988 (she discusses the evolution of phobias and revises and updates Freud's theories using current research in both psychology and anthropology); Snaith 1968 (he relates Freud's theory to contemporary theories of phobia); and Spira 1991 (he traces the evolution of the concept of phobia in Freud's work). For a discussion of anthropology since Freud, see Barnes 1959.

11. Elissa Marder has written an extensive essay analyzing the role of animals and the animal in Freud's presentation of the Wolf-Man case. She argues,

> Animal figures operate at every level of the case and intervene in complicated ways in its conceptual framework. Indeed, I hope to demonstrate that animals occupy a critical, albeit somewhat obscure, role in many if not most of the major theoretical issues raised by the case. . . . I hope to argue that paradoxically, the animals in the text serve as strange indices to the very specificity of the human psyche. . . . Bizarrely, in what follows, it will emerge that one of the defining traits of being human is the incorporation of animal figures within the psyche; these internal animal figures are uncanny traces of our radical alterity and separation from animals. (Marder 2009a, forthcoming)

12. For an insightful discussion of the psychoanalytic import of Freud's comparison of animals and children, particularly in the case of the Wolf-Man, see Marder 2009a, in which she identifies a "failed recognition" of species difference in children and Freud's savages that is a prerequisite for representation and thereby humanity: "In general, we do not suspect that wolves commonly dream of little boys even if little boys commonly dream of wolves" (Marder 2009a, forthcoming).

13. In her essay "The Bestiary and the Primal Scene," Elissa Marder develops a provocative and insightful interpretation of Freud's concern with the reality status of the primal scene witnessed by the Wolf-Man. There, she discusses the substitutability of humans for animals necessary for the production of sexual difference as Freud describes it. She argues that "the observation of sexual difference in the primal scene is predicated upon" confu-

sion between humans and animals and that "the only way human sexual difference can be perceived or represented in the scene is through the mediation and substitution of animal figures for human ones" (2009a, forthcoming).

In his essay "Freud's Bestiary," Gary Genosko also observes that Freud says that children are like animals in order to criticize Deleuze and Guattari's suggestion that Freud does not consider "becoming animal" only a mere resemblance (1993, 605). Genosko also responds to Deleuze and Guattari's analysis of Freud's replacement of the Wolf-Man's wolves with domesticated dogs by claiming that they miss what is crucial through their insistence on the wolf as a pack animal, namely, the real wolves in the young Russian life (1993, 613).

14. Elissa Marder (2009a) provides a stunning interpretation of the Wolf dream in relation to the role of animals as constitutive of humanity.

15. Kalpana Seshadri-Crooks discusses the connection between food and sex in her reading of the Lacanian supplement to Freud's

> Lacan seems to suggest that the Freudian myth of the primal horde is also the myth of the constitution of the cannibal and the bestialist—the transgressors of the law before the law. This submerged matrix of prohibitions comes more sharply into view when we consider that one of the functions of the moral law is to establish a mutually exclusive opposition between those we use for food and those we use for sex (that is, we may not have sex with the food object or turn our sexual object into food). In *The Savage Mind,* Claude Lévi-Strauss, though not on the track of species difference, acknowledges the "profound analogy which people throughout the world seem to find between copulation and eating." He provides several examples of languages, including French, which use the same word to denote both activities. . . . It is not so much that food prohibitions are prior in some way, but that the simultaneity of the prohibitions against anthropophagy and bestiality effectively disarticulates sex from food, leaving us with little but the meaty metaphor of ingestion and union. The extraordinary depth of the interrelation of these prohibitions is perhaps most evident in our relations with the family pet, which, like one's kin, may not be regarded as food or sex object. (2003, 103–4)

16. In the context of discussing the link between maternity and death in Freud's writing, Elissa Marder made a similar point in her presentation at the Society for Phenomenology and Existential Philosophy conference in Chicago, 2007:

> As feminist readers of *Totem and Taboo* have long observed, in this story about the founding of religion and politics, women have no active role to play. . . . But my interest in this text is somewhat different. Moving all to quickly, I would like to suggest that the "erasure" of the maternal and the feminine with which *Totem and Taboo* famously ends is both derived from and challenged by the complicated inscription of animals, maternity, eating and death throughout its earlier sections. (2009b)

Marder also discusses (2009a) the link between the figure of mother in relation to the figure of animal, arguing that in Freud's interpretation of the Wolf-Man's encounter with the primal scene, that the woman is more of an animal than the man.

17. Marsha Garrison points out that Hans is especially afraid of horses with carts, which both he and Freud associate with a "stork box" or his mother's pregnant belly (see Garrison 1978, 526).

18. Marsha Garrison reread Freud's case of Little Hans and concluded that "Hans's death wish against Hanna is, then, the most plausible roots of this fear [of horses]" (Garrison 1978, 531). As we will see in the next chapter, Julia Kristeva reinterprets Little Hans's fear in relation to the maternal body which, like Freud's interpretation, ignores the significant role of Hans's sister.

19. In terms of Julia Kristeva's theory of abjection, which I will discuss in the next chapter, we could say that the Wolf-Man's sister is his own abject self. See also Genosko's discussion of the relation between wolves and sisters in the case of the Wolf-Man (1993, esp. 616).

20. Freud takes this notion of the primal horde from Darwin. For a discussion of the tensions in Freud's theories of sexuality and instinct that result from the influence of Darwin, see Ritvo 1990 and Roof 2003.

21. For an insightful discussion of cannibalism and bestiality as the two prohibitions hidden behind the taboos against incest and murder instituted by the murder of the father, see Kalpana Seshadri-Crooks 2003.

12. Animal Abjects, Maternal Abjects

1. Freud says:

The strangest fact seems to be that anyone who has transgressed one of these prohibitions himself acquires the characteristic of being prohibited—as though the whole of the dangerous had been transferred over to him. This power is attached to all special individuals, such as kings, priests or newborn babies, to all exceptional states, such as the physical states of menstruation, puberty or birth, and to all uncanny things, such as sickness and death and what is associated with them through their power of infection or contagion. (Freud 1913, 22)

It is noteworthy that Deleuze and Guattari also discuss sex and reproduction in terms of contagion (1987, 241).

2. For introductions to Kristeva's notion of abjection, see McAfee 2004 and Oliver 1993.

3. For insightful and provocative discussions of Freud's mythology, see Paul Ricoeur's *Freud and Philosophy* (1970) and James DiCenso's *The Other Freud* (1999).

4. Kristeva uses the metaphor of the "stray" throughout *Powers of Horror* (1980) and *Tales of Love* (1987).

5. Elissa Marder makes this argument in her analysis of Freud's Wolf-Man case and concludes:

The child comes into contact with human sexuality and confronts sexual difference only when the humans involved do not appear to act like humans, but like animals. Once again, human sexuality becomes visible only when humans behave like animals. In the dream of wolves, therefore, the animal figures are distorted substitutes for human figures that are themselves imitating animal postures. (2009a, forthcoming)

Deleuze and Guattari's insistence that "becoming-animal" is neither mimesis nor imitation is relevant here (1987).

6. For discussions of Kristeva's reinterpretation of Freud's case of Little Hans, see Beardsworth 2004, 84–90; and DiCenso 1999, 69–70.

Deleuze and Guattari also interpret Little Hans's fear of horse as a network of affective relations. They say, "So just what is the becoming-horse of Little Hans? Hans is also taken up in an assemblage: his mother's bed, the paternal element, the house, the café across the street, the nearby warehouse, the street, the right to go out onto the street" (1987, 257).

7. For an insightful analysis of Kristeva's reinterpretation of Freud's theory of phobia, particularly in the case of Little Hans, see Beardsworth 2004, esp. 84–90. Beardsworth concludes: "Kristeva acknowledges Freud's indications of the presence of the oedipal problematic in phobia, but equally shows the phobic object to be a hallucinatory metaphor tied to unsymbolized drives. She calls the hallucinatory metaphor a 'proto-writing', and little Hans—deprived of others—is stage director of his own drama" (2004, 90). Beardsworth takes up Kristeva's analysis of the relation between writing and phobia.

8. Marsha Garrison makes a similar argument in her reinterpretation of Little Hans's phobia, maintaining that Hans is afraid of his mother, represented by the horse, and seeks protection from her from his father (1978, 525, 527).

9. This maternal anguish is the infant's relation to the not-yet or pre- or semi-objects of food, air, and movement that it needs. The infant experiences the deprivation of the breast, hunger, and other needs that are not satisfied "on time." As a result, the anguish or fear it feels in connection with these bodily needs or wants are associated with the maternal body and, if we follow Freud and Lacan, eventually with the fear of castration (interpreted narrowly as the fear of losing the penis or broadly as the fear of losing the object—or agent—of satisfaction). Marsha Garrison reinterprets (1978) Little Hans's phobia as a result of a fear of castration from his mother and not his father. Garrison argues that the case history demonstrates that the horse represents the maternal and not paternal threat. She concludes that ultimately Little Hans's forbidden desire for the death of his sister prompts his fear of punishment from the horse/mother.

10. For a discussion of the relation between Kristeva and Klein, see Doane and Hodges 1992.

11. Kristeva challenges some of Lacan's suggestions that language is always already there. She argues that this position discounts the drives and the primary processes that existed before the secondary processes (2000, 42–43). Her analysis of the unnamable and the

presymbolic "symbol" of the phobic animal also imply her divergence from Lacan's position on Freud's discussion of totemism in which Lacan insists that the names of the father (and mother, etc.) must exist before the totemic substitution.

12. Even while continually reminding us of the wanting or longing or negativity at the heart of language, Kristeva holds out hope that words can be connected to affects in ways that enable sublimation, love, and joy. She does point out, however, that the fetishism involved in language acquisition may be the only unanalyzable fetishism (1982, 37).

13. Here she follows anthropologist Célestin Bouglé (see Kristeva 1982, 81).

14. For a helpful discussion of Kristeva's theory of religion and the sacred in relation to Freud's, see Beardsworth 2004.

15. Sara Beardsworth discusses Kristeva's analysis of biblical abomination, saying that for Kristeva, "biblical abomination therefore iterates primal repression, carrying it into the very constitution of symbolic Law and, at the same time, revealing that the latter produces abjection, without end" (2004, 135).

16. For discussions of Kristeva's contributions to psychoanalysis pertaining to the role of the mother and the maternal function, see, e.g., Beardsworth 2004; McAfee 2004; Oliver 1993; Reineke 1997; Weir 1993; Wiseman 1993.

17. For an extended examination of, and engagement with, Kristeva's notion of creativity, genius, and revolt, see Oliver 2004.

BIBLIOGRAPHY

Abraham, Nicolas, and Maria Torok. 1986. *The Wolf Man's Magic Word.* Trans. N. Rand. Minneapolis: University of Minnesota Press.

Achenbach, Joel. 2003. "Biggest Cats in Town: Taking Risks That Were More Than Artistic, Siegfried & Roy Remade Las Vegas." *Washington Post,* October 26, D1.

Adams, Carol. 1990. *The Sexual Politics of Meat: A Feminist–Vegetarian Critical Theory.* New York: Continuum Publishing.

Adams, Carol, and Josephine Donovan, eds. 1995. *Animals & Women: Feminist Theoretical Explorations.* Durham, N.C.: Duke University Press.

Agamben, Giorgio. 1996. "Beyond Human Rights." Trans. Cesare Casarino. In *Radical Thought in Italy: A Potential Politics,* ed. Paolo Virno and Michael Hardt, 159–66. Minneapolis: University of Minnesota Press.

———. 1998. *Homo Sacer: Sovereign Power and Bare Life.* Trans. Daniel Heller-Roazen. Stanford, Calif.: Stanford University Press.

———. 2004. *The Open: Man and Animal.* Trans. Kevin Attell. Stanford, Calif.: Stanford University Press.

Allen, Jeffner. 1995. "A Response to a Letter from Peg Simons, December 1993." In *Feminist Interpretations of Simone de Beauvoir,* ed. Margaret A. Simons, 113–35. University Park: Pennsylvania State University Press.

Andrew, Barbara. 2003. "Beauvoir's Place in Philosophical Thought." In *The Cambridge Companion to Beauvoir,* ed. Claudia Card, 24–44. Cambridge: Cambridge University Press.

Armour, Ellen. 1997. "Crossing the Boundaries Between Deconstruction, Feminism, and Religion." In *Feminist Interpretations of Derrida,* ed. Nancy Holland, 193–214. University Park: Pennsylvania State University Press.

Arp, Kristana. 1995. "Beauvoir's Concept of Bodily Alienation." In *Feminist Interpretations of Simone de Beauvoir,* ed. Margaret A. Simons, 161–77. University Park: Pennsylvania State University Press.

———. 2001. *The Bonds of Freedom: Simone de Beauvoir's Existentialist Ethics.* Chicago: Open Court Publishing.

Baker, Steve. 2002. "What Does Becoming Animal Look Like?" In *Representing Animals,* ed. Nigel Rothfels, 67–98. Bloomington: Indiana University Press.

Barbaras, Renaud. 2001. "Merleau-Ponty and Nature." Trans. Paul Milan. *Research in Phenomenology* 31:22–38.

———. 2003. "Life and Perceptual Intentionality." Trans. John Cogan. *Research in Phenomenology* 33:157–66.

Barnes, J. A. 1959. "Anthropology After Freud." *Australasian Journal of Philosophy* 37, no. 1:14–27.

Bauer, Nancy. 2001. *Simone de Beauvoir, Philosophy and Feminism.* New York: Columbia University Press.

Beardsworth, Sara. 2004. *Julia Kristeva: Psychoanalysis and Modernity.* Albany: State University of New York Press.

Behnke, Elizabeth. 1999. "From Merleau-Ponty's Concept of Nature to an Interspecies Practice of Peace." In *Animal Others: On Ethics, Ontology, and Animal Life,* ed. H. Peter Steeves, 93–116. Albany: State University of New York Press.

Berger, Anne-Emmaneulle. 2005. "Sexing Differances." *differences: A Journal of Feminist Cultural Studies* 16, no. 3:52–67.

Berger, John. 1980. "Why Look at Animals?" In *About Looking,* by John Berger, 1–26. New York: Pantheon Books.

Bergoffen, Debra. 1995. "Out from Under: Beauvoir's Philosophy of the Erotic." In *Feminist Interpretations of Simone De Beauvoir,* ed. Margaret A. Simons, 179–92. Philadelphia: University of Pennsylvania Press.

———. 1997. *The Philosophy of Simone de Beauvoir: Gendered Phenomenologies, Erotic Generosities.* Albany: State University of New York Press.

———. 2000. "Simone de Beauvoir: Disrupting the Metonymy of Gender." In *Resistance, Flight, Creation: Feminist Enactments of French,* ed. Dorothea Olkowski, 97–112. Ithaca, N.Y.: Cornell University Press.

Birke, Lynda, and Luciana Parisi. 1999. "Animals, Becoming." In *Animal Others: On Ethics, Ontology, and Animal Life,* ed. H. Peter Steeves, 55–74. Albany, N.Y.: State University of New York Press.

Birraux, Annie. 2007. "L'animal et le developpement psychique." *Enfances PSY:*8–14.

Bourne, Joel. 2007. "When Damsels Don't Need Knights." *National Geographic,* March 2007, 23.

Brison, Susan. 2003. "Beauvoir and Feminism: Interviews and Reflections." In *The Cambridge Companion to Simone de Beauvoir,* ed. Claudia Card, 198–207. Cambridge: Cambridge University Press.

Brophy, Brigit. 2004. "The Rights of Animals." In *Animal Rights: A Historical Anthology,* ed. Andrew Linzey and Paul Barry Clarke, 156–62. New York: Columbia University Press.

Brown, Lori. 2007. "Becoming-Animal in the Flesh: Expanding the Ethical Reach of Deleuze and Guattari's Tenth Plateau" *PhaenEx: Journal of Existential and Phenomenological Theory and Culture* 2, no. 2 (fall/winter):260–78.

Brown, Wendy. 2002. "Suffering the Paradoxes of Rights." In *Left Legalism/Left Critique*, ed. Wendy Brown and Janet Halley, 420–34. Durham, N.C.: Duke University Press.

Buber, Martin. 1958. *I and Thou.* Trans. Ronald Gregor Smith. New York: Scribner's.

Buchanan, Brett. 2007. "Do Animals Exist? On the Essence and Existence of Humans and Animals." *Proteus* (spring):21–26.

Bulliet, Richard. 2005. *Hunters, Herders, and Hamburgers.* New York: Columbia University Press.

Butler, Judith. 1986a. "Sex and Gender in Simone de Beauvoir's *Second Sex.*" *Yale French Studies* 72:35–49.

———. 1986b. "Variations on Sex and Gender: Beauvoir, Wittig, and Foucault." *Praxis International* 5:505–16.

———. 1989a. "The Body Politics of Julia Kristeva." *Hypatia: Journal of Feminist Philosophy* 3, no. 3:104–18.

———. 1989b. "Foucault and the Paradox of Bodily Inscriptions." *Journal of Philosophy* 86, no. 11:601–7.

———. 1989c. "Gendering the Body: Beauvoir's Philosophical Contribution." In *Women, Knowledge, and Reality: Explorations in Feminist Philosophy.* ed. Ann Garry and Marilyn Pearsall, 253–62. Boston: Unwin Hyman.

———. 1989d. "Sexual Ideology and Phenomenological Description: A Feminist Critique of Merleau-Ponty's *Phenomenology of Perception.*" In *The Thinking Muse: Feminism and Modern French Philosophy*, ed. Jeffner Allen and Marion Young, 85–100. Bloomington: Indiana University Press.

———. 1990. *Gender Trouble: Feminism and the Subversion of Identity.* New York: Routledge.

———. 2000. *Antigone's Claim: Kinship Between Life and Death.* New York: Columbia University Press.

———. 2004a. *Precarious Life: The Powers of Mourning and Violence.* London: Verso.

———. 2004b. *Undoing Gender.* New York: Routledge.

Calarco, Matthew. 2000. "On the Borders of Language and Death: Agamben and the Question of the Animal." *Philosophy Today* 44:91–96.

———. 2004a. "Deconstruction Is Not Vegetarianism: Humanism, Subjectivity, and Animal Ethics." *Continental Philosophy Review* 37:175–201.

———. 2004b. "Heidegger's Zoontology." In *Animal Philosophy*, ed. Peter Atterton and Matthew Calarco, 18–30. London: Continuum Press.

———. 2008. *Zoographies: The Question of the Animal from Heidegger to Derrida.* New York: Columbia University Press.

Caputo, John. 1997. "Dreaming of the Innumerable: Derrida, Drucilla Cornell, and the Dance of Gender." In *Derrida and Feminism,* ed. Ellen Feder, Mary Rawlinson, and Emily Zakin, 141–60. New York: Routledge.

Carbone, Mauro. 2004. *The Thinking of the Sensible: Merleau-Ponty's A-Philosophy.* Evanston, Ill.: Northwestern University Press.

Carroll, David. 2006. "Remains of Algeria: Justice, Hospitality, Politics." *Modern Language Notes* 121:808–27.

Chanter, Tina. 1997. "On Not Reading Derrida's Texts." In *Derrida and Feminism,* ed. Ellen Feder, Mary Rawlinson, and Emily Zakin, 87–114. New York: Routledge.

Chaperon, Sylvie. 1995. "Simone de Beauvoir, *entre le naturalisme et l'universalisme, entre le sexisme et le feminism.*" In *La place des femme: Les enjeux de l'identité et de l'égalité au regard des sciences sociales,* by *EPHESIA,* 347–51. Paris: La Découverte.

Cheah, Pheng. 2005. "Obscure Gifts: On Jacques Derrida." *differences: A Journal of Feminist Cultural Studies* 16, no. 3:41–51.

Coetzee, J. M. 1999. *The Lives of Animals.* Princeton, N.J.: Princeton University Press.

Collier, Jane Fishburne, and Sylvia Junko Yanagisako, eds. 1987. *Gender and Kinship: Essays Toward a Unified Analysis.* Stanford, Calif.: Stanford University Press.

Compton, Allan. 1992. "The Psychoanalytic View of Phobias." *Psychoanalytic Quarterly* 61:206–29.

Conklin, Beth. 2001. *Consuming Grief: Compassionate Cannibalism in an Amazonian Society.* Austin: University of Texas Press.

Cook, Alexander. 2002. "Jean-Jacques Rousseau and 'Exotic Botany.'" *Eighteenth-Century Life* 26, no. 3:181–201.

De Beauvoir, Simone. 1949a. *Le deuxième sexe.* Paris: Gallimard.

———. 1949b. *The Second Sex.* Trans. H. M. Parshley. New York: Random House.

———. 1972. *The Coming of Age.* Trans. Patrick O'Brian. New York: Putnam.

———. 2004. *Philosophical Writings.* Ed. Margaret Simons. Chicago: University of Illinois Press.

Deleuze, Gilles, and Félix Guattari. 1977. *Anti-Oedipus.* Trans. R. Hurley et al. New York: Viking.

———. 1986. *Kafka: Toward a Minor Literature.* Trans. Dana Polan. Minneapolis: University of Minnesota Press.

———. 1987. *A Thousand Plateaus.* Trans. Brian Massumi. Minneapolis: University of Minnesota Press.

De Man, Paul. 1971. *Blindness and Insight.* Trans. Wlad Godzich. Minneapolis: University of Minnesota Press.

———. 1983. "The Rhetoric of Blindness: Jacques Derrida's Reading of Rousseau." In *Blindness and Insight,* by Paul De Man, 102–41. Minneapolis: University of Minnesota Press.

Dennett, Daniel. 1998. *Brain Children.* Cambridge, Mass.: MIT Press.

Derrida, Jacques. 1967. *De la grammatologie.* Paris: Les éditions de minuit.

———. 1972. *Dissemination.* Trans. Barbara Johnson. Chicago: University of Chicago Press.

———. 1974. *Of Grammatology.* Trans. Gayatri Spivak. Baltimore: Johns Hopkins University Press.

———. 1982. "Différance" (1968). In *Margins of Philosophy,* trans. Alan Bass. Chicago: University of Chicago Press.

———. 1986. *Glas.* Trans. John P. Leavey Jr. and Richard Rand. Lincoln: University of Nebraska Press.

———. 1987a. *"Geschlecht* II: Heidegger's Hand." In *Deconstruction and Philosophy: The Texts of Jacques Derrida,* ed. John Sallis and trans. John P. Leavey Jr., 161–96. Chicago: University of Chicago Press.

———. 1987b. "On Reading Heidegger: An Outline of Remarks to the Essex Colloquium." *Research in Phenomenology,* no. 17:171–85.

———. 1990. "Women in the Beehive: A Seminar with Jacques Derrida." In *Discourses,* ed. Russell Ferguson et al., 115–28. Cambridge, Mass.: MIT Press.

———. 1991a. "Choreographies." In *A Derrida Reader,* ed. Peggy Kamuf and trans. Ruben Bevezdivin, 440-456. New York: Columbia University Press.

———. 1991b. "Eating Well, or the Calculation of the Subject: An Interview with Jacques Derrida." In *Who Comes After the Subject,* ed. Eduardo Cadava, Peter Connor, and Jean-Luc Nancy, 96–119. New York: Routledge.

———. 1991c. *"Geschlecht:* Sexual Difference, Ontological Difference." In *A Derrida Reader,* ed. Peggy Kamuf and trans. Ruben Bevezdivin, 380–402. New York: Columbia University Press.

———. 1993. "Circumfession." In *Jacques Derrida,* trans. Geoffrey Bennington. Chicago: University of Chicago Press.

———. 1994. "Fourmis." In *Lectures de la différence sexuelle,* ed. Mara Negròn. Paris: Des femmes.

———. 1996. *Le monolinguisme de l'autre.* Paris: Galilée.

———.1997a. *Adieu: To Emmanuel Levinas.* Trans. Pascale-Anne Brault and Michael Naas. Stanford, Calif.: Stanford University Press.

———. 1997b. *The Politics of Friendship.* Trans. George Collins. New York: Verso.

———. 1998. *Monolingualism of the Other, or The Prosthesis of Origin.* Trans. Patrick Mensah. Stanford, Calif.: Stanford University Press.

———. 1999. "L'animal que donc je suis (à suivre)." In *L'animal autobiographique,* ed. Marie-Louise Mallet, 251–301. Paris: Galilée.

———. 2000. *Of Hospitality: Anne Dufourmantelle Invites Jacques Derrida to Respond.* Trans. Rachel Bowlby. Stanford, Calif.: Stanford University Press.

———. 2001a. *For What Tomorrow.* Trans. Jeff Fort. Stanford, Calif.: Stanford University Press.

———. 2001b. *On Cosmopolitanism and Forgiveness.* Trans. Mark Dooley and Michael Hughes. London; New York : Routledge.

———. 2001c. *Questioning God.* Ed. John D. Caputo, Mark Dooley, and Michael J. Scanlon. Bloomington: Indiana University Press.

———. 2002. "The Animal That Therefore I Am (More to Follow)." Trans. David Wills. *Critical Inquiry* 28, no. 2:369–418.

———. 2003. "And Say the Animal Responded?" In *Zoontologies: The Question of the Animal,* ed. Cary Wolfe and trans. David Wills, 121–46. Minneapolis: University of Minnesota Press.

———. 2004. "The Animal That Therefore I Am (More to Follow)." In *Animal Philosophy*, ed. Peter Atterton and Matthew Calacrco, 113–28. London: Continuum Press.

———. 2005. *Rogues*. Trans. Pascale-Anne Brault and Michael Naas. Stanford, Calif.: Stanford University Press.

———. 2006. *L'animal que donc je suis*. Paris: Galilée.

———. 2008. *The Animal That Therefore I Am*. Trans. David Wills. New York: Fordham University Press.

Deutscher, Penelope. 1997. *Yielding Gender: Feminism, Deconstruction and the History of Philosophy*. New York: Routledge.

———. 2003. "Beauvoir's *Old Age*." In *The Cambridge Companion to Simone de Beauvoir*, ed. Claudia Card, 286–304. Cambridge: Cambridge University Press.

Diamond, Cora. 1978. "Eating Meat and Eating People." *Philosophy* 53, no. 206:465–79.

———. 2001. "Injustice and Animals." In *Slow Cures and Bad Philosophers*, ed. Carl Elliott, 118–48. Durham, N.C.: Duke University Press.

———. 2008. "The Difficulty of Reality and the Difficulty of Philosophy." In *Philosophy and Animal Life*, by Stanley Cavell et al., 43–90. New York: Columbia University Press.

DiCenso, James. 1999. *The Other Freud*. New York: Routledge.

Doane, Janice, and Devon Hodges. 1992. *From Klein to Kristeva*. Ann Arbor: University of Michigan Press.

Dooley, Mark. 2001. "The Catastrophe of Memory." In *Questioning God*, ed. John Caputo, Mark Dooley, and Michael Scanlon, 129–49. Bloomington: Indiana University Press.

Dunayer, Joan. 1995. "Sexist Words, Speciesist Roots." In *Animals and Women*, ed. Carol Adams and Joan Dunayer, 11–31. Durham, N.C.: Duke University Press.

Fallaize, Elizabeth. 2001. "A Saraband of Imagery." In *The Existential Phenomenology of Simone de Beauvoir*, ed. Wendy O'Brien and Lester Embree, 67–84. Boston: Kluwer.

Fausto-Sterling, Anne. 1979. *Myths of Gender: Biological Theories About Women and Men*. New York: Norton.

Francione, Gary, and Alan Watson. 2000. *Introduction to Animal Rights: Your Child or the Dog?* Philadelphia: Temple University Press.

Franck, Didier. 1991. "Being and Living." In *Who Comes After the Subject*, ed. Eduardo Cadava, Peter Connor, and Jean-Luc Nancy, 135–47. New York: Routledge.

Freud. Sigmund. 1900. "The Interpretation of Dreams." Trans. James Strachey. In *The Standard Edition of the Complete Psychological Works of Sigmund Freud*, vols. 4 and 5. London: Hogarth Press.

———. 1909a. "Analysis of a Phobia in a Five-Year-Old Boy." Trans. James Strachey. In *The Standard Edition of the Complete Psychological Works of Sigmund Freud*, vol. 10. London: Hogarth Press.

———. 1909b. "Notes upon a Case of Obsessional Neurosis." Trans. James Strachey. In *The Standard Edition of the Complete Psychological Works of Sigmund Freud*, vol. 10. London: Hogarth Press.

———. 1913. *Totem and Taboo*. Trans. James Strachey. New York: Norton.

———. 1915. "Instincts and Their Vicissitudes." Trans. James Strachey. In *The Standard Edition of the Complete Psychological Works of Sigmund Freud*, vol. 14. London: Hogarth Press.

———. 1918. "From the History of an Infantile Neurosis." Trans. James Strachey. In *The Standard Edition of the Complete Psychological Works of Sigmund Freud*, vol. 17. London: Hogarth Press.

———. 1919. "The Uncanny." Trans. James Strachey. In *The Standard Edition of the Complete Psychological Works of Sigmund Freud*, vol. 13. London: Hogarth Press.

———. 1926. "Inhibitions, Symptoms and Anxiety." Trans. James Strachey. In *The Standard Edition of the Complete Psychological Works of Sigmund Freud*, vol. 20. London: Hogarth Press.

———. 1932. "Anxiety and Instinctual Life." Trans. James Strachey. In *The Standard Edition of the Complete Psychological Works of Sigmund Freud*, vol. 22. London: Hogarth Press.

———. 1933. "New Introductory Lectures on Psychoanalysis." Trans. James Strachey. In *The Standard Edition of the Complete Psychological Works of Sigmund Freud*, vol. 22. London: Hogarth Press.

———. 1939. "Moses and Monotheism." Trans. James Strachey. In *The Standard Edition of the Complete Psychological Works of Sigmund Freud*, vol. 23. London: Hogarth Press.

———. 1940. *Totem und Tabu*. London: Imago.

Friess, Steve. 2003. "Tiger Attack on Idol Shocks Las Vegas." *Chicago Tribune*, October 5, 16.

Fromm, Erich. 1970. "The Oedipus Complex: Comments on the Case of Little Hans." In *The Crisis of Psychoanalysis*, by Erich Fromm, 95–96. New York: Holt.

Fullbrook, Karen, and Edward Fullbrook. 1994. *Simone de Beauvoir and Jean-Paul Sartre: The Remaking of a Twentieth-Century Legend*. New York: Basic Books.

———. 1995. "Sartre's Secret Key." In *Feminist Interpretations of Simone de Beauvoir*, ed. Margaret A. Simons, 97–111. University Park: Pennsylvania State University Press.

Garrison, Marsha. 1978. "A New Look at Little Hans." *Psychoanalytic Review* 65, no. 4:523–32.

Gatens, Moira. 2003. "Beauvoir and Biology: A Second Look." In *The Cambridge Companion to Simone de Beauvoir*, ed. Claudia Card, 266–85. Cambridge: Cambridge University Press.

Genosko, Gary. 1993. "Freud's Bestiary: How Does Psychoanalysis Treat Animals?" *Psychoanalytic Review* 80, no. 4:603–32.

Gettelman, Elizabeth, and Dave Gilson. 2008. "Petophilia! A Shocking Glimpse of How We Let Our Furry Friends into Our Hearts, Our Pocketbooks—And Our Bedrooms!" *Mother Jones*, March/April, p. 28.

Glendinning, Lee. 2008. "Spanish Parliament Approves 'Human Rights' for Apes." *The Guardian*, June 26 (online).

Glendinning, Simon. 1996. "Heidegger and the Question of Animality." *International Journal of Philosophical Studies* 4:67–86.

Greene, Naomi. 1980. "Sartre, Sexuality and *The Second Sex*." *Philosophy and Literature* 4, no. 2:190–211.

Grosz, Elizabeth. 1997. "Ontology and Equivocation: Derrida's Politics of Sexual Difference." In *Feminist Interpretations of Derrida,* ed. Nancy Holland, 73–102. University Park: Pennsylvania State University Press.

———. 2005. "Derrida and Feminism: A Remembrance." *differences: A Journal of Feminist Cultural Studies* 16, no. 3:88–94.

Guyer, Sara. 1995. "Albeit Eating: Toward an Ethics of Cannibalism." *Angelaki* 2, no. 1:63–80.

Haraway, Donna. 1984. "Primatology Is Politics by Other Means." *Philosophy of Science Association* 2:489–524.

———. 2003. *The Companion Species Manifesto: Dogs, People, and Significant Otherness.* Chicago: Prickly Paradigm Press.

———. 2004. *The Haraway Reader.* New York: Routledge.

Heidegger, Martin. 1983. *Die Grundbegriffe der Metaphysik: Welt, Endlichkeit, Einsamkeit.* Frankfurt am Main: V. Klostermann.

———. 1993. "Letter on Humanism" (1947). In *Basic Writings,* ed. David Farrell Krell, 217–65. San Francisco: HarperCollins.

———. 1995. *The Fundamental Concepts of Metaphysics.* Trans. William McNeill and Nicholas Walker. Bloomington: Indiana University Press.

———. 1999. *On the Essence of Language* (1939). Trans. Wanda Torres Gregory and Yvonne Unna. Albany: State University Press of New York.

Herder, Johann Gottfried. 1772. "Abhandlung über den Ursprung der Sprache." Stuttgart: Reclam.

———. 1800. *Outlines of a Philosophy of the History of Man* (1784). Trans. T. Churchill. New York: Bergman.

———. 1966. "On the Origin of Language" (1772). In *On the Origin of Language,* trans. John Moran and Alexander Gode, 87–166. Chicago: University of Chicago Press.

———. 1969. "Organic Difference Between Animals and Man." In *Herder on Social and Political Culture,* by Johann Gottfried Herder, 255–57. Cambridge: Cambridge University Press.

Holland, Jennifer. 2007. "A Worm's World." *National Geographic,* February, 122.

Holland, Nancy. 1997. Introduction to *Feminist Interpretations of Derrida,* ed. Nancy Holland, 1–22. University Park: Pennsylvania State University Press.

———. 2002. "With One Headlight: Merleau-Ponty and the Philosophy of Science." *Philosophy Today,* SPEP suppl. 46:28–32.

Holveck, Eleanore. 1995. "Can a Woman Be a Philosopher? Reflections of a Beauvoirian Housemaid." In *Feminist Interpretations of Simone de Beauvoir,* ed. Margaret A. Simons, 67–78. University Park: Pennsylvania State University Press.

hooks, bell. 2007. *Ain't I a Woman: Black Women and Feminism.* Cambridge, Mass.: South End Press.

Irigaray, Luce. 1974. *Speculum of the Other Woman.* Trans. Gillian C. Gill. Ithaca, N.Y.: Cornell University Press, 1985.

———. 1985. *This Sex Which Is Not One.* Trans. Catherine Porter. Ithaca, N.Y.: Cornell University Press.

———. 1992. *Elemental Passions.* Trans. J. Collie and J. Still. New York: Routledge.

———. 1993. *An Ethics of Sexual Difference.* Trans. Carolyn Burke and Gillian C. Gill. Ithaca, N.Y.: Cornell University Press.

———. 1996. *I Love to You: Sketch of a Possible Felicity in History.* Trans. Alison Martin. New York: Routledge.

———. 2000. *To Be Two.* Trans. Monique M. Rhodes and Marco F. Cocito-Monoc. New York: Routledge.

———. 2002. *To Speak Is Never Neutral.* Trans. Gail M. Schwab. New York: Routledge.

Jaggar, Alison, and William L. McBride. 1985. "'Reproduction' as Male Ideology." *Hypatia: A Journal of Feminist Philosophy* (Women's Studies International Forum) 8, no. 3:185–96.

Jones, Emma. 2007. "In the Presence of the Living Cockroach." *PhaenEx* 2, no. 2:24–41.

Kamuf, Peggy, ed. 1991. *A Derrida Reader: Between the Blinds.* New York: Columbia University Press.

Kant, Immanuel. 1970. "Perpetual Peace." In *Kant's Political Writings,* ed. Hans Reiss and trans. H. B. Nisbet, 93–130. Cambridge: Cambridge University Press.

Kennedy, Duncan. 2002. "The Critique of Rights in Critical Legal Studies." In *Left Legalism / Left Critique,* ed. Wendy Brown and Janet Halley, 178–228. Durham, N.C.: Duke University Press.

Kintzler, Catherine, 1993. Introduction to *Rousseau, Essai sur l'origine des langues,* 5–46. Paris: Flammarion.

Kittay, Eva. 1995. "Taking Dependency Seriously: Social Cooperation, the Family Medical Leave Act, and Gender Equality Considered in Light of the Social Organization of Dependency Work." *Hypatia* 10: 8–26.

———. 1996. "Human Dependency and Rawlsian Equality." In *Feminists Rethink the Self,* ed. D. T. Meyers, 219–66. Boulder, Colo.: Westview Press.

———. 1998. "Welfare, Dependency, and a Public Ethic of Care." *Social Justice* 25, no. 71:1.

———. 1999. *Love's Labor: Essays on Women, Equality, and Dependency.* New York: Routledge.

Klaw, Barbara. 1995. "Sexuality in Beauvoir's *Les Mandarins.*" In *Feminist Interpretations of Simone de Beauvoir,* ed. Margaret A. Simons, 193–222. University Park: Pennsylvania State University Press.

Klein, Julie. 2003. "Nature's Metabolism: On Eating in Derrida, Agamben, and Spinoza." *Research in Phenomenology* 33:186–217.

Kristeva, Julia. 1982. *Powers of Horror.* Trans. Leon Roudiez. New York: Columbia University Press.

———. 1987. *Tales of Love.* Trans. Leon Roudiez. New York: Columbia University Press.

———. 1989. *Black Sun.* Trans. Leon Roudiez. New York: Columbia University Press.

———. 2000a. "The Meaning of Equality." In *The Crisis of the European Subject,* trans. Susan Fairfield. New York: The Other Press.

———. 2000b. *The Sense and Non-Sense of Revolt*. Trans. Jeanine Herman. New York: Columbia University Press.

———. 2005. *La haine et le pardon*. Paris: Fayard.

Kruks, Sonia. 1987. "Simone de Beauvoir and the Limits to Freedom." *Social Text* 17: 111–22.

———. 1992. "Gender and Subjectivity: Simone de Beauvoir and Contemporary Feminism." *Signs: Journal of Women in Culture and Society* 18, no. 1:89–110.

———. 1995. "Simone de Beauvoir: Teaching Sartre About Freedom." In *Feminist Interpretations of Simone de Beauvoir*, ed. Margaret A. Simons, 79–96. University Park: Pennsylvania State University Press.

Kuperus, Gerard. 2007. "Attunement, Deprivation, and Drive: Heidegger and Animality." In *Phenomenology and the Non-Human Animal*, ed. Corinne Painter and Christian Lotz, 13–28. Dordrecht: Springer.

Lacan, Jacques. 1987. "Names of the Father Seminar," trans. Jeffrey Mehlman. *October*, vol. 40: *Television* (spring):81–95.

———. 1988a. *The Seminar of Jacques Lacan, Book I: Freud's Papers of Technique 1953–1954*. Trans. John Forrester and ed. Jacques-Alain Miller. New York: Norton.

———. 1988b. *The Seminar of Jacques Lacan, Book II: The Ego in Freud's Theory and in the Technique of Psychoanalysis 1954–1955*. Trans. Sylvana Tomaselli and ed. Jacques-Alain Miller. New York: Norton.

———. 2006. *Écrits. The First Complete Edition in English*. Trans. Bruce Fink. New York: Norton.

Lacove-Labarthe, Philipe, and Jean-Luc Nancy. 1997. *Retreating the Political*. Ed. Simon Sparks. New York: Routledge.

Lawlor, Leonard. 2006. *The Implications of Immanence: Toward a New Concept of Life*. New York: Fordham University Press.

———. 2007. *This Is Not Sufficient: An Essay on Animality and Human Nature in Derrida*. New York: Columbia University Press.

Lázaro, Reyes. 1986. "Feminism and Motherhood: O'Brien vs. Beauvoir." *Hypatia: A Journal of Feminist Philosophy* 1, no. 2:87–102.

Leiber, J. 1988. "Cartesian Linguistics?" *Philosophia* 18, no. 4:309–46.

Leighton, Jean. 1975. *Simone de Beauvoir on Woman*. Cranbury, N.J.: Associated University Presses.

Léon, Celine. 1995. "Beauvoir's Woman: Eunuch or Male?" In *Feminist Interpretations of Simone de Beauvoir*, ed. Margaret A. Simons, 137–60. University Park: Pennsylvania State University Press.

Levinas, Emmanuel. 1986. "The Paradox of Morality: An Interview with Emmanuel Levinas." Trans. Andrew Benjamin and Tamra Wright. In *The Provocation of Levinas*, ed. Robert Bernasconi and David Wood, 168–80. London: Routledge.

———. 2004. "The Name of a Dog, or Natural Rights." In *Animal Philosophy: Ethics and Identity*, ed. Peter Atterton and Matthew Calarco, 47–50. New York: Continuum.

Lévi-Strauss, Claude. 1962. *Totemism*. Trans. Rodney Needham. Boston: Beacon Press.

Lewis, Helen Block. 1988. "Freudian Theory and New Information in Modern Psychology." *Psychoanalytic Psychology* 5, no. 1:7–22.

Linnaeus, Carolus. 1995. *Menniskans Cousiner.* Ed. Telemak Fredbärj. Uppsala: Ekenäs.

Linsenbard, Gail Evelyn. 1999. "Beauvoir, Ontology, and Women's Human Rights." *Hypatia: A Journal of Feminist Philosophy* 14, no. 4:145–62.

Llewelyn, John. 1991. *The Middle Voice of Ecological Conscience.* New York: St. Martin's Press.

Lorraine, Tamsin E. 1999. *Irigaray & Deleuze: Experiments in Visceral Philosophy.* Ithaca, N.Y.: Cornell University Press.

Lundgren-Gothlin, Eva. 1996. *Sex and Existence: Simone de Beauvoir's "The Second Sex."* Hanover, N.H.: University Press of New England.

MacKinnon, Catharine. 2004. "Of Mice and Men: A Feminist Fragment on Animal Rights." In *Animal Rights,* ed. Cass Sunstein and Martha Nussbaum, 263–76. New York: Oxford University Press.

Mader, Mary Beth. 2005. "Antigone's Line." *Bulletin de la Société de philosophie de langue française* 14, no. 2:1–32.

Mahon, Joseph. 1997. *Existentialism, Feminism, and Simone de Beauvoir.* New York: St. Martin's Press.

Marder, Elissa. 2009a. "The Bestiary and the Primal Scene." In *Philosophical Criticism(s) of the Concept of Sexuality in Psychoanalysis,* vol. 9, Figures of the Unconscious, ed. Eran Dorfman and Jens De Vleminck. Leuven University Press.

———. 2009b. "The Sex of Death and the Maternal Crypt." *Parallax: Inscr(i/y)ptions* 15, no. 1, forthcoming.

Margaroni, Maria. 2004. "The Time of a Gift." *Philosophy Today* 48, no. 1:49–62.

Marks, Elaine. 1987. *Critical Essays on Simone de Beauvoir.* Boston: G. K. Hall.

McAfee, Noëlle. 2004. *Julia Kristeva.* New York: Routledge.

McNeill, William. 1999. "Life Beyond the Organism: Animal Being in Heidegger's Freiburg Lectures, 1929–30." In *Animal Others,* ed. H. Peter Steeves, 197–248. Albany: State University of New York Press.

Mendieta, Eduardo. Forthcoming. "Philosophical Beasts, Logos, Nomos, Polemos." *Continental Philosophy Review.*

Merleau-Ponty, Maurice. 1945. *Phénoméologie de la perception.* Paris: Gallimard.

———. 1958. *Notes des cours au Collège de France: 1958–1959 et 1960–1961.* Paris: Gallimard.

———. 1968. *The Visible and the Invisible.* Trans. Alphonso Lingis. Evanston, Ill.: Northwestern University Press.

———. 1983. *The Structure of Behavior* (1942). Trans. Alden Fisher. Pittsburgh: Duquesne University Press.

———. 1994. *La Nature: Notes de cours du Collège de France.* Ed. Dominique Séglard. Paris: Éditions de Seuil.

———. 1996. *Notes de cours 1959–1961.* Paris: Éditions Gallimard.

———. 2002. *Phenomenology of Perception.* Trans. Colin Smith. New York: Routledge.

———. 2003. *Nature: Course Notes from the Collège de France.* Trans. Robert Vallier. Evanston, Ill.: Northwestern University Press.

———. 2004a. *Maurice Merleau-Ponty: Basic Writings.* Ed. Thomas Baldwin. New York: Routledge.

———. 2004b. *The World of Perception.* Trans. Oliver Davis. London: Routledge (Radio Lectures from 1948).

Milbank, John. 2001. "Forgiveness and Incarnation." In *Questioning God,* ed. John Caputo et al., 92–128. Bloomington: Indiana University Press.

Miller, Peter. 2007. "Swarm Theory." *National Geographic,* July, 126–47.

Moi, Toril. 1986. "Existentialism and Feminism." *Oxford Literary Review* 8:91.

———. 2004. "While We Wait: Notes on the English Translation of *The Second Sex.*" In *The Legacy of Simone de Beauvoir,* ed. Emily Grosholz, 37–68. Oxford: Oxford University Press.

Moran, John. 1966. Afterward: "On the Origin of Languages." In *On the Origin of Language,* trans. John Moran and Alexander Gode, 75–83. Chicago: University of Chicago Press.

Morris, David. 2005. "Animals and Humans, Thinking and Nature." *Phenomenology and the Cognitive Sciences* 4 (spring):49–72.

Mueller, Tom. 2008. "Biomimetics: Design by Nature." *National Geographic,* April, 68–91.

O'Brien, Mary. 1981. *The Politics of Reproduction.* London: Routledge & Kegan Paul.

O'Brien, Mary, and Lester E. Embree. 2001. *The Existential Phenomenology of Simone de Beauvoir.* New York: Springer.

O'Byrne, Anne. 2002. "Natality, Exchange and Labour." Invited talk for the Women's Studies Program, State University of New York at Stony Brook, November 12.

O'Carroll, Eoin. 2008. "Spain to Grant Some Human Rights to Apes." *Christian Science Monitor,* June (online), p. 27.

Oele, Marjolein. 2007. "Being Beyond: Aristotle's and Plessner's Accounts of Animal Responsiveness." In *Phenomenology and the Non-Human Animal,* ed. Corinne Painter and Christian Lotz, 29–37. Dordrecht: Springer.

Okely, Judith. 1998. "Rereading *The Second Sex.*" In *Simone de Beauvoir: A Critical Reader,* ed. Elizabeth Fallaize, 19–28. New York: Routledge.

Oliver, Kelly. 1993. *Reading Kristeva.* Bloomington: Indiana University Press.

———. 1995. *Womanizing Nietzsche: Philosophy's Relation to the "Feminine."* New York: Routledge.

———. 1997. "The Maternal Operation: Circumscribing the Alliance." In *Derrida and Feminism,* ed. Ellen Feder et al., 53–68. New York: Routledge.

———. 2001. *Witnessing: Beyond Recognition.* Minneapolis: University of Minnesota Press.

———. 2003. "Forgiveness and Subjectivity." *Philosophy Today* 47, no. 3:280–92.

———. 2004. *The Colonization of Psychic Space.* Minneapolis: University of Minnesota Press.

———. 2007. *Women as Weapons of War.* New York: Columbia University Press.

O'Neill, Tom. 2008. "Spot Check." *National Geographic,* July, p. 24.

Patterson, Charles. 2002. *Eternal Treblinka.* New York: Lantern Books.

Patterson, Yolanda Astarita. 1989. *Simone de Beauvoir and the Demystification of Motherhood.* Ann Arbor, Mich.: UMI Research Press.

———. 1992. "Who Was This H. M. Parshley?" *Simone de Beauvoir Studies* 9:41–46.

Pilardi, Jo-Ann. 1991. "Philosophy Becomes Autobiography: The Development of the Self in the Writings of Simone de Beauvoir." In *Writing the Politics of Difference,* ed. Hugh J. Silverman, 145–62. Albany: State University of New York Press.

———. 1993. "The Changing Critical Fortunes of the Second Sex." *History and Theory* 32, no. 1:51–73.

Rachels, James. 2004. "Drawing Lines." In *Animal Rights,* ed. Cass Sunstein and Martha Nussbaum, 162–74. New York: Oxford University Press.

Rawlinson, Mary. 1997. "Levers, Signatures, and Secrets: Derrida's Use of Woman." In *Derrida and Feminism,* ed. Ellen Feder, Mary Rawlinson, and Emily Zakin, 69–86. New York: Routledge.

Regan, Tom. 1983. *The Case for Animal Rights.* Berkeley: University of California Press.

———. 1987. *The Struggle for Animal Rights.* Clarks Summit, Pa.: International Society for Animal Rights.

———. 2004. *The Case for Animal Rights: Updated with a New Preface.* Berkeley: University of California Press.

Reineke, Martha. 1997. *Sacrificed Lives.* Bloomington: Indiana University Press.

Rich, Adrienne. 1977. *Of Woman Born: Motherhood as Experience and Institution.* New York: Bantam Books.

Ricoeur, Paul. 1970. *Freud and Philosophy.* Trans. Denis Savage. New Haven, Conn.: Yale University Press.

Ritvo, Lucille. 1990. *Darwin's Influence on Freud.* New Haven, Conn.: Yale University Press.

Roberts, Adam. 2005. "Too Close for Comfort." *Animal Welfare Institute Quarterly* (winter):10–11.

Roof, Judith. 2003. "From Protista to DNA (and Back Again): Freud's Psychoanalysis of the Single-Celled Organism." In *Zoontologies,* ed. Cary Wolfe, 101–20. Minneapolis: University of Minnesota Press.

Rosemont, Henry Jr. 1991. "Rights-Bearing Individual and Role-Bearing Persons." In *Rules, Rituals, and Responsibility: Essays Dedicated to Herbert Fingarette,* ed. Mary I. Bockover. La Salle, Ill.: Open Court Press.

Rousseau, Jean-Jacques. 1966. "On the Origin of Languages.'" In *On the Origin of Language,* trans. John Moran and Alexander Gode, 5–74. Chicago: University of Chicago Press.

———. 1983. *Discours sur l'origine et les fondements de l'inégalité parmi les hommes.* Paris: Éditions sociales.

———. 1984. *A Discourse on the Origins and Foundations of Inequality Among Men.* Trans. Maurice Cranston. New York: Penguin Putnam Books.

———. 1993. *Essai sur l'origine des langues.* Paris: Flammarion.

———. 1999. *Émile, ou de l'education.* Paris: Classiques Garnier.

————. 2003. *Émile.* Trans. Barbara Foxley. North Clarendon, Vt.: Everyman Press.

Sanday, Peggy Reeves, and Ruth Gallagher Goodenough. 1990. *Beyond the Second Sex: New Directions in the Anthropology of Gender.* Philadelphia: University of Pennsylvania Press.

Scarth, Fredrika. 2004. *The Other Within: Ethics, Politics and the Body in Simone de Beauvoir.* Lanham, Md.: Rowman & Littlefield.

Seigfried, Charlene Haddock. 1985. "Second Sex: Second Thoughts." *Hypatia: A Journal of Feminist Philosophy* 3:219–29.

————. 1990. "The Second Sex: Second Thoughts." In *Hypatia Reborn,* ed. Azizah Al-Hibri and Margaret A. Simons, 305–322. Bloomington: Indiana University Press.

Seshadri-Crooks, Kalpana. 2000. *Desiring Whiteness.* New York: Routledge.

————. 2003. "Being Human: Bestiality, Anthropophagy, and Law." *Umbr(a): A journal of the unconscious* 1:97–114.

Simons, Margaret A., ed. 1995. *Feminist Interpretations of Simone de Beauvoir.* University Park: Pennsylvania State University Press.

————. 1999. *Beauvoir and The Second Sex: Feminism, Race, and the Origins of Existentialism.* New York: Rowman & Littlefield.

————. 2000. "Beauvoir's Philosophical Independence in a Dialogue with Sartre." *Journal of Speculative Philosophy* 14, no. 2:87–103.

————. 2001. "The Beginnings of Beauvoir's Existential Phenomenology." In *The Existential Phenomenology of Simone de Beauvoir,* ed. Wendy O'Brien and Lester E. Embree, 17–40. New York: Springer.

————. 2006. *The Philosophy of Simone de Beauvoir: Critical Essays.* Bloomington: Indiana University Press.

Singer, Linda. 1985. "Interpretation and Retrieval: Rereading Beauvoir." *Hypatia,* special issue of *Women's Studies International* 8, no. 3:231–38.

Singer, Peter. 1975. *Animal Liberation.* New York: HarperCollins.

————. 1999. "Peter Singer." In *The Lives of Animals: J. M. Coetzee,* ed. Amy Gutmann, 85–91. Princeton, N.J.: Princeton University Press.

Smith, Janet Farrell. 1986. "Possessive Power." *Hypatia: A Journal of Feminist Philosophy.* (Motherhood and Sexuality) 1, no. 2:103–20.

Snaith, R. P. 1968. "A Clinical Investigation of Phobias." *British Journal of Psychiatry* 114:673–97.

Spivak, Gayatri Chakravorty. 1977. "Glas-piece." *diacritics* 7, no. 3:22–45.

————. 1988. "Can the Subaltern Speak?" In *Marxism and the Interpretation of Culture,* ed. Cary Nelson and Lawrence Grossberg, 271–313. Urbana: University of Illinois Press.

————. 2005. "Notes Toward a Tribute to Jacques Derrida." *differences: A Journal of Feminist Cultural Studies* 16, no. 3:102–13.

Spria, David. 1991. "The Evolution of Freud's Conceptualization of Phobias." *Psychoanalytic Inquiry* 11, no. 3:376–94.

Starobinski, Jean. 1988. *Jean-Jacques Rousseau: Transparency and Obstruction.* Trans. Robert Morrissey. Chicago: University of Chicago Press.

Sullivan, Henry. 1991. "Homo Sapiens or Homo Desiderans." In *Lacan and the Subject of Language,* ed. Ellie Ragland-Sullivan and Mark Bracher, 36–48. New York: Routledge.

Taylor, Chloë. 2008. "The Precarious Lives of Animals: Butler, Coetzee, and Animal Ethics." *Philosophy Today* 1, no. 52:60–73.

Thorens, Adèle. 2005. "La philosophie du vivant de Maurice Merleau-Ponty: La vie comme puissance créatrice de mondes." *Revue de théologie et de philosophie* 137:227–44.

Toadvine, Ted. 2007a. "How Not to Be a Jellyfish: Human Exceptionalism and the Ontology of Reflection." In *Phenomenology and the Non-Human Animal,* ed. Corinne Painter and Christian Lotz, 39–56. Dordrecht: Springer.

———. 2007b. "'Strange Kinship': Merleau-Ponty on the Human-Animal Relation." *Analecta Husserliana* 93:17–32.

Truth, Sojourner. 1851. "Ain't I a Woman?" Women's Rights Convention, Akron, Ohio, May 29.

Vallier, Robert. 2001. "The Indiscernible Joining: Structure, Signification, and Animality in Merleau-Ponty's *La nature.*" In *Merleau-Ponty: Non-Philosophy and Philosophy. Chaismi International,* vol. 3, 187–212.

Vera, Susana. 2008. "Apes Get Legal Rights in Spain, to Surprise of Bullfight Critics." *The Times* (London), June (online), p. 27.

Vintges, Karen. 1995. "The Second Sex and Philosophy," trans. Anne Lavelle. In *Feminist Interpretations of Simone de Beauvoir,* ed. Margaret A. Simons, 45–58. University Park: Pennsylvania State University Press.

———. 1996. *Philosophy as Passion: The Thinking of Simone de Beauvoir.* Trans. Anne Lavelle. Bloomington: Indiana University Press.

Wadiwel, Dinesh. 2002. "Cows and Sovereignty." *Borderlands e-journal* 1, no. 2.

———. 2004. "Animal by Any Other Name? Patterson and Agamben Discuss Animal (and Human) Life." *Borderlands e-journal* 3, no. 1.

Wallace, Edwin. 1983. *Freud and Anthropology.* New York: International Universities Press.

Ward, Julia K. 1995. "Beauvoir's Two Senses of the 'Body' in *The Second Sex.*" In *Feminist Interpretations of Simone de Beauvoir,* ed. Margaret A. Simons, 223–42. University Park: Pennsylvania State University Press.

Weir, Allison. 1993. "Identification with the Divided Mother: Kristeva's Ambivalence." In *Ethics, Politics and Difference in Julia Kristeva's Writing,* ed. Kelly Oliver, 79–91. New York: Routledge.

Weston, Kath. 1991. *Families We Choose.* New York: Columbia University Press.

Whitty, Julia. 2007. "In 93 Years, Half of All Life on Earth Will Be Extinct. So What?" *Mother Jones,* May/June 2007, 36–45, 88.

Wilson, Catherine. 2006. "Kant and the Speculative Sciences of Origin." In *The Problem of Animal Generation in Early Modern Philosophy,* ed. Justin Smith, 375–401. Cambridge: Cambridge University Press.

Wiseman, Mary Bittner. 1993. "Renaissance Paintings and Psychoanalysis" In *Ethics, Politics and Difference in Julia Kristeva's Writing,* ed. Kelly Oliver, 92–115. New York: Routledge.

Wittig, Monique. 1992. *The Straight Mind and Other Essays.* Boston: Beacon Press.

Wolfe, Cary. 2008. *Philosophy and Animal Life.* New York: Columbia University Press.

Wolfe, Cary, et al., eds. 2003. *Zoontologies: The Question of the Animal.* Minneapolis: University of Minnesota Press.

Wood, David. 1999. "*Comment ne pas manger*—Deconstruction and Humanism." In *Animal Others: On Ethics, Ontology and Animal Life,* ed. Peter Steeves, 15–35. Albany: State University of New York Press.

———. 2004. "Thinking with Cats." In *Animal Philosophy: Ethics and Identity,* ed. Peter Atterton and Matthew Calarco, 129–44. New York: Continuum.

Yousef, Nancy. 2000. "Natural Man as Imaginary Animal." *Interpretation* 27, no. 3: 206–29.

Zakin, Emily. 2000. "Bridging the Social and the Symbolic: Toward a Feminist Politics of Sexual Difference." *Hypatia; a journal of feminist philosophy* 15, no. 3:19–44.

Zammito, John. 2006. "Kant's Early Views on Epigenesis." In *The Problem of Animal Generation in Early Modern Philosophy,* ed. Justin Smith, 317–54. Cambridge: Cambridge University Press.

Zerilli, Linda M. G. 1992. "A Process Without a Subject: Simone de Beauvoir and Julia Kristeva on Maternity." *Signs* 18, no. 1:111–35.

symbolic, the, 10, 177–79, 184, 213

symbolization, 178

taboo: incest, 250, 251, 275, 297

talking cure, the, 179

taste, 97–100; for a certain pronunciation, 114; and morality, 55, 97, 101, 108

third sex, 166

Thorens, Adèle, 237, 327n1

Toadvine, Ted, 224, 328n3, 330n9, 330nn11–12

Torok, Maria, 268

totemism, 248–53, 255, 256, 262, 263, 269, 271–73, 275, 276; reverse, 253. *See also* animal phobias

trace, 188, 189; behavior, 177

translation, 66, 88; of the name, 65. *See also* substitution

transposition (transposability), 202, 203, 206

trauma, 175, 262; birth, 265

trophe, 3, 125–27, 129, 130

trophy, 103, 104, 124, 126, 127, 129

truth, 68, 175, 185, 186, 199

Uexküll, Jakob von, 201, 208, 210, 211, 214, 215

uncanny, the (*Unheimlich*), 10, 14, 263, 264. *See also* Sand-man

unconditionality, 124, 137–39, 319n30; of the incalculable, 114, 138

unconscious, the, 121, 200, 248, 255, 272, 298

unnamable, the, 283, 287, 291, 337n11; and fear, 281, 284

upright posture (standing erect), 83, 93, 145, 146

Vallier, Robert, 221, 222, 329n5, 329n7, 330n13, 331n15, 332n12

veganism, 107

vegetarianism (vegetarian diet); benefits of, 54, 55, 60, 99; and the chief, 103, 104; Derridian, 105–107, 238; as symptomatic of a spiritual power, 87

violence, 230–32, 239, 295, 303, 304; establish one's existence through, 172; of excluding animals, 244; our own investments in, 44; pleasure in, 298; toward animals, 34, 36, 42, 48, 230, 231, 296; and unexamined traumas, 171; and vulnerability, 313n29; the worst, 105

virtue(s), 127, 306; of language, 118; of milk, 54, 99

vulnerability (vulnerable), 41–46, 128; embodied, 42, 46; primary, 42. *See also under* humanity; Kristeva; violence

Wadiwel, Dinesh, 231, 232, 331n3, 332n6, 332n10

war, 59, 60, 171

Wills, David, 103, 149

Wilson, Catherine, 314n3

Wolfe, Cary, 46, 310n17, 312n23

Wolf-man, the, 14, 254, 258–61, 263, 264–69, 282. *See also* animal phobias; primal scene

womb envy, 14

Wood, David, 106, 107, 150

working through, 5

world, 193, 196, 198; forming/formation, 195, 196, 199, 202, 212, 233; poverty/poor in, 193, 195, 196, 233